IRAN'S LOOK EAST POLICY

IRAN'S LOOK EAST POLICY

New Directions

Edited by Mehran Kamrava

CORNELL UNIVERSITY PRESS
Ithaca and London

Copyright © 2025 by Cornell University

All rights reserved. Except for brief quotations in a review, this book, or parts thereof, must not be reproduced in any form without permission in writing from the publisher. For information, address Cornell University Press, Sage House, 512 East State Street, Ithaca, New York 14850. Visit our website at cornellpress.cornell.edu.

First published 2025 by Cornell University Press

Librarians: A CIP catalog record for this book is available from the Library of Congress.

ISBN 9781501784538 (hardcover)
ISBN 9781501784545 (paperback)
ISBN 9781501784569 (pdf)
ISBN 9781501784552 (epub)

GPSR EU contact: Sam Thornton, Mare Nostrum Group B.V., Mauritskade 21D, 1091 GC, Amsterdam, NL, gpsr@mare-nostrum.co.uk.

Contents

Introduction *Mehran Kamrava* 1

1. Iran Looks East: Context, Causes, and Consequences
   Mehran Kamrava 13

Part I **Sanctions, Regionalism, and Risks**

2. Sanctions, Complexity, and Uncertainty in Iran's Eastward Trade *Karim Eslamloueyan* 33

3. Sanctions, the Look East Policy, and Economic Performance in Iran *Zahra Karimi Moughari* 51

4. Regional Multilateralism and Iran's "Look East" Policy Under Raisi: Recontextualization of India–Iran Relations *Deepika Saraswat* 70

5. Counterbalancing the West: The Risks of Iran's Eastern Policy *Mahmood Monshipouri and Javad Heiran-Nia* 90

Part II **Iran–China Relations**

6. Iran's Pivot Toward China: Neoclassical Realist Perspectives *Niloufar Baghernia* 115

7. The China–Iran Twenty-Five-Year Agreement and the Strategic Rebalance of the Persian Gulf
   Degang Sun and Sarvenaz Khanmohammadi 132

8. China's Response to Iran's Look East Policy: An Explanation of the Partner–Community Framework *Jianwei Han* 148

Part III **Iran–Russia Relations**

9. A Risk-Seeking Iran: Explaining Iran's Military Support for Russia in the Ukraine War *Mazaher Koruzhde and Eric Lob* 167

10. The Defense Sector and Foreign Policy Decisions: The Case of Iran's Policy Toward Russia *Abdolrasool Divsallar* 191

Part IV **Iran's Relations with Central Asia and the South Caucasus**

11 Iran and the South Caucasus *Gawdat Bahgat* 211

12 Conflicts Along Iran's Northern Corridors: Implications for National Security, Regional Order, and the Look East Policy *Banafsheh Keynoush* 225

13 Iran–Turkmenistan Relations: Geostrategic Dynamics Under the New Regional Order *Hessam Habibi Doroh* 245

Part V **Iran's Relations with Malaysia and Indonesia**

14 Consistency Through Instability: Malaysian–Iranian Relations *Rowena Abdul Razak* 269

15 Looking Beyond Beijing: Iranian Overtures to Indonesia *Fred H. Lawson* 290

Part VI **Iran and a New World Order?**

16 Iran's Look East Policy and the Emerging New World Order *Diana Galeeva* 309

Acknowledgments 325
List of Contributors 327
Index 333

IRAN'S LOOK EAST POLICY

INTRODUCTION

Mehran Kamrava

This book explores the causes, manifestations, and consequences of Iran's Look East policy. Spurned and sanctioned by the West, for more than two decades now the Islamic Republic has sought to deepen its diplomatic relations and economic ties with any state not strictly within the American orbit, be it in Latin America, Africa, South and Southeast Asia, or any other part of the world. What in the early years was broadly referred to in Iran as the Look East policy assumed an increasingly coherent format under successive presidential administrations beginning in the late 1980s. The increased tensions between Iran and Western powers over the nuclear issue during the Mahmoud Ahmadinejad years, from 2005 to 2013, were temporarily halted in the years that followed. By 2015, when a landmark nuclear agreement was signed between Iran and the major world powers, formally known as the Joint Comprehensive Plan of Action (JCPOA), a new era of reduced tensions and even investments involving Iran, the European Union, and the United States seemed at hand.[1]

Hopes for a reset of Iran's relations with the West were unceremoniously dashed when in 2018 President Donald Trump boastfully tore up the agreement and launched the "maximum pressure campaign" against the Islamic Republic.[2] As in their earlier iterations, the American sanctions had a secondary component, punishing any state or private firm outside of the United States that traded with Iran.[3] The European Union dutifully followed the United States in reimposing its own sanctions and withdrawing its meager post-2015 presence from the Iranian market. Literally all other countries with friendly diplomatic relations or economic ties with the United States soon fell in line and complied with the comprehensive sanctions regime against Iran.

The unilateral American withdrawal from the JCPOA had manifold ramifications for Iran domestically, regionally, and internationally. Domestically, the steady collapse of the JCPOA had political, as well as economic, consequences. Politically, after having spent so much of their political capital convincing Ali Khamenei and the other factions that reaching a deal with the European Union and the United States was a viable and lasting option, the American withdrawal from the JCPOA led to the rapid loss of popularity and legitimacy by Iran's reformists and moderates. Having found a new lease on life after Ahmadinejad's tumultuous presidency, Iran's more moderate politicians could hardly justify their efforts at rapprochement with the West after Trump and other documented Iranophobes vowed to bring the Islamic Republic to its knees through comprehensive sanctions.[4]

The consequences of the reimpositions of sanctions in 2018 on the Iranian economy have been fully documented elsewhere.[5] Briefly, in the weeks immediately following the sanctions, Total, the French energy giant, withdrew from a US$4.8 billion joint venture project to develop Iran's South Pars gas field in the Persian Gulf.[6] Italian, Spanish, Greek, and German companies soon followed suit, and the State Bank of India announced it would stop dealing with Tehran. The German conglomerate Siemens and Italy's Danieli both soon canceled their contracts upgrade Iran's infrastructure and supply the country with industrial equipment.

The impact on the Iranian economy was nearly immediate. Black market premiums for currencies such as the Euro and the US dollar rose dramatically, and the national currency's value fell precipitously. Declining oil experts and depreciations in the local currency led to substantial rises in prices of imported goods, including medicine and medical equipment.[7] Annual inflation jumped from 9.6 percent in 2017 to 41.2 percent in 2019, remaining high, at 46.5 percent, in 2022.[8] The supply chain, particularly of industrial and high-tech equipment, was seriously disrupted, and the informal sector, generally made up of the more vulnerable segments of society, suffered a great deal.[9]

By far the greatest impact of the sanctions has been felt by the average Iranian citizen and not by the government per se. Economists have long known that "economic sanctions severely harm the most vulnerable" members of society.[10] In relation to Iran, economic studies have repeatedly shown that "sanctions do not punish the government or well-connected groups of the target's economy but rather increase the suffering of the poorer households and powerless classes."[11] After 2018, the number of rural households and households in the low- and middle-income groups that slipped into poverty increased substantially.[12] Within a year of the reimposition of the sanctions, in 2019, poverty in Iran stood at 27 percent, a 5 percent increase over the previous year.[13] As a direct result of the sanctions, between 2018 and 2021 to 2022, real public investments contracted by an annualized rate of 20 percent.[14] In September 2023, the rate of inflation was officially placed at 46.1 percent, continuing to put pressure on the purchasing powers of most middle- and lower-class Iranians.[15]

President Ebrahim Raisi came to office in 2021 in what were generally seen in Iran as highly "engineered" elections that saw the lowest voter turnout for a presidential election in the history of the Islamic Republic. According to official data provided by the government, only 49 percent of eligible voters went to the polls—compared to 85 percent in 2009 and 73 percent in both 2013 and 2017—and voter turnout in major metropolitan areas was considerably lower. In Greater Tehran, for example, only 24 percent of voters bothered voting. After Raisi, the second highest number of votes cast, at 13 percent, were blank ballots, showing the Islamic Republic's serious crisis of legitimacy.[16] Raisi started his presidency with two promises: to contain and deal with the COVID-19 pandemic, and to fix the country's broken economy. In the first endeavor, the new administration was relatively successful, engaging in widespread vaccination and significantly lowering the daily death rate from the pandemic, even earning praise from the World Health Organization.[17] But, especially in the early months of the new presidential term, the currency's slide continued, inflation persisted above 40 percent, and the lower and middle classes continued to suffer. By 2021 to 2022 the Iranian economy was showing modest signs of a gradual recovery from the adverse effects of the COVID-19 pandemic, the gross domestic product (GDP) growing that year by 4.7 percent, and the government's fiscal deficit declined to 5.3 percent of the gross domestic product, as compared to 6.3 percent the year before.[18] But this meant little to the person in the streets whose purchasing power, home ownership, and even calorie intake continued to decline.[19] Deeper, structural problems with the economy have also continued to persist. Iranian economists, investors, and merchants alike agree on the urgent need for rapid investments in the country's aging infrastructure, curbing inflation, and restoring the confidence of domestic and international investors.[20] Increasing economic options by looking Eastward, and deepening ties with international friends wherever they could be found, was one of the few viable options open to the new president and his team.

At the regional and international levels, the Hassan Rouhani administration persisted in its efforts to pursue a balanced relationship between America's European and regional allies on the one hand, and Russia, China, and other nonaligned states on the other. Nonetheless, Iran's relations with the West and with other regional friends of the United States became increasingly more difficult after 2018. President Rouhani's proposal in 2019 for a regional security architecture dubbed the Hormuz Peace Endeavor, HOPE, found no takers.[21] Trump's loss in the 2020 US presidential elections and the inauguration of the Joe Biden administration resulted in a change in the US rhetoric against Iran but not the substance of its policies against the Islamic Republic. In fact, a hurriedly articulated "Biden Doctrine" identified Iran as a disruptive international actor and a threat to US allies and interests around the world.[22] By the time Rouhani's two-term administration was coming to an end in 2021, drawing itself closer to countries outside of the Western orbit seemed like Iran's only viable option.

The election of Raisi to the presidency solidified and soon formalized an Eastward trend in Iran's foreign policy that had started a couple of administrations earlier. The Raisi administration pursued two parallel, complementary foreign policy objectives, one good neighborly relations, and the other looking East.[23] When Raisi and his foreign minister, Hossein Amir-Abdollahian, died unexpectedly in a helicopter crash in May 2024, Masoud Pezeshkian, who hailed from the reformist camp, was elected president. Pezeshkian promised a presidency altogether different from Raisi's, but not in the pursuit of the Look East policy. The president called for dialogue with the West and especially a resumption of negotiations with the United States. This should not come, however, he maintained, at the expense of deepening relations with the East. Repeatedly, both during the election campaign and after he took office, Pezeshkian reiterated the importance of Iran's relations with Russia, China, India, and other actors in the East. As the chapters in this book make clear, the new president's continuity of the Look East policy is structurally rooted. Given the West's unchanging approach to the Islamic Republic regardless of who its president might be, Iranian foreign policy's Eastward tilt is unlikely to change anytime soon.

By far the biggest justification for the Look East policy, as this summary indicates, has been the US withdrawal from the JCPOA, and the broader hostility that has persistently marked US policy toward Iran from one administration to another. A host of other justifications have since followed—ideological, economic, diplomatic, and even civilizational. Given the secondary nature of American sanctions on Iran, which punishes any non-American public or private entity that engages in commercial trades with the Islamic Republic, few firms with business interests in the United States see any benefits in any trade involving Iran. This includes almost all businesses based in or doing commerce in Europe, North and South America, and East Asia. Even private and public entities in India and China, as this book's chapters demonstrate, have largely shied away from the Iranian market for fear of running afoul of the watchful eyes of the US government's Treasury Department.

As an overarching strategy, therefore, the underlying logic of the Look East policy owes its genesis to the animus between Iran and the US in general and the 2018 reimpositions of the sanctions in particular. There is also a related economic logic at work. Iran hopes that improved relations with its neighbors, and also with states not fully absorbed into the orbit of the United States, will bring it greater possibilities for international trade irrespective of the sanctions regime. Membership in ostensibly non-Western multilateral bodies, such as the Shanghai Cooperation Organization and BRICS, is assumed to only enhance Iran's chances of circumventing sanctions or somehow rendering them ineffective.

A number of ex post facto justifications for the Look East policy have also been offered. Cultural and civilizational affinity between Iran and countries like India and China has been one of the more common themes running through the speeches of diplomats and dignitaries visiting each other's capitals. This theme has even been picked up by some of the scholars seeking to explain Iran's "rediscovery" of the East in recent decades.[24] Another, similar theme has been historical continuity, premised on the assumption that Iran never really left the East and has long been a critical node in a resilient network of commerce, trade, and cultural and political exchanges stretching from China in the East to the Levant and beyond in the West. In her contribution to this book, for example, Deepika Saraswat demonstrates how the Look East policy is part of a broader effort by Iran to (re)articulate a "new Asian identity."

These and other causes and justifications for Iran's Look East policy are examined in the chapters that follow, as are the processes and ways in which the policy has manifested itself and its manifold consequences. The book starts with my own analysis of the Look East policy, in which I define its precise meaning, trace its evolution since the late 1980s and its formal adoption in 2021, and examine the underlying causes for its development. Insofar as Iranian policymakers are concerned, any country not under Western hegemonic influence, regardless of its precise geographic location, is part the "the East." The Look East policy, therefore, signifies a strategic reorientation of Iranian foreign policy away from the West as much as it denotes attention to rising economic powers such as China and India. This strategic reorientation has been necessitated by what the Islamic Republic considers to be the West's innate hostility toward its very existence. Even in those rare instances when Iran has compromised and has forged a modus vivendi with the United States and the European Union, as it did over its nuclear program in 2015, the West has refused to abide by its end of the bargain, as made starkly clear by the US withdrawal from the JCPOA agreement in 2018. I end the chapter by highlighting some of the internal debates over the Look East policy inside Iran, asking whether partners such as Russia and China will be any more reliable than either the United States or Europe.

The four chapters that follow focus on the interconnections between domestic dynamics and the evolution and consequences of the Look East policy. They respectively examine the impact of the sanctions on the Iranian economy and on the country's foreign policy, the Islamic Republic's emphasis on Asian regionalism as opposed to bilateralism, and its efforts aimed at counterbalancing against the West. This group of contributions starts with Karim Eslamloueyan's focus on the relationship between Western-imposed sanctions on the Iranian economy and on Iran's increased trade—and therefore political ties—with the East. According to Eslamloueyan, Iran's Eastward trade is less a matter of strategic choice and more a result of economic necessity. The economic impact of the sanctions has been manifold. Sanctions have directly led to higher trade volumes between Iran and the countries of the East, while at the same time they have increased levels of uncertainty in Iran's international trade. Eslamloueyan demonstrates that the increased complexity of the Iranian economy results in declines in trade between the two sides, indicating that Iran's knowledge-based products are more likely to be traded in less advanced economies.

Along similar lines, Zahra Karimi focuses on the deleterious economic effects of the sanctions, especially insofar as Iranian trade is concerned. According to Karimi, increased trade with the East does not fully satisfy Iran's growing industrial needs given that most Iranian industries continue to use Western-supplied machinery and technical equipment through indirect imports. Utilizing data from an original field study she conducted in 2023, Karimi discovered that, at much greater costs and frequently without any after-sales services, more than 60 percent of Iranian industrial firms continue to use Western machinery. There is a marked preference, for example, for industrial equipment imported indirectly from the West over direct imports from China. Karimi's research shows that while the government's Look East policy may be economically driven, therefore, the preferences of large swaths of the industrial sector continue to lie in the opposite direction.

The reluctance to import industrial machinery from China notwithstanding, the Islamic Republic has sought to use its geographic location in order to emerge as an important "bridge" in the trade between South and East Asia on the one side and the South Caucasus on the other. Using Iran's relations with India as a case study, Deepika Saraswat focuses on Iran's renewed efforts at regional integration *within Asia*. This "Asian multilateralism" is anchored in an identity that has at its basis common Asian or Eastern civilizational features, similar security concerns, and parallel developmental synergies. Iran's hope is to help forge and deepen a new, favorable "Eurasian convergence" that is at once post-Western and posthegemonic.

Mahmood Monshipouri and Javad Heiran-Nia round up the cluster of chapters on the nexus between domestic politics and foreign policy by offering a sober assessment of Iran's Eastward tilt. Iran's Asian pivot is a result of three key factors, the chapter authors maintain, namely the country's refusal to diplomatically capitulate to the United States, the increasing primacy of security concerns over economic development, and preoccupation with regime security. These are inherently shortsighted considerations, Monshipouri and Heiran-Nia maintain, running the risk of overestimating Iran's position in Chinese strategic calculations, and also the Islamic Republic's overreliance on Russia. The authors conclude by cautioning that the Eastern policy may not be consistent with Iran's broader national interests.

As Asia's rising giant and the main global economic competitor to the United States, China occupies a central place in Iran's Look East policy. Niloufar Baghernia's contribution, the first of three chapters on the topic, traces the evolution of Iranian–Chinese relations under the Raisi presidency. Employing a neoclassical realist perspective, Baghernia argues that regional and international variables have been more significant in shaping Iranian foreign policy as compared to domestic factors. These international factors include synergies in increased Iranian and Chinese attention to regions such as Latin America and Africa. Given these considerations, according to Baghernia, Iran is likely to continue giving high priority to China, even if there are improvements in its relations with the West in general and with the United States in particular.

In March 2021, as the Rouhani administration was drawing to a close, Iran and China signed a twenty-five-year strategic agreement meant to cement their bilateral relationship in various arenas. Degang Sun and Sarvenaz Khanmohammadi focus on this landmark agreement, whose precise terms have not been made public, as a pivotal hallmark in Iran–China relations. From China's perspective, the agreement with Iran is part of a broader effort to forge strategic alliances with key actors in the Persian Gulf, including Saudi Arabia. This is occurring at a time when the US is increasingly more focused on the Indo-Pacific region.

Whereas Sun and Khanmohammadi focus on great power rivalry, and especially on the role of the United States in China's strategic calculations, in examining Iranian–Chinese relations, Jianwei Han highlights China's concepts of "partner" and "community" to explain Iran's position in Chinese strategic calculations. "Alliance," Han maintains, does not adequately explain the nature of the relationship between Iran and China. The People's Republic of China, however, sees Iran's Look East policy as perfectly complementary with its own foreign policy objectives in relation to the Persian Gulf and the greater Middle East, with Iran being a *partner* within a neighborhood *community* order in which China can pursue its policy objectives. China's brokering of Saudi–Iranian rapprochement in March 2023, according to Han, represented its efforts at conflict resolution between two of its regional community partners.

Besides China, another pillar of Iran's Look East policy revolves around its relations with Russia. If the twenty-five-year strategic agreement is the hallmark of Iran–China relations so far, Iran's military assistance to Russia since its 2022 invasion of Ukraine is emblematic of Russo–Iranian relations. The contributions by Abdolrasool Divsallar and by Eric Lob and Mazaher Koruzhde focus on the Ukraine war to analyze different aspects of Iranian–Russian relations under the auspices of the Look East policy. Lob and Koruzhde examine the underlying reasons for Iran's decision to lend extensive support to Russia despite the considerable diplomatic and even military risks involved in provoking various forms of reaction from Ukraine's Western allies, especially the United States and the European Union. The decision to support Russia militarily, the authors maintain, came on the heels of three negative developments for Iranian policymakers, namely the "maximum pressure campaign," which Trump launched and Biden never abandoned; domestic protests over antiwomen social strictures; and enhanced diplomatic and security cooperation between Israel and a number of Iran's neighbors. Perceiving themselves as operating in the domain of losses, as prospect theory also maintains, Iranian policymakers became more risk-seeking in both domestic and international affairs.

While the risks of a close military alliance with a warring Russia are real, there are also a number of advantages for Iran in closely aligning itself with Russia. For some time now, and especially after Raisi's election, Iran's security establishment and military–industrial complex have become steadily more influential in shaping the country's domestic politics and foreign policy. Divsallar's contribution highlights several advantages that key actors inside Iran's military–industrial complex see in Iran's close military cooperation with Russia. These perceived advantages include receiving Russian arms supplies and technology, utilizing Russia as a source of inspiration for military doctrine and tactics, and receiving support from Russia in articulating and implementing Iran's military doctrine. Popular Iranian perception to the contrary notwithstanding, Divsallar argues, Russian–Iranian security cooperation is extensive, multilayered, and in a number of respects advantageous to Iran's military–industrial complex.

The contributions by Banafsheh Keynoush, Gawdat Bahgat, and Hessam Habibi Doroh examine the Look East policy in relation to Iran's immediate north. Bahgat and Keynoush focus on different aspects of Iran's relations with the South Caucasus and Eurasia. Bahgat points to the active pursuit of national and strategic interests in the South Caucasus by a number of diverse actors ranging from Armenia and Azerbaijan to Turkey, Israel, Russia, the United States, and the European Union. Amid sanctions and other forms of pressure from the West, Iran has found its relations with the states of the South Caucasus to be particularly important, especially insofar as trade and transit routes are concerned. In furthering its national interests in the region, Bahgat argues, Iran's foreign policy toward the South Caucasus has featured a mixture of ideology and strategic interests, resulting in what he calls a remarkable degree of pragmatism.

Along similar lines, Keynoush points to Iran's belated realization that it needs a complementary "Look North" policy that would secure its interests in light of the conflict between Armenia and Azerbaijan over the Nagorno–Karabakh region. Officially, Iran adopted a policy of passive and positive neutrality toward the South Caucasus, pragmatically maintaining contacts and exchanges with multiple actors designed to secure its northern border and key logistics and transport corridors. But these policies have provoked suspicion from the United States and the European Union, and also from Russia. At best, Keynoush maintains, Iran's foreign policy in the region has been less than successful in advancing the country's stated interests.

A long-shared border, water and sea diplomacy, and the potential for foreign influence have all combined to prompt Iran to also pay close attention to another one of its northern neighbors, namely Turkmenistan. As Habibi Doroh makes clear in his contribution, Iran sees its relations with Turkmenistan through the same prism as its Look East policy. Doroh presents a rare insight into some of the most salient debates among Iranian policymakers and academics on the merits and demerits, and the challenges and opportunities, involving Iran's relations with Turkmenistan. At a practical level, both countries are drawn together through many common security and geostrategic interests, not the least of which include the Caspian Sea and the fluidity of politics in Afghanistan, with which both countries share long borders. For Iran, Turkmenistan is the gateway to the rest of Central Asia, and from there to both Russia and China. As Doroh explains, Iran hopes to utilize its geographic, transit, and political ties with Turkmenistan to deepen its Eastward orientation.

Contributions on two additional countries, Malaysia and Indonesia, round up the case studies on Iran's Look East policy. In her analysis of Iran-Malaysia relations, Rowena Abdul Razak demonstrates how despite a number of key differences in their policy preferences and their larger regional and global profiles, pragmatism and strategic interests have fostered close relations between the two states since before Iran's 1979 revolution. Neither differing identities—for example, Iranian Shiism and Malaysian Sunnism—nor divergent global profiles—Iran's apparent anti-Westernism and Malaysia's pro-Western orientation—have prevented the emergence of relatively strong links between Iran and Malaysia, which have been only deepened under the auspices of Iran's Look East policy.

Fred Lawson's contribution on Iran's relations with Indonesia points to the challenges Iran faces in maintaining close relations with a country that has a complicated geostrategic location and robust relations with some of Iran's main adversaries and competitors, especially the United States, Saudi Arabia, and the United Arab Emirates. Lawson demonstrates how the Look East policy has highlighted the importance of the Indo–Pacific to the Islamic Republic. On a number of occasions, however, Iran's efforts to expand relations with Indonesia, not unlike its relations with many other states, have experienced setbacks because of policies pursued by other ostensibly unrelated actors. Nevertheless, efforts at forging a strategic partnership between the two states continue.

The book concludes with a largely theoretical contribution by Diana Galeeva, whose chapter examines the role of Iran's Look East policy in fostering a new, emerging world order. Judging by the narratives and speeches supporting Tehran's foreign policy pursuits, creating a new world order, one that is posthegemonic and postliberal, is one of the central motivations for Iran's Look East policy. Although not as bluntly stated in Moscow and Beijing, this is not too different from the perspectives that underlie the foreign policies of Russia and China. It is little surprise that Iranian, Russian, and Chinese foreign policies share a number of common interests and objectives. Framing Iran's Look East policy as an effort to carve out a new world order, Galeeva demonstrates that in reality the effort is more reactionary than visionary, a product of pragmatism more than visionary aspirations.

Together, the contributions in this book demonstrate how Iran's Look East policy came about; what its main features and characteristics are; and how it has so far manifested itself in relation to China, Russia, Central Asia, the South Caucasus, and Southeast Asia. As the chapters collectively demonstrate, rhetorical justifications notwithstanding, Iran's Eastward gaze is more a matter of necessity rather than ideological preference, fueled by economic sanctions and diplomatic pressures from the United States and its allies, meant to ameliorate Iran's isolation, and, in the process, perhaps even help create a post-Western new world order. Economically and diplomatically pushed away by the West, pragmatism has been the main driver of Iran's Look East policy.

Not unlike leaders elsewhere, the Islamic Republic's policymakers often exaggerate the successes of their policies, magnifying the importance of minor achievements and explaining away setbacks. The state's bluster aside, as the contributions here show, Iran's efforts at fostering closer diplomatic—and even economic and security—ties with the states of the East have in recent years borne tangible results. For the foreseeable future, the enmity between Iran and the United States, and by implication between Iran and the European Union and the rest of what constitutes the West, shows no signs of abating. Iran is likely to continue its efforts at forging new friends and allies where it can find them, be they in Africa or Latin America or, as this book highlights, in the global East. Through its efforts, Iran may indeed emerge as a key transit node in a reemerging East, and, if its current arms buildup continues, perhaps as one of its main military powers. How this may play into a potentially renewed East–West divide, or, more aptly, a reemergence of older global divisions, is far from clear. The structure of the regional system within which Iran finds itself remains particularly fluid, as does the structure and future of Iran's own domestic politics. For the foreseeable future, nonetheless, Look East is likely to remain a feature of Iranian foreign policy.

NOTES

1. By far the most comprehensive discussion of the JCPOA to date, complete with copies of official documents and memos, has been published in six volumes by four of the principal Iranian negotiators involved, namely Foreign Minister Mohammad Javad Zarif, his deputy and head of the Iranian negotiating team Abbas Araghchi, head of the Iranian Atomic Agency Ali Akbar Salehi, and Iran's former ambassador to the United Nations, Majid Takht-Ravanchi. See Javad Zarif, Ali Akbar Salehi, Abbas Araghchi, and Majid Takht-Ravanchi, *Raz-e sar beh mohr: BARJAM koshesh-haye setarg baraye hoquq, amniyat va Tose'h-e Iran* [The nuclear deal: The untold story of JCPOA reflecting Iran's security, rights, and development], vols. 1–6 (Entesharat-e Ettela'at: 1400/2021). Of course, the volumes present the perspectives of the Iranian negotiators. Nevertheless, both in presenting these views and in the documentary evidence they provide, for scholars and researchers the volumes are invaluable.

2. Mohammed Nuruzzaman, "President Trump's 'Maximum Pressure' Campaign and Iran's Endgame," *Strategic Analysis* 44, no. 6 (2020): 573–76.

3. The US Treasury Department's Office of Foreign Asset Control maintains a detailed website of these sanctions, which can be accessed at: Office of Foreign Asset Control, "Iran Sanctions," US Department of Treasury, https://bit.ly/40AkQK9.

4. Reza Khalili, Mahmoud Yazdanfam, and Morteza Bakhshalizadeh, "U.S. Foreign Policy and Regional Power and Influence of Iran: A Comparison of Bush, Obama and Trump Administrations," *Geopolitics Quarterly* 19, no. 2 (Summer 2023): 207.

5. An excellent survey of studies on the economic consequences of the sanctions can be found at Mohammad Reza Farzanegan and Esfandyar Batmanghelidj, "Understanding Economic Sanctions on Iran: A Survey," *The Economists' Voice* 20, no. 2 (2023): 197–226, https://doi.org/10.1515/ev-2023-0014.

6. "French Energy Giant Total Officially Pulls Out of Iran," DW, August 21, 2018, https://shorturl.at/jmM0.

7. Although technically medicine and medical equipment are exempt from sanctions, banking sanctions on Iran make impossible the transfer of funds for international purchase of drugs, as documented in a number of cases. Francisco Rodriguez, *The Human Consequences of Economic Sanctions* (Center for Economic and Policy Research, 2023), 50.

8. Central Bank of Iran, Time Series Inflation Rate, https://bit.ly/47gDYiX.

9. Farzanegan and Batmanghelidj, "Understanding Economic Sanctions on Iran," 216.

10. Rodriguez, *Human Consequences of Economic Sanctions*, 13.

11. Farzanegan and Batmanghelidj, "Understanding Economic Sanctions on Iran," 207.

12. Rodriguez, *Human Consequences of Economic Sanctions*, 49.

13. World Bank, "Poverty & Equity Brief: Islamic Republic of Iran," April 2023, https://bit.ly/40yk00H.

14. World Bank, *Iran Economic Monitor: Managing Economic Uncertainties* (World Bank, 2022), 4, https://bit.ly/4kR5GtT.

15. Statistical Center of Iran, "Iran—Main Indicators," https://bit.ly/40CHCRB.

16. For an analysis of Raisi's election, see Mehran Kamrava and Hamideh Dorzadeh, "Back to the Future in Iran: Political and Policy Implications of the 2021 Presidential Elections," *The Muslim World* 113, nos. 1–2 (2023): 6–18.

17. "WHO Head Praises Iran Success in Fighting Covid-19," Mehr News Agency, May 24, 2022, https://bit.ly/3FVy4Ib.

18. World Bank, *Iran Economic Monitor*, ix.

19. Annual per capita consumption of red meat, for example, has gone from thirteen kilograms in 2001 to six kilograms in 2023, a decline attributed to its unaffordability rather than to health reasons. "Kahesh-e tavan-e mardom baraye kharid-e gosht va morgh" [Decline of people's purchasing power to buy beef and chicken], Salamat News, August 13, 2023, https://bit.ly/3QY7LHC.

20. For a revealing look at views by Iranian economists on the country's economic needs, see "Cheshmandaz-e eqtesad-e Iran dar sal-e 1402" [Outlook of the Iranian Economy in 2023], Fararu, July 23, 2023, https://bit.ly/3FZlWWu.

21. On HOPE, see Saeed Khatibzadeh, *HOPE for a New Regional Security Architecture: Toward a Hormuz Community* (Istituto Affari Internazionali, 2020), https://bit.ly/47ba6EL.

22. Elham Rasooli Saniabadi, "National Role Perceptions and Biden's Foreign Policy Towards Iran," *Iranian Review of Foreign Affairs* 12, no. 1 (Winter–Spring 2021): 141.

23. On the "good neighborly" relations as pursued by the Raisi administration, see Mehran Kamrava and Ali Bagheri Dolatabadi, "Iran's Neighborhood Policy: Parameters, Objectives, and Obstacles," *Middle East Policy* 31, no. 4 (2024): 56–73.

24. Ali Adami, "Rahbord-e negah beh sharq dar siyasat-e khareji-ye jomhuri-ye Eslami-e Iran: Didgah-ha, zamineh-ha, va forsat-ha" [The Look East strategy in the foreign policy of the Islamic Republic of Iran: Perspectives, contexts, and opportunities], *Faslnameh-e Motale'at-e Siyasi* 2, no. 7 (1389/2010): 112–16.

1

IRAN LOOKS EAST
Context, Causes, and Consequences

Mehran Kamrava

In February 2017, Iran's supreme leader, Ayatollah Ali Khamenei, who holds the highest office in the Islamic Republic, made the following statement: "In foreign policy, preference for the East over the West, preference for neighbor over the distant, preference over nations and countries that have commonalities over others, is one of our present-day priorities."[1] He thus enshrined the "Look East" policy (*Negah-e beh sharq*) as the official guideline for the conduct of Iranian foreign policy. As an overall policy orientation, an Eastern orientation of sorts has been in effect in Iranian foreign policy for a number of years.

Although not officially called Look to the East at the time, starting with the second administration of President Akbar Hashemi Rafsanjani (1993–97), Iran began making friendly gestures toward China, India, and Russia, resulting in the subsequent signing of a number of important trade agreements between Iran and all three countries.[2] Successive presidential administrations—headed by Mohammad Khatami, Mahmoud Ahmadinejad, and Hassan Rouhani—all followed suit, paying increasing attention to the importance of diplomatic, economic, and commercial ties with countries outside of the West's orbit.[3] In 2021, when Ebrahim Raisi was elected president, the policy became part of the formal doctrine of the Islamic Republic's foreign policy. Its formal adoption as one of the central pillars of Iran's foreign policy has reignited debate in the country's academic and policy circles over the country's approach to the East.

This chapter explores the precise meaning of the policy, the domestic and especially international contexts within which has been adopted, and its practical manifestations. What exactly do Iranian policymakers mean by "the East?"

As we shall see shortly, the Islamic Republic's conception of the East appears to be deliberately imprecise, broad and flexible enough to include whatever country and geographic region that is not considered to belong to the traditional West. This includes, therefore, not just Russia, which is technically located north of Iran, as well as India and China, but also the countries of the so-called Global South. Nevertheless, in Iranian calculations, the essence of the Look East policy means closer strategic and commercial relations with Russia, China, India, and other Asian states. The chapter then explores the reasons behind the adoption of the policy, zeroing in on the threat perceptions of Iranian policymakers, especially in relation to the United States, and the comprehensive economic sanctions with which they have had to grapple in recent decades. It ends with a preliminary balance sheet of some of the main achievements and shortcomings so far of the Islamic Republic's foreign policy (re)orientation toward the East.

What the Policy Means

Three perspectives have been recurring themes in Iranian foreign policy. In one way or another, these perspectives have guided the overall direction of Iranian foreign policy. At the very least, since the early days of the Rafsanjani presidency, and especially after the end of the war with Iraq in 1988, they have shaped assumptions about how to best further the country's national interests.[4] By far the most historically salient of the three approaches has been a policy pointed in the direction of the West. Although this Western orientation was assumed to be the norm in the country's foreign policy before the revolution, especially in its final years the prerevolutionary, ancien régime actually pursued a more nuanced, balanced diplomacy toward the different ideological camps that existed at the time.[5] In response to this assumed Western orientation, in its early decades, the postrevolutionary Islamic Republic claimed to abide by the revolutionary slogan of "neither the East nor the West" in its foreign policy pursuits. Most recently, first informally and then in more formal ways since 2021, the state has adopted the Look East policy.[6]

The Look East policy entails more than a geographic focus; it is a theoretical recalibration of Iran's foreign policy orientation away from the West. In the words of one of the Islamic Republic's former ambassadors, it is premised on the assumption of "how Iran can utilize the cooperation of different states around the world, along with the capacities that are inherent in the international order, for the benefit of its own national interests."[7] In Iranian foreign policy conception, the East can be defined at the micro level as the states of East Asia, as in China, Taiwan, Japan, and North and South Korea. At the meso level, in addition to East Asia, the East is assumed to also include Southeast, Central, and South Asia. These states, plus those in West Asia, North Africa, Latin America, and Africa, comprise the East at the macro level.[8]

Within this context, Look East can be seen through a number of different perspectives. It can be seen as a geographic–ideological bloc that is being assembled not necessarily in opposition but in somewhat of a contradistinction to the West. Alternatively, it could be seen as a purely ideological bloc against the West. This conception of the East is often assumed to align with the discourse of the Iranian hard right, both the so-called traditional right and the modern rightist camps. Khamenei, to take the most well-known example, represents the traditional right, while former President Ahmadinejad hailed from the modern right. Still, others view the East in civilization terms and see the Look East policy as a form of a loose, civilizational alliance.[9]

According to Iranian policymakers, Look East does not mean ignoring the West but rather paying attention to the East also, much the same way that the United States does.[10] President Masoud Pezeshkian, in fact, has made restarting dialogue with the West a cornerstone of his foreign policy while ensuring the continuity of the Look East policy. The policy calls for expanding the capacity of Iranian diplomacy by paying equal attention to the states of the East and the West.[11] Khamenei's endorsement of Look East, according to the supreme leader's own website, stems from "pragmatism and a deep understanding of the larger national interests of the country."[12] Khamenei sees the policy as a practical, pragmatic perspective and as an opportunity to establish relations with different countries.[13] Not surprisingly, the Look East policy is an outgrowth of and is closely related to a second pillar of a foreign policy emphasis of former President Raisi, namely good neighborly relations.[14]

In a practical sense, the Look East policy is meant to increase the options available to Iranian foreign policy. Starting especially with the Ahmadinejad administration, this was the primary driver behind efforts to improve relations with neighboring countries, with the states of Latin America, and with China and Russia.[15] The policy's primary objectives are to minimize Iran's vulnerabilities to sanctions, reduce security threats facing the country, and increase opportunities for interstate trade and commerce. It is also meant to strengthen cooperation with the states of the East in scientific fields and the exchange of knowledge, deepen cooperative arrangements in energy security, and enhance Iran's geopolitical and geoeconomic positions. It is also designed to facilitate long-term infrastructural cooperation with Eastern economic powers such as China.[16]

In pursuit of the Look East policy, whether in effect informally or as an official plank of the country's foreign policy doctrine, over the last three decades or so Iranian policymakers have taken a series of concrete steps to draw the Islamic

Republic closer to the East. Beginning in the final years of the twentieth century, in fact, the Iranian Foreign Ministry decided that it needed to enhance the country's strategic depth by improving relations with China, India, Malaysia, and Japan. This was taking place at the same time as there were declines in the consumption of fossil fuels in the West.[17] Throughout the first two decades of the 2000s, Iran also sought to deepen its commercial and diplomatic relations with Indonesia, especially due to the latter's strategic location in relation to the Strait of Malaga, through which most Iranian oil shipments to China travel. In June 2005, Iran attained observer status in the Shanghai Cooperation Organization (SCO).[18] After nearly two decades of trying, in June 2023 Iran finally became a full member of the SCO. Starting in 2011, Iran also sought to expand its ties with the Association of Southeast Asian Nations, ASEAN, and in 2016 became a signatory to the group's Treaty of Amity and Cooperation.

Under the auspices of the Look East policy, Iran has also improved its diplomatic relations and commercial ties with Sri Lanka.[19] After ten years, Iranian president Khatami visited Pakistan in 2002, resulting in improvements in a relationship that had been complicated by the presence of the Taliban in Afghanistan and the migration of large numbers of Afghan refugees to Iran.[20] The trend continued during Ahmadinejad's two-term presidency from 2005 to 2015. In order to strengthen a supposed resistance front against Western neocolonial machinations, Ahmadinejad improved Iran's relations with Venezuela, Cuba, Nicaragua, Sudan, Zambia, and North Korea.[21] This emphasis on South–South relations led some of the president's detractors to accuse him of pursuing a "Look to the South" policy at the expense of both the West and the East and, more detrimentally, the country's national interests.[22]

It can be argued that much of the actual groundwork for the Look East policy was laid during the Rouhani administration. Despite frequent accusations by some of Iran's conservative, hardline media that he was an advocate for closer ties to the West, President Rouhani did much to informally advance Iran's relations with the countries of the East. As part of what he called "constructive moderation," Rouhani sought to balance negotiations with the European Union and the United States over Iran's nuclear program with close attention to relations with China, Russia, and India.[23] He also enhanced Iran's ties with the Eurasian Economic Union (EAEU), and the Asian Infrastructure Investment Bank (AIIB).[24] Most notably, Rouhani was responsible for the state visit of China's President Xi Jinping to Tehran in 2016 and the introduction of the concept of a "comprehensive strategic partnership" between Iran and China.[25]

Soon after taking office in 2021, the central pillars of Raisi's foreign policy agenda began to take shape, some of which included decoupling the overall performance of Iran's economy from the fate of the nuclear negotiations, strengthening ties with countries and actors identified as part of an axis of resistance, and Look East.[26] Within two years of assuming office, the Raisi administration had signed a raft of trade and commercial agreements with states as diverse as Armenia, Belorussia, Iraq, Kazakhstan, Oman, Qatar, and Turkmenistan. No less than twenty such agreements were also signed with China, seventeen with Tajikistan, and twelve with Oman. Another twenty-eight agreements were signed in June 2023, when Raisi traveled to Cuba, Nicaragua, and Venezuela.[27] In March 2023, in what was hailed as a landmark agreement to put an end to years of hostility, Iran and Saudi Arabia announced the restoration of diplomatic relations. The secret negotiations had been brokered by none other than China. Raisi also oversaw an upgrading of diplomatic ties with Libya, which had previously been anemic, and with Sudan, which had broken off diplomatic ties with Iran in 2016.

Undoubtedly, the central dimensions of the Look East policy revolve around deepened relations with Russia and China. Examples of such deep relations include close military cooperation and coordination with Russia in Syria, and more recently in Ukraine; expansive trade with China; and naval exercises with both Russia and China in the Gulf of Oman in March 2023.[28] Iran–Russia relations have become particularly close along multiple fronts in recent years. Prior to its invasion of Ukraine, Russian foreign policy was generally guided by a sense of pragmatism that, by and large, kept the country out of unnecessary entanglements in the affairs of other states. At the same time, Russia gave priority to its relations with first the Balkan states, then the European Union, and followed by the United States. This pattern of prioritization resulted in Russia adopting different positions in relation to Iran at different times. Moreover, Russia saw itself as a key member of various multinational institutions, especially the United Nations, and demonstrated a deep commitment to their resolution.[29] Beginning in the late 2010s, however, Russia's changing threat perceptions drew it closer to Iran in a number of international issues. According to a former Iranian ambassador to Moscow, today Iranian–Russian relations are based on three sets of common denominators. They include necessities, as in logistics and transit routes through the Caspian; opportunities, such as cooperation in industry and security fields; and challenges, of which terrorism, radicalism, and American regional military foothold stand out.[30]

Iranian policymakers are aware that Russia often plays the "Iran card" in its relations with the Western states.[31] For the last several years, nevertheless, a marriage of convenience between the Kremlin and Tehran has drawn the two countries increasingly closer to one another. The Raisi presidency has resulted in a much more contained and constrained political atmosphere domestically, and the concomitant rise of securocrats in domestic and foreign policy arenas. This has occurred with the support of the supreme leader. The influence of security-minded individuals in the foreign policy arena has meant closer military cooperation with Russia during its war with Ukraine.[32] In 2023, in fact, reports began circulating that Iran and Russia were in the process of hammering out a new comprehensive agreement that would include cooperative arrangements in areas such as culture, the arts, and tourism, as well as economy, diplomacy, and the security field.[33]

Looming equally large in Iran's Look East policy, though for different reasons, is China.[34] The Islamic Republic's relations with Beijing date back to the early years of the Iran–Iraq war, when China supplied armaments to both sides. Because of sanctions, however, China could not sell weapons to Iran directly and therefore did so mostly through North Korea.[35] Today, the key commonality between Iran and China is having similar foreign policy positions in relation to global politics.[36] For Iranian policymakers, Iran has been a main recipient of pressure from American unilateralism. It is therefore important for the Islamic Republic's efforts to draw itself strategically closer to China.[37] An important example includes American influence and military presence in Central Asia, about which both Iran and China are concerned.[38] These common concerns resulted in the signing in June 2020 of the "Twenty-Five-Year Comprehensive Strategic Partnership" between Iran and China. Although the terms of the treaty have never been made public, strategic cooperation between the two sides is supposed to result in $400 billion worth of Chinese investment in Iran over the next twenty-five years.[39]

Ironically, prior to Donald Trump coming to office in the United States, China and Russia consistently voted in favor of these and other UN resolutions that in Tehran were seen as seriously harmful to Iranian national interests.[40] These included the referral of Iran's nuclear file to the United Nations Security Council (UNSC) and the passage of repeated UNSC resolutions against the Islamic Republic—Resolutions 1696 and 1737 in 2006, 1747 in 2007, 1803 and 1835 in 2008, and 1929 in 2010. In 2020, however, both China and Russia voted against a US proposal to amend Resolution 2231, originally adopted in 2015, which sought to extend the embargo on the supply of conventional arms to the Islamic Republic.[41] For Iranian policymakers, incidentally, successive UN resolutions against the country's interests were instrumental in pushing them to adopt the Look East policy.[42]

In recent years, the Look East policy has further deepened the Islamic Republic's drive toward regionalism, as Iran has sought to capitalize on geostrategic, geoeconomics, and geopolitical opportunities.[43] In addition to enhanced bilateral ties with the states of Central Asia and the Caucasus, as well as with neighboring Arab countries, the Look East policy also means increased attention to regional forums and cooperative arrangements.[44] The assumption has again been that strengthening regionalism will be an important guarantor of Iranian security.[45] The Look East policy, therefore, is intimately linked to Iran's regional cooperation and integration, and the desire to create mutual networks of roads, railways, air corridors, and commercial and financial links between Iran and other countries of the region.[46]

Before ending the discussion on the meaning of the Look East policy, mention should be made of the robust debate within Iranian policy circles as to whether the new policy is a short-term tactical move or part of the Islamic Republic's longer-term strategic outlook. Within Iran, the policy is often explained from one of three perspectives. The first is an ideological perspective, which has roots in intellectual and cultural assumptions about appropriate foreign policy objectives to pursue. A second perspective is based on the perceived economic and industrial needs of the country and where and how technological networks can be strengthened. A third and final one revolves around strategic considerations that arise out of political and military concerns.[47]

Whichever perspective is adopted, Look East is seen as a strategic outlook that goes far beyond Iran's eastern and northeastern borders.[48] It is a product of the changing architecture of the international system, some of the most important of which include the collapse of the Soviet Union, Iran's evolving regional position, the normative underpinnings of Iranian policy, and unrelenting pressure on Iran by the West.[49] For Tehran's policymakers, it is also an outcome of the post-Western world rather than a shortsighted, instrumentalist look at current international alignments. As evidenced by Iran's substantive collaboration with Russia in the Syrian civil war, the Look East policy is much more than a mere tactic and is meant to further the country's strategic depth in relation to its immediate environment and beyond.[50] The policy is part of a long-term strategic objective that is meant to last beyond short-term fluctuations in the international system.[51]

Critically, this was not always the case. Especially well into the 1990s, Iran's approach to the East was not strategic. It was merely tactical and grew out of policy responses to domestic economic pressure and international developments. At the time, due to the continued influence of the Western states over Iran's trade partners in the East, Iran's initial forays into Look East had little success.[52] As the summary presented here indicates, however, in recent decades there has been a measure of success in expanding Iran's diplomatic and trade ties with non-Western states. This trend has only picked up pace since 2021.

Raisi's endorsement of the Twenty-Five-Year Strategic Cooperation Agreement with China, Iran's full membership in the SCO and BRICS, expanded commercial trade with Russia, the Russia–Ukraine war, intensified Chinese–US competition, Iranian assumptions about the decline of the West, and expansive US sanctions on Iranian trade, entities, and politicians, all have combined to deepen Iran's commitment to the Look East policy as a long-term strategic objective.[53] There is also an increasing awareness in Tehran that US and EU-led sanctions on Iran are unlikely to be lifted in the foreseeable future. One of the primary means through which sanctions are imposed on Iran is through the US dollar, and many of the sanctioning states also use the euro. The Look East policy is therefore especially useful in deepening trade and commercial ties with many states that have strong currencies Iran uses in its trades.[54]

Causes

Let us look more closely at the underlying reasons behind the adoption of the Look East policy by Tehran. It goes without saying that for the past several decades—beginning with the storming of the US embassy in Tehran in 1979, Western arms supplies to Iraq during the Iran–Iraq war, the ratcheting up of the Iranian nuclear program in the early 2000s, Ahmadinejad's ideological presidency, and Trump's confrontational style and overt hostility toward Tehran—Iran has found itself increasingly isolated from and with steadily fewer friends in the West.[55] Under current global circumstances, Iran needs friends wherever it can get them, and it is now the countries of the East that are friendlier, or at least less hostile, to Iran.[56] Within this context, three broad sets of factors have combined to result in the adoption of the Look East policy. They include, first and foremost, being shunned and feeling threatened by the West. Second has been the country's need for rapid economic and industrial growth as it finds more of the West's commercial and trade avenues closed to it. Third is the increased global powers, and especially industrial and technological prowess, of the countries of the East.[57]

By far the most important reason for the increasing tilt toward the East in Iranian foreign policy has been the country's deteriorating relations with the West and increasing perceptions of threats directed at Iran from the United States and its regional allies, especially Israel. Until 2023, the Kingdom of Saudi Arabia was also seen as a key American ally determined to harm Iranian interests globally, within the Persian Gulf region, and even inside Iran itself.[58] Regardless of what Iran does, Iranian policymakers maintain, the West remains convinced that Iran has a "fundamentalist" and "extremist" state that is determined to acquire nuclear weapons.[59] These Western perceptions were solidified during Ahmadinejad's presidency, when he tried to position Iran as the vanguard of the global resistance against American unilateralism and hegemony.[60] The thaw in Iran's relations with the West during the Rouhani years, from 2013 to 2021, which culminated in the 2015 signing of the nuclear agreement, proved only temporary. Critically, for Tehran, the fleeting nature of the thaw was a product of Western unreliability and untrustworthiness. In 2018, the United States withdrew from the nuclear accord, and the European signatories to the agreement lacked the backbone and resolve to stand up to the Americans.

President Trump's subsequent launching of what he called "the maximum pressure campaign" on Iran did not end with his presidency. The Joe Biden administration maintained the substance of the campaign against Iran, and the European Union continued to dutifully follow suit. As far as Tehran is concerned, the United States has also encircled Iran with its military presence across the Persian Gulf, in almost every direction along the country's borders, and its military reach extends all the way from Australia to South Korea and beyond. Within this context of overwhelming American military, diplomatic, and economic pressure on the country, Iran's efforts to forge alliances with China and Russia are meant to enhance its security in an overwhelmingly hostile international environment.[61] It is little surprise, therefore, that increased threat perceptions from the West have been highly instrumental in prompting Iran to look for friends elsewhere, especially in the East.[62]

Meant to safeguard Iranian independence and sovereignty, the Look East policy is based on the assumption that it will compensate for Iran's strategic deficiencies and enhance its national interests.[63] Ultimately, the policy is a security-based arrangement that is designed to enable Iran to proactively pursue its national interests in the international arena.[64] In fact, at an indeterminate point in the future, the Iranian government would like to see the establishment of an Asian collective security arrangement that would act as a counterpart to multilateral and bilateral Western military alliances.[65] Not coincidentally, Raisi's Look East policy has at times been called an "Asian policy."[66]

Importantly, the Look East policy is being pursued at a time when there are increasing assumptions in Iran about the decline of the West. Right or wrong, some of the highest echelons of Iran's leadership, from the supreme leader on to the president and the commanders of the Revolutionary Guards, are convinced that the West is in actual decline. They point to social developments in the United States as a sign of its decline as a global power.[67] They further cite structural difficulties in global capital markets, and the failures that the United States encountered in its invasions of Iraq and Afghanistan, compared to the East's less militaristic and more diplomatic solutions to global issues, as evidence of the West's decline.[68] As the West in general and the United States in particular experience precipitous declines, and as the East and especially China rise, the Look East policy is assumed to accrue maximum benefit to Iran.[69]

Directly related to increased threat perceptions from the West are the expansive trade and economic sanctions to which Iran is subject. Being by far the most comprehensively sanctioned state in the world because of the United States, frequently threatened with American military action, and subject to an array of diplomatic, political, and economic pressures that are brought to bear by the United States and its allies, Iranian policymakers consider their country to be the biggest victim of American global hegemony.[70] In response, beginning with the Ahmadinejad presidency, one of the key assumptions of Iranian foreign policy has been to employ economics in the service of diplomacy.[71]

For Iran, which sees itself as a consequential actor in the world energy markets, the Look East policy affords the opportunity to establish a secure regional environment in which the Islamic Republic can deepen its geopolitical and geoeconomic interests.[72] The rapid growth of the Chinese and Indian economies has opened up some space for Iranian oil and gas exports.[73] Moreover, the Iranian government has set an ambitious goal for itself to be an advanced industrial state and be in a preeminent position in West Asia by 2025.[74] After the nuclear agreement was signed in 2015, Iran assumed that investments by the Europeans would be a guarantee for the future longevity of the sanctions not being reimposed. Once the United States pulled out of the accord, however, the Europeans were powerless to stand up to the United States and to live up to their end of the bargain.[75]

From Rafsanjani to Pezeshkian, for each president, the Look East policy has been a product of domestic circumstances on the one hand and evolving international developments on the other.[76] The goals of the policy have not always been easy to reach. Many states and companies alike have been reluctant to substantively engage with Iran lest they run afoul of American secondary sanctions. Between 2014 and 2022, for example, at least ten high-tech Chinese companies found themselves heavily fined by the United States for allegedly violating American sanctions by selling Iran technology that could be used in its missile program.[77] Earlier, in 2012, the banking giant HSBC was fined $1.9 billion for a host of alleged infractions, among them allowing sensitive financial transactions involving Iran.[78] Within this rather constrained international context, tallying up the successes and failures of Iran's Look East policy is somewhat problematic.

A Preliminary Balance Sheet

For Iranian policymakers, the Look East policy has brought a number of perceived advantages and has presented Iran with several strategic opportunities. According to the political scientist Ali Adami, at the civilizational level, the policy has fostered the forging of closer ties with countries such as India and China that have historical and cultural commonalities with Iran.[79] In addition to facilitating the reemergence of a somewhat coherent Eastern civilizational front, the policy is enabling Iran to tap into the economic and industrial prowess of the states of the East and to emulate their developmental models.[80] And if that were not enough, the policy provides further opportunities for highly beneficial political, economic, and military cooperation between Iran and Eastern powerhouses.[81]

These perceived advantages, however, fail in comparison with the chorus of criticisms that have been leveled against the policy by Iranian scholars and policy pundits. According to Elaheh Koolaee, a political science professor at the University of Tehran, the Look East policy's reliance on Russia and China is shortsighted. Ignoring the economic fruits of the West is "Easternization" not Look East.[82] Although Iran must have a balanced relationship between both the East and the West, unlike the Pezeshkian administration, Raisi showed little or no intention to balance the Look East policy with deepening or even repairing relations with the West.[83] Others maintain that if the Look East policy is being pursued in furtherance of ideological goals and objectives, it is bound to fail. Similarly, if the policy is simply meant as an economic stopgap measure that is meant to address short-term needs, in the long run it is also bound to be counterproductive.[84]

Whether a tactic or a strategy, others charge, the Look East policy will neither address Iran's economic needs nor its strategic objectives.[85] It is unclear, they argue, to what extent Russia, China, and even India would welcome a powerful, confident Iran.[86] A number of critics maintain that China and Russia have warmed up to Iran because for the time being it is in their economic and strategic interests to do so.[87] But China and Russia have not been, nor will they ever become, strategic partners to Iran in the long run.[88] The Chinese and Russian governments both assume that Iran's Look East policy is being implemented out of desperation and necessity, and believe that Iran will abandon them as soon as its relations with the West improve.[89] Neither country thinks of Iran as a strategic partner; nor, for that matter, is either state likely to enter into strategic partnerships with any other country. They are even less likely to enter into an ideological alliance with Iran that places them in opposition to the West. At best, they are open to developing cooperative arrangements with strategically located countries such as Iran, so long as it serves their interests.[90]

The Look East policy needs to be realistic, therefore, in realizing the limits of strategic alliances with Russia and China. Both states, critics point out, have come out with statements in support of the United Arab Emirates' position in relation to the three disputed islands in the Persian Gulf, China has far deeper economic and commercial relations with many of Iran's adversaries, and Russia cooperates closely with Israel in regards to its presence and its actions in Syria. Importantly, neither China nor others considered as part of an Eastern camp are willing to abandon a superpower like the United States, and the vast investment and commercial opportunities it presents, in favor of a country like Iran.[91]

Lastly, the critics charge, the Look East policy's assumption of the decline of the West is based on false premises. If there is a decline of the West, its practical consequences for Iranian diplomacy and strategy are overblown. It is, at any rate, a mistake to assume that the West in general and the United States in particular can be replaced by the East more broadly or by China in specific. For the foreseeable future, the West remains a powerful global force to be reckoned with.

In specific relation to China, it has been consistently unwilling to risk its global financial position by entering into major trade and investment agreements with Iran. Because of comprehensive international sanctions on the country, and due to Iran's steadfast refusal to join the international anti–money laundering organization the Financial Action Task Force (FATF), China's Belt and Road Initiative completely bypasses Iran, and Chinese investments in Iran remain at best minimal. Given that China's relationship with the West and especially with the United States are already complicated by technological competition and diplomatic tensions, China is reluctant to draw itself even closer to Iran lest it further complicates its foreign relations and its economic interests around the world. The contrasts in Chinese commercial dealings with Iran and Pakistan are quite revealing. In Pakistan, Chinese companies engage in multiple mega projects, and start and complete them relatively quickly. In Iran, by contrast, Chinese companies are few and far in between, and when they do enter into a project, they deliberately delay its completion indefinitely.[92]

More ominously, despite Iranian efforts to draw itself closer to China, it has at times continued to adopt positions inimical to Iranian interests. When Xi traveled to Saudi Arabia in December 2022, for example, China and Saudi Arabia issued a joint statement in which they called on Iran to cooperate with the International Atomic Energy Agency in order to ensure the peaceful nature of the Islamic Republic's nuclear program. During the same trip, which was timed to coincide with a Gulf Cooperation Council summit in Riyadh, China also signed on to a GCC resolution calling on Iran to negotiate with the UAE in good faith over the three disputed islands of the Lesser and Greater Tunbs and Abu Musa. In Iran, many saw China's seeming moves against Iran as clear evidence of the Look East policy's failure.[93]

Russia's approach to Iran, skeptics maintain, appears to be equally instrumentalist. It appears that under no circumstances does Russia want Iran's national power to be strengthened. Instead, Russia wants to use Iran as a bargaining chip with the West, and it often has no desire whatsoever to add substance to its relations with Iran. Not surprisingly, Russia's relations with Iran remain at the level of "cold peace."[94] In fact, Russia's recent closeness to Iran is because it needs friends in its war against Ukraine. However, the critics point out, as its conduct during the nuclear negotiations showed, Russia will not hesitate to harm Iran's interests when it is to its advantage.⁹⁵ Russia has in fact repeatedly proven itself to be an unreliable friend to Iran, as evidenced through its lack of cooperation in relation to the Caspian Sea and its refusal to sell advanced, SAM-300 missiles to Iran. These indications bode ill for the Look East policy.

The Look East policy represents the latest phase in the evolution of the Islamic Republic's foreign policy since 1979. For a number of years, under the auspices of "Neither Eastern nor Western," Iran saw itself as a stalwart member of the nonaligned movement. Nevertheless, while nonalignment informed Iranian foreign policy, Iran's economic and military needs, both legacies of the prerevolutionary era, remained firmly anchored in the West. In the 1990s, after the war with Iraq had ended and the era of reconstruction had begun, Iranian foreign policy, pretty similar to its domestic politics, remained captive to the vagaries of factional infighting and, by and large, policy paralysis.⁹⁶ Although in the early 2000s Iranian diplomacy achieved notable successes, with the 2015 nuclear agreement as its crowning achievement, it was only after 2021, when the system acquired factional uniformity under the auspices of conservative dominance, that Iranian foreign policy became far more proactive than ever before. With the blessing of the country's highest authority, Ayatollah Ali Khamenei, President Raisi and his foreign minister, Hossein Amir-Abdollahian, made the Eastward tilt of the country's foreign policy of the previous two decades into official policy.

Evidence shows that Iran's Look East policy goes beyond geographic limits and is meant to denote a broadly non-Western, if not anti-Western, outlook. In this sense, it entails commercial and diplomatic ties with whatever state or nonstate actor that stands outside of the Western political and ideological orbit. This spans countries in the geographic north such as Russia and Belarus; in the south such as Cuba, Nicaragua, Venezuela, Brazil, and South Africa; and in the east such as India, Malaysia, and China. For Iran, Look East means orientation toward an amorphous front that has not yet formed but stands increasingly opposite, or at least apart from, the Western alliance, the Washington Consensus, and the liberal world order.

Insofar as Iranian policymakers are concerned, the Look East policy has evolved into one of the Islamic Republic's strategic objectives for the foreseeable future. From the perspective of the Raisi administration, the unrelenting and comprehensive sanctions that are being vigilantly imposed by the United States and the European Union will not be lifted anytime soon in the coming years. The West, in fact, inheres a built-in hostility to the very essence of the Iranian state. At the same time, there are many opportunities for trade and investments that the fast-growing economies of Asia and South America present. Moreover, there are potentials for synergetic security relations with Russia and perhaps even China.

Therefore, it is only natural to strategically pursue deepening diplomatic, trade, and security relations with Eastern states. This strategy is anchored in China and Russia, but is hardly limited to them. It also includes states such as those that are part of the SCO and BRICS, to both of which Iran was formally admitted in 2023.[97]

Successes such as those of accession to the SCO and BRICS notwithstanding, the road ahead for Iranian foreign policy is far from smooth. The extent to which Iran seems to rely on its relations with China and Russia, and how these two powers perceive and relate to the Islamic Republic, continue to remain unclear and problematic. Also uncertain is whether overwhelming reliance on non-Western states can fully address Iran's mounting economic needs. Moreover, despite vast improvements in Iran's relations with its neighbors, tensions between Iran and Saudi Arabia and Iran and Azerbaijan remain beneath the surface. For now, the Look East policy, being vigorously pursued by Iran, seems to be succeeding in its objectives. But whether this success will continue into the future remains to be seen.

NOTES

1. Quoted in Mehdi Poursafa, "Chera negah-e beh sharq tabdil beh siyasat-e rahbordi-e Iran shod?" [Why Look to the East became Iran's strategic policy?], Javanan Online, February 13, 2018, https://bit.ly/48UvUWz.

2. Quoted in Poursafa, "Chera negah-e beh sharq."

3. For a brief survey of the Look East policy from the Rafsanjani to the Ahmadinejad presidencies, see Majid Divsalar, "Roykard-e negah-e beh sharq dar ravabet-e khareji-yeh Iran" [The Look East outlook in Iran's foreign relations], *Pegah-e Howzeh*, no. 237 (1387/2008), https://bit.ly/46s3f96.

4. See, for example, Divsalar, "Roykard-e negah-e beh sharq."

5. See, for example, Roham Alvandi, "The Shah's détente with Khrushchev: Iran's 1962 missile base pledge to the Soviet Union," *Cold War History* 14, no. 3 (2014): 423–44.

6. Mohammad Hossein Hajiloo, "Shekanandeghi-e hamkari dar faza-ye hezhemonik va nagah-e beh sharq dar siyasat-e khareji-yeh jomhuri-e Eslami-e Iran" [Fragile cooperation in a hegemonic environment and Look to the East in the foreign policy of the Islamic Republic of Iran], *Rahyaft-e Enqelab-e Eslami* 11, no. 38 (1396/2017): 72–73.

7. Rasool Musavi, "Negah-e ma be sharq mobtani bar manafe'-e ma ast" [Our Look to the East is based on our interests], Khamenei.ir, July 5, 2021, https://bit.ly/3PGaEuy.

8. Rahim Baizidi, "Rahbord-e negah-e beh sharq dar siyasat-e khareji-yeh Iran" [Look to the East strategy in Iranian foreign policy], *Faslnameh-e ayandeh pazhohi-e rahbordi* 1, no. 2 (2022): 144–45.

9. Ali Adami, "Rahbord-e negah-e beh sharq dar siyasat-e khareji-yeh jomhuri-e Eslami-e Iran" [Look to the East strategy in the foreign policy of the Islamic Republic of Iran], *Faslnameh-e motale'at-e siyasi* 2, no. 7 (1389/2020): 98.

10. Musavi, "Negah-e ma be sharq mobtani bar manafe'-e ma ast."

11. Hajiloo, "Shekanandeghi-e hamkari dar faza-ye hezhemonik," 70.

12. Musavi, "Negah-e ma be sharq mobtani bar manafe'-e ma ast."

13. Mohsen Paak-Aeen, "Roykard-e negah-e beh sharq az didgah-e rahbar-e enqelab" [The Look East outlook in the revolutionary leader's perspective], Khabaronline, January 25, 2022, www.khabaronline.ir/xhzMg.

14. "Nagah-e beh sharq va ta'mol-e mantaqeh-i" [Look to the East and regional interactions], Student News Network, June 20, 2023, https://snn.ir/fa/print/1081648. For more on Iran's good neighborly relations, see Mehran Kamrava and Ali Bagheri Dolatabadi, "Iran's Neighborhood Policy: Parameters, Objectives, and Obstacles," *Middle East Policy*, 31, no. 4 (2024): 56–73.

15. Nowzar Shafiee and Zahra Sadeqi, "Gozineh-haye Iran dar ravabet-e khareji bar asas-e siyasat-e negah-e beh sharq" [Options for Iranian foreign policy on the basis of the Look East Policy], *Rahbord-e Yas*, no. 22 (1389/2020): 310.
16. Baizidi, "Rahbord-e negah-e beh sharq," 145–48.
17. Shafiee and Sadeqi, "Gozineh-haye Iran dar ravabet-e khareji," 310.
18. Shafiee and Sadeqi, "Gozineh-haye Iran dar ravabet-e khareji," 326.
19. Shafiee and Sadeqi, "Gozineh-haye Iran dar ravabet-e khareji," 328.
20. Shafiee and Sadeqi, "Gozineh-haye Iran dar ravabet-e khareji," 329.
21. "Payamad-e sharq-garaye Irani" [Consequences of Iranian Easternization], Fararu News, September 18, 2023, https://bit.ly/3tvGl2x.
22. Shafiee and Sadeqi, "Gozineh-haye Iran dar ravabet-e khareji," 333.
23. "Payamad-e sharq-garaye Irani."
24. "Payamad-e sharq-garaye Irani."
25. Hamidreza Azizi, "Do negah beh negah-e beh sharq" [Two looks at the Look East], *E'temad*, January 19, 2020, https://bit.ly/3Qfmxtc.
26. Mohammad Hussein Malaek, "Arzyabi-e siyasat-e khareji-e do saleh-e dowlat-e sizdahom" [Evaluating the two-year foreign policy of the thirteenth government], *Diplomacy-e Irani*, May 28, 2023, https://bit.ly/3PJng4g.
27. "Nagah-e beh sharq va ta'mol-e mantaqeh-i."
28. Malaek, "Arzyabi-e siyasat-e khareji-e."
29. Mehdi Sanaie, "Siyasat-e 'negah-e beh sharq' dar howzeh-e amniyati va eqtesadi sahih ast" [The Look East policy is correct in the security and economic fields], Fararunews, December 24, 2011, https://bit.ly/3RIqgjX.
30. Sanaie, "Siyasat-e 'negah-e beh sharq' dar howzeh-e amniyati."
31. Sanaie, "Siyasat-e 'negah-e beh sharq' dar howzeh-e amniyati."
32. "Payamad-e sharq-garaye Irani."
33. "Negah-e beh sharq hamchenan mehvar-e siyasat-e khareji-e jomhuri-e Eslami-e Iran" [Look to the East as a continuing pillar of the foreign policy of the Islamic Republic of Iran], *Mardomsalari*, December 24, 2021, https://bit.ly/46qavCc.
34. Sanaie, "Siyasat-e 'negah-e beh sharq' dar howzeh-e amniyati."
35. Ehsan Fallahi and Mohsen Rostami, "Rahbord-haye defai-e amniyati-e jomhuri-e Eslami-e Iran ba negah beh sharq: Motale'at-e moredi-e Chin and Rusiya" [Security strategies of the Islamic Republic of Iran and the Look East policy: China and Russia as case studies], *Nashriyeh-e Elmi Afaq-e Amniyat*, 15, no. 54 (2022), 142.
36. Sanaie, "Siyasat-e 'negah-e beh sharq' dar howzeh-e amniyati."
37. Fallahi and Rostami, "Rahbor-haye defai-e amniyati-e jomhuri-e Eslami-e Iran," 141.
38. Hajiloo, "Shekanandeghi-e hamkari dar faza-ye hezhemonik," 75.
39. Fallahi and Rostami, "Rahbor-haye defai-e amniyati-e jomhuri-e Eslami-e Iran," 148.
40. "Payamad-e sharq-garaye Irani."
41. The proposal was defeated, with US allies the United Kingdom, Germany, France, Belgium, and Estonia abstaining from the vote and only the Dominican Republic voting in favor.
42. Shafiee and Sadeqi, "Gozineh-haye Iran dar ravabet-e khareji," 315.
43. Quoted in Poursafa, "Chera negah-e beh sharq."
44. Shafiee and Sadeqi, "Gozineh-haye Iran dar ravabet-e khareji," 311.
45. Sanaie, "Siyasat-e 'negah-e beh sharq' dar howzeh-e amniyati."

46. Keyhan Barzegar, "Rahbord-e siyasat-e khareji-e Iran dar tavazon-e qova-ye mantaqeh-i" [Strategy of Iranian foreign policy in relation to the regional balance of power], *Faslnameh-e motale'at-e rahbordi* 21, no. 4 (1397/2018): 186.
47. Shafiee and Sadeqi, "Gozineh-haye Iran dar ravabet-e khareji," 312.
48. Hadi Sayyadi and Ardeshir Sanaei, "Jaygah-e goftenam-e negah-e beh sharq dar taghiir-e roykard-e siyasat-e khareji-e Iran" [The position of the Look East policy in strategic shifts in Iranian foreign policy], *Motale'at-e oroasiya-e markazi* 12, no. 1 (1398/2019): 116.
49. Sayyadi and Sanaei, "Jaygah-e goftenam-e negah-e beh sharq," 115.
50. Quoted in Poursafa, "Chera negah-e beh sharq."
51. "Siyasat-e nehagh-e beh sharq jadid nist" [The Look East policy is not new], IRIB News Agency, January 25, 2021, https://bit.ly/3LOFDUi.
52. "Payamad-e sharq-garaye Irani."
53. "Payamad-e sharq-garaye Irani."
54. Poursafa, "Chera negah-e beh sharq."
55. Javid Qorbanoğlu, "Charkhesh-e ma'nadar-e siyasat-e negah-e beh sharq dar dowlat-e sizdahom" [The meaning turn of the Look to the East policy in the thirteenth government], *Setareh-e sobh*, January 23, 2022, https://bit.ly/3QflpFY.
56. Emad Abshenas, "Rahbord-e negah beh sharq" [The Look East strategy], International Quran News Agency, January 27, 2022, https://bit.ly/3PL3kOB.
57. Adami, "Rahbord-e negah beh sharq," 106.
58. Banafsheh Keynoush, *Iran and Saudi Arabia: Friend or Foe* (Palgrave Macmillan, 2016), 137.
59. Shafiee and Sadeqi, "Gozineh-haye Iran dar ravabet-e khareji," 320.
60. Ali Taqavi, "Rahbord-e negah beh sharq ya e'telaf-e siyasi 'alayh-e gharb" [Looking to the East or political alliance against the West], Jahan-e San'at, June 12, 2022, https://bit.ly/46mulis.
61. "Nagah-e beh sharq va ta'mol-e mantaqeh-i."
62. Shafiee and Sadeqi, "Gozineh-haye Iran dar ravabet-e khareji," 309.
63. Hajiloo, "Shekanandeghi-e hamkari dar faza-ye hezhemonik," 69; Musavi, "Negah-e ma be sharq mobtani bar manafe'-e ma ast."
64. Hajiloo, "Shekanandeghi-e hamkari dar faza-ye hezhemonik," 85.
65. Shafiee and Sadeqi, "Gozineh-haye Iran dar ravabet-e khareji," 314.
66. "Payamad-e sharq-garaye Irani."
67. Azizi, "Do negah beh negah-e beh sharq."
68. Shafiee and Sadeqi, "Gozineh-haye Iran dar ravabet-e khareji," 316.
69. Malaek, "Arzyabi-e siyasat-e khareji-e."
70. Hajiloo, "Shekanandeghi-e hamkari dar faza-ye hezhemonik," 74.
71. Shafiee and Sadeqi, "Gozineh-haye Iran dar ravabet-e khareji," 311, 331.
72. Adami, "Rahbord-e negah-e beh sharq," 120–22.
73. Shafiee and Sadeqi, "Gozineh-haye Iran dar ravabet-e khareji," 313.
74. Shafiee and Sadeqi, "Gozineh-haye Iran dar ravabet-e khareji," 321.
75. Abshenas, "Rahbord-e negah beh sharq."
76. "Payamad-e sharq-garaye Irani."
77. Fallahi and Rostami, "Rahbor-haye defai-e amniyati-e jomhuri-e Eslami-e Iran," 143.
78. "US Fines UK Bank HSBC over Money Laundering," Middle East Business Intelligence, December 13, 2012, https://bit.ly/3ttKELx.
79. Adami, "Rahbord-e negah beh sharq," 112.
80. Adami, "Rahbord-e negah beh sharq," 117.
81. Adami, "Rahbord-e negah beh sharq," 118.

82. Quoted in Danial Delavari, "Tekiyeh beh sharq nemitavanad ta'min konandeh-e manafe'-e keshvar-e ma bashad" [Reliance on the East cannot provide for our country's interests], Eco Iran, July 15, 2023, https://bit.ly/46CNNqC.
83. Qorbanoğlu, "Charkhesh-e ma'nadar-e siyasat-e negah-e beh sharq."
84. Qorbanoğlu, "Charkhesh-e ma'nadar-e siyasat-e negah-e beh sharq."
85. Azizi, "Do negah beh negah-e beh sharq."
86. Hajiloo, "Shekanandeghi-e hamkari dar faza-ye hezhemonik," 69.
87. Qorbanoğlu, "Charkhesh-e ma'nadar-e siyasat-e negah-e beh sharq."
88. Shahab Shahsevari, "Zehniyat-e siyasatgozaran dar 'negah-e beh sharq' ghalat ast" [Assumptions of policymakers regarding "Look to the East" is mistaken], Aftab News, April 1, 2023, https://bit.ly/3PM1b55.
89. Shahsevari, "Zehniyat-e siyasatgozaran."
90. Taqavi, "Rahbord-e negah beh sharq."
91. Shahsevari, "Zehniyat-e siyasatgozaran."
92. Shahsevari, "Zehniyat-e siyasatgozaran."
93. Javad Heiran-Nia, "Zaman-e tajdid-e nazsar dar negah-e beh sharq?" [Time for rethinking the Look East policy?], Fararunews, December 29, 2022, https://bit.ly/3RAyKJW.
94. Shafiee and Sadeqi, "Gozineh-haye Iran dar ravabet-e khareji," 324–25.
95. Delavari, "Tekiyeh beh sharq nemitavanad."
96. Mehran Kamrava, "National Security Debates in Iran: Factionalism and Lost Opportunities," *Middle East Policy* 14, no. 2 (Summer 2007): 84–100.
97. Iran became an official member of BRICS starting on January 1, 2024.

Part I
SANCTIONS, REGIONALISM, AND RISKS

2

SANCTIONS, COMPLEXITY, AND UNCERTAINTY IN IRAN'S EASTWARD TRADE

Karim Eslamloueyan

Diverse factors impact Asia's share in Iran's total trade, including economic sanctions imposed on Iran by the West and trade uncertainty in the global economy. Moreover, economic complexity, capturing the productive knowledge embedded in produced goods and measuring the diversification of exported commodities, is another determinant of trade relations between Iran and the major Asian economies. Some researchers argue that economic complexity further advances economic growth and underscores the role of human capital in producing sophisticated goods. The effect of these variables on Iran's trade with the East has not been studied in the literature. More specifically, this chapter focuses on Iran's trade ties with South and East Asia, which include fifteen of Iran's trade partners, such as China, India, Japan, South Korea, Malaysia, Indonesia, Thailand, Vietnam, Singapore, and Pakistan.

Yunling Zhang and Minghui Shen highlight the contribution of Asia to regional and global economic development.[1] Monireh Shariatinia and Hamidreza Azizi focus on Iran's role as a bridge in the ancient Silk Road and argue that it has great potential to connect the East and the West through the new Silk Road.[2] They study the factors affecting Iran–China cooperation and underscore the new Silk Road's strategic role in improving Iran's status in the world economy. Aside from Iran's role in connecting Asia to the West, as an oil-rich economy, it is also important for China and other South and East Asian economies due to their increasing dependency on world energy. Undoubtedly, energy is a significant constraint for future economic development in China and the rest of the world.[3]

Several questions regarding the Iran–Asia trade relationship have to be addressed. Has Asia's share in Iran's total trade increased over time? What is the role of harsh economic sanctions imposed on Iran in shaping Iran–Asia trade ties? Does world trade uncertainty contribute to Iran's trade with the East? Does improving Iran's economic complexity, showing the relationship between knowledge and the diversity of export products in each country, affect Asian trade with Iran? How did the COVID-19 crisis shape Iran's trade with South and East Asia?

The literature on Iran's international commerce lacks research that examine why Iran's trade has shifted from the West to the East. Some researchers have studied trade relationship between Iran and some of its partners. For example, Bijan B. Aghevli and Cyrus Sassanpour study the effect of an increase in oil prices on inflation, trade balance, and output growth in Iran during the period 1960 to 1977.[4] Their results show that the oil shock of 1973 to 1974 led to higher inflation and imports in Iran. Higher imports also decreased the competitiveness of Iran's non–oil trade sector in the international markets.

Mohammad Reza Farzanegan uses Multiple Indicators, Multiple Causes (MIMIC) modeling and trade misinvoicing to examine the causes and consequences of import and export smuggling.[5] He also estimates the relative size of smuggling in Iran from 1970 to 2002. He finds that a higher penalty rate and better quality of economic and political institutions reduce smuggling, while higher tariffs increase illegal trade. According to him, smuggling trade constituted approximately 13 percent of Iran's total trade from 1970 to 2002.

Using a J-curve test, Hasan Heidari and Fatemeh Zarei investigate the commercial relations between Iran and its major trading partner.[6] More specifically, they use an Error Correction model to study the short- and long-run trends of the trade balance between Iran and its major Asian trading partners during 1991 (quarter 2) to 2007 (quarter 3). They find a J-curve effect in the bilateral trade balance between Iran and its two partners, namely China and Japan.

Gholamreza Fathipour and Ali Ghahremanlou study the Iran–India trade relationship from 2001 to 2010.[7] They show that comparative advantage was the main driver for trade ties between the countries. More specifically, they find that mineral fuels form a large part of Indian imports from Iran. Moreover, inorganic chemicals, articles of iron or steel, drugs, and pharmaceuticals were India's main exports to Iran.

Using Asian International Input–Output (IIO) tables, Nahid Pourrostami investigates trade interdependency among East Asian countries.[8] She calculates interdependency and self-sufficiency indicators by employing IIO data published in 2005. The author shows that the interdependency increased in East Asia from 1990 to 2005 but decreased in other parts of the world. She also finds that self-dependency indicators in East Asian countries are high. The results show that trade interdependency between East Asian economies has increased with China but decreased with Japan.

Shekoofeh Nagheli et al. examine the impact of political institutions on Iran's exports to West Asian countries over the period 2000 to 2015 using a mixed regressive–spatial autoregressive model.[9] They find that the governance index, as a measure of good political institutions, significantly affects Iran's exports.

Using network analysis, Monireh Rafat studies the trade position of Iran and its partners in West Asia in the World Trade Network (WTN) from 2010 to 2019.[10] She shows that only the United Arab Emirates is at the core of the global trade network. According to her findings, Kuwait is in the inner periphery, and other countries, including Iran, are outside the WTN.

Researchers have yet to study the main determinants of Iran's trade shift from the West to the East. To fill this gap in the literature, I employ an Autoregressive Distributed Lag (ARDL) model to study factors affecting the short- and long-run changes in Asia's share in Iran's trade with the world. The results of my research indicate that there is a long-run equilibrium relationship among the different variables. The long-run model estimation shows that the imposition of economic sanctions by the West leads to a rise in Asia's proportion of Iran's total trade. Moreover, I show that an improvement in the Iran-specific complexity index reduces the share of Asian economies in Iran's trade.

Furthermore, the results show that world trade uncertainty increases Iran's relative trade with Asia. This implies that in an uncertain trade world, the relative risk of Iran's trade with the West increases compared to the East (South and East Asia). We also find that the COVID-19 pandemic reduced Asia's share in Iran's total trade. Finally, the results show that when an exogenous shock hits the model, it quickly returns to equilibrium. The chapter concludes that Iran's economic ties with the East are not necessarily a strategic choice but a necessity that dictates its will. The hostility between Iran and the West, and the harsh sanctions imposed on Iran by the West, have left no choice for Iran but to boost its economic relationship with the East. However, as the other contributions in this volume make clear, diplomatic tensions and sanctions are not the only factors contributing to the rise of Iran–East trade. The Iran–West conflict may accelerate Iran's trade with the East, but is not the sole determinant of Iran's "Look East" policy.

Iran's Trade Ties

Figure 2.1 shows the changes in Iran's degree of openness. It shows that after the first global oil shock of 1973, the share of trade in Iran's economy increased to about 76 percent in 1975. Because Iran was a significant oil exporter, this shock

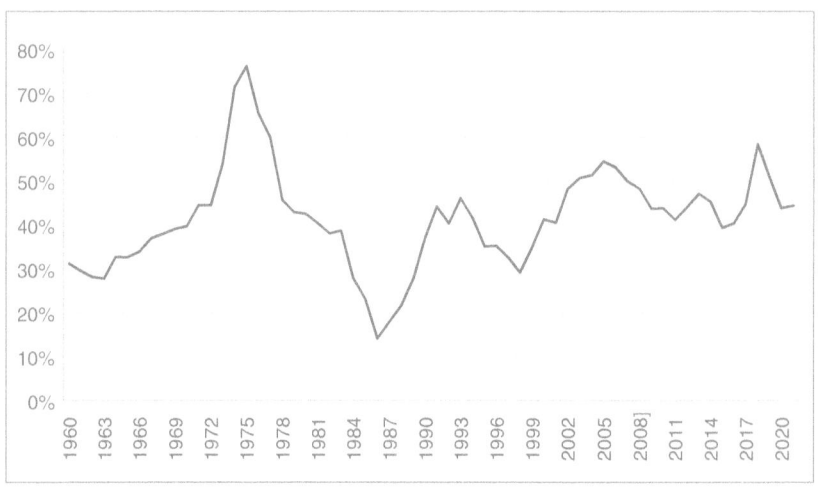

FIGURE 2.1. Iran's trade (% of GDP)
Source: World Development Indicators (WDI)—World Bank.

increased the oil price from $3 per barrel to about $10. The oil boom dramatically raised Iran's exports due to the crucial role of oil revenues in its total trade with the world. After 1975, the degree of trade openness dropped steadily, down to 45 percent in 1979. After the victory of the 1979 revolution and the start of the Iran–Iraq war in 1981, the degree of openness reached 14 percent in 1986. Since then, Iran's trade share as a percentage of gross domestic product (GDP) has witnessed an increasing trend. Its highest level was 58 percent in 2018. After the US withdrawal from the nuclear deal (JCPOA) in 2018 and the outbreak of the COVID-19 pandemic, Iran's trade as a share of GDP reached as low as 43 percent.

Iran's Trade with the West

According to the International Monetary Fund (IMF [DOTS]), Iran's trade with the West in 1966 was about 50 percent of its total trade. However, as figure 2.2 shows, the West's share in Iran's total trade reached less than 10 percent in 2021, indicating a dramatic shift in Iran's trade with the West.

Iran's Trade with South and East Asia

Figure 2.3 shows that the share of South and East Asia in Iran's total trade has had an upward trend in the last forty years. Figure 2.4 provides a comparison of the East and West shares in Iran's trade with the world. As the figures show, the

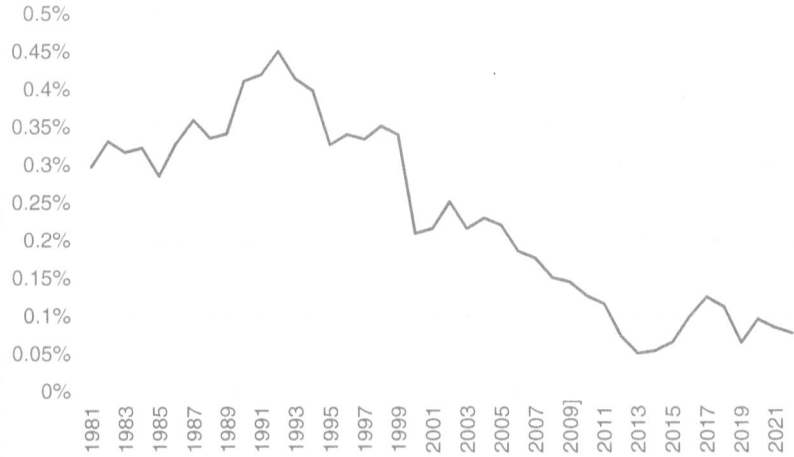

FIGURE 2.2. The West's share in Iran's total trade
Source: Direction of Trade Statistics (DOTS)—IMF.

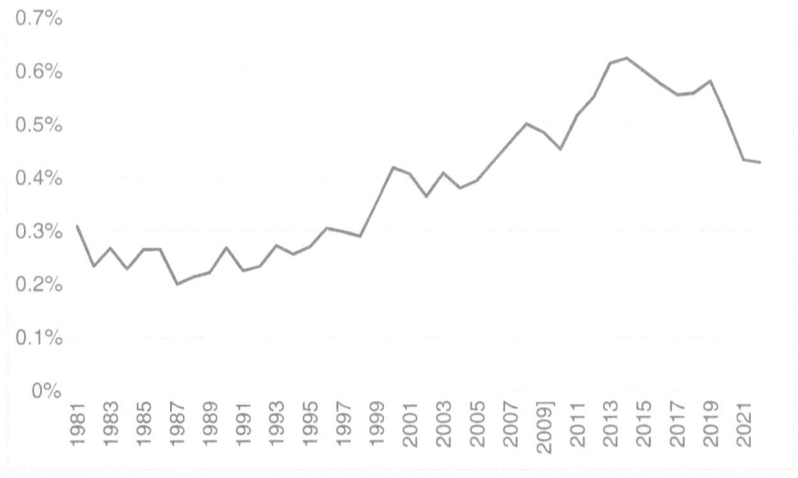

FIGURE 2.3. The share of South and East Asia in Iran's total trade
Source: Direction of Trade Statistics (DOTS)—IMF.

composition of Iran's main trade partners has dramatically shifted from the West to the East.[11]

The evidence also underscores that the share of emerging and developing Asia in Middle Eastern and Central Asian trade has increased over time.[12] Nasser Saidi

FIGURE 2.4. The shares of the West and the East in Iran's trade with the world
Source: Direction of Trade Statistics (DOTS)—IMF.

and Aathira Prasad show that the share of trade between the Middle East and North African countries, such as Saudi Arabia, the UAE, and Egypt, and Asia has also risen during the last thirty years.[13] This indicates that the share of the East in world trade has increased, and it is worth noting that this trend is not limited to Iran and might be part of a broader Look East policy in the region.

The Model Specification, Data, and Methodology

I use an econometric model to examine whether economic sanctions, uncertainty, complexity, and the COVID-19 pandemic affect the share of Asia in Iran's trade. This section discusses the logic behind choosing the key variables to explain the dependent variable.

As the literature shows, economic sanctions negatively affect the trade of the sanctioned countries and harm their well-being.[14] Consumer and intermediate goods shortages due to the trade embargo leads to higher inflation and production costs. These, in turn, reduce economic growth. Hence, a sanctioned country needs to find a way to offset the harmful effect of sanctions on trade. In the case of Iran, the model also examines how economic sanctions affect Iran's Look East policy by changing the share of Asia in Iran's total trade.

Economic complexity is one indicator that shows a country's success in achieving a knowledge-based economy, which occurs when all sectors, including agriculture, industry, and services, are knowledge-intensive. In knowledge-based economies, knowledge determines how to allocate resources, and produce and distribute goods. The economic complexity measures the direct relationship between knowledge and the diversity of the country's export products.[15] The literature highlights the role of economic complexity and trade openness in resource depletion and economic growth.[16] For example, Buhari Doğan et al. show that economic complexity boosts economic growth.[17] Along similar lines, Xiuping Guo et al. find that economic complexity nullifies the adverse effects of globalization on resource consumption.[18]

Other studies focus on the effect of uncertainty on trade. They show that uncertainty might have important implications for the direction of trade among countries.[19] Hence, one should consider world trade uncertainty when examining the trade dynamics between Iran and its partners in the East. Hence, to avoid possible model misspecification, world trade uncertainty is used as another explanatory variable.

Finally, the COVID-19 pandemic led to supply chain disruptions and severely lowered international trade.[20] The model introduces a dummy variable to capture the effect of the pandemic crisis on Asia's share in Iran's trade. Hence, the model tests the following hypotheses:

> *Hypothesis 1:* Economic sanctions increase the share of Asia in Iran's trade. In other words, sanctions decrease the ratio of Iran's trade with the West to its trade with the East.
>
> *Hypothesis 2:* World trade uncertainty changes the direction of Iran's trade share with the East.
>
> *Hypothesis 3:* Iran's economic complexity affects its trade share with the East.
>
> *Hypothesis 4:* An increase in output in South and East Asia affects Iran's share of trade with Asia.
>
> *Hypothesis 5:* Iran's gross domestic product influences Iran's trade share with Asia.

The dependent variable is the Asian share of Iran's total trade. Explanatory variables include Iran's GDP, Asia's GDP, economic sanctions, Iran's economic complexity, world trade uncertainty, and the COVID-19 pandemic. The following model is estimated:

$$TS_t = F(Y_t, YSEA_t, SAN_t, ICI_t, WTUI_t, COVID), \tag{1}$$

in which *TS* denotes the Asian share of Iran's total trade with the world; *Y* and *YSEA* are Iran's GDP and the GDP of major South and East Asian economies

(Iran's partners); *SAN* is a dummy variable capturing the economic sanctions imposed on Iran, *ICI* and *WTUI* indicate Iran-specific Complexity Index and World Trade Uncertainty Index; *COVID* is a dummy variable that captures the impact of the COVID-19 pandemic; and α_i is parameter i and ε denotes the disturbance term.

I use an ARDL model to study the evolution of Asia's share in Iran's trade. This model allows us to estimate the long-run equilibrium and short-run relations simultaneously. Moreover, we can also find the error correction term that captures the speed of adjustment toward long-run equilibrium.

Moreover, the ARDL and bound testing approaches to the analysis of level relationships proposed by M. Hashem Pesaran et al. allow us to use a combination of I(1) and I(0) variables in our model.[21] In addition, provided that long-run equilibrium among variables exists, we can examine how fast the error from equilibrium is corrected. In other words, three different models, namely, a short-run model, a long-run model, and an error correction model (ECM), are estimated.

Consider the following ARDL $(p,q_1,\ldots,q_5)$ model, in which α and β' s are parameters, and u_t is a white noise:

$$TS_t = \alpha_0 + \sum_{i=1}^{p} \alpha_i TS_{t-i} + \sum_{j=0}^{q_1} \beta_{1j} Y_{t-j} + \sum_{j=0}^{q_2} \beta_{2j} YSEA_{t-j}$$
$$+ \sum_{j=0}^{q_3} \beta_{3j} SAN_{t-j} + \sum_{j=0}^{q_4} \beta_{4j} ICI_{t-j} \qquad (2)$$
$$+ \sum_{j=1}^{q_5} \beta_{5j} WTUI_{t-j} + \beta_6 COVID + v_t$$

At this stage, different criteria such as Akaike Information Criterion (AIC), Schwarz Bayesian Criterion (SBC), and Hannan–Quinn Criterion (HQC) can be used to select the appropriate lags $(p,q_1,\ldots,q_5)$ for the short-run model.[22]

In the second stage, provided that the model passes the diagnostic tests, estimation results of the short-run model can be used to derive the long-run parameters. Next, the bounds test proposed by Pesaran et al. is conducted to examine whether a long-run equilibrium relationship exists among the variables.[23] If the null hypothesis of no levels relationship is rejected, the following ECM is estimated:

$$A(L)\Delta TS_t = B(L)\Delta X_t + (1-\Pi) ECT_{t-1} + \Gamma' W_t + v_t \qquad (3)$$

where $A(L) = 1 - \alpha_1 L - \alpha_2 L^2 - \ldots - \alpha_p L^p$, and $B(L) = 1 - \beta_{k1} L - \beta_{k2} L2 - \ldots - \beta_{kj} L^{qj}$ $(k=1,\ldots,5)$, $X = (Y_t, YSEA_t, SAN_t, ICI_t, WTUI_t)$, Δ denotes the first difference, ECT_{t-1} is the error correction term, $\Pi = (\alpha_1 + \alpha_2 + \ldots + \alpha_p)$, and W_t is a vector of deterministic variables such as the constant term and exogenous variables with fixed lags (*COVID*). L is a polynomial lag operator, Γ is a vector of parameters, and v_t denotes the disturbance term.

Empirical Results

The sample comprises fifteen South and East Asian countries, including China, India, Japan, South Korea, Malaysia, Indonesia, Vietnam, Philippines, Thailand, Taiwan, Sri Lanka, Singapore, Afghanistan, and Pakistan. The ARDL model is estimated for the period between 1995 and 2020.[24] The definition and data sources are presented in table 2.5 in the appendix. Prior estimating the ARDL model, we should examine whether the variables are stationary. To this end, different unit root tests are performed without and with breaks. The results of these tests are reported in tables 2.6 and 2.7 in the appendix. As the results show the variables TS, Y, and Y^A are integrated of order one, I(1). It means that their first order differences are stationary. However the variables $IranComp$ and $WTUI$ are integrated of order zero, I(0). It means that these variables are stationary at level.

The ARDL model is sensitive to problems of autocorrelation and heteroscedasticity. A Lagrange multiplier (LM) is used to test the null hypothesis of no autocorrelation of disturbance term. The Breusch-Godfrey Serial Correlation LM test is reported in table 2.1A. As the table shows, the F-statistic p-value is 0.18245. Hence, the null hypothesis of no autocorrelation is not rejected, and the residuals are serially uncorrelated. Next, we test whether the residuals are homoscedastic.

Table 2.1B presents the result of the Breusch–Pagan–Godfrey heteroskedasticity test. Since the F-statistic p-value is 0.4406, the null hypothesis of homoscedasticity is not rejected.

Since we have a combination of I(0) and I(1) variables, bound testing, proposed by Pesaran et al., is used to examine whether the variables are cointegrated. AIC is used to determine the lag order of the ARDL model.[25] The result of this test is presented in Table 2.2. The result of the bounds test shows that the calculated

TABLE 2.1A. Breusch-Godfrey Serial Correlation LM test

F-statistic	3.201628	Prob. F(3,3)	0.18245
Obs*R-squared	17.52593	Prob. Chi-Square(3)	0.0006

Source: Author's calculation

Note: Null hypothesis: No autocorrelation

TABLE 2.1B. Heteroskedasticity test: Breusch-Pagan-Godfrey

F-statistic	1.195207	Prob. F(16,6)	0.4406
Obs*R-squared	17.50709	Prob. Chi-Square(16)	0.3535
Scaled explained SS	0.810604	Prob. Chi-Square(16)	1.0000

Source: Author's calculation

Note: Null hypothesis: Homoskedasticity

TABLE 2.2. The result of the bounds test (F-Bounds test)

TEST STATISTIC	VALUE	SIGNIF.	I(0)	I(1)
F-statistic	4.598862	10%	2.08	3
k	5	5%	2.39	3.38
		2.5%	2.7	3.73
		1%	3.06	4.15

Source: Author's calculation

Note: Null hypothesis: No levels relationship

TABLE 2.3. The long-run estimation of the ARDL model

VARIABLE	COEFFICIENT	STD. ERROR	T-STATISTIC	PROB.
SAN	0.255879	0.083051	3.080992	0.0216
ICI	−0.333808	0.111574	−2.991805	0.0243
WTUI	0.027127	0.014289	1.898485	0.1064
Y	−2.08E-12	9.15E-13	−2.271269	0.0636
YSEA	2.36E-14	7.87E-15	2.997254	0.0241
C	0.188139	0.074361	2.530064	0.0447

EC = TS—(−0.0000*Y + 0.0000*YSEA + 0.2559*SAN −0.3338 *ICI + 0.0271*WTUI + 0.1881)

Source: Author's calculation

F-statistic is 4.598862. Since it falls outside the critical value bounds, the null hypothesis of no levels relationship is not accepted. Hence, the presence of a long-run equilibrium relationship among the variables is confirmed. It implies that the variables are cointegrated.

Finally, to examine the structural stability of estimated parameters in the ECM model, the CUSUM (cumulative sum) and CUSUMSQ (cumulative sum of squares) tests are performed. The first test checks whether there is a systematic change in the estimated coefficients. The second test is useful when there is a sudden and random departure from the constancy of the parameters. The results of these tests are presented in figures 2.5 and 2.6 in the appendix. The figures exhibit a pair of straight lines drawn at a 5 percent significance level. The regression equation is correctly specified if CUSUM or CUSUMSQ do not cross these lines. As the figures indicate, the model passes the stability test.

Now, I present the estimation results of our long-run model and the ECM, respectively. Table 2.3 reports the estimation results of the long-run model. As the results of the long-run model show, the associated coefficient of economic sanctions (*SAN*) is positive and statistically significant. It implies that economic sanction is one of the primary determinants of Asia's share in Iran's trade with the world.

Table 2.3 indicates that a higher Iran-specific complexity index is associated with a lower Aisa share in Iran's trade. Since the complexity index of Iran's main trade partners in Asia, such as Japan, South Korea, China, and India, is much higher than Iran, an increase in Iran's complex index leads to higher trade with other parts of the world.[26] In other words, Iran's knowledge-based products have more opportunities to be traded in less advanced economies. The result is a lower share of Asian countries' trade with Iran. Moreover, the results show that world trade uncertainty ($WTUI$) increases Iran's relative trade with Asia. It implies that in an uncertain trade world, the relative risk of Iran's trade with the West increases compared to the East (South and East Asia).

As Iran's GDP rises, Asia's share in Iran's total trade experiences a negative impact. Economic theory suggests that a rise in domestic income in a small open economy typically leads to more imports. The long-run result shows that Iran's imports from Asia appear to be growing at a slower rate compared to other regions. However, Iran's GDP has a negligible impact on Asia's trade share with the country, as indicated by the coefficient of Y in table 2.3. Finally, the results show that, as predicted, South and East Asia's GDP ($YSEA$) has a statistically significant positive effect on the share of Asia in Iran's total trade. Nonetheless, the impact of South and East Asia's gross domestic product on trade with Iran is minimal, as shown by the associated coefficient of $YSEA$ in table 2.3.

The estimation results of the Error Correction model (ECM) are reported in table 2.4. According to the table, the coefficient associated with COVID-19 is significant and negative. It implies that the pandemic had a negative effect on Asia's share in Iran's total trade. Additionally, Table 2.4 indicates that the coefficient associated with the error correction term, CointEq(−1), is negative and statistically significant. It suggests that approximately 87 percent of errors are corrected within one period.

Different economic and political factors affect Iran's trade ties with Asian countries. Among these factors are economic sanctions imposed on Iran by the West and increasing trade uncertainty in the global economy. The uncertainty captures significant world events such as the outbreak of US–China trade tensions, Brexit, and the 2020 US presidential election. Moreover, economic complexity is another determinant of trade relations between Iran and the main Asian economies. The chapter has used an ARDL analysis of cointegration to study the effect of economic sanctions, complexity, world trade uncertainty, and the COVID-19 pandemic on Asia's share in Iran's trade with the world. More specifically, it has focused on Iran's trade ties with South and East Asia, including Iran's main trade partners, such as China, India, Japan, South Korea, Malaysia, Indonesia, Thailand, Vietnam, Singapore, and Pakistan.

TABLE 2.4. The estimation results of Error Correction model: $D(TS)$ is dependent variable

VARIABLE	COEFFICIENT	STD. ERROR	T-STATISTIC	PROB.
D(SAN)	0.032505	0.010218	3.181154	0.0190
D(SAN(-1))	−0.141393	0.027501	−5.141279	0.0021
D(ICI)	−0.164992	0.025901	−6.370009	0.0007
D(WTUI)	−0.001389	0.000406	−3.417641	0.0142
D(WTUI(-1))	−0.015398	0.003086	−4.988811	0.0025
D(Y)	6.65E-13	3.89E-13	1.711036	0.1379
D(Y(-1))	1.97E-12	4.72E-13	4.166398	0.0059
D(YSEA)	1.59E-13	2.94E-14	5.415724	0.0016
D(YSEA(-1))	9.96E-14	2.25E-14	4.426650	0.0044
COVID	−1.309191	0.358095	−3.655989	0.0106
CointEq(-1)	−0.868633	0.108255	−8.023969	0.0002
R-squared	0.902244	Mean dependent var.		0.009201
Adjusted R-squared	0.820781	S.D. dependent var.		0.038704
S.E. of regression	0.016385	Akaike info criterion		−5.078947
Sum squared resid	0.003222	Schwarz criterion		−4.535884
Log likelihood	69.40789	Hannan-Quinn criterion		−4.942368
Durbin-Watson stat	2.353959			

Source: Author's calculation

The estimation results show that a long-run equilibrium relationship exists among variables. Specifically, the estimation of the long-run model indicates that economic sanctions have a positive and statistically significant impact on Asia's share in Iran's total trade. Moreover, the higher the complexity index, the lower the share of Asia in Iran's total trade. It implies that Iran's knowledge-based products have more opportunities to be traded in less advanced economies. In addition, in an uncertain world of trade, the risk of Iran's trade with the West increases, raising Asia's trade with Iran.

The higher output in South and East Asia region only slightly increases Asia's share in Iran's trade. The analysis using the ECM indicates that the COVID-19 pandemic reduced the share of Asia in Iran's total trade. Furthermore, the error correction term shows a swift move toward long-term equilibrium after an exogenous shock hits the model. It shows that approximately 87 percent of errors are corrected in each period.

Finally, by comparing the increasing Iran–East trade with the decreasing Iran–West trade, the chapter concludes that Iran's move toward the East is not necessarily a strategic choice but a necessity. Iran is forced to strengthen its economic ties with the East due to its hostile relations with the West, as well as the severe economic and noneconomic sanctions imposed on the country by the West. However, sanctions are not the only factor contributing to the rise of trade between Iran and the East.

It is important to note that the shift in trade toward Asia might be part of a global trend. The evidence shows that many Middle Eastern countries, with no history of conflicts with the West, have also increased their trade with the East. This means that the share of Asia in world trade has increased and that the Look East policy is not necessarily confined to Iran. The results have important policy implications for both policymakers and academics given the Look East policy has become more prominent in the region and beyond.

Appendix

TABLE 2.5. Data definitions and sources

VARIABLES	DEFINITION	SOURCE
Y	Real Gross Domestic Product (GDP)	World Development Indicators (WDI) published by the World Bank
YSEA	Real Gross Domestic Product (GDP) in South and East Asian	Authors' calculation using data obtained from World Development Indicators (WDI) –World Bank
Trade	Trade (% of GDP)	World Development Indicators (WDI) published by the World Bank
WTUI	World Trade Uncertainty Index	H. Ahir, N. Bloom, and D. Furceri (2018), "World Uncertainty Index," Stanford mimeo.
ICI	Iran's Economic Complexity Index (ECI)	Harvard Growth Lab's Country Rankings, https://atlas.cid.harvard.edu/rankings
TS	The share of South and East Asia's trade in Iran's total trade with world	Authors' calculation using data obtained from IMF: Direction of Trade Statistics (DOTS)

TABLE 2.6. Augmented Dickey-Fuller (ADF) tests without and with breaks for variables at level

VARIABLES	ADF TEST INCLUDING AN INTERCEPT*	ADF TEST INCLUDING AN INTERCEPT & A LINEAR TREND*	UNIT ROOT TEST WITH BREAKS INCLUDING AN INTERCEPT**	UNIT ROOT TEST WITH BREAKS INCLUDING AN INTERCEPT & A TREND**	INTEGRATION
TS	−1.006720	−1.880793	−2.835165	−3.248471	I(1)
	(0.7420)	(0.6462)	(0.7703)	(0.8255)	
Y	−0.029506	−1.952940	−2.011513	−3.729380	I(1)
	(0.9501)	(0.6084)	(0.9818)	(0.5457)	
YSEA	6.198445	0.000685	1.166759	−1.497980	I(l)
	(1.0000)	(0.9949)	(> 0.99)	(> 0.99)	
ICI	−2.347440	−3.241854	−5.949158	−5.949158	I(0)
	(0.1660)	(0.0993)	(< 0.01)	(< 0.01)	
WTUI	−3.611437	−3.906406	−49.03521	−49.13305	I(0)
	(0.0126)	(0.0264)	(< 0.01)	(< 0.01)	

Source: Author's calculation
Note: Null hypothesis: Variable has a unit root. P-values are in parentheses
* MacKinnon (1996) one-sided p-values
** Vogelsang (1993) asymptotic one-sided p-values

TABLE 2.7. Augmented Dickey-Fuller (ADF) tests without and with breaks for first differences

VARIABLES	ADF TEST INCLUDING AN INTERCEPT*	ADF TEST INCLUDING AN INTERCEPT & A LINEAR TREND*	UNIT ROOT TEST WITH BREAKS INCLUDING AN INTERCEPT**	UNIT ROOT TEST WITH BREAKS INCLUDING AN INTERCEPT & A TREND**	INTEGRATION
DTS	−6.306963	−6.305478	−6.739807	−6.654412	I(1)
	(0.0000)	(0.0000)	(< 0.01)	(< 0.01)	
DY	−5.285766	−5.301237	−5.733479	−5.872217	I(1)
	(0.0001)	(0.0005)	(< 0.01)	(< 0.01)	
DYSEA	−1.907157	−6.385286	−6.901423	−7.826315	I(1)
	(0.3256)	(0.0000)	(< 0.01)	(< 0.01)	
DICI	−7.321516	−7.151165	−8.554526	−8.548729	I(0)
	(0.0000)	(0.0000)	(< 0.01)	(< 0.01)	

Source: Author's calculation
Note: Null hypothesis: Variable has a unit root. P-values are in parentheses
* MacKinnon (1996) one-sided p-values
** Vogelsang (1993) asymptotic one-sided p-values

TABLE 2.8. The estimation results of ARDL model: TS is dependent variable

VARIABLE	COEFFICIENT	STD. ERROR	T-STATISTIC	PROB.*
TS(−1)	0.131367	0.236463	0.555550	0.5986
Y	6.65E-13	9.72E-13	0.683794	0.5196
Y(−1)	−5.06E-13	1.27E-12	−0.399244	0.7035
Y(−2)	−1.97E-12	1.11E-12	−1.777587	0.1258
YSEA	1.59E-13	5.69E-14	2.799759	0.0312
YSEA(−1)	−3.92E-14	8.04E-14	−0.488068	0.6428
YSEA(−2)	−9.96E-14	5.92E-14	−1.681835	0.1436
SAN	0.032505	0.026988	1.204456	0.2738
SAN(−1)	0.048367	0.039116	1.236504	0.2625
SAN(−2)	0.141393	0.056204	2.515706	0.0456
ICI	−0.164992	0.051361	−3.212407	0.0183
ICI(−1)	−0.124965	0.057532	−2.172102	0.0729
WTUI	−0.001389	0.000964	−1.440757	0.1997
WTUI(−1)	0.009555	0.007436	1.285002	0.2462
WTUI(−2)	0.015398	0.008123	1.895519	0.1068
COVID	−1.309191	0.861657	−1.519387	0.1795
C	0.163424	0.062262	2.624759	0.0393
R-squared	0.983327	Mean dependent var.		0.480717
Adjusted R-squared	0.938866	S.D. dependent var.		0.093718
S.E. of regression	0.023172	Akaike info criterion		−4.557208
Sum squared resid	0.003222	Schwarz criterion		−3.717929
Log likelihood	69.40789	Hannan-Quinn criterion		−4.346132
F-statistic	22.11663	Durbin-Watson stat		2.353959
Prob(F-statistic)	0.000509			

Source: Author's calculation

The Stability Test

The regression equation is correctly specified because CUSUM and CUSUMSQ do not cross a pair of straight lines drawn at a 5 percent significance level.

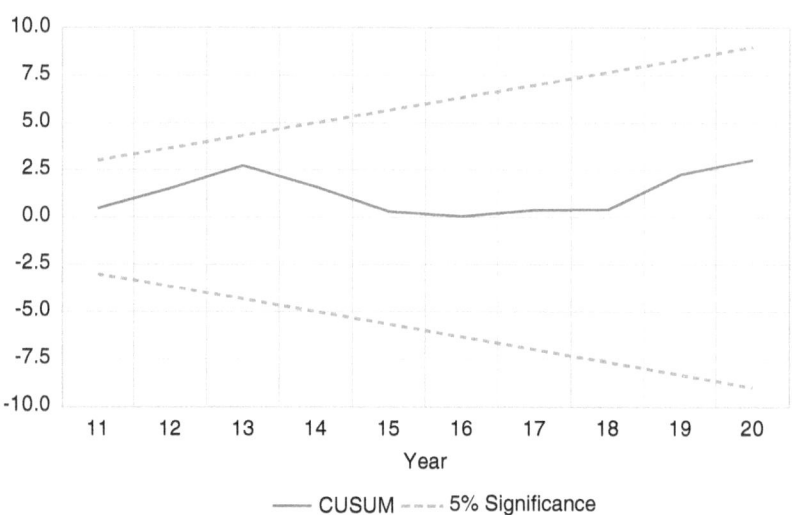

FIGURE 2.5. CUSUM (cumulative sum) test. Note: The figure exhibits a pair of straight lines drawn at a 5 percent significance level. CUSUM does not cross the straight lines.

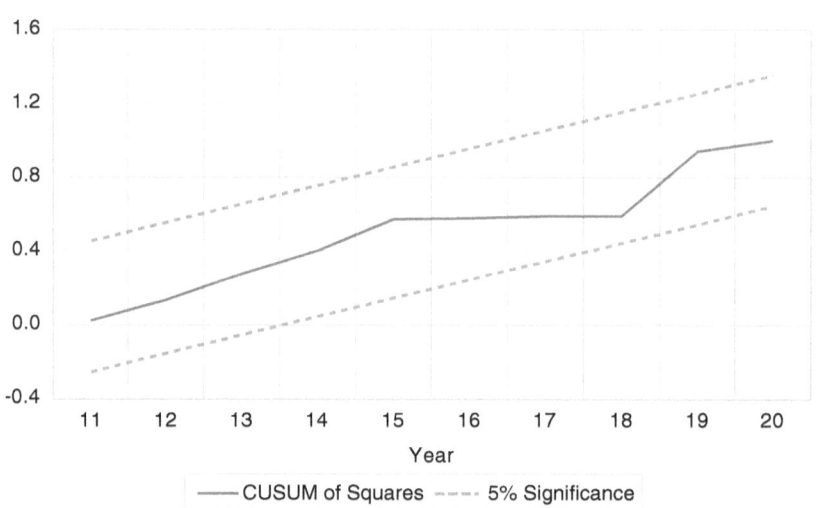

FIGURE 2.6. CUSUMSQ (cumulative sum of squares) test. Note: The figure exhibits a pair of straight lines drawn at a 5 percent significance level. CUSUMSQ does not cross the straight lines.

NOTES

1. Yunling Zhang and Minghui Shen, "Emergence of ASEAN, China and India and the Regional Architecture," *China & World Economy* 20, no. 4 (2012): 92–107.

2. Mohsen Sharuatinia and Hamidreza Azizi, "Iran–China Cooperation in the Silk Road Economic Belt: From Strategic Understanding to Operational Understanding," *China and World Economy* 25, no. 5 (2017): 46–61.

3. Fanand He and Donghai Qin, "China's Energy Strategy in the Twenty-first Century," *China & World Economy* 14, no. 2 (2006): 93–104.

4. Bijan B. Aghevli and Cyrus Sassanpour, "Prices, Output and the Trade Balance in Iran," *World Development* 10, no. 9 (1982): 791–800.

5. Mohammad Reza Farzanegan, "Illegal Trade in the Iranian Economy: Evidence from a Structural Model," *European Journal of Political Economy* 25, no. 4 (2009): 489–507.

6. Hasan Heidari and Fatemeh Zarei, "Barrasi-ye ravābet-e tejāri-ye Irān bā mohemtarin sherkā-ye tejāri-ye Āsiyā bā tamarkoz bar āzmūn-e monhani-ye J," Faslnāmah-i Mudalsāzī-i Iqtiṣādī (Investigating the Commercial Relations between Iran and Its Other Major Trading Partner Focusing on J-Curve Test), *Quarterly Journal of Economic Modelling*, 6, no. 18 (2011): 83–103.

7. Gholamreza Fathipour and Ali Ghahremanlou, "Economical-Regional Integration: An Overview on Iran-India Trade Relation," *Procedia-Social and Behavioral Sciences* 27, no. 157 (2014): 155–64.

8. Nahid Pourrostami, "Darajah-i vābastegī-e tejārī-i kishvarhā-ye sharq-e āsiyā bā estifādah az jadval-e dādah-stāndah-i baynolmelalī-e āsiyāyī" [An analysis of trade interdependency among East Asian countries using Asian international input–output table], *Iqtiṣād va Tijārat-i Nauīn*, 13, no. 2 (2018): 1–27.

9. Shekoofeh Nagheli, Majid Maddah and Esmaiel Abounoori, "Ta'sīr-e nihādhā-yi siyāsī bar sādārāt-i irān bih keshvarhā-yi gharb-i āsiyā: rūykard-e eqtiṣādsanjī-ye faḍāyī" [The effect of political institutions on iran's exports to West Asian countries: Spatial econometric approach], *Pazhūhesh-hāye Eqtiṣādī-ye Īrān*, 24, no. 79 (2019): 107–41.

10. Monireh Rafat, "Taḥlīl-e Jāygāh-e Tejārī-e Īrān va Shurakā-yi ān dar Gharb-i Āsiyā bar Asās-e Shākhiṣ-hāye Vazn-dāri Shabakah-e Tejārī" (Analysis of Iran and its Partners in West Asia Trade Position Based on Weighted Trade Network Indicators), *Naẓarīyah-hā-yi Kārburdī-i Iqtiṣād*, 8, no. 28 (2021): 145–64.

11. See: "Direction of Trade Statistics (DOTS)," International Monetary Fund, accessed July 23, 2023, https://data.imf.org/?sk=9d6028d4-f14a-464c-a2f2-59b2cd424b85.

12. The figures are not presented here but are available upon request. For details, see "Direction of Trade Statistics (DOTS)."

13. Nasser Saidi and Aathira Prasad, "Trends in Trade and Investment Policies in the MENA Region. MENA-OECD," *SSRN*, 2018, https://bit.ly/40nBNHC.

14. Gary C. Hufbauer, Jeffrey J. Schott, Kimberly Ann Elliott, and Barbara Oegg, *Economic Sanctions Reconsidered*, 3rd ed. (Peterson Institute for International Economics, 2007); and Matthias Neuenkirch and Florian Neumeier, "The Impact of US Sanctions on Poverty," *Journal of Development Economics* 121 (2016): 110–19.

15. César A. Hidalgo and Ricardo Hausmann, "The Building Blocks of Economic Complexity," *Proceedings of the National Academy of Sciences of the United States of America* 106, no. 26 (2009): 10570–75.

16. Buhari Doğan, Daniel Balsalobre, and Muhammad Ali Nasir, "European Commitment to COP21 and the Role of Energy Consumption, FDI, Trade and Economic Complexity in Sustaining Economic Growth," *Journal of Environmental Management* 273 (2020): 111146.

17. Mosab I. Tabash, Ekundayo Peter Mesagan, and Umar Farooq, "Dynamic Linkage between Natural Resources, Economic Complexity, and Economic growth: Empirical Evidence from Africa," *Resources Policy* 23, no. 78 (2022): 102865.

18. Xiuping Guo, Xianglei Meng, Qingfeng Luan, and Yanhua Wang, "Trade Openness, Globalization, and Natural Resources Management: The Moderating Role of Economic Complexity in Newly Industrialized Countries," *Resources Policy* 85 (2023): 103757.

19. Fengxiu Zhou and Huwei Wen, "Trade Policy Uncertainty, Development Strategy, and Export Behavior: Evidence from Listed Industrial Companies in China," *Journal of Asian Economics* 82 (2022): 101528; and Jungho Baek and Jee Hee Yoon, "Shocks of Crude Oil Prices and World Trade Policy Uncertainty: How Much Do They Matter for China's Trade Balance with Its Three Largest Partners?," *Economic Analysis and Policy* 78 (2023): 914–921.

20. Mary E. Hancock and Jesse Mora, "The Impact of COVID-19 on Chinese Trade and Production: An Empirical Analysis of Processing Trade with Japan and the US," *Journal of Asian Economics* 86 (2023): 101596.

21. M. Hashem Pesaran, Yeongchol Shin, and Richard J. Smith, "Bounds Testing Approaches to the Analysis of Level Relationship," *Journal of Applied Econometrics* 16, no. 3 (2001): 289–326.

22. For details, see: M. Hashem Pesaran and Bahram Pesaran, *Working with Microfit 4.0: Interactive Econometric Analysis* (Oxford University Press, 1997).

23. M. Hashem Pesaran, Yeongchol Shin, and Richard J. Smith, "Bounds Testing Approaches to the Analysis of Level Relationship," *Journal of Applied Econometrics* 16, no. 3 (2001): 289–326.

24. The period is chosen based of data availability.

25. Selected lags are: ARDL(1, 2, 2, 2, 1, 2). The estimation results of short-run model is reported in table 2.8 in the appendix.

26. According to the Economic Complexity Index 2021, China is ranked twenty-fifth, and Iran is ranked sixty-seventh; see: "Country & Product Complexity Rankings," Atlas of Economic Complexity, accessed July 23, 2023, https://atlas.hks.harvard.edu/rankings.

3

SANCTIONS, THE LOOK EAST POLICY, AND ECONOMIC PERFORMANCE IN IRAN

Zahra Karimi Moughari

Trade is an important engine of growth. Political ties shape economic relations between countries. Trade with "hostile countries" is generally forbidden and punishable. Before the 1979 revolution, the United States and the Federal Republic of Germany were Iran's biggest trading partners. Iran imported high-tech machinery and equipment from advanced Western countries. The storming of the US embassy in Tehran in November 1979 was the beginning of numerous, protracted international sanctions against Iran. Consequently, Iran decided to expand its economic and political relations with countries such as China, Russia, and India. Neighboring countries, especially the United Arab Emirates (UAE) and Turkey, became the informal channels for indirect trade with Western countries. Since 2012 harsh nuclear-related sanctions have created severe obstacles for Iran's trade with the West; so, Iran's trade is highly concentrated in Eastern developing countries.

This substitution has been very costly, as Eastern countries also rely on Western countries for advanced machinery and technologies. When Iran faced harsh sanctions in 2012, big Chinese and Indian companies were obliged to obey the sanctions, as they have direct ties with international markets and cannot ignore the huge benefits of trade with Western countries. Iran trades with a limited number of medium-sized Eastern firms and tolerates the high costs. Even though many big Iranian firms, especially state- or semi-state-owned enterprises, attempted to improve their technical knowledge to produce their previously imported machinery and parts, macroeconomic variables show that Iran's economic performance has been weak, particularly compared to its neighboring countries that have friendly relations with the rest of the world.

This chapter investigates the strengths and weaknesses of Iran's orientation to the East in relation to the country's economy. The chapter starts with an analysis of the impacts of foreign policies on Iran's economic performance, focusing specifically on the impact of sanctions-driven foreign policy on gross domestic product (GDP) growth in Iran, as well as investments, productivity, and real wages in the country. The chapter concludes by presenting findings from a survey conducted on Iran's businesses regarding the success or failure of substituting the East for the West in order to procure modern machinery and technology.

The results of the study show that, despite harsh and prolonged sanctions, a large majority of Iranian firms still use Western machinery and equipment. Chinese products, however, could not be substituted. Although many firms pay high costs for indirect import of their required Western merchandise, ultimately sanctions have negatively impacted the quality of their imported raw materials and intermediate goods and reduced the quantity and quality of their products. As a result, if sanctions remain in place, Iran's economic activities will deteriorate further.

Changes in Iran's Major Trade Partners

Because of various sanctions, Iran stopped its direct traditional exports such as carpets, pistachios, and saffron, to the United States, Canada, and Europe. Iran's nonoil exports are concentrated on Eastern developing countries, while oil exports to Europe continued until 2012. Yet, Iran's nonoil traditional exports are carried through brokers. The UAE, as a small country, is one of the main destinations of Iran's nonoil exports and the origin of its imports. In fact, it is a route for Iran's indirect trade. Hostilities with the Western countries resulted in Iran's increasing reliance on the UAE for indirect export of nonoil goods and imports of required machinery and equipment. As an example, in 2001 about $600,000 of Iran's total nonoil exports were shipped to the UAE. This amount reached to $4.5 billion in 2019; meanwhile the final destinations of such exports are generally advanced countries.[1]

As mentioned earlier, beginning in the late 1980s, the Islamic Republic has tried to establish relatively friendly relations with European countries. In 2001, more than 30 percent of Iran's imports arrived directly from European countries and Japan. After the nuclear row and the imposition of new international

TABLE 3.1. The country of origin of Iran's imports

	2001		2011		2022	
	AMOUNT	SHARE (PERCENT)	AMOUNT	SHARE (PERCENT)	AMOUNT	SHARE (PERCENT)
United Arab Emirates	1.6	8.9	17.5	30.4	18.4	30.9
China	0.9	5	7.4	12.9	15.7	26.4
South Korea	1	5.6	4.7	8.2	0	0
Germany	1.8	10	3.5	6.1	2	3.4
Turkey	0.3	1.7	3.1	5.4	6.1	10.3
Switzerland	0.4	2.2	2.5	4.3	0	0
France	1.1	6.1	1.8	3.1	0.3	0.5
Italy	1	5.6	1.7	3	0	0
Japan	1.2	6.7	1.3	2.3	0.08	0.13
India	0.6	3.3	1.2	2.1	2.8	4.7
Total (10 countries)	9.9	55	44.7	77.7	45.4	76.3
Other countries	8.1	45	12.8	22.3	14.1	23.7
Sum total	18	100	57.5	100	59.5	100

Source: Tehran Chamber of Commerce, 2023 (in billion USD)

sanctions in 2012, the share of Western countries in Iran's imports declined considerably (see table 3.1). The nuclear deal with the P5+1 (US, Germany, France, Rusia and China) countries in 2015 increased Iran's imports from the European Union and Japan by 42 percent between 2016 and 2017. But this was short lived. In 2018, the United States withdrew from the agreement and Iran faced severe sanctions again. This increased pressure forced Iran to engage more with the East. From 2017 to 2022, imports from the European Union and Japan dropped to less than half (from approximately $9 billion to $4.3 billion) and reached to less than 4 percent of Iran's total imports in 2023.[2] Adversely, China's share in Iran's international trade increased noticeably. While Iran's nonoil exports to China amounted to about $180 million (4.3 percent of total nonoil exports) in 2001, it raised to more than $14.5 billion (27.4 percent of total nonoil exports) in 2022. Russia, as a major oil and gas exporter, did not have significant trade ties with Iran until 2020. In 2022, with approximately $1.6 billion exports and $744 million imports, Russia became one of the main trade partners of Iran.[3]

At present, Iran imports a great part of its required modern machinery and equipment indirectly from other developing countries, with the help of several brokers, instead of direct imports from Western countries. From 2016 to 2022, China's exports to Iran increased by 20 percent from $13.1 billion to $15.7

billion.[4] Many European countries such as Italy, Switzerland, and France almost completely stopped their trade with Iran after 2018. Iran's reliance on a few Asian countries for trade increased the cost of its imports and exports.

As we shall see shortly, more than 85 percent of the respondent firms in our field study paid "higher or much higher" prices for indirect imports of Western machinery and equipment compared to average prices, and 82.7 percent spent "much or very much" time compared with regular and ordinary purchases that do not require indirect import. Eastward orientation increased Iran's vulnerability in trade, as any policy change of its major trade partners, like China and the UAE, could create more obstacles for Iran's access to required goods and services.

It must be noted that brokers who help Iran escape sanctions make huge profits by importing needed machinery and spare parts indirectly. The prices of Western imported goods in Iran generally is more than double the original, and the number of trading firms is increasing considerably. These indicate the high profits that can be earned in indirect imports. Therefore, antagonism against the West has created a fertile ground for widespread corruption and weakened the incentives of domestic and foreign firms for productive investment in Iran. Figure 3.1 shows the sharp decline of investment from 2011 to 2021. The country cannot attract foreign direct investment to diversify and renovate its economy in the past decade, and it also has faced rising capital flight.

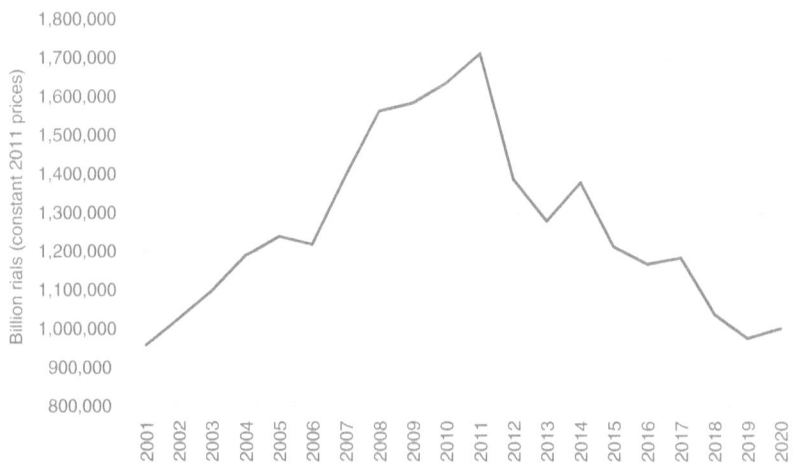

FIGURE 3.1. Investment changes (2004–21)
Source: Iran Central Bank 2023.

The Costs of Comprehensive Sanctions

Since 1988 (the end of Iran–Iraq war) until 2012, the beginning of harsh economic sanction under Barack Obama's presidency, Iran's annual GDP growth was 4.8 percent, and the average growth of fixed capital formation was 6.8 percent. Although the growth rates were not high enough to narrow the gap between Iran and emerging countries like South Korea and Turkey, the standard of living was improving and the number of households under the poverty line was decreasing.

Iran's oil revenues declined from about USD 113 billion in 2011 to about USD 63 billion in 2012 and about USD 26 billion in 2015.[5] Additionally, Iran faced a severe shortage of hard currencies following the 2012 sanctions. Restrictions on Iran's banking transaction with the world deteriorated the situation and further reduced the import of intermediate and capital goods. Production, per capita income, and investment decreased accordingly. Rising budget deficit and high growth of liquidity fueled escalating inflation and the country slipped into the crisis of stagflation.

From 2011 to 2020, GDP growth was about zero, and per capita income dropped by about 35 percent. In the same period, total investment was reduced by 4.6 percent annually, while depreciation in fixed capital increased by 3.2 percent each year (figure 3.1). Therefore, investment was not enough to cover the depreciation of the fixed capital, and production capacity started to shrink. Old and outdated machinery and equipment affected the production and labor productivity of public and private firms.

Transformation of the Labor Market

Since 2011, despite the challenges of international sanctions and prevailing stagflation, the number of employed workers has been rising.[6] From 2011 to 2021, the annual GDP growth was about 0.4 percent. Nevertheless, employment increased about 2.3 percent per annum and the number of employed workers increased from 20.5 million people in 2011 to 23.5 million people in 2021. This change in employment showed that during recession, most people cannot afford to stay unemployed for long, and even many highly educated youth became self-employed, as they had to start a business. In these years, the share of self-employment increased from 32.2 to 36.3 percent of total employment. As an example, in 2021 internet taxi companies alone had about five million taxi drivers that are considered self-employed, as they are not in a formal wage earning contract with the companies. They have their own cars and pay part of their income to these companies for their internet services.[7]

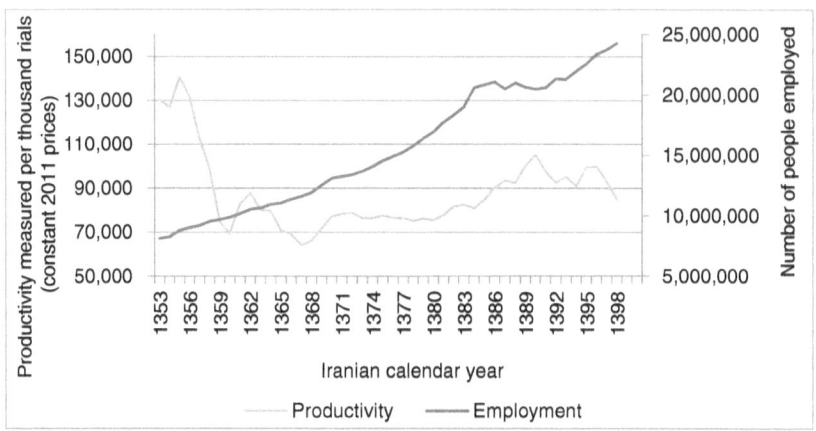

FIGURE 3.2. Employment and productivity
Source: Statistical Centre of Iran 2023 and Iran Central Bank 2023.

In this same period, labor productivity plummeted by 9.1 percent (an average of 0.9 percent each year), as annual GDP growth was 0.4 percent and employment increased by 1.5 percent per annum. While production declined in many state-owned factories, they did not fire excess workers to prevent the imposed negative economic and social effects of sanctions on Iranian households. A large share of employment in private sector moved from high value–added, formal, and stable jobs to low value-added, informal, and precarious work. Employment increased at the cost of a decline in productivity and an expansion of informal and low-paid employment (figure 3.2).

Negative productivity growth, combined with increased employment from 2011 to 2021, is comparable to the Iran–Iraq war period, when the economy was devastated, the government employed excess workers, and a large portion of the workforce became self-employed, like street vendors and taxi drivers. Western-imposed sanctions have destroyed many secure jobs, especially in small- and medium-sized firms. As most workers cannot afford to stay unemployed, they have moved from industrial employment to low value–added informal sectors.[8]

Firms in sectors such as clothing, leather, and furniture have benefited from Western countries' sanctions against Iran, as rival goods have become very expensive due to the depreciation of the rial in relation to other currencies and difficulties in imports and restrictions on Iran's international banking transactions. While the growth of industrial sector value-added was −2.1 percent during the period 2011 to 2019, this negative trend changed in the recent years and the growth rate of industrial output was 21.2 percent from 2019 to 2022.[9]

The output of large state-owned industries that were highly dependent on imports of Western machinery and equipment have dropped significantly, but they have not been allowed to reduce their personnel. Therefore, in total the number of industrial workforce increased under the sanctions.

Iran's orientation toward the East has winners and losers across different Iranian industries. Foodstuffs, clothing, and furniture industries benefited from trade barriers and high exchange rates. These products became more competitive compared to foreign rival commodities. Exporting industries such as petrochemicals and basic metals also experienced growth and gained needed hard currencies. From 2015 to 2019, exports of iron and steel increased from USD 2.8 billion to USD 4.9 billion. These figures for aluminum and copper were USD 0.4 billion and USD 1.2 billion accordingly. Exports of petrochemical industries also witnessed a mild growth and increased from USD 3.7 billion in 2015 to USD 4 billion in 2018.[10] The number of employees in the winning industries started to rise. Vehicle industries are among the losers as their production dropped because of sanctions.[11] The COVID-19 pandemic added to the economic hardship, and more than one million jobs were lost between 2019 and 2020.[12]

Falling Real Wages

Sanctions took a toll on different groups within the labor force. From 2011 to 2021, the number of entrepreneurs dropped from 814,000 to 740,000. In other words, more than 70,000 firms were closed and their workers lost their jobs. In the same period, more than 180,000 women and more than 1.5 million men were added to the group of self-employed.[13] Self-employment generally needs small capital and low skills. Many fired workers who could not get a suitable new job in other firms had to start a new business as sole proprietors. Most self-employed people are not covered by any type of pension scheme and are informal workers. A great part of these laborers are highly educated people who are unemployed, as they cannot use their skills and talents in their new jobs; self-employment is their last resort.

Unfavorable labor market conditions are reflected in real wages. Throughout 2011 to 2021, because of the high inflation rates, nominal wages increased rapidly, yet the rise in wages could not cover escalating living costs. Increasing proportion of the workforce, even among highly educated youth, receive the formal minimum wage and even less, especially in small- and medium-sized companies

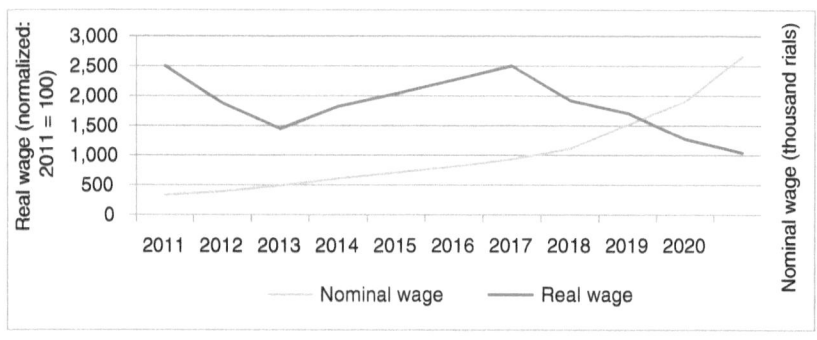

FIGURE 3.3. Nominal and real formal minimum wage
Source: Iran Ministry of Cooperatives, Labor and Social Welfare, *Minimum Wage and Household Expenditure 2011–2021* (Ministry of Labor Publishing Centre, 2022).

and in remote and deprived regions. Figure 3.3 shows the changes in nominal and real formal minimum wage from 2011 to 2021. As the formal minimum wage was not adjusted by inflation rates, the real minimum wage lost about 30 percent of its purchasing power (see the right axis of figure 3.3). Between 2013 and 2017, because of improved international relations, inflation rates declined and real minimum wage rose. However, as a result of the US withdrawal from the JCPOA (Joint Comprehensive Plan of Action), real wages declined considerably, as inflation rates were much higher than increases in the minimum wage.

An increasing proportion of wage earners in private firms, especially in small firms with less than 50 workers in some of the country's more deprived regions, do not receive the formal minimum wage and are not covered by any form of social insurance. According to Iran's Parliament Research Center, about 60 percent of workers are not protected by labor laws. About 65 percent of Iran's labor force works in small firms with less than five workers.[14] Most of these workers are informal employees, and are not covered by any kind of social insurance schemes. In a highly risky and discouraging business environment and rising uncertainty about the future, Iranian entrepreneurs prefer to employ workers temporarily and with informal status. Increasing numbers of educated youth in middle- and low-income families cannot afford lengthy job searches and have to accept unskilled jobs. Therefore, sanctions have accelerated the expansion of low-paid, temporary, and informal employment in Iran rather than rising unemployment, and increased poverty even among families with employed members. Therefore, the most vulnerable segments of Iran's workforce bear the brunt of the animosity between Iran and the United States and its allies, as well as the harsh sanctions imposed by the West.

The Impacts of Iran's Orientation Toward the East on Technology Transfer

Sanctions have considerable negative effects, especially on large private firms that use Western technologies. For example, Iran's vehicle production has dropped significantly since 2012. Substitution of low-quality and inexpensive auto parts, usually imported from China, has reduced the quality of Iranian cars.[15] Production of Chinese cars and trucks was substituted for Western manufacturers. It is worth noting that big Chinese companies with investments in the United States are cautious not to work with Iranian companies to avoid sanctions. Therefore, only Chinese medium-sized companies supply what Iran needs. As an example, Chery, a Chinese vehicle manufacturer whose cars are assembled in Iran by a private Iranian manufacturer, has prevented the use of the Chery brand on assembled cars.[16] At present, various Chinese cars and trucks are assembled in Iran, but due to their generally low quantity, Iranian autoparts manufacturers are not interested to invest in producing their parts. So far, orientation toward the East has not provided a meaningful opportunity for knowledge transfer to Iran's car industry.[17]

Iran's big mining companies are also hit hard by sanctions. Before the revolution, major mining firms could import heavy machinery from the United States, Japan, and other advanced industrial countries. The mining industry is currently facing a challenge with outdated machinery and equipment, and it needs to procure new heavy machinery and spare parts. There are about 5,000 mining machines that are more than thirty years old. These machines are often overhauled eight or even ten times and cannot be repaired anymore. Large mining firms need to substitute them with new and high-tech machines that are mainly manufactured in a few Western countries.[18]

Many Iranian small- and medium-size private firms pay the high price of sanctions also. They cannot import high-quality raw materials and other intermediate goods. For example, shrimp farms cannot import the best quality of modified shrimp gene. Because of the low-quality shrimp larvae and cheap shrimp feed, the majority of the farms have faced huge losses due to the higher shrimp mortality in the past years. Shrimp farms in Saudi Arabia are strong competitors of Iranian shrimp producers. Saudi farms that have access to high-quality materials can protect their shrimps and export them to international markets.[19]

Computer service providers, who supply security software and hardware for banks and other institutions, are dependent on special items, such as high-quality modems, graphic cards, motherboards, network equipment, printers, and laptops that are produced in the United States. They cannot substitute Chinese computer components and software for American products. They have to import the items indirectly and at considerably higher prices, and when problems arise with the imported items they cannot be fixed easily. Sometimes they have to travel to the UAE, Turkey, or other countries to solve the software problems which can be fixed by the suppliers' online advice and without any cost.[20]

Big refineries, petrochemical industries, and producers of large electric manufacturers cannot import all the required items from the East. They need advanced Western technology for improving the quality of their products, while food and building material industries generally can import their needed machinery and intermediate goods from China. Many big firms import advanced machinery from the West, using several brokers and transporting the machines through a number of countries to escape sanctions. Formal guarantees of such machinery are not usable in Iran. Furthermore, modern machinery generally has electronic parts and programs. If there is any problem in the machine or software, the buyer must pay a high price and spend a long time to fix it. Therefore, there is a lot of damaged machinery and equipment in factories that can be repaired if sanctions are lifted.[21]

Field Study

Although transactions with the East generally mean trade with three big countries—China, Russia, and India—it is really China that is the most important trading partner for Iran. In the past decade, many Iranian firms have expanded their ties with Chinese companies. But the majority of enterprises in Iran's private sector, which largely relied on Western machinery and equipment in the past, have not been able to use Chinese products as substitutes and have been negatively impacted by the sanctions. There is no precise data on the costs of the sanctions on Iran's private sector. Therefore, in 2023 I conducted a survey to determine which groups of private firms have been hit the hardest, and which private activities have suffered the least negative impact of the sanctions. Iran's Chamber of Commerce and Industry assisted me with contacting other chambers of commerce, such as the *German–Iranian Chamber* of Industry and Commerce, and the Swedish–Iranian Chamber of Commerce, and encouraged their members to answer the questionnaire of the survey (see appendix 1). Several members of the Iran Entrepreneurs' Association also completed the questionnaires.

The questionnaires were filled by 128 private firms; some of the respondents did not answer the questions completely. The ultimate number of acceptable questionnaires is 110. About 43.6 percent of the sample companies were small firms with a workforce size of less than 50, while 6.4 percent were medium-sized

TABLE 3.2. Use of Western machinery and equipment

	FIRMS WITH MORE THAN 20 YEARS OF EXPERIENCE		FIRMS WITH LESS THAN 20 YEARS OF EXPERIENCE		P-VALUE
	NUMBER*	PERCENT	NUMBER	PERCENT*	
Very and very much	30	65.2	35	58.3	0.7662
Moderate	12	26.1	10	16.7	0.8786
Few and very few	4	8.7	10	16.7	0.1049
Not at all	0	0.0	5	8.3	0.0098
Total	46	100	60	100	

Source: Survey data. Four firms did not indicate their year of establishment.

enterprises with fifty-one to one hundred workers. More than 45 percent of the respondents were big private firms with more than one hundred workers. About 42 percent of the sample firms had more than twenty years of experience, while newly established companies (within less than five years) consisted about 11 percent of the sample. A majority of the respondents belonged to highly experienced and large size enterprises.

About 61 percent of the respondents used Western machinery "much or very much" (65 percent of firms with more than twenty years of experience and 58 percent of firms with less than twenty years). About 12.7 percent used Western machinery "few and very few" (8.7 percent of firms with more than twenty years of experience and 16.7 percent of firms with less than twenty years). While it seems that firms with more than twenty years of experience are more dependent on Western machinery and equipment, compared to younger firms, the difference is not statistically significant. Approximately 8.3 percent of younger firms do not use Western machinery at all, which has a statistically significant difference (95 percent confidence interval) with older firms that neither of them announced that does not use (0 percent) Western machinery and equipment (see table 3.2).

Table 3.3 presents the use of Western machinery and equipment by Iranian firms that can be divided into two categories: firms with more than one hundred workers, and firms with less than one hundred workers. More that 60 percent of big and small companies in the sample use Western machinery and equipment "much and very much." Although the proportion of larger firms that use Western products (64 percent) is bigger than smaller firms (60 percent), the difference is not statistically significant. Similar to table 3.2, only five respondents among smaller firms announced that they do not use Western machinery at all. The difference in not using Western items between bigger firms (0 percent) and smaller firms (9.1 percent) is statistically significant (95 percent confidence interval).

TABLE 3.3. Use of Western machinery and equipment

	MORE THAN 100 WORKERS		LESS THAN 100 WORKERS		P-VALUE
	NUMBER*	PERCENT	NUMBER*	PERCENT	
Very and very much	32	64.0	33	60.0	0.6636
Moderate	14	28.0	7	12.7	0.9752
Few and very few	4	8.0	10	18.2	0.576
Not at all	0	0.0	5	9.1	0.0095
Total	**50**	**100**	**55**	**100**	

Source: Survey data. Five respondent firms did not indicate the number of their employees.

More than 45 percent of the Iranian firms, which buy their required Western machinery and equipment indirectly, are not able to receive proper after-sale services, 19.4 percent of such companies cannot get any after-sale services at all. Computer service provider firms involved in network security need special components and software that are mainly imported from the United States and other advanced Western countries. They have to buy their required items indirectly and have severe difficulties to get license and software from Western companies. However, several Iranian firms can escape sanctions and import Western goods indirectly, but they have to wait a longer time in the import process and pay higher expenses for these imports. More than 85 percent of the respondents paid "higher or much higher" prices for indirect imports of Western machinery and equipment compared to average prices, and 82.7 percent spent "much or very much" time compared with regular and ordinary purchases that do not require indirect import.

Severe restrictions on Iran's imports have reduced "much and very much" the quantity and quality of the products of 61.8 percent of respondent firms, and increased the costs of repair and maintenance of the machinery and equipment "much and very much" for 75.5 percent. Only three respondents (2.7 percent of the sample) announced that sanctions have not had any negative impact on the quantity and quality of their products. These are the firms in the packaging industry and services sector that started their work during the harsh international sanctions and followed the government's orientation toward the East and used mainly Chinese technology.

The technical capability of 74.5 percent of the sample firms has declined "much or very much" due to the sanctions and restriction of access to advanced Western technology. About 73.6 percent of the firms in the sample need Western machinery and equipment "much and very much" to expand their production capacities. Only 2.7 percent of the respondents can increase their production level without using Western technologies.

TABLE 3.4. Substitution of Chinese machinery for Western ones

	FIRMS WITH MORE THAN TWENTY YEARS OF EXPERIENCE		FIRMS WITH LESS THAN TWENTY YEARS OF EXPERIENCE		P-VALUE
	NUMBER	PERCENT	NUMBER	PERCENT	
Very and very much	5	10.9	8	13.3	0.3490
Moderate	13	28.3	13	21.7	0.7809
Few and very few	21	45.7	32	53.3	0.2158
Not at all	7	15.2	7	11.7	0.7013
Total	46	100	60	100	

Source: Survey data

Substitution of Eastern Products for Western Machinery and Equipment

China's economic development and its relatively low-priced goods have encouraged an increasing proportion of Iranian companies to use Chinese products instead of Western machinery and equipment. Yet, about 50 percent of the firms in the sample could substitute "a few or very few" Chinese products for Western items. It seems that younger firms (13.3 percent) more than older ones (10.9 percent) replaced "much and very much" Western machines for Chinese ones, but this difference is not significant (table 3.4). In other words, there is no statistically significant difference between older and younger firms in the sample regarding the ability to use Chinese products instead of Western ones. However, more than 12 percent of the firms could not find any substitution for Western machinery and equipment.

Twelve percent of the firms (with more than one hundred employees) and 14.5 percent of smaller firms (with less than one hundred employees) replace Chinese machinery and equipment for Western ones "much and very much." Although it seems that a bigger proportion of smaller firms can substitute Chinese machinery for Western ones, this difference is not statistically significant. Thirty-two percent of big enterprises and 16.4 percent of smaller firms in the sample could "moderately" substitute Chinese products for Western items. The difference between these two groups is significant and explains that a large proportion of big companies, compared to smaller ones, could moderately replace Chinese products for Western machinery and equipment (table 3.5).

In sum, there is no considerable difference between the impact of sanctions on newly established and older companies, and between big firms and smaller ones. Therefore, our survey shows clearly that harsh international sanctions that inevitably intensified the Iran's Look East policy has imposed a heavy burden on the majority of private firms, reducing their incentives for new investment and decreasing their competitiveness.

TABLE 3.5. Substitution of Chinese machinery for Western ones

	MORE THAN 100 EMPLOYEES		LESS THAN 100 EMPLOYEES		P-VALUE
	NUMBER	PERCENT	NUMBER	PERCENT	
Very and very much	6	12.0	8	14.5	0.6499
Moderate	16	32.0	9	16.4	0.0293
Few and very few	23	46.0	29	52.7	0.755
Not at all	5	10.0	9	16.4	0.8344
Total	**50**	**100**	**55**	**100**	

Source: Survey data

In a highly globalized world, all countries try to strengthen their position in the international markets and pursue foreign policies that are interconnected with economic goals. By economic diplomacy, countries try to maximize opportunities and minimize the costs of the world's competitive markets for their businesses. Iran's diplomacy since the 1979 revolution has been based on the ideology that necessitates the fight against imperialism (the Western world) and support for the oppressed. This very costly ideology has created long-lasting hostilities with the United States and its European allies, and has shaped Iran's foreign policy orientation toward the East (mainly Russia, China, and India). This policy created exceptional opportunities for Chinese firms to supply their various products in Iranian markets, in the absence of Western rivals.

Hostility with the West imposed heavy costs on Iran's economy; and various international sanctions weakened the country's position in the global arena. Sanctions on Iran's oil exports and severe restriction on international banking transactions have limited the country's oil revenue and increased budget deficit significantly, leading to rapid growth of liquidity and inflation rates. Declining oil income, uncertainty about the future, and restriction of imports and exports hammered investment, production, and employment. Although job opportunities increased during the past decade, it was at the cost of falling productivity. A large proportion of high value–added jobs in several factories disappeared and instead millions of low value–added jobs, such as street vendors and taxi drivers created. As people cannot afford to be unemployed for a long time, they become underemployed, as they cannot utilize their skills and talents in their new jobs.

Developmental foreign policy is one of the most important means to expand mutual relationship with other countries for improving Iran's position in the global economy. Resolving political problems with Western countries and lifting the economic and financial sanctions is the necessary condition of

Iran's development. Having mutually fruitful economic and political relations both with the East and the West is in the best interest of Iran. Pragmatic and development-oriented foreign policy based on peaceful coexistence with other countries can facilitate the access of Iranian firms to international markets and expand tourism industry by showcasing Iranian tourist attractions.

To study the impacts of sanctions and the approach of the Look East foreign policy on Iran's economy, a survey was conducted with Iranian private firms. The results of this survey show that the majority of Iranian firms use Western machinery and equipment. Sanctions increased the costs of indirect imports of Western products and restricted the access of businesses to after-sale services of Western companies. Yet, most Iranian firms could not substitute Western products with Chinese ones. Therefore, sanctions have negatively impacted the quantity and quality of products in a big proportion of Iranian firms, and have discouraged investment. If this unfavorable situation continues, Iran's economic activities will decline further.

Over the years, there have been a number of attempts by neighboring countries like Oman and Qatar to facilitate direct talks between Iran and United States. It seems that a new consensus is also being formed among political elites that economic aims must be prioritized in Iran's foreign policy. Opening the path for trade with United States, European Union, and their allies will be a turning point in Iran's economic reconstruction. With balanced foreign relations, Iran can benefit the opportunities of trade with the East and the West simultaneously.

Appendix: Questionnaire

Part 1. Firms' Information

Products/Services (Please write your main products or services):

TABLE 3.6. Question 1

Q. NO.		VERY MUCH	MUCH	MODERATE	FEW	VERY FEW	NOT AT ALL
1	To what extent do you need to import machinery, equipment and software? If your answer is "not at all" please do not answer other questions.						

Part 2. Use of Western Technology

TABLE 3.7. Questions 2–5

Q. NO.		VERY MUCH	MUCH	MODERATE	FEW	VERY FEW	NOT AT ALL
2	How much do you use machinery, equipment and software of companies from the United States, Europe, and Japan in your firm?						
3	How much do you use the license of companies from the United States, Europe, and Japan in your firm?						
4	How much of your required machinery and equipment can be imported indirectly from Western countries?						
5	To what extent are you indirectly able to receive after-sales service for repairing of your machinery and equipment?						

Part 3. Use of Eastern Technology

TABLE 3.8. Questions 6–10

Q. NO.		VERY MUCH	MUCH	MODERATE	FEW	VERY FEW	NOT AT ALL
6	How much of your required software can be supplied by companies from China, Russia, or India?						
7	Can Eastern machinery and equipment be substituted for Western products?						
8	To what extent can you receive a license from China, India and other developing countries to use advanced technologies?						
9	To what extent do Eastern companies offer reliable guarantee for their machinery and equipment?						

TABLE 3.8. (Continued)

Q. NO.		VERY MUCH	MUCH	MODERATE	FEW	VERY FEW	NOT AT ALL
10	To what extent do Eastern companies offer training for your personnel to work with imported machinery and equipment?						

Part 4. Costs of Indirect Imports from Western Countries

TABLE 3.9. Questions 11–17

Q. NO.		VERY MUCH	MUCH	MODERATE	FEW	VERY FEW	NOT AT ALL
11	How much time (more than ordinary process) do you spend for indirect imports of Western machinery and equipment?						
12	How much money (more than ordinary price) do you pay for indirect imports of Western machinery and equipment?						
13	How much negative impact do sanctions have on your technical capabilities?						
14	How much do sanctions increase costs of repair and maintenance of your machinery and equipment?						
15	How much negative impact do sanctions have on the quality of your imported raw materials?						
16	How much negative impact do sanctions have on the quality of your imported intermediate goods?						
17	How much negative impact do sanctions have on the scale of your production?						

Part 5. Impacts of Eastern and Western Technologies on Future Investment

TABLE 3.10. Questions 18–20

Q. NO.		VERY MUCH	MUCH	MODERATE	FEW	VERY FEW	NOT AT ALL
18	How much Western and Eastern companies are different regarding after-sale services?						
19	How much access to Western machinery and equipment is necessary for the improvement and expansion of your business?						
20	How much access to Western machinery and equipment is necessary for attraction and satisfaction of your potential customers?						

Source: https://tradingeconomics.com/iran/

NOTES

1. "Amar varedat va saderat" [Imports and exports data], Tehran Chamber of Commerce, 2023, https://tccim.ir/stats.

2. "Amar varedat va saderat."

3. N. Saghafi Ameri and A. Ahadi, *Iran va siyasat-e negah be shargh* [Iran and its orientation toward the East] (Expediency Discernment Council) (Tehran Center for Strategic Studies, 2008).

4. "Amar varedat va saderat."

5. "Seri zamani tejarat-e khareji" [Time series data, international trade], Central Bank of Iran, 2023, https://tsd.cbi.ir/Display/Content.aspx.

6. Zahra Karimi, "Iran's Labor Market Under the Sanctions," *International Journal of New Political Economy* 3, no. 1 (2022): 183–202.

7. "Tedad ranandegan snap va tapsi bishtar az uber" [Number of Snap and Tapsi drivers higher than Uber], *Tejarat News*, November 20, 2021, https://tejaratnews.com/startup/.

8. Karimi, "Iran's Labor Market Under the Sanctions."

9. Central Bank of Iran, "Hesab-haye melli-e Iran" [Iran's national accounts], 2023, https://www.cbi.ir/simplelist/4454.aspx.

10. Central Bank of Iran, "Taraznameh va gozaresh-e eghtesadi" [Economic report and balance sheet 2019], September 7, 2023, https://www.cbi.ir/Category/EconomicReport_fa.aspx.

11. Karimi, "Iran's Labor Market Under the Sanctions."

12. Statistical Centre of Iran, "Amar-e nirou-ye kar" [Workforce data], 2023, https://bit.ly/3PxnBXw.

13. Statistical Centre of Iran, "Amar-e nirou-ye kar."

14. Parliament Research Center, "A perspective of Iran's economic situation: Challenges and solutions," 2020.

15. Parliament Research Center, "Vaaredaat ghat'aat bi keyfiat chini khiyaanat be eghtesaad keshvar ast" [Imports of low-quality auto parts is very dangerous for Iran's economy], 2016, https://bit.ly/49B5idk.

16. "'arzeh mahsoolaat cheri ba naam am vey am tavassot modiraan khodro; am vey am tigoo" [Supply of Chery cars under the MVM brand by Modiran Vehicle Manufacturing Company], Khodrobank.com, 2021, https://bit.ly/3QArLP0.

17. Author interview with manager of auto part procurement in SAIPA Car Manufacturing Company, 2023.

18. "Gharar bud khodkafa shvim, khodfena shodim" [We wanted to be self-sufficient, but we became self-destructive], Birunit.com, March 5, 2021, https://bit.ly/46mQb4L.

19. Author interview with owner of a shrimp farm in Bandar Abbas, 2023.

20. Author interview with expert in a IT service provider in Tehran, 2023.

21. Author interview with top manager in a big manufacturing company owned by a public institution in Tehran, 2023.

4

REGIONAL MULTILATERALISM AND IRAN'S "LOOK EAST" POLICY UNDER RAISI

Recontextualization of India–Iran Relations

Deepika Saraswat

In the wake of the US withdrawal in 2018 from the Iran nuclear agreement, formally known as the Joint Comprehensive Plan of Action (JCPOA), and return of unilateral sanctions, the Hassan Rouhani administration framed Iran's outreach to China and Russia in terms of defending multilateralism against the American unilateralism. Under the Ebrahim Raisi administration, especially following the approval of Iran's Shanghai Cooperation Organization (SCO) membership at Dushanbe summit in 2021, Iran's "Look East" has been reframed in terms participating in Asian regionalism or continentalism and "Asian multilateralism." In this context, Iran's pursuit of long-term strategic partnership with China and Russia is aimed at furthering Iran's wider geoeconomic aspirations of integrating it into and also shaping the emerging regional order in Eurasia.

This chapter maps the transformation in Iran's Look East policy, first by analyzing Iran's increasing focus on multilateralism since the Rouhani administration's negotiation of an interim nuclear deal in the first year of his government in 2013, and how it transformed into "Asian multilateralism" under Raisi's presidency. Second, the chapter examines Iran's idea of regionalism, focusing on three aspects: (1) Iran's notion of Asia as comprising of diverse civilizations, and articulation of "new Asian identity" based on the exclusion of the West; (2) common, indivisible security concept, and development–security nexus at the regional level; and (3) utilizing Iran's geographical advantage, while projecting Iran as a "bridge" linking different regions, and connectivity initiatives. Finally, the chapter examines how Iran's vision of regional integration has recontextualized India–Iran relations, creating both new challenges and possibilities of convergence.

Iran's Turn to "Multilateralism" and the "Look East" Policy

Over the last decade, one notable trend in Iran's foreign policy narrative, and to some extent at the level of practical conduct, has been the prominence of multilateralism. However, since first embraced by the Rouhani administration, Tehran's approach to multilateralism has changed substantially. As Robert Murray argues, despite the liberal characteristics of regimes and institutions, multilateralism is essentially "a strategic choice made by self-interested states about how to advance their interests and influence world order."[1] A corollary of this instrumentalist or strategic approach to multilateralism is that "trends and preferences around multilateralism are not static."[2] Murray explains the varying commitments of states to and changing form of multilateralism at international and regional levels by referring to system-level changes:

> the structure of international system at any given point in history will impact if and how states use multilateralism as a strategy, what kind of order states strive to create and negotiate, and what norms will be focussed on by those states that make up multilateral arrangements and institution.[3]

The foreign policy of the moderate Rouhani administration was cast in a "liberal" mold to the extent it prioritized "constructive engagement" internationally, and supported cooperation-based, non–zero-sum approach to regional security. By engaging world powers in multilateral negotiations to resolve the nuclear issue, including the United States, the broader goal was to de-securitize and normalize Iran's broader international relations. As Rouhani's Foreign Minister Mohammad Javad Zarif noted of the transformation of the global environment, as a result of globalization and mutual interdependence among states, and how "zero-sum" and unilateral approaches of great powers had proven ineffective, while the rising trend of collective action and cooperative approaches had reduced the significance of hard, military power, and created new conceptions of ideational and soft power accessible to larger pool of states.[4] Iran's détente with the United States on the nuclear issue enabled the Rouhani administration to transform Iran's traditional view of the international system as hegemonic and a source of threat for independence and sovereignty of the Islamic Republic to one "moving towards a state of mutual interdependence," and where "the Western once unchallenged monopoly over international relations and in shaping and directing developments has been broken."[5] Such a view of the international system justified a balanced policy of engaging and expanding Iran's relations with all major powers, including Europe and the United States, on the basis on mutual respect and mutual interest.[6]

When the Iran–US normalization process came to a grinding halt following the Donald Trump administration's withdrawal from the nuclear agreement in 2018 and the reimposition of US sanctions on Iran, the Rouhani administration remained committed to the agreement. It sought to mobilize remaining signatories including Europeans by calling for common defense of multilateralism against the US "unilateralism."[7] However, Supreme Leader Ayatollah Ali Khamenei, who sets the directions of the national security and foreign policy of the country, now vindicated in his distrust of engaging the West in nuclear negotiations, called for prioritizing ties with the East and neighboring countries: "In foreign policy, top priorities for us, today, include preferring the East to the West, preferring the neighboring countries to the far reached locations, preferring nations and countries that share in our common goals. We should not be dependent on foreign countries."[8]

The Rouhani administration framed its outreach to China, which was engaged in a trade war with the United States, in terms of their shared commitment to multilateralism against the US unilateralism. In the context of intensifying US–China great power competition, Iran's emphasis on multilateralism was increasingly framed in terms of contestation between rival visions of "cooperative, international law-based and democratic international relationships," and one based on relative gains and hegemony. Iran projected itself as a "responsible international actor" willing to play by rules.

Notwithstanding the return of the US sanctions, Iran hoped to play a pivotal role in China's Belt and Road Initiative–related infrastructure projects. The Rouhani administration increasingly referred to Iran and China's broader geopolitical convergence at regional, and continental level.[9] Foreign Minister Zarif wrote in the *Global Times* of the "shared vision" that binds Iran–China ties: "China and Iran share a vision of sovereign states with independent foreign policies across the Asian continent being connected, prospering together and realizing their potential and their true places in the world."[10] Subsequently, the Rouhani administration initiated negotiations on the Iran–China Comprehensive Strategic Partnership four years after the joint statement on Comprehensive Strategic Partnership was made during President Xi Jinping's visit to Iran in 2016. Notably, after attending the G7 Summit in Biarritz in August 2019, where President Emmanuel Macron unsuccessfully tried to push the US administration for a "pause" in its pressure campaign on Iran, Zarif left for Beijing to discuss the roadmap for the twenty-five-year strategic partnership. Earlier, in February 2019, Ali Larijani, then–Iranian parliament speaker, had visited China at the head of a high-level delegation that included Zarif, Oil Minister Bijan Zanganeh, Central Bank Governor Abdolnasser Hemmati, and a number of parliamentarians.[11] President Xi noted in his meeting with Larijani that China was resolved to develop comprehensive strategic partnership with Iran irrespective of the change in the international regional situation. Larijani, who, in his position as the secretary of the Supreme National Security Council in 2005, had launched Iran's "Look East" policy, was appointed by Rouhani as special representative for strategic ties with the People's Republic of China.

In June 2020, after Rouhani's cabinet approved a preliminary draft of the Twenty-Five-Year Cooperation Agreement, unconfirmed reports emerged in the international media about China receiving a 32 percent discount on crude purchases along with a two-year payment break and $400 billion in Chinese investment in Iran's oil, gas and transport sectors, and Chinese control over one of Iran's Persian Gulf islands.[12] The subsequent debate in Iran, both among political circles and the public, predictably focused on issues that have acted as constraints on Iran's "Eastern strategy," namely ideological principles of independence enshrined in Iran's constitution and captured in the slogan "neither East nor West."[13] There was also widespread pessimism about serious relations with major powers in terms of dependence on China. Former President Mahmoud Ahmadinejad was first to bring the issue into public sphere, as he denounced the Rouhani administration for "secretly signing a deal" with a foreign state and violating the fundamental principles of the Islamic Revolution that were meant to "withhold nothing from the nation."[14]

Significantly, Rouhani administration's defense of the agreement went beyond the traditional logic of the Look East policy as "responding to U.S. sanction pressure," by adding the logic of global power transition to the East. Explaining the rationale behind the agreement in the parliament, Foreign Minister Zarif argued that "the point that has to be taken into consideration in our foreign policy is the shift in global power."[15] The government spokesperson claimed that the plan proves the failure of the US policies to isolate Iran and sever its relations with the international community.[16] The final agreement was signed in March 2021, coinciding with the fiftieth anniversary of diplomatic ties between Iran and China. It was hailed as beginning a "new chapter of cooperation" for the second half of the century of relations.[17] Undoubtedly, Iran placed a long-term "strategic partnership" with China at the core of its Look East policy, which itself had transformed from an expedient means of countering Western sanctions to a long-term strategy responding to the systemic shift.[18] Furthermore, as a result of decisions at the highest levels of power, and the political ascendancy of the Principlists faction internally, the Look East policy was placed front and center as a strategy for Iran's international engagements.

On the eve of the presidential election in 2021, Supreme Leader Ayatollah Khamenei stated that those calling on the country and the revolution to "normalize" itself—in other words, to become closer to international norms—were essentially rejecting revolutionary principles in the name of transformation.[19] This was a nod to the Principlists, whose support for an "Eastern strategy" stems from their ideological antagonism towards the West and a suspicion of the reformists and moderates focus on the engagement with Europe and the United States. The victory of the Principlist candidate Raisi in what was historically the least competitive presidential election in Iran marked a generational shift in Iranian politics. The conservatives and Principlists, having monopolized the judiciary, the parliament, and executive power, embarked on the "second phase of the revolution" proclaimed by Khamenei in 2019 on the fortieth anniversary of the Islamic revolution.[20] Khamenei's overarching discourse of the "second phase of revolution" called for the continued management of economy, society, and culture by adhering to revolutionary principles of national dignity, independence and freedom, with the goal of making the Islamic Republic a "model of comprehensive Islamic government." As Khamenei steered Iran's politics along the path of ideological revival, he dismissed and even delegitimized diplomacy with the West. While defining the US and "a number of European countries" as "unreliable and deceiving," with which Iran must be extremely cautious, Khamenei stated that "in the case of the United States, no problem with them is seen to be resolved, and any negotiation with the U.S. will have no outcome but material and spiritual harms."[21] As a result, the Look East policy, with a focus on Iran's neighbors and Asian countries, came to define the foreign policy orientation of the Raisi administration from its very inception.

The approval of Iran's full membership of the SCO at the 21st Council of the Head of the State meeting in Tajikistan in September 2021 was a transformative development in Iran's multilateral engagement. It was the first time that the Islamic Republic had joined a regional organization alongside major powers, with a focus on security cooperation.[22] Undoubtedly, the renewed efforts toward resolving political impediments to Iran's membership, especially differences with Tajikistan over Iran's support for the banned opposition Islamic Renaissance Party of Tajikistan, had been made during the Rouhani administration, with Ali Shamkhani, secretary of Supreme National Security Council, spearheading these efforts through the change of administration. But the approval of the membership at the beginning of the Raisi administration gave an institutional platform to Iran's Asia focus while redefining Islamic Republic's overall geopolitical engagement at both regional and international levels.

Iran's traditional geopolitical imagination defined by an East–West polarity, within which Iran had historically devised policies of positive and negative equilibrium and balance, or alignment with one against threats from the other, was now reworked by a geopolitical logic of integration within the Eurasian region. During a visit to China in September 2022, Foreign Minister Hossein

Amir-Abdollahian, in an op-ed in a Chinese daily, noted how international power transitions and the emergence of a multipolar world had made East–West geopolitical thinking redundant:

> In today's world, East and West have lost their traditional implications and, in a way, have been replaced by regionalism or even continentalism. Hegemonic control and unilateralism are waning and the international community's transition towards a multipolar world and the redistribution of power in favor of independent countries are becoming inevitable trends.[23]

Iran sees structural changes in the international system brought about by China's economic rise and an assertive Russia. These developments have resulted in the emergence of a multipolar world and an increasing salience of economic and security multilateralism in Eurasia. Iran's convergence with Russia and China-led initiatives, which include institutionally driven links such as the Eurasian Economic Union and the SCO and connectivity projects such as Beijing's Belt and Road Initiative, is based on its assessment that by asserting their leadership through multilateral and regional arrangements, Russia and China contain the US power and influence in Iran's Asian neighborhood. Such regional multilateral initiatives fall into the category of "rival regionalism" for providing "an alternative to the U.S. and Western leadership by creating or revitalising non-Western organisations."[24] Moreover, Iran sees Russia and China binding themselves in multilateral regional organizations, and a plurality of regional initiatives led by different powers, as conducive for emergence of a horizontal, decentered, multipolar order in Asia.

The SCO and Iran's Asian Regional Vision

Edmund Herzig traces Iran's interest in regionalism at the end of the Cold War to Iranian policymakers' anxieties about structural changes at the global level.[25] The collapse of the Soviet Union not only brought about changes at the level of the international system, the emergence of independent states in Central Asia and the Caucasus substantially transformed Iran's regional environment. The next few paragraphs briefly discuss four dimensions of Iranian vision of regionalism in the early 1990s: geopolitical, functional, cultural, and a recognition of centrality of Russia in the post-Soviet space.

In the 1990s, as Iran, alongside Iraq, became the target of the "dual containment" policy of the United States, it dreaded the prospects of an emerging unipolar world order and globalization dominated by a single and hostile superpower.

Tehran, therefore, maintained that the bipolar order should rather give way to a multipolar one, and articulated its vision of regionalism within a broader perspective of a multipolar world. Herzig explains this conception of the world "as a set of interlinked and overlapping regions." "The emergence and reinforcement of these regions and their internal and mutual linkages is held to be a part of a benign globalization process that will limit the capacity of any single power to dominate the system."[26] First, in the post–Cold War international system, Iran saw its location at crossroads between four different regions of Central Asia, the Caucasus, and the Persian Gulf and South Asia. This was seen as assuring Iran's status as a major regional power and a crucial partner in any security arrangement in these regions.[27] In its regional projects dealing with security issues, such as the Caspian Sea Cooperation Organisation, Tehran advocated for a multilateral approach in order to address negative security externalities and common interests in regional stability. But Iran's insistence on self-reliance among regional states and the exclusion of the extraregional powers, meaning the United States, did not find resonance with Iran's neighboring states, which did not share Iran's security concerns vis-à-vis the United States.

Second, Tehran realized that cultivating economic interdependence in trade, energy, transport, and infrastructure with its neighboring states and regions was a sustainable strategy of integrating with the global economy and countering the US strategy of isolating Iran. Iran's efforts at functional regionalism—that is, promoting economic and political cooperation through regional organizations, including the Economic Cooperation Organisation, and the Association of Persian-Speaking States—found some acceptance among the newly independent states in Central Asia and Caucasus.

Third, Iran attached importance to culture and civilizational aspects in regional identity construction.[28] Apart from leveraging Iran's ethnic and religious bonds with some of the neighboring states in furthering regional cooperation, the cultural–civilizational narrative also stems from Iran's view of the world as comprising of a pluriverse of historical civilizations, and its rejection of the Western normative universalism based on liberal democracy.

Fourth, Iran pursued a Russia-centric regional policy in the post-Soviet space, whereby Iran's engagement with the new republics was based on an implicit recognition of Russia's real and potential power over the Commonwealth of Independent States.[29] Tehran therefore was careful not to pursue policies that could jeopardize its relationship with Moscow.[30] The geopolitics of Iran–Russia relations had been fundamentally reworked with the collapse of the Soviet Union, as the two countries no longer had a common land border after nearly two centuries.[31] Since 1722, when the czarist Russian Empire took advantage of a weakening Ottoman Empire and disintegrating Safavid Empire in Iran to make inroads into Iran's northern Caucasian provinces, and after periodic occupations successfully annexed them into Russian Empire a century later. Territorial loss and Russia's presence on Iran's northern borders had placed Russia as the primary threat to Iran's territorial integrity and sovereignty, therefore at the center of Iran's foreign policy.[32] In the post–Cold War context, on the one hand Tehran had an interest in perpetuating the dissolution of the former Soviet Union and in preventing the rebirth of a new Russian Empire adjoining its border. On the other hand, Tehran saw the pursuit of cooperation with Moscow on regional issues, for instance in civil war in Tajikistan and later in Afghanistan, as a matter of national interest. It also viewed Russian leadership and influence in the region through the prism of countering US hegemonic ambitions in the region.[33]

Western observers, who view the SCO primarily through a geopolitical prism, and focus on its defense–security nature as an "anti-NATO," anti-Western, revisionist club centered on "Russia-China entente," see Iran's membership as part of an emerging "Russia-China-Iran axis."[34] Other readings focus on the institutional dimension of the SCO as gradually developing into "a new model of multilateral cooperation" that will arguably constitute the backbone of future Eurasian governance, and play the role of harmonizing strategies of long-term economic integration of Asia.[35] From the latter perspective, Iran has made a "strategic choice" to proactively engage and even shape an Asian multilateral order. While broadly concurring with both these readings, the remaining part of this section examines how Iran is framing its SCO membership and future role in the organization in regional and continental terms. It observes a continuity in Iran's concept of regionalism, focusing on three aspects: (1) Iran's vision of Asia as comprising of diverse civilizations, and articulation of a "new Asian identity" based on the exclusion of the West; (2) common, indivisible security concept, and development–security nexus at the regional level; and (3) utilizing Iran's geographic and locational advantage, while projecting Iran as a "bridge" linking different regions, and connectivity initiatives.

Emphasis on Civilizations in Asian Identity Construction

Iran's conception of culture-based regionalism leverages shared religious, cultural, linguistic, and ethnic ties with its neighbors. It is in equal measures driven by geopolitical consideration of promoting interdependence and autonomy among regional states. Also, Iran routinely frames its bilateral ties with other Asian powers such as India and China in civilizational terms. Arguably, in so doing, Iran legitimizes its religio-political system as rooted in unique religious and civilizational heritage, buttressing Iran's claim as historical actor in its own right. Tehran also draws on a romanticized vision of harmonious civilizational interactions into the contemporary context of a cooperative and inclusive order in Asia. From Tehran's point of view, a major accomplishment of the SCO, which has been historically centered on Russia, China and the five Central Asian republics, is its stabilizing role and restoring Central Asia, and by extension Iran's role, in facilitating pan-Asia trade of the previous two millennia.[36] Raisi spoke of the SCO's role in terms of restoration of Asia's "historical cohesion" in the Dushanbe summit:

> This region has had a great cohesion throughout history, and the restoration of this cohesion is one of the features of the Shanghai Pact and emphasised by the Islamic Republic of Iran. Asia is a land rich in civilisations and values. Asia's role in the international stage requires maintaining harmony between its nations and civilizations.[37]

Notwithstanding Iran's emphasis on diversity of civilizations and nations in Asia, it sees the SCO in ideational terms of realizing a "new Asian identity," which is autonomous and exclusive of the West. In other words, Iran's support for regionalism and continent-wide integration in Asia is at the intersection of its global and regional strategy. At the international level, Tehran sees its membership in non-Western institutions such SCO as an opportunity to participate in the creation of a more equitable international order, and advancing alternative normative values (the centrality of the state, respect for sovereignty, and the noninterference principle).[38] At the regional level, Iran's support for "Asian multilateralism" is about emphasizing regional autonomy, as well as collective approach to issues of security and development, with the objective of limiting the security role of extraregional players—notably the United States and NATO—in Eurasia.

Regional Security–Development Nexus

Against realist, state-centric notion of security, which are based on relative and hard or military power, the SCO's focus has been on nontraditional challenges, such as terrorism, extremism, cross-border organized crime, and drug trafficking, which pose threats to territorial integrity, as well as social and political stability, of states. Given the transnational character of these threats, multilateralism has found acceptance among the member states. As the SCO's mandate expands to promote economic cooperation in Eurasian region, there is also increasing support for an approach based on security–development nexus.[39]

Iran's view that mega-connectivity and infrastructure projects such as Beijing's Belt and Road Initiative can address the region's development deficit and, thus, contribute to security, is broadly in agreement with the Chinese notion of "development peace," or the SCO's concept of "security through development."[40] Tehran's support for the security–development nexus also stems from its criticism of the failed US attempts at democracy promotion and its "war against terror" in Afghanistan and elsewhere in West Asia.[41] Iran considers stabilization of Afghanistan, broadly conceived in terms of security of its international borders, as well as political stability based on effective participation of all ethnic groups in the future governance of the country, as inextricably linked to regional security, along with prospects of economic cooperation and integration in the region.[42] Even as it pragmatically engages Taliban on border, trade, and humanitarian issues, Tehran has actively engaged in multilateral mechanisms, especially the Foreign Ministers of Neighboring Countries of Afghanistan, and the SCO, for a collective approach to prevent the spillover of insecurity into the neighboring countries and seek support for an "inclusive government" in Afghanistan. Given that Russia remains the primary security partner for Central Asian states, Iran sees its experience of military–technical cooperation with Russia during their coordinated campaign in support of Bashar al-Assad's government in Syria as a "valuable experience," and a successful model of fighting terrorism and extremism, which can be replicated with other regional and supraregional partners.[43]

In the same vein of the security–development nexus, Raisi identified sanctions as economic terrorism, and "a key obstacle to promoting regional harmony."[44] This is in line with Iran's view that US sanctions are designed to undermine social and political stability of the country, while also seeking to isolate Iran from the region economically and politically. Therefore, a key agenda for Iran at the SCO has been to call on the organization to focus on expanding economic cooperation and develop mechanisms as a collective response to sanctions.

Iran as a "Bridge" Linking Different Connectivity Initiatives

Since the early twentieth century, when the Trans-Iranian Railway linking Iran's Caspian Sea to the Persian Gulf coasts was constructed, Iran has claimed a unique geographical advantage in north–south transit and connectivity.[45] Since the late 1990s, Iran, Russia, and India have been driven by convergent interests in developing the multimodal International North–South Transportation Corridor (INSTC) via Iran. Notably, their coordinated approach to fostering regional connectivity is part of their combined efforts to expand access to new markets and resource regions, while shaping a more balanced geoeconomic dynamic in Eurasia. In the absence of a supranational dynamic, or intensity of trade and economic interdependence between them, connectivity of national transport systems, including road, railways, and ports was seen as the most viable solution for regional as well as transregional transport and logistics development.

Over the last decade, since China announced China–Central Asia–West Asia as one of the six corridors of its Belt and Road Initiative, Iran has been keen to restore its historic status in the old Silk Road as a bridge between the East and the West.[46] As Tehran tried to leverage its geopolitical influence in Iraq and Syria to create an overland trade and transport corridor stretching from the Persian Gulf to the Mediterranean Sea, it was also drawing Beijing's attention to this southern land route for the China–Central Asia–West Asia Corridor.[47]

The economic benefits available to a transit economy depend on the extent of integration between international transport corridors with regional and national logistics infrastructure. Not surprisingly, therefore, Iran seeks to avoid a competitive dynamic between these different connectivity initiatives, and is projecting itself as the link between the INSTC and other East–West latitudinal corridors, especially Central Asia–West Asia Corridor of the Belt and Road Initiative.

Russia's invasion of Ukraine and comprehensive European Union (EU) sanctions on the country have made the Northern Corridor (China–Kazakhstan–Russia–Belarus–Poland–Germany), which has been the primary artery of China–EU rail trade, a risky proposition. Central Asian states are increasingly turning to Iran to either protect or enhance their transit role by diversifying transport routes via Iran.[48] In June 2022, Kazakh President Kassym-Jomart Tokayev was in Tehran to jointly launch with President Raisi the Kazakhstan–Turkmenistan–Iran (KTI) transit corridor, as part the Southern Caspian Sea Corridor to Europe via Turkey.[49] Interestingly, Iran and Russia see the KTI railway as a north–south railway corridor. Earlier, during Raisi's visit to Russia in January 2022, Moscow pledged to revive the credit line it had promised in 2017 to finance electrification of a 500-kilometer stretch from the city of Incheh Borun on the Iran–Turkmenistan border to Garmsar on the Tehran–Mashhad main line.[50]

Furthermore, Iran and India are jointly developing Chabahar Port as regional transshipment hub between the landlocked Central Asian republics, Afghanistan, and India. Just before the return of the US sanctions on Iran, in December 2018, India took over the operations of a part of the Shahid Beheshti Port.[51] Despite the challenges posed by sanctions, India's port operator had tried to acquire the necessary equipment and has used the port facilities for delivering humanitarian assistance to Afghanistan.[52] In recent years, India has pushed for connecting Chabahar with an eastern branch of the INSTC to Central Asia. A few months before the Taliban's takeover of Afghanistan, at an event marking "Chabahar

Day," India's External Affairs Minister S. Jaishankar proposed the inclusion of the port in the INSTC. While welcoming the interest of Uzbekistan and Afghanistan in joining the twelve-member, multimodal corridor project, the minister noted that an "eastern corridor through Afghanistan" would maximize the potential of the project.[53]

Even as Iran's self-projection as a "bridge" between various connectivity initiatives on the continent has been argued with a certain "historical-geographical determinism," it is to be seen as Iran's attempt to navigate the dynamic of geo-economic competition inherent to these projects. In his first address at the SCO summit in Dushanbe, Raisi described Iran as the link between three major infrastructure projects, within a broader vision of development-oriented, cooperative, and networked order in Eurasia:

> Peace and development are achieved through the cooperation and coordination of key countries in the region. In this direction, the formation and strengthening of infrastructure bonds between different countries is important and necessary. The One Belt-One Road Initiative, the Eurasian Economic Union and the North-South Corridor, as key projects in the field of infrastructural links, can play a role in strengthening the common interests of developing countries and strengthening peace in the region. These projects are not competitors but complement each other.[54]

Iran has also downplayed the competition between Chabahar and the Chinese-developed Gwadar Port, located only seventy-two kilometers apart on Pakistan's side of Makran coast. As two deep-oceanic ports outside the Strait of Hormuz choke point, they compete as potential gateways connecting Eurasian hinterland to the northern Indian Ocean. Just after India had assumed operational control of a terminal in Chabahar, then–Foreign Minister Zarif, during a visit to Pakistan, proposed to connect Chabahar Port with the Gwadar Port, in effect linking with China Pakistan Economic Corridor (CPEC), the "flagship project" of the Belt and Road Initiative.[55] Given India's principled opposition to the CPEC, which runs through Gilgit-Baltistan in the Pakistan-occupied Kashmir violating Indian sovereignty, Zarif's proposal was widely seen as a response to India's compliance with the US sanctions by stopping crude imports from Iran. At the SCO summit in 2021, Raisi invited member states to utilize Chabahar as trade and transshipment hub, as he described the port as a "symbol of cooperation" of all members of the organization.[56]

To sum up, Iran's projection of itself as the "bridge" can be explained as an interest-driven policy aimed at maximizing Iran's transit potential through integration of different infrastructure and economic corridors through the country.

Iran's "gateway" role in facilitating India's connectivity with Central Asia also underscores Iran's wider interest in geoeconomic balance in Eurasia. Iran's strategy can be seen as a continuation of its historical role of playing off rival powers in order to maintain its long-term autonomy and freedom of action.

Recontextualization of India–Iran Ties

Since the 2003 "New Delhi Declaration," which came in the wake of growing convergence between India and Iran in Afghanistan and the wider region, and mentioned for the first time their interest in jointly developing the Chabahar Port, Iran has been feted by Indian strategic community as India's "gateway" to Central Asia and wider Eurasia.[57] Notwithstanding the geoeconomic dimension foregrounded in the official declarations, the strategic significance of Chabahar was widely understood. First, by participating in the development of Chabahar, and hinterland connectivity to Afghanistan and Central Asia, India was to a great extent able to neutralize Pakistan's strategic denial of overland transit to India aimed at limiting New Delhi's role in Afghanistan.

Secondly, China's development of Pakistan's Gwadar Port—later as part the CPEC stretching from China's landlocked western provinces to the Arabian Sea—caused alarm in New Delhi. Beyond the declared aims of addressing China's internal development priorities and mitigating strategic vulnerabilities on choke points, Gwadar was seen from the prism of India–China strategic rivalry in the Indian Ocean. The CPEC has been seen in India as part of a wider China-led economic and strategic integration of much of the Eurasian littoral, fundamentally transforming the traditional character of Indian Ocean as a semi-closed strategic space capable of domination by a single naval power.[58]

To avoid getting caught up in the zero-sum geopolitical rivalry between China and India, Iran has embraced the narrative of development-oriented regional connectivity and cooperation. By promoting Chabahar as a "symbol of cooperation" for all members of the SCO, Raisi sought to put the port project above the geopolitical fray. At the same time, Iranian officials describe Chabahar as the centerpiece of "strategic partnership" between India and Iran, as they seek Indian investment in the development of the port infrastructure, hinterland connectivity, and routing more cargo through the port to make it commercially viable.[59]

Against the backdrop of electoral defeat of the incumbent US President Trump by Joe Biden, who was keen to reengage Iran on the nuclear issue, India and Iran intensified their diplomatic outreach to Central Asian countries, especially Uzbekistan, to participate in Chabahar and the INSTC.[60] Soon after a virtual summit held between Indian Prime Minister Narendra Modi and Uzbek

President Shavkat Mirziyoyev on December 11, 2020, India, Iran, and Uzbekistan had their first Trilateral Working Group Meeting on the joint use of Chabahar Port.[61] Following the Taliban's takeover and a worsening humanitarian crisis in Afghanistan, India, in cooperation with the United Nations World Food Program, used Chabahar to send wheat and humanitarian assistance to Afghanistan. In an adjustment to the changes in Afghanistan, India outlined its vision to make Chabahar Port a transit hub under the INSTC.[62] The Iranian section of the branch runs from Chabahar to Sarakhs on the Iran–Turkmenistan border. Uzbekistan, which has built a railway linking its border town of Termez with Maza-e-Sharif in Afghanistan is keen to link with Herat, which upon the completion of the 222-kilometer-long Khaf–Herat railway, will have railway connectivity with Iran.[63]

With the Russia–Ukraine war and Western sanctions impacting Russia's role in East–West transit and Iran's membership of the SCO, Central Asian states have actively engaged Iran to diversify their connectivity to Europe and India. The first meeting of the India–Central Asia Joint Working Group on Chabahar Port was held in Mumbai in April 2023.[64] The next round is to be hosted in Tehran. In January, 2024 when the external affairs minister visited Iran, he noted regional connectivity as the "critical pillar" of India–Iran ties and had called for monitoring the progress on Chabahar under the direct supervision of the highest political leadership of the two countries. Subsequently, Indian Ports Global Limited (IPGL) and Iran's Port and Maritime Organisation signed long-term main contract valid for ten years concerning operation of the Shahid Beheshti terminal in the Chabahar Port Development Project. IPGL will invest $120 million in Chabahar Port, while offering a credit window equivalent to $250 million for mutually identified projects aimed at improving Chabahar related infrastructure.[65] Since 2021, India has supplied six mobile harbor cranes (two of 140-ton and four of one hundred–ton capacity) and other equipment worth $25 million. With significant improvements in the cargo-handling capacity of the port, Indian operations at the port were declared commercially viable in 2023, paving the way for serious discussions culminating in a long-term contract.[66]

In the geopolitical flux of Eurasia, Iran's stance of regional multilateralism emphasizes a collective approach to resolve regional security issues. In doing so, Iran seeks to claim an active role in maintaining its security interests in Central Asia and the Caucasus and at the same time, ensure Iran's freedom of choice in engaging in interest-based cooperation with a diverse set of regional countries, including India. At a time when Iran has prioritized long-term strategic partnership with China and deepening ties with neighboring Pakistan, its narrative of regional multilateralism also grants Tehran the flexibility of engaging India in Afghanistan, Central Asia, and the Caucasus in a way that balances the influence of China and Pakistan in the region. Both India and Iran have a shared interest in maintaining a geopolitical and geoeconomic balance in Eurasia.

In September 2018, soon after the Trump administration started negotiating a peace deal with the Taliban, Iran helped launch multilateral consultations among regional countries concerned about security challenges, especially the threat of terrorism emerging from Afghanistan. It was four days after the ISIS-linked gunmen opened fire on Iranian military parade in the southwestern city of Ahvaz, Shamkhani hosted a "Regional Security Dialogue," which was attended by senior security officials from Russia, China, India, and Afghanistan.[67] Shamkhani emphasized that regional states need to take security matters into their own hands and have a closer security and intelligence coordination. Given the involvement of India and the elected government of Afghanistan, which was critical of Pakistani backing for the Taliban, Islamabad saw the regional format as designed by India to target Pakistan.[68] The second round of dialogue held in Tehran was also joined by Tajikistan and Uzbekistan. New Delhi hosted the third round two months after Taliban's military takeover of Afghanistan. It saw expanded participation of Iran, Russia, and the five Central Asian republics.[69]

Apart from stressing collective efforts to address humanitarian situation in the country, the Delhi Declaration on Afghanistan emphasized on three crucial aspects: (1) respect for sovereignty, unity and territorial integrity of Afghanistan and noninterference in its internal affairs; (2) Afghanistan's territory should not be used for sheltering, training, planning, or financing any terrorist acts; and (3) necessity of forming an open and truly inclusive government that represents the will of all the people of Afghanistan and has representation from all section of their society including major ethno-political forces in the country. While countries like Pakistan and China do not welcome India's role in Afghanistan, Iran and Central Asian countries also find multilateral frameworks suitable for engaging India on a crucial regional security issue and to put "inclusive government" in Afghanistan as a key regional agenda on Afghanistan.[70]

After the Second Karabakh War, in which Azerbaijan gained control of Armenian-occupied territories surrounding Nagorno-Karabakh, Iran backed the "3 + 3" model, including the three South Caucasus countries of Armenia, Azerbaijan, and Georgia, plus Russia, Turkey, and Iran, which could serve as a new postwar regional integration platform.[71] The November 2020 tripartite ceasefire agreement brokered by Russia that ended the war included a clause stating that "all economic and transport links in the region shall be unblocked," including those between the "western regions of the Republic of Azerbaijan and the Nakhchivan Autonomous Republic."[72]

On the basis of the agreement, Azerbaijan has pushed for the so-called Zangezur Corridor via Syunik, the southernmost province of Armenia bordering

Iran, to its Nakhchivan exclave. Baku has equated such a connection with the Lachin corridor, which had connected Nagorno-Karabakh to Armenia. Armenia opposes the corridor through which Baku claims extraterritorial rights on its territory.[73] Yerevan fears the emergence of a militarized corridor running through its territory with no border or customs checks in contravention of Armenian law.[74] The proposed corridor will violate Armenia's territorial integrity, while facilitating a direct link between its neighboring enemies, Turkey and Azerbaijan.[75] Both Iran and Armenia have been alarmed by irredentist tone of Baku's revival of historical, territorial designation of Zangezur as a lost Azerbaijani ethno-space, which has belonged to Armenia since the Soviet period.[76] Iran fears that Baku's irredentist claims on the Armenian territory through which the corridor is to pass will deprive Iran of its forty-kilometer border with Armenia, which has so far prevented the formation of a "Turkic belt" on Iran's northern borders.[77] Iran sees the dire security implications in terms of Turkey and Israel entrenching themselves on its northern borders, potentially allowing them to destabilize its northern Azeri-populated provinces. In the aftermath of its invasion of Ukraine, Russia has taken a more flexible approach toward the Zangezur Corridor, mainly because of its growing reliance on Azerbaijan and Turkey for east–west transit.

Iran's strategy has been to jointly work with Armenia to engage India within the framework of the INSTC, as well as the Persian Gulf–Black Sea Transit and Transport Corridor. These efforts culminated into the first India–Iran–Armenia trilateral consultation in Yerevan in April 2023.[78] Apart from cooperation in the military–technical sector, trade and transit cooperation was the focus of the trilateral political consultations.[79] Analysts see the emergent India–Iran–Armenia trilateral cooperation on regional connectivity as a soft balancing strategy to frustrate Turkey and Azerbaijan's plans for the Zangezur Corridor.[80] The aim is to secure Armenia's territorial integrity and balance what is seen as an emergent Turkey–Azerbaijan–Pakistan axis without provoking a direct confrontation.

The signing of the long-term contract on India's operation of Chabahar despite numerous challenges is the most important development highlighting that both India and Iran see mutual strategic value in forging a long-term partnership. It also underscores India's delicate balancing between it and the United States. However, as India forges new minilateral partnerships and mega-connectivity projects with the United States its allies in West Asia, it will have to maintain its own independent strategic view of Iran. Unlike Washington, which continues with a strategy of sanctions and pressure on Iran, New Delhi's interest are served by an "Iran which is well integrated in the region rather than an isolated, weakened Iran which falls into Chinese economic, and thus geopolitical, orbit."[81] Furthermore, India will have to convince Tehran that its participation in regional connectivity and trade technology cooperation with the United States and its allies in West Asia is driven by the same vision of advancing regional alternatives to a potential hegemon that informs its engagement in Eurasia.

Iran's framing of its membership in the SCO under the rubric of "Eurasian convergence" and "Asian multilateralism" underscore that Iran's Look East strategy has increasingly acquired a regional dimension. While Iran sees its integration within the neighborhood and wider Eurasia as a long-term strategy to counter US sanctions, it also seeks to play the role of a responsible, active stakeholder in addressing regional security issues and shaping a multilateral economic and security order conducive to Iran's long-term interests. The regional dimension, and emphasis on multilateralism, underscore Iran's preference for shared responsibility in addressing key regional security issues and a vision of development-oriented regional economic integration. Undoubtedly, Iran's approach responds to the extant dynamics of multilateralism and a variety of regional connectivity initiatives led by major regional actors. It allows Iran to simultaneously deepen its participation in various Chinese and Russian–led infrastructure and economic integration projects, as it continues cooperation with India in north–south connectivity and development of Chabahar Port. In a nutshell, for Tehran, a favorable order in Eurasia is not only a post-Western, but also a posthegemonic order.

By simultaneously strengthening geoeconomic ties with the three main actors of China, Russia, and India, Iran hopes to consolidate its status as an independent regional power not beholden to any single great power. Iran's strategy of positioning itself as a bridge will allow it to a more geoeconomically balanced Eurasia, while also being useful in terms of navigating the potential scenario of a multipolar rivalry among various regional actors.

NOTES

1. Robert W. Murray, "Whither Multilateralism? The Growing Importance of Regional International Societies in an Emerging Multipolar Era," in *Seeking Order in Anarchy* ed., Robert W. Murray (University of Alberta Press, 2016), 99.
2. Murray, "Whither Multilateralism," 15.
3. Murray, "Whither Multilateralism," 15.
4. Mohammad Javad Zarif, "What Iran Really Wants: Iranian Foreign Policy in the Rouhani Era," *Foreign Affairs* 93 (2004): 49–60.
5. Mohammad Javad Zarif, "Multilateralism and Ideational Power," *International Studies Journal* 14, no. 2 (Fall 2017), https://bit.ly/3FLzAwd.
6. Zarif, "What Iran Really Wants," 56.
7. Hassan Rouhani, "Europe Should Work with Iran to Counter US Unilateralism," *Financial Times*, November 1, 2018, https://bit.ly/40sD0xF.
8. "Preference of East over West is a priority for Iran: Ayatollah Khamenei," Khamenei.ir, February 18, 2018, https://bit.ly/3Mx9r8l.

9. Jacopo Scita, "From Bilateralism to Multilateralism: Iran's Place in China's Eurasian Projects," *Middle East Insight*, April 21, 2020, https://bit.ly/49g3rKK.

10. Mohammad Javad Zarif, "Shared Vision Binds Iran-China Relations," Press TV, August 25, 2019, https://bit.ly/3G61OlL.

11. Mehdi Sepahvand, "Xi Stresses 'Comprehensive Strategic Ties' with Iran," *Tehran Times*, February 20, 2019, https://bit.ly/40t7n6M.

12. "Iran Government Squeezed over 'Secretive' Deal with China," Al-Monitor, July 10, 2020, https://bit.ly/3QpEZhA.

13. Mehdi Sanaei and Jahangir Karami, "Iran's Eastern Policy: Potential and Challenges," *Russia in Global Affairs* 19, no. 3 (2021): 42, https://bit.ly/3tUGtIU.

14. "Iran Government Squeezed."

15. "Iran Government Squeezed."

16. "No Hidden Issue in Iran-China Agreement, Zarif Says," *Tehran Times*, July 5, 2020, https://bit.ly/3StodR1.

17. "Wang Yi Meets with Iranian Supreme Leader's Advisor Ali Larijani," Ministry of Foreign Affairs of the People's Republic of China, March 28, 2021, https://bit.ly/47hC01m; and "Iran, China Enjoy Good, Stable, Strong Relationship: Iranian FM Abdollahian," *Global Times* (January 13, 2022), https://bit.ly/3SrkL9G.

18. Hongda Fan, "China–Iran Relations from the Perspective of Tehran's Look East Approach," *Asian Affairs*, 53, no. 1 (2022): 55.

19. "Only Those Who Believe in the People and Youth and Who Pursue Justice Should Hold Executive Power," Khamenei.ir, May 11, 2021, https://bit.ly/47m1NW6.

20. "A New Day Has Come," *Tehran Times*, August 6, 2021, https://bit.ly/46QXJ0l.

21. "The 'Second Phase of the Revolution' Statement Addressed to the Iranian Nation," Khamenei.ir, February 11, 2019, https://bit.ly/40uEhEb.

22. Vali Kaleji, "What Iran's Shanghai Cooperation Organization Membership Really Means," *National Interest*, November 28, 2021, https://bit.ly/3sqVhi0.

23. Hossein Amir Abdollahian, "SCO: An opportunity to bolster Eurasian convergence," CGTN, September 16, 2022, https://bit.ly/47kh9uh.

24. Ellen L. Frost, *Rival Regionalisms and Regional Order: A Slow Crisis of Legitimacy*, NBR Special Report no. 48 (National Bureau of Asian Research, 2014), 20–21, https://bit.ly/46ZKt9M.

25. Edmund Herzig, "Regionalism, Iran and Central Asia," *International Affairs* 80, no. 3 (2004): 510.

26. Herzig, "Iran and Central Asia," 510.

27. Seyed Kazem Sajjadpour, "Iran, the Caucasus and Central Asia," in *The New Geopolitics of Central Asia and its Borderlands*, ed. Ali Banuazizi and Myron Weiner (Indiana University Press, 1994), 200.

28. R. K. Ramazani, "Iran's Foreign Policy: Both North and South," *Middle East Journal* 46, no. 3 (1992): 405.

29. Sajjadpour, "Iran, the Caucasus and Central Asia," 201.

30. Sajjadpour, "Iran, the Caucasus and Central Asia," 201.

31. Jahangir Karami, "Iran and Russia: Past Experiences and Future Prospects," *Journal of Iran and Central Eurasia Studies*, 2, no. 1 (Summer 2019): 14.

32. Abbas Amanat, *Iran: A Modern History* (Yale University Press, 2017), 140.

33. Nicole Grajewski, "Russia and Iran in Greater Eurasia," *Middle East Insights* (2020): 2, https://bit.ly/3FKa0HQ.

34. Mohammadbagher Forough, "What the West Gets Wrong About the SCO," *National Interest* (September 24, 2022), https://bit.ly/40uFIT5; and Aslı Aydıntaşbaş, Marie Dumoulin, Ellie Geranmayeh, and Janka Oertel, "Rogue NATO: The New Face of

the Shanghai Cooperation Organisation," European Council on Foreign Relations, September 16, 2022, https://bit.ly/3SrZJHW.

35. Mei Xue and Benjamin Mwadi Makengo, "Twenty Years of the Shanghai Cooperation Organization: Achievements, Challenges and Prospects," *Open Journal of Social Sciences* 9, no. 10 (2021), https://bit.ly/45ZojTS; and Ruslan Izimov Yussupzhanovich and Zamira Muratalieva Tulkunovna, "Role of the SCO in the Eurasian Continent," *India Quarterly: A Journal of International Affairs* 75, no. 1 (2019): 44, https://bit.ly/47oDlUl.

36. Anoushiravan Ehteshami, "Asianisation of Asia: Chinese-Iranian Relations in Perspective," *Asian Affairs* 53, no. 1 (2022): 16.

37. "President Raisi Addressing 21st SCO Summit," Islamic Republic of Iran Ministry of Foreign Affairs, September 17, 2021, https://bit.ly/40uFrzx.

38. Jingdong Yuan, "Forging a New Security Order in Eurasia: China, the SCO, and the Impacts on Regional Governance," *Chinese Political Science Review* 8 (2023): 434, https://bit.ly/3QpH3Gm.

39. Forough, "What the West Gets Wrong."

40. Mohsen Shariatinia and Hamidreza Azizi, "Iran and the Belt and Road Initiative: Amid Hope and Fear," *Journal of Contemporary China* 28, no. 120 (2019): 987–88.

41. Forough, "What the West Gets Wrong"; and "President Raisi Addressing 21st SCO Summit."

42. Mohsen Pakaein, "The Need for Stability and Security in Afghanistan," Islamic Republic News Agency, November 20, 2021, https://bit.ly/3StqhZh.

43. "President Raisi Addressing 21st SCO Summit."

44. "President Raisi Addressing 21st SCO Summit."

45. Szczepan Lemańczyk, "The Transiranian Railway—History, Context and Consequences," *Middle Eastern Studies* 49, no. 2 (March 2013): 239.

46. Mohsen Shariatinia, Hamidreza Azizi, "Iran–China Cooperation in the Silk Road Economic Belt: From Strategic Understanding to Operational Understanding," *China and World Economy* (2017): 49, https://doi.org/10.1111/cwe.12213.

47. Deepika Saraswat, "Iran's Ties with China: Synergising Geoconomic Strategies," Arab Center for Research & Policy Studies, July 7, 2022, https://bit.ly/3u8wxvq.

48. Deepika Saraswat, "Iran's Central Asia Policy Gains Momentum amid Russia–Ukraine War," Manohar Parrikar Institute for Defence Studies and Analyses, July 19, 2022, https://bit.ly/3MxvrzU.

49. "Iran, Kazakhstan Inaugurate Rail Transit Route," Tasnim News Agency, June 20, 2022, https://bit.ly/3QMaovR.

50. "Iran, Russia to Complete Garmsar-Incheh Borun Railway," Iran Front Page, August 28, 2022, https://bit.ly/40uizAq.

51. Rezaul Laskar, "India Takes Over Operations of Iran's Strategic Chabahar Port, Can Bypass Pak on Way to Afghanistan," *Hindustan Times,* December 24, 2018, https://bit.ly/49lcjyS.

52. Parul Chandra, "Iran Extends Lease for India to Operate Chabahar Port," StratNews Global, August 10, 2020, https://bit.ly/40s7krT.

53. Dipanjan Roy Chaudhury, "India Proposes Inclusion of Iran's Chabahar Port in International North South Transport Corridor," *Economic Times,* March 5, 2021, https://bit.ly/471DMnw.

54. "President Raisi Addressing 21st SCO Summit."

55. Anirban Bhaumik, "Iran Goes to Pakistan with Chabahar Link Plan," *Deccan Herald,* May 28, 2019, https://bit.ly/4710A6V.

56. "President Raisi Addressing 21st SCO Summit."

57. "The Republic of India and the Islamic Republic of Iran 'The New Delhi Declaration,'" Ministry of External Affairs, January 25, 2003, https://bit.ly/47eYmjW.

58. David Brewster, "Silk Roads and Strings of Pearls: The Strategic Geography of China's New Pathways in the Indian Ocean," *Geopolitics* 22, no. 2 (2017): 271–72.
59. "India Can Easily Resist Western Sanctions: Iranian Envoy," NewsBharati, March 18, 2023, https://bit.ly/4bz0e9N.
60. "First Trilateral Working Group Meeting Between India, Iran and Uzbekistan on Joint Use of Chabahar Port," Ministry of External Affairs, December 14, 2020, https://acr.ps/1L9zR2x.
61. "First Trilateral Working Group Meeting."
62. Dipanjan Roy Chaudhury, "India invites C Asian, Iranian, Afghan Envoys on Chabahar Day," *Economic Times*, August 2, 2022, https://bit.ly/3KdDxfz.
63. "New Section of Khaf-Herat Railway Launched," *Tehran Times*, July 12, 2023, https://bit.ly/4dYiUSi.
64. "Iran Deputy FM Joins 1st Meeting of India-Central Asia Joint Working Group on Chabahar Port," Islamic Republic of Iran Ministry of Foreign Affairs, April 13, 2023, https://bit.ly/3QZakZo.
65. "India Signs Long-Term Bilateral Contract on Chabahar Port with Iran," *Hindu Business Line*, May 13, 2024, https://acr.ps/1L9zQjE.
66. Shubhajit Roy, "What Are India's Stakes in Iran's Chabahar Port?," *Indian Express*, May 15, 2024, https://bit.ly/4dWnz71.
67. "Indian NSA Ajit Doval Meets Russian, Iranian, Afghan Officials at Regional Security Dialogue," *Eurasian Times*, September 27, 2018, https://bit.ly/4e9lll5.
68. Ayjaz Wani, "Regional Multilateral Consultations on Afghanistan," Observer Research Foundation, February 17, 2023, https://bit.ly/3R1kjNI.
69. "Delhi Declaration on Afghanistan," Ministry of External Affairs-Government of India, November 10, 2021, https://bit.ly/4bWzK21.
70. "Conversations on the Afghan Peace Process: Iran's Role in Afghanistan," Institute of Strategic Studies, August 17, 2021, https://bit.ly/44ZHCxj.
71. Vali Kaleji, "Iran and the 3+3 Regional Cooperation Format in the South Caucasus: Strengths and Weaknesses," *Eurasia Daily Monitor* 18, no. 96 (June 16, 2021), https://bit.ly/4dTIzeK.
72. Onnik James Krikorian, "Baku, Yerevan and Moscow Clash over Regional Transit," *Eurasian Daily Monitor* 21, no. 12 (January 25, 2024), https://bit.ly/3yCPkBt.
73. Eldar Mamedov, "Perspectives: Iran Adapting to Altered Geopolitical Landscape in South Caucasus," *Eurasianet*, April 4, 2024, https://bit.ly/3KdDJvj.
74. Krikorian, "Baku, Yerevan and Moscow."
75. "IntelBrief: Border Skirmish Between Armenia and Azerbaijan Reignites Dispute over Zangezur Corridor," Soufan Center, February 23, 2024, https://bit.ly/44YUQKP.
76. Laurence Broers, "Augmented Azerbaijan? The Return of Azerbaijani Irredentism," *Eurasianet*, August 5, 2021, https://bit.ly/4bTllmW.
77. Vali Kaleji, "Iran and the 3+3 Regional Cooperation Format in the South Caucasus: Strengths and Weaknesses," *Eurasia Daily Monitor* 18, no. 96 (June 16, 2021), https://bit.ly/4dTIzeK.
78. Dipanjan Roy Chaudhury, "India–Iran–Armenia Launch Trilateral to Create Corridor to Russia and Europe," *Economic Times*, April 22, 2023, https://bit.ly/3yt7HZq.
79. "Armenia Hosts First Trilateral Meeting with Iranian and Indian Officials," *Tehran Times*, April 23, 2023, https://acr.ps/1L9zQHy.
80. Vali Kaleji, "New Trilateral Cooperation for Iran, Armenia and India in the South Caucasus: From 'Soft Balancing' to Regional Transit Balance," *Eurasia Daily Monitor* 20, no. 100 (2023), https://bit.ly/3UZ6cd2.
81. Deepika Saraswat, "The US Challenge to India's Ties with Iran," *The Round Table* 111, no. 6 (2022): 734.

5

COUNTERBALANCING THE WEST
The Risks of Iran's Eastern Policy

Mahmood Monshipouri and Javad Heiran-Nia

Since the inception of the Islamic Republic, Iran's foreign policy of negotiating its interests by balancing the East and the West has gradually shifted toward the former. China and Russia have exploited Iran's isolation, largely a result of ongoing US sanctions, by looking for ways to challenge frayed US–Iran ties. The US withdrawal from the Iran nuclear deal in 2018 under the Donald Trump administration further reinforced this shift. Iran has become increasingly a key participant in a network of alliances built by Beijing to counterbalance US hegemony. Iran regards the Belt and Road Initiative as a sign of China's growing economic and geopolitical power. Tehran's view of strengthening its relations with Moscow, however, is based on an entirely different consideration—largely aimed at doubling down on its military ties with Russia. We argue that there are multiple risks associated with Iran's "Look East" policy. Iran's claim to have a special place in China's geoeconomic orbit is overblown if not fundamentally misguided, and Iran's economic and political ties with China are unlikely to save Iran from its isolation by the West. China's "positive balance" approach toward all countries in the Middle East, as well as its extensive trade ties with the West, are integral to its foreign policy.

In recent decades and years, such a shift has manifested itself not just in Iran's desire to strengthen its relationship with China and Russia to circumvent international sanctions and isolation, but also in countering a US-led world order. The move, which has set off a major controversy within Iran's foreign policy establishment, is part of a larger and ongoing debate about whether the long-standing policy of equilibrium between the East and the West should—or should not—adapt to new political realities in the region.

While the debates regarding the country's foreign policy orientation have been restricted to intimately linked circles within the top echelon of ruling elites, it is possible to identify three discernible stances behind Iran's East Asia pivot policy: (1) refusing to capitulate to or make extensive concessions to the United States; (2) prioritizing security concerns over economic development goals; and (3) preserving the continuity of the domestic political system—often referred to as regime survival.[1]

China's protracted international rivalry with the United States, while far from becoming a new cold war, has the potential to develop into difficult regional tensions.[2] China has also viewed the Middle East and North Africa (MENA)—in the words of one expert, a region with many "non-Western" Global South countries—as an ally to forestall what it considers the Global North's disproportionate advancing influence.[3]

Similarly, Russia appears intent on exploiting Washington's political divide and dysfunction while also fueling US decline.[4] Although Iran's vision of the world order reflects shared beliefs and interests with China and Russia, several key differences highlight the difficulties of reconciling these countries' stated objectives of regional peace and security with those of Iran. These difficulties will most likely render Iran's "East policy" unsettled at best and precarious at worst.

Iran's partnership with Russia on multiple fronts—including the Caspian Sea, the South Caucasus, the MENA region, and the war on Ukraine—appears rooted in political expediency. Similarly, despite closer Iran–China cooperation on energy, trade, and some shared geopolitical interests, the two countries have potentially contrasting interests on a number of issues. Beijing's recent attempt to build stronger relations with Riyadh and Abu Dhabi suggests that China seeks to gain a new foothold in the Middle East, one based on increasing its trade ties with the region's oil-rich countries without facing international sanctions.

We argue that there are multiple risks associated with Iran's "Look East" policy. Iran's claim to have a special place in China's geoeconomic orbit is overblown, and Iran's economic and political ties with China are unlikely to prevent them from being isolated by Western countries. We question the assumption that Washington's "maximum pressure campaign" under the Trump administration, which pressured European firms to leave Iran, created a vacuum that Chinese investors and traders successfully filled. That prediction never materialized.

Furthermore, China's "positive balance" in its regional policy toward all countries in the Middle East, as well as its extensive trade ties with the West, have proven to be integral to its foreign policy.[5] Insofar as Russia is concerned, Tehran's

Eastward policy likely risks deepening its dependency on Moscow, a possibility that would significantly compromise Iran's national interests. Our purpose in this chapter is to demonstrate that the risks involved with turning to the East should not be underestimated.

Drivers of the Look East Policy

Due to its revolutionary nature and emphasis on political Islam, Iran's system formed itself in opposition to the West and the liberal order, and its foreign policy was no exception. Washington–Tehran relations in the aftermath of the Trump administration's unilateral withdrawal from the JCPOA has pushed Tehran further in the direction of bolstering ties with more countries in the East. Arguably, "Look East" could create a breathing space for Iran against the West and meet some of the country's economic, political, and security needs.

In this section, the internal and international reasons for strengthening the focus on the East in Iran's foreign policy are discussed. One internal reason for the pivot is the weakening and elimination of reformists from Iran's political structure, in part because reformers seek to normalize Iran's relations with the West. Also, the middle class, which provides the bedrock of support for the reformers, has become very weak in recent years, especially during the second term of Hassan Rouhani's presidency.[6] The size of the middle class has noticeably shrunk from 58.4 percent in 2011 to 48.8 percent in 2019. Some eight million middle-class people have fallen into the lower middle class, while the ranks of the poor have swelled by more than four million.[7]

Furthermore, the increase in inflation caused by Trump's withdrawal from the JCPOA has made this class markedly poorer. As a result of the Trump administration's "maximum pressure" campaign, Iran's gross domestic product (GDP), which had stagnated sharply during the first phase of sanctions under the Barack Obama administration, has been steadily declining. Sanctions have dealt a severe blow to Iran's economy and the living standards of ordinary people by reducing oil exports and curbing its foreign trade. The COVID-19 pandemic further exacerbated the impact of sanctions on Iran. In the short period between the reduction of sanctions in 2016 and their reimposition in 2018, Iran's GDP growth rate dropped from 13 percent per year to negative 6 percent.[8]

Gholamhossein Shafei, head of the Iran Chamber of Commerce, has noted:

> According to the Parliamentary Research Center, the Gini coefficient has been on the rise since 2013, which means a significant increase in inequality and social gap. According to official statistics, the rate of capital formation has been incessantly declining since 2011. The rate of

capital formation in machinery in the last 9 months of 2019 compared to the same period last year had a negative growth of 15 percent, while this rate in 2018 was a negative growth of 7 percent. This comparison means that the productive sector in the country is not motivated enough to invest. Despite the increase in the nominal income of households, it seems that despite the increase in its purchasing power, the country's middle class is disintegrating.[9]

Another critical perspective is provided by Hashem Pesaran, who believes that "the most obvious way to crush the middle class is to grind them between the two millstones of taxation and inflation."[10] When the middle class is destroyed, everything will collapse, and the middle class will no longer be left to read books, travel, learn, teach, or carry democratic values and culture. Iranian society is now going to be divided into two classes: the upper and the lower. Still another critic, Asef Bayat, professor at the University of Illinois, argues that the current middle class in Iran can be better explained by the concept of the "middle class poor." He believes that the sense of abandonment, the lack of hope for the future, the awareness of the prevailing corruption, the economic class gap, and the degrading living standards of this angry class have turned it into a powder keg.[11]

The first proposed budget (2022) of the Ebrahim Raisi administration also demonstrates the lack of support for the poor and middle class. The nature of this budget shows that the process of weakening the middle class will continue. Along this line, Kamran Naderi, director of the Islamic Banking Department at the Central Bank's Monetary and Banking Research Institute, writes: "Raisi's first budget will put a lot of pressure on the middle class, and a large part of this class will fall into low-income deciles."[12]

In fact, over time, the deteriorating economic situation has paved the way for the conservatives to become stronger, as they have attributed the Rouhani administration's poor economic performance to the result of trust in and reliance on the West, especially Washington. According to a study in 2021, economic pressure has reduced popular support for moderate parties, as well as support for integrating into the global economy. Naturally enough, support for the JCPOA has significantly declined from 80 percent to 50 percent.[13] This has contributed to pursuing the "Look East" policy, further strengthening relationships with China and Russia. One example of this tendency has been a twenty-five-year agreement with China and a twenty-year agreement with Russia. Iran's membership in the Shanghai Cooperation Organization (SCO) and the Eurasian Economic Union (EEU) needs to be viewed in this context.

Regardless, many Iranian policymakers have come to believe that China and Russia are the future poles of the international system. That may explain why Iranian ruling elites have prioritized "Look East" over direct talks with the West concerning the nuclear deal in the short term better than coming years. Regarding the change of polarization in international system, Iran believes that Russia's invasion of Ukraine is a sign of declining—if not diminishing—US hegemony. Supreme Leader Ayatollah Ali Khamenei has recently stated: "The issues of the recent war in Ukraine should be seen more deeply and in the context of the formation of a new world order."[14]

The "Look East" policy is also predicated on the assumption that the West's problem with Iran is an existential one and that the West has always tried to isolate, weaken, and ultimately overthrow the Islamic Republic. Tehran believes that the West's problem with the Islamic Republic was predominantly ideological and that such an identity and normative conflict with the liberal hegemonic order has prevented the formation of an institutionalized relationship between Iran and the West, while also forcing Iran to realize that no meaningful technical or economic support from the West would ever be granted to it. Several developments have reinforced such a pessimistic perception in Iran. These include, among others, the failed attempts by both Presidents Hashemi Rafsanjani and Mohammad Khatami to establish normal ties with the West; President George W. Bush's labeling of Iran as part of an "axis of evil"; the growing Western pressure on Iran in the form of draconian economic sanctions before, during, and after the nuclear talks; and persistent criticisms leveled against Iran's human rights conditions.[15]

The East in the policy of "Look East" was therefore ideological, as well as geographical. In normative terms, "Look East" seeks to unite with ideologies opposed to liberalism, thus confronting the current Western order and norms of the international system led by Europe and the United States. The principles and teachings of the Islamic revolutionary identity of Iran after the 1979 revolution, such as the centrality of Islam in the state's governing infrastructure and mission, were in clear opposition to liberalism. Moreover, proponents of the "Look East" policy tend to believe that the Islamic Republic of Iran, by favoring Asian civilizations and sharing cultural and historical identity with this region, can more easily build political alliances and form ideological convergence with them.[16]

It is worth noting that the Masoud Pezeshkian administration has underscored the importance of interaction with the world, even as it has afforded a higher priority to the relations with the countries of the Global South.[17] Despite the emphasis on a balanced foreign policy, the new government of Iran considers the "Look to the East" foreign policy as a strategic approach and not a tactical one.[18] Regarding the relationship with Russia and China, Pezeshkian writes that both countries "have consistently stood by us during challenging times. We deeply value this friendship. Our 25-year roadmap with China represents a significant milestone toward establishing a mutually beneficial comprehensive 'strategic partnership,' and we look forward to collaborating more extensively with Beijing as we advance toward a new global order."[19]

Building a Bulwark Against Isolation

Iran's pivot to the East policy has positive and negative consequences. Forging closer relations with Russia and China to challenge the post–Cold War, Western-led world order has effectively sheltered Iran from complete isolation while providing it with political, military, and economic ties that it cannot develop elsewhere.[20] While Russia, China, and Iran seek to present an alternative worldview and vision to the US-led Western world order, their commitment to counteract it and capacity to do so vary. Both Moscow and Beijing have exploited the backbreaking international sanctions imposed on Iran to bolster their position and influence in the country. Efforts to create non-Western, nonliberal international institutions such as the SCO, along with strengthening security cooperation, are emblematic of shared views to curb the spread of Western economic influence and political power in Eurasia and the Asia–Pacific region.[21]

Some experts, however, have warned that although gaining full membership in the SCO can be widely regarded as a psychological victory for a country that has long been under sanctions, it is unlikely to solve the country's sanctions problem any time soon. Iran's current trade and financial bottlenecks caused by external sanctions cannot be resolved solely by membership in the SCO, as investors and enterprises in countries such as China, Russia, and India will be driven by the economic realities on the ground—that is, by their commercial interests and legal feasibility, especially in light of the impacts of sanctions.[22]

China, Russia, and Iran all resent an international order they had no role in building and which they believe falls short of reflecting their interests. Separately, and in different ways, each rejects the universality of Western liberal principles, as they also push for alternative economic, political, and security institutions and arrangements.[23] Yet despite closer cooperation between China and Iran in various sectors, including energy, economy, trade, and military, these "relations have stopped far short of a formal political and strategic alliance."[24] Iranian–Russian relations are similarly characterized as "a suspicious partnership, rather than a strategic alliance."[25] A key limit on the relationship between the two countries includes the lack of any formal strategic alliance including common defense and military cooperation in the event of an attack.

Russia, China, and Iran clearly follow competing security approaches to regional issues. Much of the relationship between Iran and China, on the one hand, and Iran and Russia on the other, are marked by their interactions with the West more broadly, and with the United States in particular.[26] Nothing is more divisive in Russia–Iran relations than the two countries' control over the Caspian Sea resources and sovereignty. Iran and Russia adamantly pursue their own goals in the region. While Tehran and Moscow share the goal of keeping Western presence—military or otherwise—out of the Caspian Sea region, their long-term goals noticeably differ. Russia has kept exploiting Iran's isolation due to the stringent Western sanctions, while it has also entered into bilateral agreements with Kazakhstan and Azerbaijan on dividing up the body of water there.[27]

In recent years, especially after the Russian invasion of Ukraine, Moscow and Tehran have expanded their military cooperation. The disclosure of the news that Iran had sold drones to Russia that have been deployed and are still being used to attack Ukraine has rekindled a debate about whether this level of cooperation with Russia is in Iran's national interest. The drone sales have led to additional sanctions against Iran by the United States, Switzerland, and the European Union. Some observers have even accused Iran of violating UN Security Council resolution 2231, which maintains restrictions on the export of Iranian missiles until 2023.[28]

Some Iranian experts have asserted that Russia has held Iran's foreign policy captive. Following the Russian lead in certain foreign policy arenas, they argue, could significantly restrict Iran's maneuverability, holding Tehran accountable for Moscow's adventures. Heshmatullah Falahat Pisheh, a conservative political activist and former head of the National Security and Foreign Policy Commission of the Iranian parliament, has pointed out that Russia benefits from both hampering Iran's return to the 2015 nuclear deal, as well as maintaining Iran's isolation over the Ukraine war. In fact, Russia views any improvement in relations between Iran and the West as a threat to its interests. Along these lines, Rajab Safarov, a former member of the Russian Federation Presidential Political Council and head of the Iran Commission at the Moscow Chamber of Commerce and Industry, has noted that a pro-West Iran is more dangerous for Russia than a nuclear Iran: "Iran is like an iron defense shield for us [Russia] against the West and, if a pro-Western government comes to power in Iran, the collapse of Russia will begin from that moment."[29]

From a different perspective, one expert has argued that a close Tehran–Moscow relationship has in fact enabled Iran to hinder US pressures and avoid war in the course of the nuclear negotiations. However, the prospects of Iran's increased dependency on Russia for its military and food security has meant that Iranian power has been eclipsed by broader Russian interests.[30] Historically, when Russian and Iranian interests have converged to bolster their mutual security goals, Iran has been able to function as a stable state despite the ongoing sanctions.

If those interests, however, have collided in cases where Iran has decided to pursue its own military and security interests, regardless of the Russian position, the dynamics of that relationship have tended more often than not to favor Moscow—not Tehran.

China's Rising Presence in Iran

The Twenty-Five-Year Strategic Cooperation Agreement between Iran and China—signed in March 2021 and worth $400 billion—has fueled widespread speculation about its longer-term impact on Iran's state sovereignty. While Iran and China share a similar view on the liberal international order, fostering anti-US hegemony while also underscoring the importance of sovereignty, China will most likely resist much deeper economic ties with Iran given the risky business context and the ongoing threat of sanctions. Moreover, Iran's political activities in espousing proxy networks in the MENA region serve as a brake on furthering political support for Tehran along these lines. There is a broad consensus that Washington serves as a significant constraint on deepening Iran–China relations, given Beijing's desire to maintain extensive trade ties with the United States and ongoing Chinese observance of US sanctions on Iran. For the Islamic Republic, the strategic deal between Tehran and Beijing is viewed as Iran's "insurance policy" if US sanctions continue and US–China trade tensions escalate.[31]

As a result, China has been Iran's largest trading partner for ten consecutive years. In 2021, Iran's largest export value was with China, which had great leverage on Iran's economic and foreign policy, indicating nearly 84 percent of Iran's export value (see table 5.1).

TABLE 5.1. Top trade partners of Iran

COUNTRY	PERCENTAGE OF VOLUME OF TRADE
China	42.4
Turkey	19.4
Pakistan	4.39
Armenia	2.9
India	2.71
Azerbaijan	2.69
Kuwait	2.57
Germany	2.50
United Arab Emirates	2.48
Oman	1.74

Source: OEC, "Iran: 2021," https://bit.ly/3s6XVJW

However, since January 2023, Russia has become the major foreign investor in Iran, accounting for some 45 percent of the total foreign investment attracted by Iran (more on that later).³² Bilateral economic ties between Iran and Russia have intensified since sanctions were placed on Russia after its invasion of the Ukraine. The lack of any tangible progress toward the restoration of the JCPOA has driven Iran and Russia closer together than ever.

Opportunities: Bilateral Trade

China has pursued an active political role in the MENA region with the aim of securing the acquisition of oil and expanding commercial and trade ties with the region's countries. Most recently, other goals such as bolstering its geostrategic and great power status in the region, as well as ensuring domestic stability, have become critical to China's overall Middle East strategy. Closely related to this goal has been China's intention to maintain steady political and commercial ties with Muslim countries of the region in the hope of containing the twelve million Uyghur Muslims and their related separatist movement within China.³³ It is worth noting that China detains millions of Muslim Uyghurs in numerous camps.

It is within this context that one needs to understand why China has growing stakes in Iran and its energy sector, and why it has constantly opposed UN sanctions against Iran over its nuclear program. The Chinese have proposed building a rail link that will stretch nearly 2,000 miles, from Urumqi, the capital of China's western region of Xinjiang, to Tehran. The line would connect Kazakhstan, Kyrgyzstan, Uzbekistan, and Turkmenistan along the way.³⁴

Iran and China traded $15.795 billion worth of commodities in 2022, which indicated a 7 percent increase in the trade volume compared to 2021.³⁵ In December 2022, China exported $893 million and imported $312 million from Iran, resulting in a positive trade balance of $581 million. Iran's share within China's total global trade in 2022 was only 0.25 percent. China, with over $11 billion of imports from Iran, has been the number one importer of Iranian produce, which constitutes around 27 percent of the Islamic Republic's total outbound commodities.

China is also Iran's biggest oil customer. To dodge sanctions, most of Iran's crude exports to China are rebranded as crude from other countries. For instance, in 2021 China only constituted 28 percent of Iran's total oil exports, with Russia, rebranded Malaysian oil, and other countries such as the United Arab Emirates and Syria making up the difference. Iran is expected to increase its oil sales to China, while also facing tough competition from Russia, which has also tried to sell reasonably low-priced oil to China.³⁶

China's relationship with Iran, as some observers have pointed out, has included many examples of Beijing using arms sales in order to gain access to Iran's energy supplies and markets.[37] Over time, the arms component of the Sino-Iranian relationship has assumed an even greater importance. While arms trade has partially helped sustain China's economic growth, Beijing has also claimed that such transactions with Iran, which are strongly opposed to the US unilateral policies, are intended to create a multipolar world conducive to peace and an expanding global economy. As such, Beijing views its weapons transfers, to Iran and other countries, as part of a larger strategy of strengthening developing countries against Western hegemony and not necessarily a mechanism for increasing its wealth and/or securing its energy resources.

An opposing view underscores the importance of how China's policies toward Iran have been driven principally by Beijing's domestic calculations in which China has regularly kept its distance from Iran's contentious politics at home and in its international activities. While maintaining their partnership, the Sino-Iranian relationship has been driven by a necessary and calculated intention to "build economic leverage in order to face the capitalist Western world."[38] The Twenty-Five-Year Strategic Cooperation Agreement between Iran and China, signed on March 27, 2021, was concluded less so because of Iran's desire and more so spurred by China's own interests, as most elements of the agreement reflected concessions to Beijing. In exchange, China reaffirmed the agreement's significance, indicating that the era of unrestrained cooperation between Washington and Beijing has ended.[39]

By avoiding major disruptions that have been caused by the tensions in US-Iranian relations before, during, and after the nuclear deal, Beijing has managed to expand its influence over Tehran.[40] A major reservation raised about the Beijing-Tehran partnership is that there is no guarantee that transactional ties between the two countries would lead to the empowering of their strategic and security ties in the global arena, unless these relations could ensure the long-term advancement of Iranian security and its nuclear program.[41]

China's President Xi Jinping has emphasized his commitment to the goal of building what he describes as a "fairer and more just" international system—one supported by Chinese power rather than US power and one that represents norms more consistent with Marxist–Leninist values and ideology. Most relevantly, Beijing has pushed for building a new set of China-centric international institutions, such as the Belt and Road Initiative, the Asian Infrastructure Investment Bank, and the SCO, to compete and eventually replace Western-dominated ones. This ideological quest for a "more just" world also frames China's promotion of its own national development model across the Global South to serve as an alternative to the "Washington Consensus" of free markets and democratic governance.[42]

Chinese institutions have publicly pledged as much as $1.4 trillion to finance New Silk Road projects through 2049.[43] Using the New Silk Road Initiative as a diplomatic route, experts point out, China can advance projects that for their success to be ensured require close cooperation between Sunni and Shiite countries, such as the Iran–Pakistan gas pipeline, the port of Gwadar on the coast of the Arabian Sea, and a Silk Road high-speed railway connecting Xinjiang and Tehran through the Sunni majority countries of Central Asia: Kazakhstan, Uzbekistan, and Turkmenistan. China has played a key role in promoting Iran's membership in the SCO, whose other members are predominantly Sunni, a development made possible when UN sanctions against Iran were removed following the original signing of the nuclear deal.[44] The New Silk Road campaign has significantly boosted Beijing's economic clout, and its considerable geopolitical importance is now acknowledged throughout the region. The economic future of many Asian countries appears increasingly dependent on goodwill from Beijing.[45]

The Chinese have become fully cognizant of the fact that they can still afford to underestimate their interests and neglect the region as a whole. They are no longer willing to be outsiders and watch the Middle East descend into political instability. Given its dependency on the region's oil reserves, Beijing puts a special premium on stability and peace in the Middle East. With the United States and Russia unable to effect rapprochement between Iran and Saudi Arabia, China, which remains on good terms with both, has filled the vacuum.[46] The days when the United States was the single most important market for all the major Asian economies and when Japanese multinational companies were among the most dominant foreign investors across Southeast Asia are long gone. China, according to one study, has now become the most important trading partner for South Korea, Japan, Australia, and virtually all Southeast Asian countries.[47]

Critics have in the past accused both the Mahmoud Ahmadinejad and Rouhani administrations of having no economic policy other than "job creation for Chinese."[48] Furthermore, Iranian governments have in recent years fueled anti-China sentiments by inordinately importing low-quality Chinese products that have competed with domestic production, resulting in the displacement of national brands, job losses, and safety standards.[49] Far from a "comprehensive strategic partnership," as critics note, Iran–China relations can be best described as "mutual ambiguity." Beijing has been cautious in its policy approaches to demonstrate that a good relationship with Iran would not undermine its burgeoning interests in the MENA region, especially in the Gulf Cooperation Council members states. By hedging via "strategic ambiguity," China has helped maintaining equilibrium in the region.[50]

The Largest Investor in Iran

Russia has overtaken China to top the list of foreign investors in Iran.[51] As a result of the Russian invasion of Ukraine in February 2022, and resulting sanctions imposed on Russia, trade relations between Russia and Iran have dramatically increased. Both countries' economic and military ties, largely a result of the Western world's sanctions, have significantly increased. Ali Fekri, deputy minister of finance, in an interview with *Shargh Daily*, pointed out that Russian investments in Iran have noticeably increased compared to that of China. More specifically, since the government of President Raisi took office in August 2021, Russia has made the largest volume of investment in Iran. "With $2.7 billion worth of investments, more than half of all foreign direct investments, Russia is the biggest investor in Iran. The United Arab Emirates is the second-largest investor, followed by Turkey, China, and Afghanistan."[52]

On January 29, 2023, Central Bank Governor Mohammad-Reza Farzin tweeted: "A direct link was established between banks in Iran and Russia. Within the framework of cooperation between the central banks of Iran and Russia, apart from the direct link to Russian banks, our country's banking network will be linked with 106 foreign non-Russian banks."[53]

Constraints: Economic Uncertainties and Geopolitical Risks

Some experts have called our attention to the risks of dependency on China in the face of the ongoing international sanctions on Iran. Following the US withdrawal from the JCPOA, big Chinese companies—such as Huawei and Zhonggu Storage and Transportation Co. Ltd—were forced to draw down some of their activities in Iran. Only small- and medium-sized Chinese companies with little or no presence in Western markets and less connections with the global financial system have been active in Iranian markets.[54] The expansion of China's share of Iranian imports has led to the economic domination of China and the reduced competitiveness of Iranian industries, resulting in partial loss of local employment.[55] Furthermore, critics go on to argue that the "Chinese plan to establish rail and road links between Central Asian countries, Russia, and Europe on the one hand and to connect those countries to the South Caucasus through the Caspian Sea, followed by their connection to Turkey and Europe on the other, will have negative impacts on the Iranian transit position in the region."[56]

Yet another important competitive aspect related to the Belt and Road Initiative is the rivalry between the projects aimed at developing the Gwadar and

Chabahar Ports. Gwadar Port has been managed by China under the China–Pakistan Economic Corridor, whereas Chabahar Port is funded by India under the tripartite Preferential Trade Agreement with Iran and Afghanistan, signed on May 23, 2016. Both are expected to serve as the international energy trading route, providing links to Central Asia, the Middle East, Africa, and Europe. The competition between the two in the long term will be inevitable.[57]

Additionally, a part of the East–West Corridors that China seeks to build is in direct competition with the proposed North–South Corridor with Iran as its pivotal center. Some Iranian officials have argued that if the transportation projects near Iran, including those of the Belt and Road Initiative (BRI), are constructed, Iran is certain to lose its transit position in West Asia within the next decade.[58] While Iranian experts view the challenges facing the liberal order as an opportunity to bolster China–Iran cooperation, their main concern remains Beijing's lackadaisical attempt to invest in Iran. For its part, China will continue its cautious approach to its relationship with Iran knowing full well that Tehran has few choices but to stick with Beijing and Moscow as viable balances to Western political pressures.

The Iranian government has expressed much dismay over a recent joint statement issued by Beijing and the Arab states of the Persian Gulf in which China overtly sides with the Gulf states. The Gulf Cooperation Council and China made a reference to three small islands in the Persian Gulf that Iran has controlled since 1971, but which the United Arab Emirates claims as its own. Additionally, Iranian authorities have expressed their unease—albeit not publicly—regarding China's uncertain position on Iran's nuclear program and the stalled negotiations with the West.[59] Many Iranian experts and politicians continue to call into question the benefits of the twenty-five-year comprehensive investment agreement. It is rather a mere accord, they argue, bent on luring Iran into China's regional influence while the latter continues to fail to invest in Iran's oil and gas and railway and port infrastructure. Meanwhile, Tehran struggles with the question of how to recalibrate its foreign policy built mostly around the idea of finding common ground with the Eurasian powers.

Iran–India Partnership

Although India lacks the central position of Russia and China in Iran's new foreign policy of "Look East," it is not outside of Tehran's strategic realm and in some cases is considered a complement to this complex, multidimensional policy. Some Iranian politicians even believe that relations with India carry more potential benefits for Tehran than China.[60] It is within this context that the Raisi administration has proposed a twenty-five-year long-term agreement to Delhi. It should be noted that Iran has signed long-term agreements with China, Venezuela, and Russia as well.[61]

Increasingly, Iran and the Persian Gulf region have come to figure prominently in India's foreign policy considerations. Consider, for example, the domestic and international significance of the Chabahar port in the region. This port, which is located in Iran's southeastern Sistan and Baluchestan provinces and on the edge of the Gulf of Oman and Indian Ocean, constitutes Iran's key outlet to the Arabian Sea and connects it to Afghanistan through a trade and transport corridor. This port is in fact the sole deep-sea port in Iran with direct access to the ocean. When constructed, this port could establish a corridor based on a 628-kilometer-long Chabahar–Zahedan rail line, which would allow India to use Iran as a channel for access to Afghanistan and Central Asia, while bypassing Pakistan.

Its geographic proximity to Afghanistan, Pakistan, and India, as well as its location as a major transit center on the growing International North–South Transport Corridor (INSTC), renders it one of the most significant commercial hubs in the region. More crucially, Chabahar is exempt from US sanctions, providing Iran with an opportunity to facilitate further trade with other countries.[62] Experts insist that Chabahar Port has the capacity to transform trade ties in South and Central Asia. Its proposed land-based trade routes will connect the port to Afghanistan and Central Asian markets.

Additionally, Chabahar Port connects the Indo–Pacific countries to the market of Central Asian countries and ultimately European countries. However, the importance of the European route of this corridor has been questioned with the signing of memorandum of understanding on the India–Middle East–Europe Economic Corridor, or IMEC, by the European Union, India, Saudi Arabia, the United Arab Emirates, the United States, and other G20 partners at the last G20 meeting on September 9, 2023. Based on this corridor, India will be able to connect to Europe through the United Arab Emirates, Saudi Arabia, Jordan, and Israel.[63]

It is noteworthy that, for both Iran and India, this port is largely seen as central to the Indo–Pacific trade route. This area has also taken on a new importance for Iran's "Look East" policy. Although India is not ideologically aligned with this policy, it is of interest to Iran, as it pertains to geopolitics, transit, and circumventing of sanctions. Both India and Iran are members of the SCO. Tehran has also become a member of the organization of regional economies of Brazil, Russia, India, China, and South Africa (BRICS). These two organizations are central to Iran's East policy. India can also connect the SCO to the EEU through the INSTC that passes through Iran.

It should also be noted that Iran's and India's views on BRICS are not the same. Although India has supported Iran's membership in this organization, each of them pursues their own specific agenda. India, whose interests are mainly aligned to those of the United States through the Quad, along with Australia and Japan, who trade heavily with the West, rarely if ever views BRICS as an anti-Western bloc. Iran, by contrast, considers this organization an instrument to confront the West.[64]

Additionally, in the future perspective of India's strategic partnership with Iran, the link and connection of the Iran route and transit plans from Chabahar to Sarakhs, the INSTC, and other related routes, India's access to Central Asia through Iran will be guaranteed in the shortest and most cost-effective routes.[65] Accordingly, New Delhi is seeking to use the SCO to promote the INSTC and the Chabahar Port Project.[66] Furthermore, this corridor makes it possible for India to bypass Pakistan and to compete with China in creating international corridors, including the Belt and Road Initiative and the China Pakistan Economic Corridor (CPEC). Accordingly, a tripartite committee was established in 2020 by India, Iran, and Uzbekistan for closer cooperation in Chabahar Port and other projects.[67]

Similarly, new developments in the Suez Canal and the Russian invasion of Ukraine have expedited the launching of the INSTC. Subsequently, in June 2022, trade in this corridor officially started with a shipment from Russia to India via Iran.[68] This corridor has also brought Iran and India much closer in their views on the South Caucasus. The two countries have shown some concerns about the cooperation of the Republic of Azerbaijan, Pakistan, and Turkey and their attempts to create the so-called Zangezur Corridor, which is also favorable to China and could possibly disrupt the INSTC. That may explain why India, like Iran, has taken the side of Armenia in its war with the Republic of Azerbaijan.[69]

India has also created an independent credit line with Iran based on the rupee. India appears to share with Iran the policy of seeking an alternative to the US dollar. Tehran's incentive to do so stems from the fact that such an alternative will significantly diminish the pressure of the US sanctions. In recent years, appreciating the shift of power from the West to the East, Iran has decided to frame its national interests in terms of establishing a close relationship with the East, especially with its neighbors. Concerns about the Taliban gaining power is another factor that brought India and Iran closer together. India's foreign minister was the first foreign dignitary to meet with Raisi after his victory in the Iranian presidential election. The developments in Afghanistan received considerable attention in this meeting, just as the talks surrounding Chabahar Port were given high priority.[70]

Iran and India consider themselves the biggest losers since the Taliban came to power in Afghanistan, which is why the two countries have expanded their coordination in this regard. Especially during the twenty years of US military presence, Tehran and New Delhi have invested in the economy, security, and military in Afghanistan. One of these investments was the development of Iran's Chabahar Port to become India's access window to Afghanistan and Central Asia, and a competitor to Pakistan's Gwadar Port, in which China has invested in order to access the Afghan and Central Asian markets. Seen from this perspective, some observers have described the targeting of Chinese engineers by an Iranian team in Baluchistan as part of the port war between Gwadar, Chabahar, and Jebel Ali in the United Arab Emirates.[71]

Following the Iran nuclear deal, especially since the international sanctions on Iran were lifted in 2016, Iran, India, and Afghanistan agreed to develop Chabahar Port. The railway project, which was initially to be built by the Iranian Railways and the Indian Railways Construction Ltd., failed to proceed as planned in large part due to the US withdrawal from the nuclear deal and the subsequent renewal of US sanctions on Iran. The Iranians then proceeded without India's cooperation, turning to a twenty-five-year strategic partnership deal with China worth $400 billion to replace the former. Nevertheless, Iran and India have reached an agreement on drawing a roadmap for long-term cooperation, and according to Hossein Amir-Abdollahian, Iran's foreign minister, one of Iran's main foreign policy objectives is dialogue and consultation with New Delhi regarding finalizing this roadmap.[72]

As a potential global trading hub, the construction of this port is likely to become an arena for geopolitical competition. New Delhi views the port as a way to access Afghan and Central Asian markets without becoming dependent on Pakistan's land routes. Most importantly, the port could buttress Indo–Iranian ties, which could counterbalance growing Sino–Pakistani cooperation.[73] The fact remains that China has become increasingly influential in Iran, especially by signing a deal with Iran, making it possible for China to gain access to critical natural resources and shipping lanes.

Insofar as Iran is concerned, the port could provide new diplomatic and economic opportunities given its pariah status in the West. The question persists: Can Iran exploit the competition between China and India in an attempt to boost its own regional and international standing while not becoming dominated by either one of these powers? Chabahar Port could offer an invaluable and unique regional trade route, while at the same time it could ironically intensify regional rivalries.[74]

Under pressure from Washington, however, New Delhi has remained modestly accommodating toward Iran and its efforts to protect the peaceful aspects of the Iranian nuclear program. New Delhi has prioritized more cooperative relations with Washington over furthering economic deals with Tehran.[75] India has sought stronger ties and energy partnerships with US allies in the Persian Gulf region, enabling it to reverse its energy dependency on Iran while also diversifying its oil supply sources.[76] By the end of 2021, India's quest for major security guarantees in the Persian Gulf and the Indian Ocean, and the growing threats of its domestic Muslim extremists, some of whom were pro-Iranian Muslims, pushed India to search for partners other than Tehran. With the rise of a Hindu nationalist government, India has increasingly viewed Israel as an important trade and security partner. With the collapse of the nuclear talks in 2018, India's economic ties with Iran have substantially dwindled.[77]

Is Iran navigating the impossible with pursuing the "Look East" strategy? This strategy contains inherent limits, as Iran's close economic, political, and military ties with Russia and China face clear restrictions. While Moscow, Beijing, and Tehran share similar approaches to international order, their diverging national interests and regional politics have precluded and most likely will impede the formation of a cohesive alliance. The absence of institutionalized structures typical of alliances or formal alignment negatively affects the dynamics of any enduring cooperation in the coming years. Additionally, Russia and China pursue divergent approaches to diplomacy with Iran, further highlighting the challenges to the realization of a triple entente or a durable alignment.[78]

The fact remains that the leaders of these three countries are moved by a complex mix of ambitions, interests, and agendas, which are sometimes in tandem with each other and at times less congenial. One cannot be blind to the fact that there is no coherent vision built around a common strategic plan that brings these three powers together. While some Western experts tend to describe Iran's "Look East" strategy as a form of asserting its civilizational challenge to the Western liberal democratic order, we have shown that Iran's Look East pivot policy was and is driven more by economic expediency than ideological compatibility.[79] Iran's crippled economy, a result of the effects of international sanctions, has forced it into closer ties with China and Russia.

Furthermore, according to many Iranian experts, Beijing has proven that it is not prepared to pay a hefty political and economic cost to support partners such as Iran. Despite the festering media hype on the Iran–China twenty-five-year Comprehensive Strategic Partnership Plan or Iran's full membership in SCO, these are highly unlikely to significantly alter the balance of power in favor of Iran vis-à-vis the United States insofar as China's long-term strategic and economic interests are concerned.[80]

Critics of Iran's Eastern pivot have also rightly noted that leaning on one or more powers under the assumption that they could help Iran in confrontations with others is fundamentally misguided given that Iran's geostrategic position rationally calls for a balanced and comprehensive policy. Political realities on the ground, as well as foreign policies pursued by China and Russia, amount to no clear vision for Iran's Eastern policy as a reliable, long-term survival and development strategy.[81] As critics warn, this is unlikely to push back Western pressure in the long term or help Iran successfully forge an anti-Western coalition.

To be sure, China's relations with other Gulf Cooperation Council members have precluded Beijing from forging a stronger alliance with Iran. Underlining this point, one expert correctly points out that "Chinese diversification of its energy sources and Iran's vulnerability to Western pressures could prevent the full materialization of a new [regional] order."[82] In short, this strategy cannot be regarded as a long-term and effective blueprint.[83]

Concerned about Iran's growing economic and political ties with China and Russia, the Joe Biden administration has chosen a different diplomatic approach toward Iran, endorsing an "informal" and unwritten agreement with Tehran by resuming talks over the nuclear deal. Tehran has pledged, among other things, not to enrich uranium beyond its current level of 60 percent purity, refrain from supplying ballistic missiles to Russia, and engage in the prisoner exchange with Washington.[84]

For its part, Washington has partially lifted some sanctions on Iran by unfreezing $20 billion in Iranian assets held in foreign banks in Iraq and South Korea, largely for humanitarian purposes. Of this amount, Iraq has released $2.7 billion in gas and electricity debt to Iran after receiving a sanctions waiver from the United States.[85] The Biden administration had hoped the new agreement will deescalate regional tensions and avoid a full-blown conflict with Iran, as well as reduce Iran's dependency on Russia and China, while opening up new energy supplies for Europe at a time when Russian oil and gas exports to Europe have been banned as a result of the Ukraine war.

Tehran's uneven geopolitical foreign policy reorientation, however, has raised several questions: Should foreign policy reflect the interests of ordinary people and not just specific groups or factions? Will the Iranian public, social forces, professional organizations, intellectual groups, and the country's small private sector—all mostly familiar with Western ideas, systems, and cultures—be willing to embrace and adapt themselves to this Eastward shift harbored by Iran's political and security elites?[86] While it is too early to definitively answer these questions, the evidence thus far points to one key conclusion: The risks of Iran's Eastern policy remain irreducibly unpredictable.

NOTES

1. Mahmood Sariolghalam, "Diagnosing Iran's Emerging Pivot Toward Russia and China," Middle East Institute, June 1, 2023, https://bit.ly/3QK8rAk.
2. Hal Brands and John Lewis Gaddis, "The New Cold War," *Foreign Affairs* 100, no. 6 (November/December 2021): 10–20.
3. Tuvia Gering, "Full Throttle in Neutral: China's New Security Architecture for the Middle East," Atlantic Council, February 15, 2023, https://bit.ly/3SoBafd.
4. Fiona Hill, "The Kremlin's Strange Victory," *Foreign Affairs* 100, no. 6 (November/December 2021): 36–47.
5. Gering, "Full Throttle in Neutral."
6. Javad Heiran-Nia, "How Iran's Middle Class Shapes Its Foreign Policy," *Manara Magazine*, April 12, 2022, https://bit.ly/3QmfJZp.
7. Djavad Salehi-Isfahani, "Iran's Middle Class and the Nuclear Deal," Brookings, April 8, 2021, https://bit.ly/46Sqjyr.
8. Djavad Salehi-Isfahani, "Impact of Sanctions on Household Welfare and Employment," Rethinking Iran, 2020, https://bit.ly/49gUrFg.
9. "Shāfeʻī: Tabaghe-ye motavasset-e keshvar dar hāl-e tajziye shodan ast" [Shafei: The middle class of the country is disintegrating], ISNA News Agency, June 7, 2020, https://bit.ly/47jObed.
10. Quoted in Hashem Ouraei, "Peyvand-e nāmeʻmun-e qodrat va servat" [The unfortunate link between power and wealth], *Jahan Eghtesad*, December 31, 2021, https://bit.ly/3QiwaWN.
11. Asef Bayat, "The Fire That Fueled the Iran Protests," Atlantic, January 27, 2018, https://bit.ly/3SvZCuS.
12. "Hoshdār nesbat be awāreq-e towrami-ye budje-ye sāl-e 1401" [Warning about the inflationary consequences of the 2022 budget], ILNA News Agency, December 11, 2020, https://bit.ly/3siPE5A.
13. Masoud Mosavi Shafaei and Hajar Ardestani, "Naqsh-e tabaghe-ye motavasset dar siyāsat-e khāreji-ye jomhuri-ye eslāmi-ye irān" [The Role of the Middle Class in the Foreign Policy of I.R. Iran], *Foreign Policy Quarterly* 28, no. 2 (Summer 2013): 237–63.
14. "Rahbar-e enqelāb: Emruz jahān dar āstāne-ye yek nazm-e jadid-e beyn-ol-melali ast/jang-e ukrāyn rā bāyad amiq-tar did" [Leader of the revolution: Today the world is on the verge of a new international order/Ukraine war should be looked at more deeply], Iran Diplomacy, April 26, 2022, https://bit.ly/3MrhOSL.
15. Javad Heiran-Nia, "Iran Won't Break with Russia over Ukraine. Here's Why," Atlantic Council, March 30, 2022, https://bit.ly/3QpJA38.
16. Javad Heiran-Nia, "The Enduring—and Growing—Strength of Iran's 'Look to the East' Foreign Policy," *Manara Magazine*, February 21, 2022, https://bit.ly/3MsXVLc.
17. Javad Heiran-Nia, "How Iran's Next President Sees an Emerging 'New World Order,'" Stimson, July 17, 2024, https://www.stimson.org/2024/how-irans-next-president-sees-an-emerging-new-world-order/.
18. Naser Kanaani, "Ertebāt bā sharq dar avvaliyyat-e dowlat va dastgāh-e diplomāsi ast" [Relations with the East is the priority of the government and the diplomatic system], Official Website of the President of the Islamic Republic of Iran, September 9, 2024, https://dolat.ir/detail/451223.
19. Masoud Pezeshkian, "Ravābet-e irān va rusīye samīmāne va rāhbordi ast" [The relationship between Iran and Russia is sincere and strategic], Official Website of the President of the Islamic Republic of Iran, October 11, 2024, https://president.ir/fa/154527.
20. Dina Esfandiary and Ariane Tabatabai, *Triple Axis: Iran's Relations with Russia and China* (I. B. Tauris, 2018), 2.
21. Esfandiary and Tabatabai, *Triple Axis*, 6–7.

22. Bijan Khajehpour, "Iran's Membership in Asian Security Body Won't Solve Sanctions Problem," Al-Monitor, September 22, 2021, https://bit.ly/3tZn1eh.
23. Esfandiary and Tabatabai, *Triple Axis*, 14.
24. Esfandiary and Tabatabai, *Triple Axis*, 32.
25. Esfandiary and Tabatabai, *Triple Axis*, 36.
26. Esfandiary and Tabatabai, *Triple Axis*, 74–75.
27. Richard Weitz, "Tehran and Moscow: Alignment and Divergence in the Caspian," Middle East Institute, June 9, 2021, https://bit.ly/47dwDjD.
28. Javad Heiran-Nia, "Drone Sales to Russia Spark a Debate in Iran," Atlantic Council, November 23, 2023, https://bit.ly/3MsZ0me.
29. Heiran-Nia, "Drone Sales to Russia."
30. Banafsheh Keynoush, *The World Powers and Iran: Before, During and After the Nuclear Deal* (Palgrave Macmillan, 2022), 108.
31. Alex Vatanka, "Making Sense of the Iran-China Strategic Agreement," Middle East Institute, April 26, 2021, https://bit.ly/45Zj46m.
32. "Russia Becomes Largest Foreign Investor in Iran," Iran's Ministry of Foreign Affairs, January 29, 2023, https://bit.ly/3u4bcTP.
33. Chunlong Lu and Jie Chen, "China's Middle East Policy Since the Post-Mao Reform," in *Strategic Interests in the Middle East: Opposition and Support for US Foreign Policy*, ed. Jack Covarrubias and Tom Lansford (Ashgate, 2007), 93.
34. Thomas Erdbrink, "For China's Global Ambitions, Iran Is at the Center of Everything," *New York Times*, July 25, 2017, https://bit.ly/3QkkByo.
35. Emil Avdaliani, "China's 2023 Trade and Investment with Iran: Development Trends," Silk Road Briefing, February 8, 2023, https://bit.ly/3SsQZRV.
36. Avdaliani, "China's 2023 Trade and Investment with Iran."
37. Manochehr Dorraj and James English, "Iran-China Relations and the Emerging Political Map," in *Iranian Foreign Policy Since 2001: Alone in the World*, ed. Thomas Juneau and Sam Razavi (Routledge, 2013), 179–95; see especially page 181.
38. Keynoush, *World Powers and Iran*, 137.
39. Keynoush, *World Powers and Iran*, 135–36.
40. Keynoush, *World Powers and Iran*, 118.
41. Keynoush, *World Powers and Iran*, 139.
42. Kevin Rudd, "The World According to Xi Jinping: What China's Ideologue in Chief Really Believes," *Foreign Affairs* 101, no. 6 (November/December 2022): 8–21; see especially page 17.
43. Chas W. Freeman, "China's Current Problems and Prospects," Middle East Policy Council, accessed May 20, 2023, https://mepc.org/speeches/chinas-current-problems-and-prospects.
44. Gal Luft, "China's New Grand Strategy for the Middle East," Foreign Policy, January 26, 2016, https://bit.ly/46Q3kUC.
45. For further information on that, see Mahmood Monshipouri, *Middle East Politics: Changing Dynamics* (Routledge, 2019), 296–301.
46. Luft, "China's New Grand Strategy for the Middle East."
47. Mark A. Green, "China Is the Top Trading Partners to More Than 120 Countries," Wilson Center, January 17, 2023, https://bit.ly/49g1w8Z.
48. Shirzad Azad, *Iran and China: A New Approach to Their Bilateral Relations* (Lexington Books, 2017), 81.
49. Azad, *Iran and China*, 87.
50. Azad, *Iran and China*, 88.
51. "Russia, Largest Foreign Investor in Iran," Iran Press, January 29, 2023, https://bit.ly/3QI5vUM.

52. Ali Alfoneh, "Abandoned by China, Iran Gravitates Toward Russia's Orbit," Arab Gulf States Institute in Washington, February 7, 2023, https://bit.ly/49xf7cr.

53. Alfoneh, "Abandoned by China."

54. Mohsen Shariatinia and Hamidreza Azizi, "Iran and the Belt and Road Initiative: Amid Hope and Fear," *Journal of Contemporary China* 28, no. 120 (2019): 984–94; see especially page 989.

55. Shariatinia and Azizi, "Iran and the Belt and Road Initiative," 990.

56. Shariatinia and Azizi, "Iran and the Belt and Road Initiative," 990.

57. Mir Sherbaz Khetran, "Gwadar and Chabahar: Competition or Cooperation," *Strategic Studies* 38, no. 2 (Summer 2018): 43–55.

58. Shariatinia and Azizi, "Iran and the Belt and Road Initiative," 991.

59. Avdaliani, "China's 2023 Trade and Investment."

60. "Iran's Relationship with India Has 'Far More Potential' Than China: Ex-President Ahmadinejad," New Indian Express, August 3, 2021, https://bit.ly/3tXjnl3.

61. "Pīshnehād-e qeyr-e montazere-ye irān, tavāfoq-e bist-o-panj sāle īn bār bā hend?" [Iran's unexpected offer, twenty-five-year agreement this time with India?], Donya-e Eqtesad Daily, December 21, 2022, https://bit.ly/3tZ8W0t.

62. Soroush Aliasgary and Marin Ekstrom, "Chabahar Port and Iran's Strategic Balancing with China and India," *Diplomat*, October 21, 2023, https://bit.ly/40tmBZF.

63. Nandita Bose, "US, India, Saudi, EU Unveil Rail, Ports Deal on G20 Sidelines," Reuters, September 9, 2023, https://bit.ly/3se7arJ.

64. Javad Heiran-Nia, "What Can Iran Achieve from BRICS Membership?" Stimson, August 30, 2023, https://bit.ly/3QGK6uU.

65. Hossein Pourahmadi Meibodi, Abdul Ali Qavam, and Mahmood Khani Joyabad, "Eqtesād-e siyāsi-e siyāsat-e khāreji-ye hend va rāhbordhā-ye peyvand va ertebāt-e ān bā āsiā-ye markazi" [The political economy of India's foreign policy and its linking and communication strategies with Central Asia], *Central Asia and the Caucasus Journal* 23, no. 98 (Summer 2017): 1–32.

66. "Iran Can Bring Russia, India Closer Through INSTC," Financial Tribune Daily, January 12, 2020, https://bit.ly/3Sr1qpi.

67. "India, Iran and Uzbekistan Hold Meet on Joint Use of Chabahar Port," Business Standard, December 15, 2021, https://bit.ly/40sRZrm.

68. "North-South Corridor Begins Op. with 1st Shipment," Mehr News Agency, June 11, 2022, https://bit.ly/3SoVRr5.

69. Omar Ahmed, "Is the South Caucasus a New Battleground for India and Pakistan?," Middle East Monitor, October 3, 2022, https://bit.ly/45YcPjs.

70. "Vazir-e omur-e khāreji-ye Hend bā ra'is-e jomhur-e montakhab-e Irān didār kard" [The Indian foreign minister met with the president-elect], IRNA News, July 7, 2021, https://bit.ly/3FJH1ny.

71. Ahmad Movafagh Zeidan, "Pākestān, Īrān va Hend be Afghānestān negāh mīkonand" [Pakistan, Iran and India view Afghanistan], Arabi 21, September 27, 2021, https://bit.ly/49jvysn.

72. "Amir-Abdollahian: Be donbāl-e naqshe-ye rāh-e hamkāri-e bolandmodat bā Hend hastim" [Amir-Abdollahian: We are looking for a roadmap for long-term cooperation with India], Fars News Agency, June 8, 2022, https://bit.ly/49dkltD.

73. Soroush Aliasgary and Marin Ekstrom, "Chabahar Port and Iran's Strategic Balancing with China and India," *Diplomat*, October 21, 2023, https://bit.ly/40tmBZF.

74. Aliasgary and Ekstrom, "Chabahar Port."

75. Keynoush, *World Powers and Iran*, 146–47.

76. Keynoush, *World Powers and Iran*, 158.

77. Keynoush, *World Powers and Iran*, 164.

78. Nicole Grajewski, "An Illusory Entente: The Myth of a Russia-China-Iran 'Axis,'" *Asian Affairs* 53, no. 1 (2022): 181.

79. Gary J. Schmitt, "Introduction: The Challenge Ahead," in *The Rise of the Revisionists: Russia, China, and Iran*, ed. Gary J. Schmitt (AEI Press, 2018), 5.

80. Ali Omidi, Ehsan Fallahi, and Kourosh Ziabani, "Analyzing the Contrast Between Chinese Economic Pragmatism and Iranian 'Look to East' Optimism," *International Journal of China Studies* 12, no. 21 (December 2021): 295–318; see especially page 313.

81. Mehdi Sanaei and Jahangir Karami, "Iran's Eastern Policy: Potential and Challenges," *Russia in Global Affairs*, no. 3 (July/September 2021), https://eng.globalaffairs.ru/articles/irans-eastern-policy/.

82. Keynoush, *World Powers and Iran*, 138.

83. Sanaei and Karami, "Iran's Eastern Policy."

84. Michael Crowley, Farnaz Fassihi, and Ronen Bergmen, "Hoping to Avert Nuclear Crisis, U.S. Seeks Informal Agreement with Iran," *New York Times*, June 14, 2023, https://bit.ly/3FI6vli.

85. "Iraq Releases $2.7 Billion of Iran's Frozen Assets: Official," Tasnim News Agency, June 10, 2023, https://bit.ly/3snzLuv.

86. Sariolghalam, "Diagnosing Iran's Emerging Pivot."

Part II
IRAN–CHINA RELATIONS

6

IRAN'S PIVOT TOWARD CHINA
Neoclassical Realist Perspectives

Niloufar Baghernia

Iran's "Look East Policy" drew the world's attention to Tehran's shifting foreign policy since Mahmoud Ahmadinejad's presidency in 2005. The Islamic Republic's "Neither East Nor West" policy, the primary slogan of the Islamic revolution in 1979, has been altered to the Look East policy, shifting its focus to the non-Western growing powers. In doing so, Tehran has aimed to strengthen ties with Beijing, which led Iran to sign the twenty-five-year agreement with China. With the victory of hardliners in Iran and the onset of Ebrahim Raisi's presidency, improving ties with China has further become Tehran's foreign policy priority. As such, this chapter explores the key factors that have played a role in China's significance in Iran's Look East policy during Raisi's presidency. In so doing, this research employs neoclassical realism theory to study elites' decision-making preferences, both internally and externally. The study then moves on to the structural factors of the international system and the Middle East—such as Middle Eastern power dynamics, China's rise, and Iran's countering the United States' power—in order to analyze how these internal and external factors affected Iran's decision-making toward China during President Raisi's term. In addition, the chapter examines the potential long-term implications of this partnership on Iran's policymaking toward China. The research has relied on speeches and comments by current Iranian government officials, as well as documents regarding the significance of China in analyzing China's rising importance in Iranian foreign policy considerations.

After Raisi's return from a trip to China in February 2023, in his speech at Mehrabad airport in Tehran, he claimed that China showed a willingness to add

Iran as a new member of BRICS. He also maintained that in light of economic interests and trade, Iran should forge closer ties with China as a rising economic power in Asia and the world more broadly.[1] Chinese officials also declared that the two sides signed several bilateral collaboration agreements in agriculture, tourism, trade, environmental protection, culture, sports, and health.[2] In many ways, this mutual declaration of cooperation was no surprise—over the past two decades, Iran and China have maintained fairly high levels of cooperation, which was illustrated as "20 centuries of cooperation" by Chinese newscasters to depict Sino-Iranian ties.[3]

Regarding Iran–China relations, considerable research has been conducted. By focusing on China's role in fulfilling Iran's interests, first, some researchers argue that China is seen as an exceptional country in Iran's eyes. Anoushiravan Ehteshami and Gawdat Bahgat, for example, argue that Iran is unique among rising Middle Eastern countries in seeing Asia's rise as an opportunity for fostering an alternative future. Particularly, after decades of isolation, Tehran sees the reemergence of China as a leading global economic and growing political power as the most advantageous path to prosperity. In addition, Tehran views deepening Asian ties as a means of detaching its political economy from the West.[4] Jon Alterman also claims that, for Iran, China serves as a counterweight in global affairs, and almost every country in the Middle East assumes that it would benefit from a rising Chinese role in the region.[5] Along similar lines, John Garver maintains, apart from the economic motivations behind Iran's inclination toward China, "the civilizational solidarity between Iran and China forms a kind of spirit of Sino-Iranian ties, a worldview that stems from the fact that they were both most accomplished, powerful and wealthy kingdoms in the past which were brought low by Western powers in the modern period."[6] In addition to its economic needs and its global isolation, Iran's similar outlooks with China have made Tehran pursue the Look East policy instead of the earlier "Neither East Nor West" slogan.

In a second strand of research on Sino–Iranian ties, scholars have employed various international relations theories to analyze the relationship. Employing neoclassical realism, Bahareh Sazmand and Maryam Goudarzi compare the presidencies of Ahmadinejad and Hassan Rouhani, arguing that the relationship with China has been heavily affected by the structure of the international system. They also contend that Iran turned more toward China during Rouhani's presidency.[7] However, Fariborz Arghavani Pirsalami, using defensive realism, argues that during Ahmadinejad, the international system and internal decision-makers simultaneously influenced Iran–China ties.[8]

In contrast with this literature on Iran's ties with China, utilizing neoclassical realism, this chapter goes beyond the mere importance of China for Iran and critically investigates the key factors that played a role in China's significance in Iran's Look East policy during President Raisi's term. In other words, the chapter asks why Iran shifted more toward China at this time period. Little research has been done on Iranian–Chinese ties during this time. As such, this chapter contributes to better understanding the relations between these countries via the lens of neoclassical realist theory by making the following points:

1. Iran tilted more toward China during Raisi's term and aspired to strengthen the relationship between the two countries.
2. Although domestic factors played a role in Iran's foreign policy toward China, the structure (international system and the Middle East) played a more significant role in this behavior.
3. In contrast with other presidents, it appears that the Raisi administration seemed more inclined to continue close relations with China regardless of any reconciliation with the West.

A Neoclassical Realist Framework

Three fundamental assumptions underpin neoclassical realism theory. First, it intends to shed light on certain foreign policy behaviors rather than merely explaining broad international structural outcomes. Second, it portrays the international system as the primary, long-term causality of transformations in any country's foreign policy behavior. At last, the theory layers domestic-level factors into their explanatory models for the purpose to attain a higher level of predictive and empirical accuracy.[9] Therefore, while power is paramount in explaining shifts in any state's foreign policy conduct, it is inadequate because each state has a different combination of domestic-level politics, interests, regime types, institutional configurations, cultural legacies, and preferences.[10] These factors typically have a substantial impact on foreign policy behavior, functioning as a "filter" between the international environment and the results of strategic policy.

It is true that countries have relative power in the international system. However, this power has uncertainties in terms of how decision-makers interpret such a reality and how much they mobilize their resources to accomplish foreign policy objectives. Neoclassical realism, therefore, brings the state back into theoretical analysis and opens the "black box" of the state.[11] It revisits how crucial unit-level variables are in determining foreign policy outcomes. Every state encounters a two-level game in conceiving and enforcing foreign policy: On the one hand, states must react to the limited options provided by the international system, while, on the other, they have to extract and mobilize domestic resources from domestic society and simultaneously maximize their ability to satisfy domestic pressures. Neoclassical realists hold that decision-makers' calculations and perceptions of relative power and domestic restrictions are intervening variables between international pressures and a country's foreign policy.[12]

To neoclassical realists, in order to understand the path states analyze and react to their external environment, one must examine how systemic pressures are translated through unit-level intervening variables such as decision-makers' perceptions and the domestic state structure.[13] In this world, leaders can be restrained by both international and domestic politics. International anarchy, moreover, is neither Hobbesian nor peaceful but somewhat ambiguous and challenging to understand. In this vein, according to neoclassical realists, the first intervening variable is the decision-makers' perceptions, through which systemic pressures must be filtered. To them, the international distribution of power can compel countries' behavior only by influencing the decisions of flesh-and-blood officials, and would-be foreign policy analysts, hence, have no alternative but to investigate in detail how each country's policymakers comprehend their situation. In practical terms, this means that the translation of capabilities into national behavior is frequently imprecise and uneven over the short and medium terms.[14]

The second dimension of state strength concerns its central policymaking apparatus: Fareed Zakaria asks whether the state maintains adequate capacity and cohesion to carry out its wishes. While the general underpinnings of great-state capacity are sovereignty, stability, and a reliable and professional bureaucracy, two critical factors stand out. One is the state's ability to extract wealth; the other is the extent of centralization of decision-making power within the state.[15] Zakaria asks if there is fierce competition among bureaucratic agencies and the branches of government between the federal and local governments. Without centralized decision-making and access to material resources, no state can be deemed strong. Thus, at one end of the spectrum lie those states that are cohesive, independent, wealthy, and maximal, and at the opposite end lies those that are divided, society-penetrated, poor, and minimal.[16]

Thomas Christensen also introduces a brand-new idea of "national political power" in his book. He defines the concept as "the ability of state leaders to mobilize their nation's human and material resources behind security policy initiatives."[17] *He contends that* the overemphasis on national economic and military power has handicapped realism's ability to handle several intriguing policy outcomes that might be connected to domestic mobilization or the creation or maintenance of national political power. A significant shortcoming of the realist analysis is that they suppose that states can simply mobilize their material and human resources in responding to international challenges and opportunities. Rather, Christensen offers a model that treats the state's ability to mobilize the populace as a crucial intervening variable between the international challenges facing the nation and the strategies eventually adopted by the state to meet those challenges.[18] These intervening variables, however, have been categorized differently by scholars. Some such as Norrin Ripsman, Jeffrey Taliaferro, and Steven Lobell have considered state–society ties, domestic institutions, strategic culture, and leader images.[19] Others, including Michiel Foulon,[20] have focused on policymakers' cognitive filters, ideology, and the interest groups.[21]

In this vein, neoclassical realism provides the most thorough analysis of Sino–Iranian ties since it takes into account both international and domestic developments as contributing factors in state behavior. This research, however, goes a step further and challenges the theory utilizing Iran–China ties. The pressure from the United States and China's rise have been considered as critical factors in understanding the shift during Raisi's presidency. Regional pressures, such as the ascent of Saudi Arabia and its strengthening ties with China and Israel, are other factors that have accelerated Iran's policymaking meant to enhance relations with Beijing. This means that the Islamic Republic had concerns over changing the Middle East's balance of power in favor of its adversaries, such as Saudi Arabia, which pushed the regime to seek to lessen the pressure from the region through enhancing relations with China during President Raisi's term. I have also employed three variables, including status, regime identity, and state unification (parties), to analyze the foreign policy transformations toward China.

The Significant Role of Systemic Factors

When applying neoclassical realism, systemic pressure is one of the most critical variables in which the starting point is to determine the international system's effects on countries' behavior. After the Cold War, unipolarity has become a distinguished element of the international system. In Birthe Hansen, Peter Toft, and Anders Wivel's argument, this system features a highly asymmetric distribution of relative capabilities in which the United States is a dominant superpower, exerting power that is challenging for others to counterbalance.[22] Because of the influence of a rising power such as China, the changing polarity of the international system can affect like-minded countries in regions such as the Middle East. Iran is one of the key countries wherein officials are opposed to the United States' unilateral supremacy.

There is considerable literature on whether the international system is changing or whether or not China will become a superpower. However, this is not in the scope of this chapter, and the subsequent part aims to analyze how China's rise as a structural factor influences other countries' foreign policy behavior with a similar outlook as China. As such, the following sections critically analyze the international and regional (i.e., China's increasing leverage in the Middle East) impact of the possible changes of the power from the United States to China on Iran's foreign policy toward Beijing.

International Structure Motivations

After the establishment of the Islamic Republic, the US–Iranian relationship deteriorated with the new government's revolutionary ideas and with the students supporting the Islamic Republic overrunning the American embassy in Tehran, which cut off the diplomatic ties with Iran in April 1980.[23] Within this context, according to neoclassical realism, the Islamic Republic's primary goal is to secure its survival and security in the anarchic and self-help international system. Iran's survival in the Islamic Republic's standpoint can be ensured through political independence and the expansion of influence in the international environment. These goals prompt Iran, similar to other countries, to pursue its national and strategic interests.[24] As such, one significant threat that the Islamic Republic's survival has faced is the United States' interference inside the country. Throughout the postrevolutionary years, Tehran has intentionally avoided any moves toward reconciliation except in the face of imminent threat or a conceivable US military operation against the Islamic Republic.[25] Tehran's underlying calculus maintains that normalization with Washington would profoundly impact the current Iranian political system, from disrupting its internal politics to overwhelming its economy and reshaping its culture.[26] This has made the Islamic Republic seek other like-minded countries to counter the United States' power. As an illustration, in Raisi's visit to Latin America in June 2023, he claimed, "The common issue for all four nations [Iran, Cuba, Venezuela, and Nicaragua] is sovereignty. Americans do not want us to be independent." He further added, "Sanctions are a type of war against countries, but the weapon has changed. Yesterday [in the past], it was a military weapon; now, today, it is a sanctions weapon. Sanctions seek to break the people. So, we have to increase relations between sanctioned countries, which counteracts and neutralizes sanctions."[27]

According to Randall Schweller and Xiaoya Pu, when rising powers' relative capabilities are not strong enough to directly face the hegemon, they endeavor to shape the environment by resisting a superpower.[28] They call the strategy alternatively as "everyday resistance" and "rightful resistance." Everyday resistance happens when weak actors resent the hegemonic order, and condemn its legitimacy and the hegemon's authority to govern. The weak actor counters the hegemon and its associated notion of the inevitability of the existing structure using a revolutionary consciousness. The latter, however, occurs when weak actors somewhat and temporarily accept the legitimacy of the hegemon, and take advantage of opportunities and authorized channels within the order to make relative gains and challenge particular behaviors of the hegemon. To overcome the United States' threatening power, the Islamic Republic has therefore aimed to follow the Look East policy and turn to China and Russia. Although there are other reasons for pursuing the policy, America's unilateral power has caused Iran to turn to China, which increased after Donald Trump's withdrawal from the Joint Comprehensive Plan of Action (JCPOA).

China's rise is another critical structural factor contributing to Iran's tilt toward China. China's material capability has gradually increased, marking it as a second-tier power in the international system. It resists the unipolar system in two dimensions: pragmatically accepting US hegemony and, at the same time, by actively and vocally contesting its validity.[29] In addition, Xi Jinping, in his speech in April 2021, hinted to the United States that the international balance of power is changing. He urged the Joe Biden administration and the international community to accept China as both a rising superpower and an equal partner in solving global challenges.[30] This strategy is adopted by the Islamic Republic as well. The more extensively China creates spheres of influence in strategically important regions such as the Middle East and challenges the United States' role, the more Iran is willing to pursue its Look East policy, particularly focusing on China. This can be seen in the speeches and social media accounts of Ali Khamenei, Iran's supreme leader. In one of his tweets on his official account, he claims, "The international order is changing. Everyone in the world repeats this."[31] Focusing on China, he continues, "Today there are influential countries in the world which share similar outlook toward the international politics with us. This is new and significant. We should appreciate this and strengthen our relations with these countries that accompany us in critical international events."[32] In one of his speeches, Khamenei claimed that "the United States' power in this new world order will be isolated, and the political, economic, cultural and scientific power is changing from the West to Asia."[33]

In addition to Khamenei, Raisi, in his visit to Latin America in June 2023, stated, "In the new world that is being formed, imperialism is falling and the countries that have resisted the arrogance of the arrogant are on the verge of victory."[34] Ali Bagheri, deputy foreign minister for political affairs, similarly claimed that "While the West dreams of the end of history, the rest of the world is about to witness history at a new outset. The new world is emerging from soft tools and non-military confrontations rather than from war and hard military warfare." "No doubt, the new international system will no longer be unipolar," he noted.[35] In addition:

> Becoming a member of the Shanghai Cooperation Organization was finalized during the 13th government when Iran had spent years trying to start this process. At the same time as this initiative, cooperation with

the BRICS member countries was also included in the foreign policy's serious agenda to provide diversity in access to international facilities and tools to meet economic, monetary, and financial needs. Thus, by being a member of the largest political-security and economic mechanisms against unilateralism, Iran is determined to play an influential and essential role in forming multilateral structures and mechanisms.[36]

Hence, a rising China and its increasing sphere of influence in strategically important regions made the Islamic Republic tilt more toward China during Raisi's presidency. Considering China's rising influence in the Middle East, Dawn Murphy argues that China gradually creates spheres of influence and challenges the rules of the international system by building a new international order. She adds that if the current liberal order excludes China, this new order could be the base of China's economic, political, and military relations with the world.[37] Thus, considering what the officials in Iran argue about China's rise and declining powers of the United States, it appears that the rise of China, its growing influence, and its ability to change the global order has risen the importance of China for authorities in Iran in recent years. In addition, going back to Schweller and Pu's argument, as both China and Iran follow "resistance" against the United States and the current international system, officials in Iran have become more inclined to pursue China's desired order and decrease the threat of United States to Iran's political system with China's support.

The Growth of Regional Pressure

The ongoing development of China and Iran's rivals' ties, such as Saudi Arabia in the Middle East, is on the rise. Saudi Arabia and Iran's relations deteriorated after the emergence of the Islamic Republic in 1979. As Iran's biggest regional rival, Saudi Arabia has increasingly pursued to develop ties with China in recent years.

In March 2023, state oil giant Saudi Aramco declared two significant deals to expand its multibillion-dollar investment in China and strengthen its rank as China's top crude provider. The deals were the greatest reported since Chinese President Xi's visit to Saudi Arabia in December 2022, when he called for oil trade in yuan, a move that would weaken the dollar's supremacy.[38] However, Chinese investments in Iran have dropped precipitously since the United States withdrew from the nuclear deal: China invested only $185 million in Iranian projects at the beginning of the presidency of Raisi.[39] Chinese trade flows with other countries in the region, such as Saudi Arabia, greatly surpass the Sino–Iranian trade. Raisi shortly indicated these issues in his remarks before departing for Beijing, noting that "Iran has to pursue compensation for the dysfunction that existed up until now in its relations with China."[40] With this message, Raisi both blamed Rouhani, his predecessor, for failing to strengthen stronger ties with China while also indicating that China had let Iran down by failing to implement a twenty-five-year Comprehensive Strategic Partnership agreement signed in 2021.[41]

Apart from boosting economic relations with China, Saudi's security and military ties with Beijing also make Iran concerned about lagging behind its rival—in other words, Riyadh—in the region. Riyadh announced in April 2023 that the government had approved a memorandum, according to the Saudis, giving it the status of a "dialogue partner" in the eight-member, Beijing-led Shanghai Cooperation Organization (SCO). The move further solidifies Saudi Arabia's increasing ties to its largest trading partner, which have seen a jump forward since Chinese President Xi visited Riyadh in 2022.[42] Although Iran is a permanent member of the organization, the new Saudi status in SCO signifies a development in Sino-Saudi relations in Iranian officials' mindset.

Militarily, Saudi Arabia has also aspired to boost its military capabilities with China's assistance. According to America's intelligence assessment on December 23, 2022, Saudi Arabia is manufacturing ballistic missiles with China's support. Although Riyadh previously purchased missiles from Beijing, this is supposed to be the first time it has constructed them locally, and the development created concerns temporarily about a new missile race in the Middle East.[43] The Fars News Agency, which is linked to the Islamic Revolutionary Guard Corps in Iran, called the Saudi missile program a "premature baby in the middle (heart of) world powers," arguing that "China's missile technological help to Saudi Arabia is part of Beijing's attempts to decrease Washington's influence on Riyadh."[44] The website also claimed that "Unlike Iran, Saudi Arabia still needs foreign help to develop its missile program, and so far, Saudis have not presented a successful record of running the program independently."

Iran's fear of Saudi Arabia's and the Gulf Cooperation Council (GCC) countries' enhancing ties with China deepened during the China–GCC summit in Saudi Arabia on December 9, 2022. One of the main issues concerning Iran the two sides addressed was to "Prevent the proliferation of weapons of mass destruction in the GCC region and ensure the peaceful nature of the Iranian nuclear programme, to preserve regional and international security and stability. They reaffirmed the call on Iran to fully cooperate with the International Atomic Energy Agency." They also shared their views about the territorial dispute between Iran and the United Arab Emirates. "The leaders affirmed their support for all peaceful efforts, including the initiative and endeavours of the United Arab Emirates to reach a peaceful solution to the issue of the three islands, Greater Tunb, Lesser Tunb, and Abu Musa, through bilateral negotiations under the rules of international law, and to resolve this issue in accordance with international legitimacy."[45]

The summit and the issues addressed about Iran received different reactions in Iran. First, the deputy chief of staff to President Raisi, Mohammad Jamshidi, claimed that "Chinese colleagues should remember that when Saudi Arabia and the United States supported ISIS and Al-Qaeda in Syria and destroyed Yemen with brutal military aggression, it was Iran that fought terrorist groups to establish stability and security in the region."[46] Nasser Kanani, Iran's Foreign Ministry spokesman, cited that:

> the statement is the repetition of failed Iranophobia policy. He then asked the council to reconsider their approaches to regional issues and choose a constructive path. He added that China's ambassador had met with Amir-Abdollahian's assistant for Asia and Oceania and conveyed dissatisfaction to China with the statement on the issue of Iran's territorial integrity and emphasized that the three islands of the Persian Gulf are an integral part of the territorial integrity of Iran and will never be the subject of negotiations with any other countries.[47]

Later, the foreign minister, Hossein Amir-Abdollahian, on his Twitter page both in Persian and Chinese, wrote that "the three islands are an inseparable parts of Iran, and we do not accept any countries' comments on that."[48] Some Reformist newspapers in Iran reacted to the summit following the statement in Riyadh. *Aftab Yazd* published an interview with four economic and political experts titled "Why are we pessimistic about China?"[49] In addition, the *Ebtekar* newspaper called the statement "The Chinese unfaithfulness,"[50] and the *Islamic Republic* published on its front page that "China did not apologize."[51] Hence, it appears that Iran's fears of regional threats because of enhanced ties between China and Saudi Arabia prompted Tehran to send a large delegation in a first state visit to China. On this visit, senior Iranian officials, including the Central Bank chief and the top nuclear negotiator, accompanied the president.[52] In addition, the Iraqi officials, after returning from Iran in November 2022, stated that Iranian officials are concerned that the increasing relations between China and Saudi Arabia might negatively affect the Sino–Iranian ties.[53]

Apart from the development of China and Saudi relations, Iran had other concerns, making Tehran lean more toward China and its desired interests in the region. In March 2023, the *New York Times* reported that "Saudi Arabia is pursuing security assurances from the United States, support with developing a civilian nuclear program and fewer constraints on U.S. arms sales as its price for normalising relations with Israel."[54] On June 8, 2023, Saudi Foreign Minister Prince Faisal bin Farhan met with the US secretary of state in Riyadh. During the meeting, Farhan reportedly said:

It is quite clear that we believe that normalisation with Israel is in the interest of the region, and it would bring significant benefits to all. . . . But without finding a pathway to peace for the Palestinian people, without addressing that challenge, any normalisation will have limited benefits. And therefore, I think we should continue to focus on finding a pathway toward a two-state solution and a pathway toward giving the Palestinians dignity and justice.[55]

Still, it is too early to indicate how the normalization will proceed. It is nevertheless significant that attempts to reconcile ties between Israel and Saudi Arabia have been seen as threatening in Iran. This can be witnessed in Saudi Arabia's foreign minister's visit to Iran and the discussions with Raisi on June 17, 2023. Raisi, in this visit, stated, "Only the enemies of Muslims, and the Zionist regime [Israel] . . . are resentful of the development of bilateral and regional cooperation between Iran and Saudi Arabia." He then continued, "The Zionist regime is not only the enemy of Palestine but is also the threat to all Muslims, and the normalisation of some countries with this regime does not create any security in the region."[56]

Hence, the fear of falling behind the Sino–Saudi ties and progress in Saudi–Israeli normalization have pressured Iran to seek security through enhancing ties with China. Saudi Arabia and Israel's enhanced ties with China place Iran in a weak and vulnerable position, leading Tehran to pursue paths to address its security concerns.

In addition to this, Iran is aware that Saudi Arabia was the world's fastest-growing large economy in 2022. The world still relies on fossil fuels. The Ukraine war and sanctions against Russia, Iran, and Venezuela have made the world depend on some countries in the Middle East, particularly Saudi Arabia.[57] The wealth created out of the current global condition for Saudi Arabia, combined with shifts in Riyadh's foreign policy, can put Iran behind its rival. Iran's position can become even more vulnerable if Saudi Arabia develops further ties in various fields with China, which can change the Middle East's balance of power in favor of Riyadh. Ultimately, as the perceived threat from these developments grew, the Islamic Republic decided to deepen ties with China, which was followed by the reconciliation between Iran and Saudi Arabia with China's support in March 2023.

Domestic Factors

Apart from structural factors, Iran's foreign policy has been affected by domestic variables as well. The following section utilizes three variables, including the different parties' roles in the current government, regime identity and status, to analyze Iran's foreign policy toward China during Raisi's term.

Iran has historically striven to be a regional power. Iran's leaders, whether from the Islamic Republic or its predecessors, have believed in a historical sense of imperial mission. The leaders of the Islamic Republic also came to power, maintaining regional aspirations. Iran thus desires to be the dominant regional power in the Persian Gulf and a pivotal power in the Middle East.[58] This goal is not new, and it is distinctive neither to the Islamic Republic nor to its hardline factions. It is rather a continuation of earlier goals. Iranian leaders are convinced that Western powers have made a concerted effort to contain the country's actions as an autonomous regional power. Tehran perceives that US policy, in coordination with American allies, inhibits Iran's role in managing regional affairs and seeks to sabotage the Islamic Republic. This has made Iran dissatisfied with the regional order and its place within it, which explains why the Islamic Republic favors a revisionist foreign policy.[59] This anti-Americanism and rejectionist identity have made Iran look for other options that also oppose US power.

A closer look at the Iranian government's seventh Development Plan (2023–27) also reveals the mindset of leaders in Iran toward the world. The document cites that Iran needs to "Create platforms and necessary conditions for diversifying and strengthening all-round ties with target countries in the world, especially countries in the neighbouring region and emerging powers in the framework of the general policies of the system."[60] Enhancing ties with the "world" evidently means emerging powers such as China, neighboring countries such as Saudi Arabia, the United Arab Emirates, and the rest of the Middle East region.[61] This excludes Europe and the United States. The text also mentions the need to design and implement diplomatic measures to support Palestine and confront Israel.[62] Israel is, therefore, another country excluded from the world in Iranian leaders' mindset in foreign policy. Hence, the Iranian leaders' dissatisfaction with their regional and international status has acted as a source pushing Iran more toward China.

The factional elites' unification has also significantly influenced Iran's pivot to China during Ebrahim Raisi's presidency. The Raisi presidency led to higher levels of policy uniformity within the Iranian political system. Even more important, it resulted in the executive branch rank and file being staffed with supporters, loyal administrators, and 1980s revolutionaries. Since the Islamic revolution, Iran's legislative and judicial branches have shown some allegiance to the status quo.[63] Nevertheless, following each change of president, the executive branch has had the chance to fill some 11,000 administrative appointments throughout the country with like-minded people. With the tenure of the more conservative Raisi government, all three branches were dedicated to maintaining the coherence and stability of the Islamic Republic.[64] However, this aim was challenged by the mass protests in Iran due to the death of Mahsa Amini, a twenty-two-year-old girl in the custody of the Morality Police in Tehran on September 16, 2022. As the scholar Mahmood Sariolghalam observes, Raisi's government's aim was to survive with all the sources of internal and external challenges. In contrast to the Western countries, China is not concerned with Iran's internal political difficulties, therefore allowing Iran the space it needs during the sensitive period of leadership transition and succession.

In this vein, considering the policies of previous administrations, a number of scholars have questioned whether the shift toward China is temporary. To be precise, the question is whether officials in Tehran will choose the West if the deal with over the JCPOA goes well or if the Look East policy will continue.[65] With structural and regional pressures imposed on the Islamic Republic, especially the role of China's increasing influence in the Middle East, it appears that China's position is rising in Iran's foreign policy considerations, even after the death of Raisi. During Raisi's presidency, officials in Iran perceived that structural changes at the international level favored China and Asia. In their official visits to countries that share their apprehension against the unilateral power of the United States, Iranian leaders repeatedly discussed changes in the international system and the apparent decline of America's supremacy.

China's rise, as noted earlier, and its increasing leverage in the Middle East further reinforced this interpretation. For instance, the GCC countries in the Middle East are deepening ties with China at different levels, departing from the unilateral ties with Washington. The first category of ties with China is Saudi Arabia and the United Arab Emirates, which openly hedge against the US departure from the Middle East. They have surpassed conventional trade and purchased missiles, drones, and military aircraft from Chinese companies. The second group consists of Qatar and Oman. Both have opened their port infrastructures at Hamad Port and Duqm Port, respectively, and their digital networks to Chinese operators.[66] Qatar has purchased Chinese ballistic missiles. Bahrain and Kuwait have correspondingly opened their economies to Chinese investors, including modernization projects such as Kuwait's Silk City. In addition, according to statistics from the Stockholm International Peace Research Institute, China has been the eight largest arms exporter to Bahrain over the last decade.[67] This becomes significant when one considers Iran's rivalry with the GCC countries. Hence, considering China's increasing rise globally and regionally, as well as Iran's rivalry with the GCC states, it is safe to say that even if any reconciliation with the West occurs, Iran is highly likely to pursue its pivot to China and bolster ties.

This chapter analyzed Iran and China's evolving ties through the perspective of neoclassical realists during the late President Raisi. The theory incorporates both external and internal factors contributing to the foreign policy behavior of states. According to neoclassical realism, external factors are insufficient in understanding a particular foreign policy by themselves. Hence, internal variables should be studied in order to comprehend the state's behavior or its policies toward others. Moreover, internal factors cannot be neglected. Having investigated Iran–China relations, this chapter argues that the pressure from the structure—the international system and the Middle East—played a more influential role in Iran's significant shift in behavior at both regional and international levels.

As neoclassical realists argue, the combination of internal and external factors has led to the Islamic Republic's pivot to China. However, a detailed analysis of official Iranian speeches and documents reveals that the significant concerns of the Iranian leaders exceed the internal factors contributing to a more in-depth relationship with China. Although the government was formed by the hardliners who were supporters of strengthening ties with China, the policy shift occurred after Trump's withdrawal from the JCPOA, during Rouhani's presidency, who was not a hardliner. In addition, although important, anti-Americanism did not play a major role, considering Iranian–American private talks in Oman in recent years. This shows that the Islamic Republic can be flexible and make unforeseen changes when pressured by the structure.

A closer look at Iran–China relations indicates that international and regional pressures imposed on Iran played a more significant role than internal variables to pivot toward China more profoundly. The rise of China, especially after the consolidation of Xi's power, made the Islamic Republic perceive the foreseeable changes in the order of the international system. Although Iranian officials were united in their belief that the system has yet to change, in their speeches and talks, they show confidence that, with the support of like-minded countries, the shift will eventually occur shortly. Secondly, China's own evolving engagement with the countries in the Middle East pushed Iran more toward China. By diversifying its ties and amplifying its economy, Saudi Arabia threatens Iran's security and Tehran's goal of becoming the superior power in the region. The fear showed itself in Raisi's 2023 state visit to China immediately after the China–GCC summit, wherein Iran's sovereignty was threatened in the Iranian leader's mindset, according to their reactions afterward. Saudi Arabia's possible reconciliation with Israel also substantially influenced Iran's shift toward China. Raisi criticized Saudi–Israeli ties and possible normalization. The fear of the possibility of Saudi Arabia's rise and reconciliation with Israel put Iran's security in danger in two ways. First, Saudi Arabia and Israel can become more powerful by enhancing ties with China. Second, Iran loses China as the only like-minded rising power to other regional states. These pressures on Iran gave Tehran a nudge to lean more toward Beijing, primarily during Raisi's term. Thus, it appears that, with China's rise both globally and in the Middle East, the Islamic Republic might continue shifting toward China, even if reconciliation with the West takes place.

NOTES

1. Ebrahim Raisi, "Sokhanan-e ra'is-jomhur dar bazghasht as safar be Chin" [The president's speech after returning from China], Mehr News Agency, February 16, 2023, https://www.mehrnews.com/xZyD9.
2. "Xi Jinping Holds Talks with Iranian President Ebrahim Raisi," Ministry of Foreign Affairs of the People's Republic of China, February 14, 2023, https://bit.ly/3sqiNM2.
3. John W. Garver, "China and Iran: An Emerging Partnership Post-Sanctions," Middle East Institute, February 8, 2016, 3–4, https://acr.ps/1L9zRj1.
4. Anoushirvan Ehteshami and Gawdat Bahgat, "Iran's Asianisation Strategy," in *Iran Looking East: An Alternative to the EU?*, ed. Annalisa Perteghella (LediPublishing, 2019), 148.
5. Jon B. Alterman. "China, the United States and the Middle East," in *The Red Star and the Crescent, China and the Middle East*, ed. James Reardon-Anderson (Oxford University Press, 2018), 47.
6. John W. Garver, *China and Iran, Ancient Partners in a Post-Imperial World* (University of Washington Press, 2006), 3–4.
7. Bahareh Sazmand, Maryam Goudarzi, "A Comparative Analysis of China's Position in Ahmadinejad and Rouhani Look East Policy," *Journal of Central Eurasia Studies*, no. 1 (Spring and Summer 2022): 127–28.
8. Fariborz Arghavani Pirsalami, "Iran and China's Relations during Mahmoud Ahmadinejad Presidency, Look East Policy and Structure Impacts" *Studies of International Relations Journal*, no. 32 (Winter 2016): 37.
9. Dean P. Chen, "Security, Domestic Divisions, and the KMT's Post-2008 'One China' Policy," *International Relations of the Asia-Pacific* 15, no. 2 (2015): 327.
10. Chen, "Security, Domestic Divisions," 328.
11. Mu Ren, "Interpreting China's (Non-)Intervention Policy to the Syrian Crisis: A Neoclassical Realist Analysis," *Ritsumeikan Journal of International Studies* 26, no. 1 (June 2014): 259–82.
12. Ren, "Interpreting China's (Non-)Intervention Policy."
13. Gideon Rose, "Neoclassical Realism and Theories of Foreign Policy," *World Politics* 51, no. 1 (October 1998): 152.
14. Rose, "Neoclassical Realism," 158.
15. Fareed Zakaria, *From Wealth to Power: The Unusual Origins of America's World Role* (Princeton University Press, 1998), 39.
16. Zakaria, *From Wealth to Power*, 39.
17. Thomas J. Christensen, *Useful Adversaries: Grand Strategy, Domestic Mobilization, and Sino-American Conflict* (Princeton University Press, 1996), 11–13.
18. Christensen, *Useful Adversaries*.
19. Norrin M. Ripsman, Jeffrey W. Taliaferro, and Steven E. Lobell, *Neoclassical Realist Theory of International Politics* (Oxford University Press, 2016), 59.
20. Michiel Foulon, "Neoclassical Realism: Challengers and Bridging Identities," *International Studies Review* 17, no. 4 (2015): 635.
21. Shiping Tang, "Neoclassical Realism: Methodological Critiques and Remedies," *The Chinese Journal of International Politics* 16, no. 3 (2023): 5.
22. Birthe Hansen, Peter Toft, and Anders Wivel, *Security Strategies and American World Order: Lost Power* (Routledge, 2008); and Ren, "Interpreting China's (Non-)Intervention Policy," 264.

23. "Photos: The Troubled History of Iran-US Relations," Al Jazeera, November 29, 2022, https://bit.ly/3QihZ41.

24. Seyyed Jalal Dehghani Firouzabadi, "Neoclassical Realism and Islamic Republic of Iran's Foreign Policy," *Foreign Policy Quarterly* 25, no. 2 (July 2011): 284.

25. Mahmood Sariolghalam, "Diagnosing Iran's Emerging Pivot Toward Russia and China," Middle East Institute, June 1, 2023, https://bit.ly/3QK8rAk.

26. Sariolghalam, "Diagnosing Iran's Emerging Pivot."

27. "Raisi Mobilizes Support for Iran in Latin America," United States Institute of Peace, June 22, 2023, https://bit.ly/3tV9zbk.

28. Randall L. Schweller and Xiaoya Pu, "After Unipolarity China's Visions of International Order in an Era of U.S. Decline," *International Security* 36, no. 1 (Summer 2011): 50.

29. Schweller and Pu, "After Unipolarity," 52.

30. Tony Walker, "Xi Jinping Sends Message to US on China's Rising Power in Boao Address," Conversation, April 21, 2021, https://bit.ly/3skt4JN.

31. Ali Khamenei (@khamenei_fa), "Nazm-e jahani dar hal-e tahavvol ast" [The international order is changing], Twitter, May 21, 2023, https://bit.ly/3MojBYA.

32. Ali Khamenei (@khamenei_fa), "Emrooz keshvarha-ye bozorg va mohemi dar ba'zi az khottut-e asasi-ye siyasat-e beynolmelali ba ma hamrah va ham-fekr-and" [Today major countries share our views on some fundamental lines of international politics], Twitter, May 21, 2023, https://bit.ly/3MqeBmh.

33. Ali Khamenei, "Bayanat dar didar-e danesh-amuzan" [Khamenei speech in meeting with students], Khamenei.ir, November 2, 2022, https://acr.ps/1L9zQUB.

34. "Iran's Raisi Hails 'New World Order' Favoring Independent States," Middle East Monitor, June 13, 2023, https://bit.ly/46UMF2m.

35. Ali Bagheri Kani, "Cheshm-andaz-e siyasat-e khareji dar partow-e nazm-e jadid-e Jahani" [The perspective of foreign policy in the light of the new world order], Islamic Republic of Iran, Ministry of Foreign Affairs, May 20, 2023, https://bit.ly/474yS93.

36. Kani, "Cheshm-andaz-e siyasat-e khareji."

37. Dawn C. Murphy, *China's Rise in the Global South: The Middle East, Africa, and Beijing's Alternative World Order* (Stanford University Press, 2022), 1–2.

38. Aziz El Yaakoubi and Maha El Dahan, "Saudi Arabia Seeks Cooperation with China, 'Ignores' Western Worries," Reuters, June 12, 2023, https://bit.ly/3FHUb4E.

39. Ali Ahmadi, "Iran-China: Deeper Economic Ties Could Lead to Slow down with Washington," Middle East Eye, 26 March 2023, https://bit.ly/3s6BwfO.

40. Saeed Azimi, "Iran's Special Relationship with China Beset by 'Special Issues,'" Bourse and Bazaar Foundation, February 16, 2023, https://bit.ly/3FDUBsO.

41. Azimi, "Iran's Special Relationship."

42. Gerald M. Feierstein, Ruba Husari, Charles Lister, Alex Vatanka, and Mohammed Soliman, "Monday Briefing: Saudi Arabia Takes New Steps to Further Strengthen Ties to China," Middle East Institute, April 3, 2023, https://bit.ly/46ccMkh.

43. Julia Masterson, "Saudi Arabia Said to Produce Ballistic Missiles," Arms Control Association, January/February 2022, https://bit.ly/45VV9on.

44. "Barname-ye moshaki-ye Arabestan; nowzadi nares dar qalb-e reghabat-e ghodrat-ha-ye Jahani" [Saudi missile program: A premature baby in the heart of the world power's competition], Fars News Agency, January 3, 2022, http://fna.ir/60wy6.

45. "Statement of the Riyadh Summit for Cooperation and Development Between the GCC and the People's Republic of China," Saudi Press Agency, December 9, 2022, https://acr.ps/1L9zQpg.

46. "Nokhostin vakonesh-e Iran be ezharat-e ra'is-jomhur-e Chin dar Arabestan" [Iran's first reaction to the statements of the Chinese president in Saudi Arabia], *Donyaye Eghtesad*, December 10, 2022, https://bit.ly/45WxbcH.

47. Nasser Kananni, "Bayaniye-ye Shora-ye Hamkari-ye Khalij-e Fars tekrar-e siyasat-e shekast-khorde-ye Iranharasi ast" [The statement of the GCC is the repetition of failed policy of Iranophobia], Islamic Republic News Agency, December 10, 2022, https://irna.ir/xjLd2j.

48. Hossein Amir-Abdollahian (@Amirabdolahian), "Jazayer-e se-gane-ye Abumusa, Tonb-e Kuchak va Tonb-e Bozorg dar Khalij-e Fars, ajza-e jodayi-napazir-e khak-e pak-e Iran ast" [The three islands are inseparable parts of Iran], Twitter, December 11, 2022, https://bit.ly/3tXDVd4.

49. Yeganeh Shogh Al-Shoara, "Chera be Chin badbin hastim?" [Why are we pessimistic about China?], *Aftab Yazd*, December 11, 2022, https://bit.ly/47bRmVa.

50. "Jafa-ye Chini dar Riyaz" [Chinese unfaithfulness in Riyadh], Ebtekar, December 11, 2022, https://bit.ly/3QCyDfX.

51. "Chin ozrkhahi nakard!" [China did not apologize], Islamic Republic Newspaper, December 14, 2022, https://bit.ly/46UO2xY.

52. Maziar Motamedi, "Iran's Raisi Leads Large Delegation in First State Visit to China," Al Jazeera, February 13, 2023, https://bit.ly/45Zl4M5.

53. Qassim Abdul-Zahra, "Saudi-Iran Talks Said to Have Stalled over Protests in Iran," Associated Press, December 19, 2022, https://bit.ly/3QEFu7s.

54. Michael Crowley, Vivian Nereim and Patrick Kingsley, "Saudi Arabia Offers Its Price to Normalize Relations with Israel," *New York Times*, March 9, 2023, https://nyti.ms/3QItPpe.

55. Helene Sallon and Louis Imbert, "Normalization with Israel: Saudi Arabia Shows Signs of Openness," *Le Monde*, June 13, 2023, https://bit.ly/3Sup8B3.

56. "Vidio; Vazir-e khareje-ye Arabestan be didar-e Ra'isi raft/Ra'isi: hich mane'I bara-ye tose'e-ye ravabet ba keshvarha-ye Eslami nadarim/ Ben Farhan: Arabestan dar talash bara-ye erteqa-ye ravabet ba Tehran be sath-e esteratezhik ast" [The video; Saudi foreign minister visited Raisi/Raisi: We have no obstacles to develop relations with Islamic countries/Bin Farhan: Saudi Arabia is trying to improve relations with Tehran to a strategic level], Al-Alam News Network, June 17, 2023, https://bit.ly/3Sn4Vgc.

57. Fareed Zakaria, "The Rise of the Persian Gulf Is Reshaping the World," *Washington Post*, June 16, 2023, https://bit.ly/3SmYiKO.

58. Thomas Juneau, *Squandered Opportunity: Neoclassical Realism and Iranian Foreign Policy* (Stanford University Press, 2015), 81–85.

59. Juneau, *Squandered Opportunity*, 85.

60. "Matn-e layehe-ye barname-ye haftom-e tose'e montasher shod" [The draft text of the 7th Development Plan is published], Islamic Republic News Agency, June 18, 2023, https://irna.ir/xjMJYF.

61. "Iran sees no limits to expanding ties with UAE: Amir-Abdollahian," Islamic Republic News Agency, June 22, 2023, https://bit.ly/47dcMkB.

62. "7th Development Plan," 2023.

63. Mahmood Sariolghalam, "Diagnosing Iran's Emerging Pivot Toward Russia and China," Middle East Institute, June 1, 2023, https://bit.ly/3QK8rAk.

64. Sariolghalam, "Iran's Emerging Pivot."

65. Bahareh Sazmand, Maryam Goudarzi, "A Comparative Analysis of China's Position in Ahmadinejad and Rouhani Look East Policy," *Journal of Central Eurasia Studies* 15, no. 1 (Spring & Summer 2022): 150.

66. Jean-Loup Samaan, "China and the GCC: An Uncertain Partnership," Gulf International Forum, December 23, 2022, https://bit.ly/47gsOuk.

67. Samaan, "China and the GCC."

7

THE CHINA–IRAN TWENTY-FIVE-YEAR AGREEMENT AND THE STRATEGIC REBALANCE OF THE PERSIAN GULF

Degang Sun and Sarvenaz Khanmohammadi

Since the outbreak of COVID-19, the international political and economic system has changed dramatically. The Western and the non-Western Asian and Eurasian powers are engaged in strategic rivalry. The three-century-long Western-dominated international system is giving way to a mixed system with Global North and Global South playing predominant roles simultaneously. In face of the changing international system, China and Iran are promoting strategic docking, and their relations have evolved from a comprehensive strategic partnership in 2016 to the Twenty-Five-Year Strategic Cooperation Agreement in 2021. Meanwhile, the China-Saudi comprehensive strategic partnership has been promoted after the first China–Arab summit was held in Riyadh in December 2022. Mediated by China, reconciliation between Iran and Saudi Arabia and their engagement in the Shanghai Cooperation Organization (SCO), and in the BRICS in the future, has promoted Beijing's political influence in the Gulf, and will dilute the US-led anti-Iranian coalition in the Middle East.

China and the United States are engaged in strategic rivalry. After entering the White House, Joe Biden called China their "most serious competitor," and Washington was ready to confront, compete and cooperate with China simultaneously in the fields of economy, security, diplomacy, human rights, intellectual property rights, and global governance. In particular, the flashpoints of the Sino–US dispute include Hong Kong, Taiwan, Xinjiang, the South China Sea, high technology, international rules, values, Asian security order, and financial orders.[1] Washington is particularly anxious by the prospect that China may reach the top of the global supply chain. In September 2023, US Secretary of Commerce

Gina Raimondo's visit to China coincided with the Huawei Mate 60 Pro's launch, indicating that that US technological blockade against Huawei may fail.

China, however, highlights cooperation with the United States and underscores to build a community of shared future for humanity with all parties in the world, and in particular seeks measures to expand cooperation and management differences with the West. According to the World Bank, China's gross domestic product (GDP) increased by 2.3 percent in 2020, a remarkable growth, while the US GDP shrank by 3.3 percent that same year.[2] Based on the annual average exchange rate of yuan (renminbi), China's economic volume reached US $14.73 trillion, while the total economic volume of US was $20.95 trillion in the same year; thus China was about 70.3 percent of that of the United States.[3]

With the accelerated pace of power shifting, China is often demonized in Western media outlets, many of which claim that China's rise, resembling that of Germany in World War Two, the Soviet Union during the Cold War, and Japan in the 1990s, is challenging the US global leadership and the monopoly of US dollars. This is further facilitated by the Biden administration's rivalry with China. Therefore, Washington is shifting its strategic pivot from the Greater Middle East to the Indo–Pacific region, and is actively building a web of coalitions designed to contain China. These include "the global democratic alliance" vis-à-vis the China-led SCO, consolidating the "Indo–Pacific Quad," forging "US–India–Israel–UAE Quad," and establishing a new global supply chain alliance that excludes China. In addition, the United States attempts to expand the "Five Eyes Alliance" by inviting Japan.[4] The United States' NATO allies, such as Germany and Britain, were also encouraged by Washington to dispatch aircraft carriers and fleets to patrol the South China Sea in the name of "free navigation," in an effort to show off their "muscles" and to exert pressure on China. In response, China has to reconsider the strategic values of Russia, Iran, Syria, and Palestine for purposes of strategic rebalance against the United States.

This chapter explores Sino–Iranian relations from the perspective of great power rivalry and argues that the updated relations is driven by the American factor. Sino–US competition and Iranian–US confrontation have stimulated Beijing and Tehran to form a tacit but de facto quasi-alliance for the purpose of balance. The methodologies employed in the chapter are process tracing, historical approaches, and interviews. Chinese and Iranian diplomats and officials were interviewed in an effort to decode the "black box" of the Sino–Iranian honeymoon and China's engagement in the Persian Gulf through the SCO's westward expansion.

Within the context of US strategy of "securitization" and strategic realignment, China seeks to strike a political coalition with the "Global East" countries. The China–Iran Twenty-Five-Year Strategic Cooperation Agreement, signed in 2021 during Chinese Foreign Minister Wang Yi's visit to Tehran, is a political, strategic and economic agreement between the Islamic Republic of Iran and the People's Republic of China. According to the agreement, China will invest in Iran's oil industry, cooperate with the National Gas Export Company and National Petrochemical Company, and assist Iran in further developing its infrastructure. The agreement also includes cooperation in the fields of economy, trade, energy, defense, and in the area of strategic cooperation and mutual support in the international and regional organizations. The ultimate goal of the accord is to build a more balanced power structure. At the invitation of President Xi Jinping, Iranian President Ebrahim Raisi paid a state visit to China in February 2023, aiming to consolidate their strategic agreement. The most salient factor that brings Tehran and Beijing closer to each other is their opposition to US hegemony in the current changing international system.[5] The spokespersons of the two sides, as well as their official media, however, deny that their cooperation targets any third parties.

This partnership comes as a part of the Belt and Road Initiative (BRI), originally proposed by President Xi in 2013 as the revitalization of the ancient Silk Road connecting China in East Asia with Iran in West Asia. The Initiative uses a network of highways, railways, and ring pipelines from Xi'an of western China to the Xinjiang Autonomous Region on the Kazakh border, and from there to Iran, Iraq, Syria, and Turkey in West Asia. The belt then connects from Istanbul to Bulgaria, Romania, the Czech Republic, and Germany, and then to Rotterdam in the Netherlands and Venice in Italy; it then joins the Maritime Silk Road extending from the South China Sea and the Indian Ocean to the Red Sea and the Mediterranean Sea. The latter is a network of ports and coastal infrastructure that connects South and Southeast Asia to East Africa and the Mediterranean countries.

According to Chinese government, the BRI covers sixty-five countries from Asia to Europe and Africa. The population of these countries is about four and a half billion, connecting three vital economic zones of Asia, Europe, and the Middle East. Striding at the crossroads of the Maritime and Land Silk Roads, Iran secures a special position in the BRI. China's grand economic blueprint for these countries is welcomed by most of the host countries.[6]

The changing international system, however, has exerted a profound impact on China's BRI and their relations with Iran. In addition to NATO, the European Union, the Group of Seven, the Organization for Economic Cooperation and Development (OECD), and other Western-led regional institutions, the developing countries have formed various political, financial and economic institutions as well, such as the SCO, BRICS, and the Asian Infrastructure Investment Bank (AIIB), to name a few.[7] The relative decline of the West and the rise of the "rest" has stimulated the developing countries, such as China, Russia, Iran,

Turkey, Kazakhstan, Egypt, Indonesia, and other to update their partnerships. Sino–Iranian relations is a case in point.

Discussions about the Sino–Iranian strategic agreement began during President Xi's visit to Iran in January 2016. Signed in March 2021, the agreement outlines only a general framework for future cooperation in various fields between the two countries. This chapter uses Persian, Chinese, and English sources to examine, and in the process demystify, the strategic agreement and its implications.

The Twenty-Five-Year Strategic Cooperation Agreement: Updating Sino–Iranian Strategic Relations

In 2020, *Petroleum Economist* reported that during the visit to China by the Iranian Minister of Foreign Affairs Mohammad Javad Zarif, Beijing and Tehran expanded the scope of the 2016 discussions. These discussions reportedly included discounts and concessions to China for its investment in Iranian oil and gas. According to the *Petroleum Economist*, the agreement gave China big discounts on oil purchases, for which Beijing could pay up to two years later. Chinese companies also reportedly have the right to be the first to choose or reject new, unfinished, or halted development projects of Iran's oil and gas fields and petrochemical projects. Furthermore, Beijing can buy any oil, gas, and petrochemical product with a guaranteed minimum discount of 12 percent for up to six months, and pay for it with Chinese yuan or any other currencies coming from trade with African and former Soviet Union countries.[8]

The report further mentioned that at least 5,000 Chinese security personnel will be deployed in Iran in order to protect Chinese projects. Iran will promote RMB internationalization. In fact, the US dollar will not be used in China-Iran trade; instead, petrodollars will be replaced with petroyuan.[9] There was news of $400 billion in Chinese investments in Iran.

There was even a report that, as part of the agreement, Iran has agreed to hand over Kish Island to the Chinese.[10] Both Chinese and Iranian officials denied news of the alleged handover, calling it groundless and absurd. Shortly after his visit to Beijing, Zarif stated that these rumors were categorically false. The Iranian media called the *Petroleum Economist*'s report a rumor based on Western concerns about relations between China and Iran.[11] Iran also denied rumors that "Tehran is handing over several islands as well as parts of its economy to attract Beijing."[12] Beijing highlighted that it adheres to nonalignment and a defensive policy and that it would never encroach on Iranian sovereignty or territorial integrity.

The initial agreement that was signed and published describes the areas of cooperation in the oil and energy sector. Some of the key provisions of the agreement include a stable supply of crude oil to China, cooperation in upstream and downstream projects in the Iranian oil industry with help from Chinese companies, participation in equipping oil and other oil products storage tanks in Iran, participation in construction and expansion of the capacity in Iran's energy transmission lines, increased exports of Iranian petrochemical products to China, and cooperation on the production of electricity and fertilizers from urban waste.[13] According to the strategic partnership, China will provide investments as well as economic and security services worth $400 billion over twenty-five years in return for a steady supply of oil from Iran to the Chinese economy.[14]

The two sides have also agreed on facilitating the implementation and completion of all previously agreed upon projects. There have been no talks about the amount of investment, discounts, or how China is going to pay and through what currency. In fact, China's $400 billion investment in Iran also seems impossible in the foreseeable future. This means that China would need to invest $16 billion on an annual basis, a task that is simply not possible. The total foreign direct investment in Saudi Arabia, for example, the world's largest oil producer and a country under no sanctions, has averaged only $5.1 billion over the past five years.[15] Considering China's relative economic slowdown in the post–COVID-19 era, Chinese investment in Iran cannot be substantial.

Insofar as Iran's free economic zones are concerned, which include Iranian islands in the Persian Gulf, the Sino–Iranian strategic agreement encourages investments in Qeshm, Arvand, and Makoo zones by Chinese investors. It also invites Chinese experts to share their knowledge and experience in establishing and administrating free economic zones. The agreement calls for supporting the cooperation and participation of the AIIB and the Silk Road Fund in Iran's free and special investment, joint investment for the establishment of additional free economic zones in Iran, and setting up a joint cross-border free zone in a third country.

Another controversy involving the agreements revolves around security and military cooperation between the two countries. China and Iran plan to hold regular meetings of the joint commission on cooperation in national defense industries and to conduct regular military–industry dialogue. Their goal is to expand educational and research cooperation between the two militaries in defense and security areas, and to exchange expertise in the fields of asymmetric warfare, counterterrorism, and transnational crimes.[16] In fact, deployment of any military forces in either country has not been mentioned in Sino–Iranian strategic agreement.

The wave of negative propaganda against the Iran–China agreement has intensified since its formal announcement. Some Iranians living abroad, the

Persian-language expatriate media, and even a few former senior officials—sometimes without the slightest knowledge of the actual provisions of the agreement—have sought to create pessimism about the agreement and have attacked its "confidentiality."[17] The Chinese media has also expressed pessimism about the agreement, arguing that China may be trapped into the US–Iran security confrontation.[18]

Also the Iranian government spokesman's explanation that the terms of the agreement were kept secret at China's request also served as an excuse to make the Chinese side appear as the party dictating its terms.[19] Some in social media platforms point out that the agreement was so colonial and had allowed China dominate Iran that many Iranians say it has "sold Iran to China."[20] However, when reactions peaked about the details not being officially published, the head of Iran's Strategic Council on Foreign Relations, Kamal Kharazi, stated that the agreement is only a roadmap to guide cooperation between the two countries in various fields over the coming years.[21]

As explained by the Iranian Ministry of Foreign Affairs, the document only contains outlines of long-term cooperation between the two countries.[22] There are other countries that have signed similar documents with China and did not reveal their contents, as they often relate to national security. Of course, when an agreement is concluded between two countries that has strategic dimensions, parliamentary approval is usually required before the agreement can go into effect.[23] Much of the accusations about the agreement that are made in the Persian and English media, therefore, are by and large the Western "media war" against Sino-Iranian cooperation.

Reza Nasri, an international lawyer based in Iran, explains the confidentiality of international agreements:

- In any international, bilateral agreements, any action needs to be taken with the consent of both parties.
- Not publishing the text of major strategic agreements—at least until there are tangible results—is a common practice in diplomacy. Sensitivity to the "confidentiality of the text until the result" is by no means limited to the Chinese government. For example, negotiations on the Transatlantic Trade and Investment Partnership (TTIP) between the United States and the European Union took place from the 1990s to 2018 without their content being made public.
- Publishing the full text of such a strategic and large-scale agreement is not in the interest of either country. In fact, rivals—especially the United States—should be kept in the dark about the depth and scope of the cooperation between Iran and China, which in essence strengthens Iran's hands in any future negotiations with the United States.[24]

The United States serve as stimulus for China–Iran solidarity. The experience of both Iran and China in recent years has shown that the more obvious the details of a project to the US government, the more successful it will be in sabotaging and preventing that project from being implemented. While public skepticism in Iran toward the agreement is understandable, especially given some of the government's misguided policies over the last forty years, in this case the government has indeed acted in accordance with the principles of bilateral agreements, confidentiality, negotiation strategy, and its own security interests. The Iranian Foreign Ministry, in fact, has tried to allay some of the public's concerns by publishing the agreement's overall framework.[25]

It should not be forgotten that in 2020, when the Iranian government signed and published the Convention of the Legal Status of the Caspian Sea, a number of media outlets accused the government of selling it and claimed that Iran's current share of oil deposits has declined from 50 percent in 1992 to around 11 percent.[26] The public's distrust toward international treaties is often fanned on multiple fronts. Domestic factional rivalry only adds fuel to international, mainly Western, narratives casting Iran in a negative light.[27]

Dynamics of the Sino–Iranian Strategic Agreement

China and Iran underscore that the updated Sino–Iranian cooperation is the outcome of their respective needs in the changing international system, and it is not targeted against any specific parties. The US disengagement from Afghanistan, the conglomeration of Turkic-speaking countries, the rise of ISIS and its affiliates, and the expansion of SCO have all combined to foster deeper interstate cooperation in Eurasia.[28] The United States has a tendency to rely on international sanctions as a strategy to put a stop on Iran's nuclear developments, but this has not always sat easy with China due to its deep partnerships with Iran. The two countries have been long-lasting partners throughout history, and in recent years China has been Iran's number one trading partner. While most of these types of cooperation comes from China's energy needs and Iran's resources, the two countries have also had nonenergy economic and defense collaborations in order to form a geostrategic balancing against the United States.

The Iran–China strategic agreement will bring China closer to the Western Asian markets, further deepening American apprehensions about Chinese economic power and global reach. It will also better enable Iran to better withstand US-led economic sanctions. The White House is worried that the relationship between its principal global rival on the one hand and its long-term antagonist in the Middle East on the other will undermine its efforts to further isolate Iran globally.

According to the *Wall Street Journal*, State Department officials believe that even if such an agreement were signed between Tehran and Beijing, Chinese private companies might not dare to enter Iran for fear of US sanctions, and billions of dollars would be lost.[29] They will jeopardize their capital and economic opportunities in other parts of the world. There are many reasons that makes this accord difficult to implement. Many private companies backed by the Chinese government, especially in the energy sector, are unable to withstand the US sanctions that will be imposed once they enter the Iranian market. In addition, Iran's economy is marked by high levels of corruption, and much of it is controlled by the Revolutionary Guards, which the United States considers to be a "foreign terrorist organization." These two factors make the profitability of investment in Iran far from certain.[30]

The answer to whether China will risk its relations by getting into this agreement lies in not only US–China relations, but also the geostrategic picture of Eurasia. It does not seem likely that a twenty-five-year deal with Iran, and assistance to a government that has one of the most hostile relations with the United States, bears any resemblance to cross-cutting conflicts. This is perhaps the biggest challenge to US power at the international level by China since the 1975 Vietnam War. Such a challenge has not been seen by any country since the end of the Cold War and the collapse of the Soviet Union. The implementation of this agreement under current circumstances means that China seeks to establish a government that is openly involved with the United States on several fronts, and considers this conflict a strategic goal. If this assumption is correct, it can be assumed that the Chinese government has prepared itself for a potentially tense period with the United States.

But another hypothesis could be that China and the United States, despite competition, are highly interdependent and that it does not make sense for them to enter a period of tension, even if the policy of "competition and cooperation" continues. Presidents Biden and Xi met virtually on November 15, 2021. As for cooperation, President Biden underscored the importance of managing strategic risks. On the one hand, he raised specific transnational challenges, such as health security, the climate crisis, global energy supplies, North Korea, Afghanistan, and Iran.[31] After Canada and Mexico, China is the third largest importer of goods and services from the United States. On the other hand, China is the largest exporter of goods and services (excluding the European Union) to the United States, which ranks fourth (after South Korea, Japan, and Taiwan) in terms of exports to China. In addition, the United States owes China more than $1 trillion, making China its second-largest creditor after Japan. Given this level and volume of entanglement and interdependence between the two countries, China's entry into a serious confrontation with the United States seems unlikely.

In recent years, trade with Iran has not been a priority for China. China invested less than $27 billion in Iran from 2005 to 2019, and its annual investment in the Islamic Republic has dropped every year since 2016. In 2019, China only invested $1.54 billion in Iran, which is much less than the amount invested in United Arab Emirates at $3.72 billion and Saudi Arabia at $5.36 billion.[32] For the most part, China has abided by the US sanctions.

If China does not intend to confront the United States, the following hypotheses might answer why it would sign such an agreement with Iran. First, China's long-term goal is to include Iran as a pivotal partner in the BRI project, and to activate the twenty-five-year agreement as soon as broad cooperation is possible. Therefore merely signing the agreement will not result in US sanctions. Second, China's short-term and political goal could be to give the Iranian leadership the confidence it needs to stand up to the US and to force it to revive the Joint Comprehensive Plan of Action (JCPOA) agreement. China insists on reviving this deal because continued US sanctions have made it difficult for China to cooperate with Iran. However, logically, the agreement should not be expected to be implemented until after US sanctions are lifted.

Third, China seeks profitable trade on the one hand and access to Iranian energy resources on the other. The inexhaustible dispute between Iran and the United States has given China a golden opportunity to take advantage of its investments for many years to come and to gain access to cheap, highly discounted Iranian oil. Naturally, this will be done cautiously by China because any long-term investments, given their experience of the Donald Trump era, could suddenly come to a sudden stop. Finally, after United States pulled out most of its forces from the Middle East, China and Iran are confronted with an uncertain Afghanistan and a volatile West Asia. They therefore need to consolidate their cooperation in Central Asia as well.

Mixed Iranian Responses to and Expectations of the Strategic Agreement

While the strategic agreement can be seen as an alternative for Iran, which is seeking a way to face the sanctions imposed by the, it is worth mentioning that President Xi's visit to Iran in 2016 was a year after the world powers and the United States came to an agreement with Iran, the JCPOA, from which the Trump administration unilaterally withdrew in 2018. This indicates Iran's pessimism concerning the nuclear deal, and an attempt to move its "Look East" approach to the next level. In place since the beginning of Mahmoud Ahmadinejad's presidency in 2005, according to this policy Iran should rely more on establishing good relations with the countries of the "Global East" in order to enhance its international position. The "Look East" approach is a response to this lack of goodwill toward Iran from the West. Also, it is a way to protect Iran's national interests in facing the Western sanctions,[33] which acquired added urgency after the US withdrawal from the nuclear deal.

The decision to enter into a unilateral strategic agreement with China was made by the supreme leader of Iran, Ali Khamenei. Iran is frustrated by the successful implementation of the US government sanctions and the inability to sell oil, lack of success in attracting foreign investments, the challenge of degrading oil and gas facilities, the risk of losing market share, project financing constraints, and barriers to banking transactions. Therefore, Iran sees China as a major "quasi-ally" against the West and its sanctions. But of course this approach for Iran is not only about getting out of a difficult predicament. The Principlists (conservative) faction believes that Iran can rely on China to build an effective defense against the United States and neutralize external pressures. Reformists, however, assume that the agreement with China will force the United States to interact with Iran because of the failure of the sanctions policy, and, as a result, through expanding agreements with Europe, there will be a balance in foreign trade and economic relations. In the meantime, some experts have a pessimistic view of the agreement, believing that if such an agreement is signed with China, there will be no space and projects left for other countries, and Iran will practically become dependent on China.[34]

Overall, there are three main perspectives in Iran regarding the agreement with China. First are those who believe that this marks a new chapter in Iran's strategic relationship with a great power like China. They think China sees Iran as a strategic ally in an extremely optimistic way. A second group fears the agreement, arguing that "the allegedly extensive concessions given by Tehran to Beijing might turn Iran into a Chinese colony."[35] Many in this group mention historical examples of how Iran has suffered in its relations with the great powers throughout its contemporary history. They maintain that the agreement with China is reminiscent of Turkmanchay, Golestan, Reuters, and Talbot treaties, all of which are examples of the country's subservience to the great powers of the time. This largely pro-Western group believes that the "unholy alliance" between Iran and China cannot serve the interests of the Iranian nation due to the deteriorating human rights situation and the lack of democracy in China. In their view, China is more dangerous in its colonial and imperial aspirations than Western powers. They see the agreement as the beginning of China's influence in Iran and Iran's loss of political independence. However, this group does not provide any evidence for this claim and only makes predictions regarding China's future behavior toward Iran.

The third and last group has more moderate and realistic views, arguing that this agreement cannot be considered as a beginning of a new era for China–Iran relations. At the same time, however, its importance cannot be undermined. This groups believes that strategies and agreements are not important; what matters is their implementation. While China can be a major partner, Iran must not forget their previous relations with China. The two countries had warm relations and both took part in a joint naval exercise in 2019 with Russia in the northern Indian Ocean.[36]

The Changing Balance of Power in the Gulf and China's Role

Apart from the United States, Israel is also closely watching the strategic agreement between Beijing and Tehran. Israeli observers have often expressed anxiety about the agreement.[37] Carice Witt, founder and executive director of SIGNAL (Sino–Israel Global Network and Academic Leadership) stated that the impact of the agreement for Israel is clear, and when the military reinforcement of Iran is in the hands of another country, this danger becomes even more ominous. She claims that the Chinese government does not think Iran is a threat to Israel, and Beijing believes that Iran is not really seeking Israel's destruction.[38]

Amos Yadlin, former head of the Israeli military intelligence service, maintains that Tel Aviv is concerned about the China–Iran agreement. He expressed his concern about joint military exercises between the two countries, as well as joint research and development and intelligence sharing. Yadlin claims that while China opposes Iran having nuclear weapons, it has done nothing to stop this. Iran also needs political protection, through which China can ease some of the US pressure on Iran. He concludes by claiming that the Chinese government, realizing the differences between the Biden and Trump administrations, may be much more "aggressive" than before.[39]

Another issue about this agreement is the regional challenges. In the plan, Tehran officials have paid close attention to shaping Iran's East–West communication route. With Chinese help, Iran can find a prominent position in meeting Indian–Pakistani and Syrian–Iraqi fossil fuels and electricity needs. But creating this special advantage, which enhances Iran's geopolitical position, is not what the regional competitors such as Saudi Arabia would favor.[40]

Iran's shift toward China is part of a broader, structural movement throughout the Middle East. Tehran's allies now see declining US interest in the region as an opportunity to confront sanctions and to strengthen Beijing. China was even able to somehow gain the trust of traditional US allies such as Saudi Arabia, the United Arab Emirates, Egypt, and Jordan through launching joint projects and weapons sales.[41] It does not appear that China will agree to make Iran the prominent power in the region, or to strengthen Iran against other regional rivals. China's presence in the Persian Gulf and the Indian Ocean seems attractive to Iran from a defense and strategic perspective. But China tends to advance it in a balanced manner between Iran and its other regional partners. Whether this can be achieved, some analysts believe, would be doubtful.[42]

China has pursued a diversified energy security strategy throughout the years, importing crude oil from a range of Middle Eastern, African, Latin American, and Central Asian countries. This indicates that even if after the twenty-five-year agreement, and even if China's share of oil imports from Iran rises, it will still continue its partnership with other energy suppliers and will not rely only on Iran. China's policy has been to keep a low diplomatic profile in the Middle East and not to take strong positions on issues such as the Israel and Palestine conflict or the Syrian civil war so that its regional commitments can remain balanced.

Since most of China's crude oil imports come from the Middle East, Beijing would like to see stability in the region. Beijing is therefore likely to oppose any action that would threaten regional stability and lead to an arms race.[43] China has similar strategic and cooperative agreements with the other countries in the Middle East, including Iraq, Saudi Arabia, and the United Arab Emirates, Iran's immediate neighbors. It also has such agreements with Russia, India, Egypt, Pakistan, Ireland, Qatar, and others. In 2023, China also established strategic partnerships with Palestine and Syria. In short, the Sino–Iranian agreement aims to align China–Iran relations with the rest of the Middle East and with China's international outreach efforts.[44]

China's relations with Iran are primarily formed by its economic interests and its expanding energy needs in particular, and this agreement secures Chinese oil supplies for years to come. The agreement is similar to the twenty-year strategic agreement between China and Iraq, signed in 2019. China's investment in Iran is not only profitable for China in terms of energy security, but will also lead to a solid relationship with a supplier that is not intimidated by the United States, nor will it cut its oil exports to China in case of any conflict between China and the West.[45]

Iran–Saudi Reconciliation and China–Iran Cooperation

The strategic agreement between China and Iran is just the first step. Beijing's second goal is to facilitate Iran–Saudi reconciliation in order to dilute the US-led anti-Iranian coalition. Since about 2021, Iran and Saudi Arabia have been negotiating with the mediation of Baghdad. With the Baghdad track seemingly deadlocked, Wang, known as the engineer of China's foreign policy during Xi's presidency, negotiated a landmark reconciliation agreement between Iran and China in March 2023, ending seven years of hostility.

China has a large presence in the region, focusing on commerce and economy, and has multiplied since the introduction of the Beijing's BRI project meant to reach global markets. Iran is one of the main crossings of the Land Silk Road that stretches from Central Asia to Europe, but the Arabian ports in the Red Sea are an important passage of the Maritime Silk Road that reaches the European ports in the Mediterranean Sea. This economic presence requires proactive diplomacy through which Beijing can demonstrate its capabilities.[46]

China–US competition is reflected in the Middle East; the rise of Turkey, Saudi Arabia, Iran, and Egypt has fostered multipolarity. China is unhappy with US decision to withdraw from the JCPOA, and top Chinese diplomats have frequently expressed their support for Iran and its position. According to the Chinese Foreign Minister Wang, the root cause of the US–Iran problem is US hegemonism; to solve the problem, the United States must honor its commitment to the Iranian people by unconditionally rejoining the JCPOA, so as to win the trust of the Iranian people and to speed up US–Iranian negotiations. China is even more irritated with US hegemonism and abuse of economic sanctions. Meng Wanzhou, daughter of Huawei's founder, was accused of breaking American sanctions on Iran. She was arrested in Vancouver in 2018 and was detained until 2021. China harshly criticized the United States for its long-arm sanctions against Huawei and oil companies that had business with Iran.

The balance of power in the Middle Eastern is changing dramatically in the new era. The US disengagement from Afghanistan and Iraq, and its pivot to the Indo–Pacific region, may prompt China to play a bigger political role in regional issues in the Middle East. China seizes the opportunity to promote Iran–Saudi reconciliation, and has sought to undermine the US-led anti-Iranian coalition. With US military disengagement from Afghanistan and Iraq, and with China's political engagement in the region, Iran, Saudi Arabia, the United Arab Emirates, Egypt, and Turkey are looking East and are embracing the SCO. The Iran and Saudi Arabia agreement has paved the road for peace in Yemen, reduced political tensions in Iraq and Lebanon, facilitated the return of Syria to the Arab countries, lessened military tensions in the Persian Gulf, and fostered the restoration of JCPOA talks. The China–Iran strategic agreement, together with updated China–Arab strategic partnership and the SCO's expansion westward, will reshape the Persian Gulf's security architecture. The "Global East" consisting of China, Iran, Russia, Central Asian countries, and others is looming in Eurasia.

NOTES

1. Wu Xinbo, "Baideng zhizheng yu zhongmei guanxi zouxiang" [The Biden administration and the prospect of Sino-US strategic rivalry], *Guoji wenti yanjiu*, no. 2 (2021): 34–35.

2. NetEase, "2020 shijie geguo GDP paiming" [The world GDP ranking in 2020], https://bit.ly/3u44QUN.

3. "2025 zhongguo GDP jiangdadao 20wanyi meiyuanma" [Will China's GDP reach $20 trillion by 2025?], 2019, https://bit.ly/3FPl72t. In 2022, the US GDP growth rate exceeded China's, the first time in the past four decades.

4. Liu Aming, "Sifang anquan duihua de xinfazhan ji qianjing fenxi" [The new development of QUAD and the its prospects], *Guoji zhanwang*, no, 1 (2021): 88–89. The Five Eyes Alliance is a cooperative intelligence network of anglophone countries, including the United States, the United Kingdom, Canada, Australia, and New Zealand.

5. Alam Saleh and Zakiyeh Yazdanshenas, "China-Iran Strategic Partnership and the Future of US Hegemony in the Persian Gulf Region," *British Journal of Middle Eastern Studies* 51 (2023): 3.

6. Ranjineh Khojasteh, "'Yek Kamarband, Yek Jaadeh' megaa-porozhe-ye tose'e-ye eghtesaadi e Cheen: Ahdaaf va chaalesh-haaye peesh e roo" ["One Belt, One Road": China's economic development mega project goals and challenges ahead], IRIB News Agency, 2019, https://bit.ly/49roVof.

7. See Tim Niblock, Alejandra Galindo, and Degang Sun, eds., *The Arab States of the Gulf and BRICS: New Strategic Partnerships in Politics and Economics* (Gerlach Press, 2016).

8. "China and Iran Flesh Out Strategic Partnership," *Petroleum Economist*, September 3, 2019, https://bit.ly/3FNFEoc.

9. "Revaayat e National Review Az Raahbord e Jadeed e Iraan va Cheen Baraye Moghaabeleh Ba Amreeca" [National Review's narration of the new strategy of Iran and China to confront the United States], Alef News Agency, July 17, 2020, https://bit.ly/3FOeQE0.

10. Lucille Greer and Esfandyar Batmanghelidj, "China and Iran Announced a New Economic and Security Partnership: That's Not as Alarming as It Sounds," *Washington Post*, April 1, 2021, https://bit.ly/3MxugjM.

11. Zahra Mirzafarjouyan, "Zarif Rejects Rumors over Sale of Kish Island to China: MP," Mehr News Agency, July 12, 2020, https://bit.ly/3sptizl.

12. "Full Text of Joint Statement on Comprehensive Strategic Partnership Between I.R. Iran, P.R. China," Official Website of the President of the Islamic Republic of Iran, January 1, 2016, https://bit.ly/3SobQG4.

13. "Zhongguo yilang zuixin xieyi, dui zhongguo yiweizhe shenme?" [The China-Iran new agreement: What's its implication to China?], Pengpai xinwen, April 1, 2021, https://bit.ly/3MAsXkb.

14. "The Iran-China 25 Year Comprehensive Strategic Partnership: Challenges and Prospects," Rasanah International Institute for Iranian Studies, April 2, 2021, 3, https://bit.ly/45ZMAcj.

15. Greer and Batmanghelidj, "China and Iran Announced a New Economic and Security Partnership."

16. "Full Text of Joint Statement."

17. See Yashir Rashid, "The Latest Status of the 25-Year Comprehensive Cooperation Agreement Between Iran and China," Center for Iranian Studies, April 22, 2022, https://bit.ly/47gUXkP.

18. See Fan Hongda, "Ruhe lijie zhongguo yiyang quanmian hezuo?" [How to understand China-Iran comprehensive cooperation?], Guanchazhe, April 20, 2021, https://bit.ly/3Srobt2.

19. Shireen Hunter, "The Iran-China Agreement: Inconsequential or a Game Changer?" Responsible Statecraft, April 5, 2021, https://bit.ly/3Sus2ph. See also "Iran Government Squeezed over 'Secretive' Deal with China," Al-Monitor, July 10, 2020, https://bit.ly/3QnhHZH.

20. Ghazal Vaisi, "The 25-Year Iran-China Agreement, Endangering 2,500 Years of Heritage," Middle East Institute, March 1, 2022, https://bit.ly/3QppDtd.

21. "Iran-China Cooperation Document, a Guiding Roadmap," Iran Press News Agency, March 31, 2021, https://bit.ly/3QnUHtv.

22. "Statement on 'Document of Comprehensive Cooperation Between Iran and China,'" Iran Watch, March 27, 2021, https://bit.ly/3slRO4p.

23. "Sanad e jame'e hamkaari ha ye 25 saale e Iran va Chin che ta'siri bar ayande e eghtesaad e Iraan khaahad daasht? Vaakonesh ha ye motefaavet be sanad e hamkaari e 25 saaleh" [What impact will the comprehensive document on 25 years of Iran-China cooperation have on the future of the Iranian economy? Different reactions to the 25-year cooperation document], *Shargh Daily*, April 3, 2021, https://bit.ly/3QJDaNM.

24. Reza Nasri, "Vaaghe'iat haa dar mored e mahraamaane boodan e gharaardaade 25 saale e Iran va Chin" [Facts about the confidentiality of the 25-year Iran-China agreement], Khabar Online News, April 1, 2021, https://bit.ly/3StVQlP.

25. Nasri, "Vaaghe'iat haa dar mored."

26. "Russia Demands Iran Ratify Caspian Sea Legal Convention," Iran International, April 8, 2021, https://bit.ly/3MTn4ir.

27. Nasri, "Vaaghe'iat haa dar mored."

28. On November 12, 2021, Turkey succeeded in reforming the "Cooperation Council of Turkic Speaking States" into the "Organization of Turkic States." The members of this organization are Azerbaijan, Kazakhstan, Kyrgyzstan, Turkey, and Uzbekistan. In addition, Hungary and Turkmenistan have observer status. See "Erdoğan Creates 'Organization of Turkic States,'" Voltaire Network, November 17, 2021, https://bit.ly/40ohLgk.

29. "The Iran-China Axis," *Wall Street Journal*, July 17, 2020, https://bit.ly/40oJ1Lu.

30. "Iran Ranks Among Most Corrupt Countries in the World," Iran International, January 28, 2022, https://bit.ly/46UHeAm.

31. The White House, "Readout of President Biden's Virtual Meeting with President Xi Jinping of the People's Republic of China," November 16, 2021, https://bit.ly/3FMeBcH.

32. Salman Parviz, "Foreign Media Reactions on Sino-Iran Partnership," *Tehran Times*, August 5, 2020, https://bit.ly/49lR145.

33. "Ravaabet e Iraan va Cheen; Forsathaaye tafaahom naameye 25 saaleh" [Iran-China relations; 25-year memorandum opportunities], Fars News Agency, April 3, 2020, https://bit.ly/3QJsSgD.

34. Ali Afshari, "Tavafegh azhodehya ve shir, ya bazi chin ba kart iran dar barabaraghab" [Agreement between the lion and the dragon, or China playing against the eagle using Iran's cards], Radio Farda News, July 20, 2020, https://bit.ly/47igny6.

35. Hunter, "Iran-China Agreement."

36. "Iran, China Sign Strategic Long-Term Cooperation Agreement," Politico, March 27, 2021, https://bit.ly/3QudF1F.

37. Ofira Seliktar and Farhad Rezaei, "The Iran-China 25-Year Plan: A Preliminary Assessment," BESA Center Perspectives paper no. 1,653, July 21, 2020, https://besacenter.org/wp-content/uploads/2020/07/1653-China-Iran-25-Year-Plan-Seliktar-Rezaei-final.pdf.

38. Sepideh Ahadpoor, "Baaztaab e hamkaari e 25 saaleh Iran va Cheen [Reflection of 25 years of Iran-China cooperation: A document that shakes the US and the Zionist regime], Young Journalists Club News Agency, July 17, 2020, https://bit.ly/3QL1LBP.

39. "Ebraaz e negaraani e Esraeel az tavaafogh e Iraan va Cheen" [Israel expresses concern over Iran-China agreement], Tabnak News Agency, March 29, 2021, https://bit.ly/3FMGu4k.

40. Afshari, "Tavaafogh e ezhdehaa va sheer."

41. "Revaayat e National Review az raahbord e jadid e Iran va Cheen baraaye moghaabele ba Amreeca" [National Review's narration of the new Iran-China Strategy to confront the United States], Alef Analytical News Community, July 17, 2020, https://bit.ly/3QNsu0o.

42. Afshari, "Tavaafogh e ezhdehaa va sheer."

43. Joel Wuthnow, "Posing Problems Without an Alliance: China-Iran Relations After the Nuclear Deal," *Strategic Forum*, February 2016, https://bit.ly/40p6qfU.

44. William Figueroa, "China-Iran Relations: The Myth of Massive Investment," *Diplomat*, April 7, 2021, https://bit.ly/49pRylK.

45. See Scott W. Harold and Alireza Nader, *China and Iran: Economic, Political, and Military Relations* (RAND Corporation, 2012).

46. Iliya Jazayeri, "Posht e parde tavaafogh e Iraan va Arabestaan baa miaanjigari e Cheen" [Behind the scenes of the agreement between Iran and Saudi Arabia with the mediation of China], Radio Farda News, April 28, 2023, https://bit.ly/3tWbU5A.

8

CHINA'S RESPONSE TO IRAN'S LOOK EAST POLICY

An Explanation of the Partner–Community Framework

Jianwei Han

This chapter uses the partner-community framework to analyze China's cognition and response to Iran's Look East policy. It aims to understand the relationship between China and Iran from China's foreign policy perspective, especially beyond the theory of alliances. "Partner" and "community" are the two critical concepts in China's diplomacy. *Partner* is taken to mean friend or collaborator, and nonalignment without targeting a third party. Building a *community* with a shared future is regarded as the highest goal of Chinese diplomacy. The idea of the community reflects the ideals of China's diplomacy to engage in "peaceful communication" with other states. Partnership is one of the primary ways of realizing this community. China believes that Iran's Look East policy is the result of the sanctions and unfair treatment by the West, in turn prompting China to treat Iran as an equal partner. In the Chinese view, Iran's policy is conducive to safeguarding Chinese interests while at the same time building a neighborhood community order. In addition, China hopes that an Eastward-looking Iran would be a responsible power in ensuring regional peace. China has also brought Iran's rival, Saudi Arabia, into the partner–community framework and brokered the reconciliation between the two countries.

In recent years, the regional order in the Middle East has undergone a profound transformation, an important manifestation of which is an Eastward shift in the foreign policies of a number of Middle Eastern countries. Especially the middle powers of the Middle East—such as Iran, Saudi Arabia, the United Arab Emirates, and Egypt—are seeking to establish closer strategic partnerships with

China and other Asian countries. Among these countries, Iran has a more prominent Look East policy and is more active in developing its relations with China, India, and Central Asian countries, while at the same time becoming increasingly distant from countries in the West.

The significant transformation of Iran's foreign policy occurred especially in 2018, as the Donald Trump administration unilaterally withdrew from Joint Comprehensive Plan of Action (JCPOA) and launched "extreme sanctions" against Iran. As the main target country in Iran's Look East policy, China has responded to Iran positively. For its part, China itself has been playing a critical role in pulling Iran's foreign policy more Eastward. China–Iran relations are, as a result, entering a new era of strengthened cooperation.

There have been many debates on the relationship between China and Iran—for instance, whether the relationship between China and Iran is an alliance. If it is not an alliance, how should this strategic partnership be positioned and described appropriately? This chapter argues that the alliance theory cannot explain the close relationship between China and Iran; it is more appropriate to understand the nature of this relationship from the China's perspective. The chapter maintains that the partner–community framework is the primary logic and concept underlying China's diplomacy. China's cognition of and response to Iran's Look East policy is based on the partner–community philosophy and is meant to serve the common interests of both China and Iran.

Alliance Theory and Chinese–Iranian Relations

Alliance theory has a strong influence on Western international relations and is one of the representative viewpoints of the realism school. Alliance diplomacy has had a profound impact on the foreign policies of Western countries. Still, it remains an important means by which Western countries have sought to maintain their dominant position in the world. The general outlines of the view hold that an alliance is a military and security bloc formed in response to external threats, with formal covenants and mutual offensive and defensive assistance agreements. These agreements support multilateral organizations, as well as collective security arrangements. Additionally, because of the military and security nature of these alliance, they are also different from international organizations mainly engaged in economic, social, and cultural affairs. In fact, alliance as a military compact is accepted by most of the principal students of international politics, such as Hans Morgenthau, Ernst B. Haas, Inis L. Claude, Arnold Wolfers, Robert E. Osgood, Robert Kaplan, Dean Acheson, William T. R. Fox, and Stanley Hoffmann.[1]

However, in reality there are a number of different types of alliances, and a completely unified concept of alliance is difficult to form. Even Stephen M. Walt, one of the main contributors to alliance theory, admitted that it is not easy to define and measure with precision.[2] The differences in alliance reflect the complexity of state-to-state relations in the real world. Especially after the end of the Cold War, there have been many new changes in the alliance between countries, new variations on the alliance theme, such as the "quasi-" or "virtual" alliance, for example, have appeared.[3] These new concepts show that many countries tend to give up traditional forms of alliance in order to achieve diplomatic goals, and adopt a fluid, vague, and reasonable way to form a "temporary alliance" or "quasi-alliance."

Although alliances have become more diverse in today's world, the reasons for them are broadly similar from the past to the present. They mainly emerge because of the existence of an enemy, and a country needs to ally with one or more countries to jointly counter the threat of that enemy. There were also debates on the specific cause of the alliance's origin within the realist school. In one of his most famous views, Morgenthau argued that alliance was a meaningful way to achieve a "balance of power." "Nation A and B, competing with each other, each country can choose a policy of alliances to maintain and improve their relative power situations."[4] Walt challenged the "balance of power" theory, however, arguing that alliances originate primarily from "balance of threat." "Although power is an important part of the equation, it is not the only one. It is more accurate to say that states tend to ally with or against the foreign power that poses the greatest threat."[5] In reality, there is no significant gap between the theory of "balance of power" and "balance of threat." Walt just expanded the scope of the explanation of the origins of the alliance, making it possible to explain both the behavior of weak countries to check the most powerful countries and the behavior of a country to balance the less powerful but threatening countries. What both views have in common is the emphasis on the nature of the alliance against a common external threat.

The impact of alliance policy on Western countries is not only noticeable but profound. So far, the United States remains the world's most adroit state at adopting alliance strategy. After the end of the Cold War, even though the Soviet Union had disappeared, the United States did not give up the alliance strategy, and it continues to use this system in response to the emergence of what it considers to be significant threats on a global scale. After the 9/11 terrorist attacks, the United States used its robust alliance system to launch successive wars in Afghanistan and Iraq, and a long-term battle against real or imagined terrorist organizations all over the world ensued. However, when Trump was elected to the American presidency, he pursued isolationism and abandoned the alliance strategy in foreign policy, which at once plunged the United States' alliance diplomacy into crisis. When Joe Biden entered the White House, the United States quickly resumed its alliance strategy, strengthening cooperation with allies such as European countries, Japan, and South Korea, at the same time intensifying its competition with Russia and China.[6]

The US adherence to the alliance strategy does not mean that alliance confrontation is still the dominant form of international relations. The main rivals of the United States, such as Iran, China, and Russia, have yet to form such an alliance in the way that it does. The three countries indeed need to draw closer to each other in order to counterbalance the United States. Still, the reality is that China firmly pursues a policy of nonalignment, and Iran claims that its policy is "neighborhood and balanced."[7] Russia, for its part, especially after the outbreak of the Ukraine war in February 2022, remains alone against Ukraine and the West as a whole.

Some scholars have expressed their views on the relations between China, Iran, and Russia from the perspective of alliance. Suren Sargsyan, for example, believes that "the possibility of Russia, Iran and China creating a new informal alliance is that this scenario is possible."[8] However, Nicole Grajewski argues that China is not in an alliance with Iran and Russia from the perspective of alliance institutionalization. "The tendency to conceive Iran, Russia and China as a cohesive bloc obscures the absence of institutionalised structures characteristic of alliances or formal alignments."[9] Other similar analyses have recognized that China and Iran (and also Russia) are not allies in the same way as the United States and European countries are. Still, the analyses lack a more precise definition for the close relationship that exists between China, Iran, and Russia.

Taking the relationship between China and Iran as an example, Iran's Look East policy has elicited a positive response from China, with the two countries strengthening cooperation at an open and multilateral level that goes beyond a relatively narrow alliance relationship. The two countries have benefited from a partnership that is better than simply being allies. In March 2023, under the mediation of China, Iran, and Saudi Arabia achieved a historic handshake and resumed diplomatic relations. China has not only maintained a close relationship with Iran, but has also facilitated the Saudi–Iran dialogue, breaking the logic of the alliance theory that the enemy of a friend is an enemy, and instead evolving it into the logic that the enemy of a friend can be a friend. In order to understand China's cognition and response toward Iran's Look East policy, it is necessary to start with an essential concept that Chinese diplomacy employs, namely the partner–community.

The Partner–Community Framework in Chinese Foreign Policy

Partner–community diplomacy, the integration of partner diplomacy and community diplomacy, is a general description of the philosophy of China's foreign policy. In 1982, at the 12th National Congress of the Communist Party of China, China declared that it would pursue an independent and peaceful foreign policy and develop its relations with other countries following the Five Principles of Peaceful Coexistence.[10] Over the decades since, China has further strengthened and consolidated its nonalignment diplomacy. Some scholars have defined this as "balanced diplomacy."[11] Balanced diplomacy is mainly based on the analysis of interests from the prism of realism, and its core point of view is that diplomacy based on balance can more effectively safeguard China's interests. However, balanced diplomacy usually fails to explain the principle of combining pragmatism and ethics in China's diplomacy. That is, China's diplomacy strives to consider the common interests of its own and other countries, and at the same time seeks to maximize the interests of both sides.

This chapter argues that Chinese diplomacy relies on a framework based on partnership and is aimed at building a community world order. Building partnership is the principal means of building a community order in the end. Partner diplomacy is also referred to as realistic idealism diplomacy.[12] After the end of the Cold War, China began to build partnerships with certain countries. Since President Xi Jinping took office, he has actively promoted the development of global partnership networks. "We should make more friends and form a global network of partnerships while adhering to the principle of nonalignment," he said in 2021.[13] By October 2020, China had already established 112 partnerships all over the world.[14]

The essential features of the partnerships in China's diplomacy are as follows:

1. *Openness*. The partnership can be established with all countries, without being exclusive or forming a closed bloc against any third country.
2. *Inclusiveness*. The partnership does not emphasize differences in political systems and ideologies, but joint development and strengthening cooperation.
3. *Flexibility*. Partnerships can be established at different levels on the basis of respecting each other's intentions.
4. *Equality*. The status of China and its partners is entirely equal.
5. *Independence*. China respects the complete independence of its partners in domestic and foreign affairs, and promises to respect each other's sovereignty and territorial integrity.

"Community" is mainly a diplomatic idea developed by President Xi. That is, building a community with a shared future for mankind is the primary goal of China's diplomacy. In March 2013, when President Xi visited Russia, he formally presented the concept of "a community of shared future" for the first time in a speech at the Moscow Institute of International Relations. "In this world," he said:

> countries are more interconnected and interdependent than ever before, and human beings live in a global village, living in the same time and space where history and reality meet. The world has formed a community with a shared future in which something of each in the other.[15]

During the past decade of Xi's administration, a community with a shared future has gradually become a core idea of China's diplomacy. The idea of a community with a shared future has its characteristic values and ways of practice. From the perspective of values, a community with a shared future regards the world as interdependent and interconnected, and believes that countries can achieve peaceful coexistence and joint development through cooperation. The idea of a community with a shared future holds that the current de facto inequality and wealth gap between countries is unreasonable. According to President Xi, "It is unsustainable that some countries are getting richer while others are chronically poor and backward."[16] Different countries should work together to deal with common global problems, and rich countries should take more responsibility. In a word, the idea of a community with a shared future holds that all countries in the world are equal members of the international community and that the relationships between countries are based on mutual cooperation on the basis of parity.

The idea of a community with a shared future sounds ideal but has its practical basis driven by common interests. It is especially desirable to those developing countries with urgent demands for peace, stability, and development, which hope to enhance their status in the international arena. The Chinese government regards the concept of a community with a shared future as an achievable goal, with the Belt and Road Initiative (BRI) serving as a critical, practical platform for building a community with a shared future.[17] So far, China has reached agreements with Southeast Asian, Central Asian, and Arab countries on building a regional community with a shared future.

Partner diplomacy and community diplomacy are highly interrelated. Generally, China first establishes a partnership with a country. When the bilateral relationship develops to a certain degree, it will elevate to the level of building a community under the premise of soliciting the will of both sides. The idea of a community with a shared future is based on multiple bilateral communities, regional communities, and multilateral transregional communities. China is also trying to encourage other countries to approve the concept of partner–community diplomacy, so that these countries can form partnerships with each other based on equality and mutual trust without targeting others, thereby gradually forming a community consciousness.

The idea of partner–community is not an idealist fantasy, but is based fully on considerations of China's practical interests. It should be pointed out that China's way of thinking about its interests is a kind of shared thinking. That is, it believes that only by taking into account the common interests of other countries can China obtain its interests too.[18] China's partner–community diplomacy is especially attractive to those countries facing Western pressure and difficulties in development. Iran's Look East policy is a case in point.

However, there have been many criticisms and doubts about China's partner–community diplomacy. For instance, some scholars argue that China's partner diplomacy is pursued unequally, primarily represented by the economic relationship between China and its partner countries.[19] It is seen mainly as a diplomatic tool for exporting Chinese goods. Many people also doubt that the establishment of a comprehensive strategic partnership between China and Iran will endanger the stability of the security order in West Asia. However, it has been proven that their partnership did not worsen the regional security, but rather promoted the easing of the situation in the region and provided some help for the Middle East countries to get out of the security dilemma.[20]

China's Perception of and Response to Iran's Look East Policy

Iran's crisis in its relations with the West is the critical driver of its Look East policy. Especially under the pressure of extreme sanctions imposed by the United States, Iran could not obtain substantial help from European countries and was forced to turn to the East in order to seek economic and diplomatic friends partners.

Before the significant shift in Iran's foreign policy, China had already formed close energy and economic cooperative relations with Iran, as it is a country with strategic importance for China. Iran's position in relation to the Strait of Hormuz is significant to the security of China's energy routes. Iran is also a vital node country for China's BRI in the Middle East. In addition, from the perspective of the great power rivalry, since the Trump administration launched a trade war against China in May 2018, China and the United States have become primary rivals in the world. China urgently needs friends and partners with whom it can compete against the United States. As a result, Iran's Look East policy has attracted significant attention and a positive response from the Chinese government.

First, China believes that Iran's Look East policy is the result of long-term sanctions and unfair treatment by the United States, and also inspired by China's policy of treating Iran as an equal partner. Regarding sanctions, the Chinese government firmly opposes the unilateral sanctions imposed by the United States against Iran. In 2020, China issued an official paper which clearly stated its political position on the Iranian nuclear issue, "Upholding the JCPOA is conducive to upholding multilateralism, safeguarding the international order based on international law, and peace and stability in the Middle East. Countries that have withdrawn from the JCPOA do not have the right to unilaterally activate the Security Council's snapback sanctions mechanism against Iran."[21]

Indeed, China has long been one of the primary beneficiaries of the US sanctions against Iran. Especially before 2010, China's trade with Iran had not been significantly affected by the sanctions, which made many Chinese goods flood into the Iranian market. Meanwhile, China was able to import oil from Iran relatively easily, and many Chinese companies were able to invest in Iran. In 2009, China became Iran's largest trading partner.[22] Mainly because of this, some scholars argue that Iran and China have formed a relationship of "asymmetric interdependence" during the sanction period.[23] Meanwhile, this is often regarded as China filling the "backfill" left by the US sanctions on Iran.[24] However, sanctions have had an increasingly negative impact on China's economic cooperation with Iran since 2018. Since the United States imposed extreme sanctions on Iran, many Chinese enterprises had to withdraw from the Iranian market under the pressure of secondary sanctions. China's trade and investments in Iran have dropped sharply.

Although interest consideration does play a role in China's opposition to sanctions against Iran, China's opposition to unilateral US sanctions is mainly based on the position of morality and justice rather than the consideration of economic interests. China's Foreign Minister Wang Yi has expressed firm opposition to unilateral sanctions. "Any unilateral sanctions violate international law, and sanctions based on lies and false information, in particular, are a provocation to human conscience and lack of morals. China stands ready to work with the Iranian side and the people of other countries to oppose bullying, safeguard international fairness and justice."[25] China once voted in favor of the UN Security Council's decision to impose multilateral sanctions on Iran due to the Islamic Republic's nuclear program. At the same time, however, China has advocated limiting the scope of the sanctions in order to limit their harmful impact to ordinary Iranian people. In 2008, after the UN Security Council passed the fourth resolution on sanctions against Iran, the Chinese representative pointed out that "the relevant sanctions do not target the Iranian people, nor do they affect the normal economic, trade and financial exchanges between countries and Iran. All sanctions are reversible."[26] At the International Atomic Energy Agency (IAEA) Board of Governors meeting in 2011, a Chinese representative declared that dialogue and negotiation were the right ways to properly resolve the Iranian nuclear issue and serve the fundamental interests of all parties.[27] China's opposition to US sanctions against Iran reflects the dissatisfaction with US hegemonic tendencies, and its belief that injustice and bullying still exist in the international order, which is not in line with China's concept of partner–community diplomacy.

China is an essential member of the mechanism of P5+1 (UN Security Council's five permanent members plus Germany) nuclear negotiations and played a constructive role in brokering the JCPOA. After the signing of the JCPOA, China believed that it was time to upgrade its partnership with Iran. In January 2016, President Xi paid a state visit to Iran and upgraded China–Iran relations to a comprehensive strategic partnership. The joint statement establishing the comprehensive strategic partnership between China and Iran showed that China regarded Iran not only as an equal partner, but also as a very critical partner. According to a joint statement that was subsequently issued, "both countries regard each other as an important strategic cooperative partner, and take the development of their relations as a priority of their foreign policies."[28] It also noted that "China appreciates Iran's constructive role in combating terrorism and maintaining regional peace and stability," and pledged to strengthen cooperation in promoting regional peace and stability. This statement is much different from the narrative of the United States and other Western countries that regard Iran as a "threat" and constantly accuse Iran of destabilizing the region, which won Iran's trust and respect for China in response.

China's positive response to Iran's predicament is an important impetus for Iran to look East. In June 2018, the eighteenth meeting of the Council of Heads of State of the Shanghai Cooperation Organization (SCO) was held in Qingdao, China. Iranian President Hassan Rouhani attended the summit mainly for seeking support, and China showed respect and understanding toward Iran at the critical moment. President Xi personally met with Rouhani, expressing strong support for developing the China–Iran comprehensive strategic partnership, as well as the JCPOA, insisting that the two sides continue to strengthen the BRI and all-around cooperation.[29] Xi pointed out that the JCPOA is an important outcome of multilateralism, conducive to safeguarding peace and stability in the Middle East and the international nonproliferation regime, which should continuously be implemented in an earnest manner.[30]

The SCO Qingdao Summit proved to be a significant source of support for Iran and a powerful incentive for it to look East. Since then, more and more

Iranian officials, think tanks, and scholars have visited China for exchanges, and have hoped to continue to enhance bilateral cooperation. With the outbreak of COVID-19 pandemic at the end of 2019, economic and cultural exchanges between China and Iran were greatly affected, but diplomatic relations between the two sides continued improving. In March 2021, China and Iran signed the Twenty-Five-Year Cooperation Agreement, further deepening their long-term and comprehensive strategic partnership.

Second, China believes that Iran's Look East policy is conducive to constructing a new neighborhood order guided by the idea of community. China has established an overall diplomatic blueprint featuring "major countries as the key, neighboring countries as the primary, developing countries as the foundation, and multilateralism as the important stage."[31] In general, China has given top priority to its relations with the United States, followed by its relations with Europe and other developed countries in the past decades. However, since President Xi took office, he has begun to emphasize the importance of neighborhood diplomacy. Xi is committed to building a neighborhood community with a shared future that features amity, sincerity, mutual benefits, and inclusiveness.[32] A neighborhood community with a shared future represents China's vision of the neighborhood with a new order of equality, inclusiveness, and cooperation.

In Chinese traditional conception, the neighborhood region generally refers to the countries bordering China's territory, such as the East Asian, Southeast Asian, South Asian, and Central Asian countries, as well as Mongolia and Russia. However, along with the strengthening of energy, economic, and infrastructure connectivity, the Middle East has gradually entered China's neighbor vision from the far west, thus changing from China's "extension of peripheral zone" to "extended neighbors."[33] China hopes to include the Middle East region in the construction of its greater neighborhood order. Therefore, Iran's Look East policy aligns with China's strategy of navigating the Middle East as a whole. In fact, Iran's attractiveness does not lie in its energy reserves only; its history, geography, and capabilities make it an integral part of China's Middle East strategy.[34]

At the same time, China's increasing emphasis on diplomacy with neighboring countries is being driven by competitive pressures from the United States. To contain the rise of China, the United States proposed the Indo–Pacific strategy, seeking to establish new alliances system in Asia to restrain China's development. The Biden administration reemphasized the importance of alliance coordination and strengthened relations with allies in European and Asian countries, with the primary goal of containing China. In May 2021, the G7 agreed on a new initiative to support global infrastructure investment, with the primary goal being to compete with China's BRI.[35]

Therefore, driven both by internal demand and external pressure, China has shown increasing interest in the Middle East and hopes to promote the establishment of a regional community order based on peace, stability, and joint development. The biggest challenge to building a community order in the Middle East is the precarious and complex security situation in the region. China has been cautious about getting deeply involved in the regional issues in the past several decades. Therefore, China sees Iran's Look East policy as an opportunity to integrate it into a new regional order based on partner–community diplomacy.

An important manifestation of Iran's Look East policy is its active application to join the SCO. During Iran's lengthy application process, China supported Iran to become a full member of the group. Finally, at its twenty-second summit in September 2022, the SCO formally admitted Iran into the organization.[36] The SCO is actually a new type of multilateral regional organization that China is trying to influence and shape with the concept of partner–community diplomacy. Within the organization, all member states are equal, so there is no distinction between weaker or more powerful states. Iran's accession to the SCO as an equal and independent member reflects the new progress of Eurasian regional integration under this framework. After joining the SCO, Iran submitted a new request to join BRICS, an international organization formed by the major emerging economies—China, South Africa, India, Russia, Brazil—on an equal and voluntary basis, with the partnership as a bond and the appeal of joint development. Iran's bid to join BRICS is a further step of its Look East diplomacy. On August 24, 2023, Iran, together with Argentina, Ethiopia, Saudi Arabia, Egypt, and the United Arab Emirates, was invited to become a member, which was achieved through the efforts of the founding members of BRICS, including China.[37]

Moreover, China hopes that with its Look East policy, Iran can become a responsible power and contribute to the realization of regional peace. The ultimate goal of partner–community diplomacy is to build a peaceful and stable order. It calls on all countries to settle disputes in a rational and moderate way, and opposes resorting to war, as well as the proliferation and use of weapons of mass destruction. However, the game between Iran and the United States is essentially a zero-sum confrontation, and long-term American pressure has led to periodic radicalization of Iran's foreign policy. Iran's Look East policy also provides China with such an opportunity to moderate Iran's foreign policy through communication and persuasion.

On the nuclear issue, China acknowledges that it supports Iran's legitimate right to use nuclear energy for peaceful purposes, while urging Iran to maintain cooperation with the IAEA, not to seek nuclear weapons, or to withdraw from the Treaty on the Non-Proliferation of Nuclear Weapons (NPT).[38] After the US unilaterally withdrew from JCPOA, Iran increased its levels of enriched uranium and broke some of the red lines imposed by the JCPOA. From 2021 to 2022, indirect negotiations between Iran and the United States in Vienna did not progress well. Iran chose to take a tough stance in response, continued to enriched uranium at higher levels, and reduced its cooperation with the IAEA. In September 2022, after widespread protests broke out in Iran due to the death of a Kurdish woman named Mahsa Amini, the European Union imposed additional sanctions on the country and even threatened to list the Islamic Revolutionary Guard Corps as a terrorist organization.[39] Internal and external pressures combined to harden the posture of the Iranian government in relation to its nuclear program. In January 2023, Iran's semi-official English-language newspaper, the *Tehran Times*, reported that "Iran is mulling a range of options, including the strategically important possibility of withdrawing from the NPT."[40]

However, during former President Ebrahim Raisi's visit to China in February 2023, the Sino–Iranian joint statement "stressed the importance of disarmament and nuclear nonproliferation to world peace and reaffirmed their respect for the inalienable rights of all states under the Treaty on the Non-Proliferation of Nuclear Weapons (NPT), to develop nuclear science and technology and acquire nuclear material, technology and equipment for peaceful purposes."[41] Following this visit, Iran resumed cooperation with the IAEA and stopped floating the possibility of withdrawing from the NPT, which indicates that there is a subtle link between the Sino–Iranian joint statement and changes in Iran's nuclear policy.

Because of Iran's control of and influence over a number of proxy militias in the Middle East, the United States regards the Islamic Republic as the biggest security threat in the region and considers it to be a state sponsor of terrorism. This is also the main justification used by the United States to impose tough sanctions on Iran. However, China's narrative about Iran presents a different scenario. China not only recognizes Iran's important contribution to regional peace and stability but also wants to strengthen cooperation with Iran in promoting the reduction of tensions and urging Iran to shoulder more responsibilities. "China supports Iran in playing a bigger role in regional and international affairs."[42] In the statement on the establishment of the comprehensive strategic partnership between China and Iran, "Both sides agreed that promoting peace and stability in the region serves the common interests of the international community, and are willing to strengthen communication on regional hotspot issues such as Syria and Yemen, as well as major regional issues such as the establishment of a zone free of weapons of mass destruction in the Middle East, and promote the political settlement of hotspot issues."[43] China has been prompting Iran to make pragmatic and responsible decisions in dealing with external relations. This exemplifies the practice of partner–community diplomacy and is in the interests of both Iran and China.

In 2023, China successfully brokered a rapprochement between Saudi Arabia and Iran, bringing the two rivals into its partner–community framework. The Middle East is widely recognized to be one of the most volatile region in the world, and many countries in the region have been suffering from multiple security dilemmas. Saudi–Iran relations have long been seen as a major issue in the geopolitical rivalry in the Middle East. The contradictions between the two countries are not only due to historical grievances, but also practical factors, such as sectarian conflicts and competition for regional influence, and the intervention of external powers has intensified ongoing tensions. However, despite the long-running feud between them, China has forged reciprocal partnerships with both countries, based mainly on energy and economic cooperation. In January 2016, China established the comprehensive strategic partnership both with Iran and Saudi Arabia, thus reflecting one of the key characteristics of partner–community diplomacy. That is, the improvement of the relationship between China and Saudi Arabia is not targeting Iran, and neither is China's relations with Iran a threat to Saudi Arabia. The philosophy of an open inclusive partnership makes China a potential intermediary to the conflict between Saudi Arabia and Iran.

In addition, China's role in the reconciliation is also closely related to two other factors. First, China's willingness to act as a facilitator for the reconciliation is not only related to Iran's Look East policy, but is also a result of Saudi Arabia's Look East policy as well. Since 2021, Saudi Arabia's diplomacy has taken a more significant turn to look East. By December 2022, China became the largest trading partner of not only Saudi Arabia but of all Arab countries.[44] At the same time, high-level interactions between China and Saudi Arabia have increased with frequent exchanges of views on issues of mutual concern. On December 2022, President Xi paid a state visit to Saudi Arabia, convened the China–Saudi Arabia summit, and issued a joint statement "stressing the need to continue joint efforts in various fields under the framework of the comprehensive strategic partnership between the two countries to deepen relations and bring them to a new and promising realm."[45] The China–Saudi Arabia summit has brought the strategic partnership between China and Saudi Arabia to a new height and laid the foundation for China to mediate the rivalry between Saudi Arabia and Iran.

Second, both Saudi Arabia and Iran have shown a strong desire for reconciliation. After Saudi Arabia broke off diplomatic relations with Iran in 2016, Iran showed a strong willingness to reconcile. However, Saudi Arabia was not keen on improving relations with Iran. Since 2021, affected mainly by the strategic contraction of the United States from the Middle East, Saudi Arabia's willingness to reconcile with Iran increased significantly, and the two sides began to hold secret talks under the mediation of Iraq and Oman. Although there was no substantial progress, the foundation had been laid for a final reconciliation between the two sides. In May 2022, Iran and Saudi Arabia held talks under Iraqi mediation and agreed on a ten-point memorandum of understanding.[46] However, the two countries still preferred a major power to witness their reconciliation, since China had played a coordinating role between the two countries, enabling China to play a decisive role in finalizing the reconciliation.

Promoting the reconciliation between Saudi Arabia and Iran is in line with China's partner–community diplomacy. China believes that this will significantly promote the improvement of the security situation in the Middle East, which not only serves the interests of most Middle Eastern countries, but also serves the interests of China to the great extent. The animosity between Saudi Arabia and Iran had become a serious obstacle for China to further integrate into the Middle East, especially as China's attempt to upgrade its relations with one country would meet with suspicion by the other side. In March 2021, China and Iran signed a Twenty-Five-Year Cooperation Agreement, which brought China–Iran relations to a new level but caused concerns among Gulf Arab countries, including Saudi Arabia. In December 2022, the summit between China and Saudi Arabia and Arab countries also caused dissatisfaction from the Iranian side.[47] This situation forced China to think prudently about the need to promote the reconciliation between the two countries.

In March 2023, under Chinese mediation, Iran and Saudi Arabia achieved a historic handshake and reestablished diplomatic relations. The three countries announced that "an agreement has been reached between the Kingdom of Saudi Arabia and the Islamic Republic of Iran, that includes an agreement to resume diplomatic relations between them and re-open their embassies and missions within a period not exceeding two months, and the agreement includes their affirmation of the respect for the sovereignty of states and the non-interference in internal affairs of states."[48]

The Saudi–Iranian reconciliation is a significant event in the transformation of the Middle East geopolitical order. Throughout the mediation process, China placed itself on equal partnership with Saudi Arabia and Iran, and indicated that the two countries could also establish equal partnerships and cooperate with each other, ultimately achieving a result of the greatest benefits for all parties involved.

From the perspective of China's partner–community diplomacy, this chapter has analyzed the underlying reasons for Iran's Look East policy in specific relation to China. China's partner–community diplomacy is not an idealistic illusion, nor is it a narrative crafted to disguise its purpose as a rising power seeking hegemony. The philosophy of China's diplomacy is to be "strong but not hegemonic," and peaceful rise is the principle connotation of China's nonalignment diplomacy. Partner–community diplomacy puts all countries on an equal footing, seeks common security for all countries based on the principles of balancing moral and practical interests, works for reconciliation between countries, and opposes forming exclusive alliances against others. As a major power in the Middle East, Iran has been sanctioned by the United States for a long time and has faced overall pressure from the West. China, however, has been a consistent help to Iran, basing its relations with the Islamic Republic on respect and understanding. This has sustained Iran's Look East policy.

NOTES

This chapter is funded by Shanghai Philosophy and Social Sciences Project—"Research on Anti-Sanctions Model and Policy Optimization of Iran and related Chinese Enterprises from the Perspective of Compliance Governance" (2022BGJ002).

1. Edwin H. Fedder, "The Concept of Alliance," *International Studies Quarterly* 12, no. 1 (1968): 69.
2. Stephen M. Walt, *The Origin of Alliance* (Cornell University Press, 1987), 14.
3. Thomas S. Wilkins, "'Alignment', Not 'Alliance'—the Shifting Paradigm of International Security Cooperation: Toward a Conceptual Taxonomy of Alignment," *Review of International Studies* 38, no. 1 (2012): 54.
4. Hans Morgenthau, *Politics Among Nations: The Struggle of Power and Peace* (McGraw-Hill, 2005), 204.
5. Walt, *Origin of Alliance*, 21.
6. Eldad Shavit and Shimon Stein, "President Biden in Europe: The United States Returns as a Leader," Institute for National Security Studies, June 23, 2021, 2, https://acr.ps/1L9zQpu ; and Tom Le, "Biden Must Assist Japan and South Korea with the History Issue," East-West Center, February 24, 2021, 1–2, https://acr.ps/1L9zOFF.
7. "'Neighborhood Policy' and 'Balanced Diplomacy' Will Continue in 1402," Government of the Islamic Republic of Iran, March 22, 2023, https://irangov.ir/detail/409068.
8. Suren Sargsyan, "Are Russia, Iran and China Creating a New Informal Alliance?" *Armenian Mirror-Spectator*, March 22, 2023, https://acr.ps/1L9zRlS.
9. Nicole Grajewski, "An Illusory Entente: The Myth of a Russia-China-Iran 'Axis,'" *Asian Affairs* 53, no. 1 (2022): 164–65.
10. Hu Changshuan, "Yi zhong guo xin fa zhan wei shi jie ti gong xin ji yu" [China's new development will provide new opportunities for the world], *Guangming Daily*, December 16, 2022, https://acr.ps/1L9zRhf.
11. Feng Liu, "Balance of Power, Balance of Alignment, and China's Role in the Regional Order Transition," *The Pacific Review* 36, no. 2 (2023): 261–83.
12. Chen Zhimin, "Huo ban zhan lue: shi ji zhi jiao zhong guo de xian shi li xiang zhu yi wai jiao zhan lue" [Partnership strategy: China's realistic and idealistic diplomatic strategy at the turn of the century], *Pacific Journal* 21 (1999): 12–20.
13. Publicity Department of the CPC Central Committee, Ministry of Foreign Affairs of the People's Republic of China, *Xi Jinping wai jiao si xiang xue xi gang yao* [Outline of Xi Jinping diplomatic thought study] (People's Publishing House, 2021), 119.
14. "180 ge jian jiao guo, 112 dui huo ban guan xi: zhong guo de peng you bian tian xia"[180 countries with diplomatic relations, 112 partnerships], Central People's Government of the People's Republic of China, October 9, 2020, https://acr.ps/1L9zQxd.
15. Xi Jinping, *Lun jian chi tui dong gou jian ren lei ming yun gong tong ti* [On persisting in promoting a community with a shared future for mankind] (Central Literary Publishing House, 2018), 5.

16. Xi, *Lun jian chi tui dong gou jian*, 132.

17. "Wo men jiang tui dong yi dai yi lu chang yi, gou jian ren lei ming yun gong tong ti"[We will advance the Belt and Road Initiative and build a community with a shared future for mankind], State Council Information Office of the People's Republic of China, April 22, 2019, http://www.scio.gov.cn/.

18. Su Changhe, "Jian chi gong shang gong jian gong xiang de quan qiu zhi li guan" [Adhering to the concept of extensive consultation, joint contribution and shared benefits in global governance], *People's Daily*, March 27, 2019.

19. Jonathan Holslag, "Unequal Partnerships and Open Doors: Probing China's Economic Ambitions in Asia," *Third World Quarterly* 36, no. 11 (2015): 2112–29.

20. Sarvenaz Khanmohammadi and Degang Sun, "China-Iran Strategic Cooperation Agreement in the Changing International System," *Asian Journal of Middle Eastern and Islamic Studies* 16, no. 1 (2022): 27–45.

21. Ministry of Public Security of the People's Republic of China, "Position Paper of the People's Republic of China on the 75th Anniversary of the United Nations," January 30, 2021, https://acr.ps/1L9zRjf.

22. Yang Li and Ren Jia, "Yi dai yi lu kuang jia xia zhong guo yi lang jing ji he zuo yu huo ban guan xi gou jian"[Construction of China-Iran economic cooperation and partnership under the framework of the Belt and Road Initiative], *New Silk Road Journal* 7 (2019): 61–62.

23. Joris Teer and Suolao Wang, "Sino-Iranian Asymmetrical Interdependence in Light of the Iran Nuclear Issue," *Asian Journal of Middle Eastern and Islamic Studies* 12, no. 2 (2018): 167–92.

24. Robert K. Figg and Danielle A. Wilson, *U.S. Led Sanctions on Iran* (Nova Science Publishers, 2011), 53.

25. "Iranian President Hassan Rouhani Meets with Wang Yi, Embassy of the People's Republic of China in the United States of America, March 27, 2021, https://acr.ps/1L9zQHP.

26. "Explanation of Vote by China at the Security Council After Taking Vote on Draft Resolution on Sanctions against Iran," Permanent Mission of the People's Republic of China to the UN, March 3, 2008, https://acr.ps/1L9zR7H.

27. "Zhong fang dai biao ren wei ying jia da jie jue yi lang he wen ti de wai jiao nu li" [The representative of the Chinese side believes that diplomatic efforts should be intensified to resolve the Iranian nuclear issue], Central People's Government of the People's Republic of China, June 9, 2011, https://www.gov.cn/jrzg/2011-06/09/content_1880057.htm.

28. "Zhong hua ren min gong he guo he yi lang yi si lan gong he guo guan yu jian li quan mian zhan lue huo ban guan xi de lian he sheng ming" [Joint statement between the People's Republic of China and the Islamic Republic of Iran on the establishment of a comprehensive strategic partnership], Central People's Government of the People's Republic of China, January 24, 2016, https://acr.ps/1L9zQIp.

29. Liang Yu, "China, Iran to Step Up Pragmatic Cooperation," *Xinhua*, June 1, 2018, https://acr.ps/1L9zQKp.

30. "Xi Jinping Holds Talks with President Hassan Rouhani of Iran," Ministry of Foreign Affairs of the People's Republic of China, June 10, 2018, https://acr.ps/1L9zQMg.

31. Dang Ruifeng and Zeng Chen, "Zhong guo de wai jiao zhan lue ge ju: zhou bian shi shou yao" [China's diplomatic strategy pattern: the neighboring countries are the first], *Around Southeast Asia* 159 (2007): 68.

32. Xi Jinping, "Jian chi zong ti guo jia an quan guan, zou zhong guo te se guo jia an quan dao lu" [Adhere to the overall concept of national security and take the path of national security with Chinese characteristics], People.cn, April 16, 2014, https://acr.ps/1L9zQRn.

33. Xing Guangcheng, "Xi Jinping wai jiao si xiang yu zhou bian ming yun gong tong ti jian she" [Diplomatic thought of Xi Jinping and the building of a community of shared future in neighboring countries], *Contemporary World* 332 (2021): 15.

34. Jacopo Scita, "China-Iran Relations Through the Prism of Sanctions," *Asian Affairs* 53, no. 1 (2022): 89.

35. Matthew P. Goodman and Jonathan E. Hillman, "The G7's New Global Infrastructure Initiative," Center for Strategic & International Studies, June 15, 2021, https://acr.ps/1L9zQPM.

36. Saeed Azimi, "Iran Officially Joins SCO," *Tehran Times*, September 17, 2022, https://acr.ps/1L9zQSR.

37. Farnaz Fassihi, "With BRICS Invite, Iran Shrugs Off Outcast Status in the West," *New York Times*, August 25, 2023, https://nyti.ms/40ovAeC.

38. "Zhong guo jiu quan mian jie jue yi lang he wen ti ti chu wu dian zhu zhang" [China puts forward five-point proposal for comprehensive settlement of Iranian nuclear issue], People.cn, February 19, 2014, https://acr.ps/1L9zQlX.

39. Maziar Motamedi, "Iran Condemns EU Vote over 'Terrorist' Designation for IRGC," Al Jazeera, January 21, 2023, https://acr.ps/1L9zRjk.

40. Mehran Shamsuddin, "NPT Withdrawal; Iran's New Option Politics," *Tehran Times*, January 22, 2023, https://acr.ps/1L9zRhh.

41. "Zhong hua ren min gong he guo he yi lang yi si lan gong he guo lian he sheng ming" [Joint statement between the People's Republic of China and the Islamic Republic of Iran], Ministry of Justice of the People's Republic of China, February 17, 2023, https://acr.ps/1L9zRk1.

42. "Zhong hua ren min gong he guo he yi lang yi si lan gong he guo lian he sheng ming."

43. "Zhong hua ren min gong he guo he yi lang yi si lan gong he guo guan yu jian li quan mian zhan lue huo ban guan xi de lian he sheng ming."

44. Lama Alhamawi, "How China Became Saudi Arabia's Top Trading Partner, Revived Ancient Silk Road," *Arab News*, December 9, 2022, https://acr.ps/1L9zRkl.

45. "Zhong hua ren min gong he guo he sha te a la bo wang guo lian he sheng ming" [Joint statement between the People's Republic of China and the Kingdom of Saudi Arabia], Ministry of Foreign Affairs of the People's Republic of China, December 9, 2022, https://acr.ps/1L9zReL.

46. "Tehran, Riyadh Reach 10-Point MoU in Fifth Round of Talks—Iraq," *Iranintl*, April 25, 2022, https://www.iranintl.com/en/202204251672.

47. Jack Lau, "Xi's China-Arab Summit Success in Riyadh Raises Temperatures in Iran," *South China Morning Post*, December 14, 2022, https://acr.ps/1L9zRaD.

48. "Joint Trilateral Statement by the People's Republic of China, the Kingdom of Saudi Arabia, and the Islamic Republic of Iran," Ministry of Foreign Affairs of the People's Republic of China, March 10, 2023, https://acr.ps/1L9zQqW.

Part III
IRAN–RUSSIA RELATIONS

9

A RISK-SEEKING IRAN
Explaining Iran's Military Support for Russia in the Ukraine War

Mazaher Koruzhde and Eric Lob

Iran's military support for Russia during the Ukraine war was a high-risk geopolitical move, especially when Iran was struggling with a crippled economy and domestic social unrest. This behavior was risky because US and NATO officials partly blamed Iran's military support for prolonging the war and raising the death toll. Despite the profits and other benefits from this support, it brought more sanctions against Iran, sent its economy into a deeper spiral or state of malaise, and, in the worst-case scenario, increased the probability of a US-led attack. The United States and other Western countries also saw this support as part of an "unholy alliance" that would potentially have to be stopped by means other than simply sanctions. That was because this alliance, as CIA Director William Burns stated, was "moving at a pretty fast clip in a very dangerous direction." He believed that Iran's support for Russia "creates obvious risks not only for the people of Ukraine, ... but also risks to our friends and partners across the Middle East as well."[1]

Iran's military support for Russia can be explained from a wide range of perspectives, which will be presented in greater detail in the second section. These perspectives, which we do not reject, partly revealed the motives behind Iran's drone transfers and other military aid to Russia. That said, we argue that Iran's behavior can be better understood if situated within the broader context of the Iran–US conflict. The latter was reignited after the election of President Donald Trump and his maximum pressure campaign (MPC) against Iran starting in 2016. The MPC culminated in the US withdrawal from the 2015 Iran nuclear deal or Joint Comprehensive Plan of Action (JPCOA) and reimposition of sanctions against Iran in 2018.

From this standpoint, Iran's drone transfers and military aid to Russia were only another geopolitical maneuver in a series of high-risk moves. After a year of "strategic patience" or "heroic flexibility," these moves included increased uranium enrichment, drone and missile attacks, tanker seizures, hostage taking, and military support for the Houthis in Yemen against Saudi Arabia and the United Arab Emirates (UAE). In addition to the actual gains from these moves in the form of funds and prestige, among others, Iran's main goal was to gain concessions from the United States and its allies and partners in Western Europe and the Persian Gulf. The purpose of these concessions was to prolong the survival of the Iranian regime, which was seriously threatened due to its loss of legitimacy for mismanaging a worsening economy following US sanctions. The 2022 to 2023 Woman, Life, Freedom protests—which started after Mahsa Amini died while in the custody of the Iranian morality police—showed that political and sociocultural issues, when coupled with economic grievances, could severely threaten the regime.

To explain Iran's military support for Russia within the framework of its geopolitical tensions with the United States and its popular protests at home, we draw on insights from prospect theory, which examines decision-making under risk. Using this theory, we argue that the convergence of three factors—the MPC, protests in Iran, and the prospect of an Arab–Israeli alliance—led Iranian officials to perceive themselves as operating in the domain of losses. The latter made these officials more risk-seeking not only in their domestic affairs, in terms of brutally repressing the protests. It also did so in their geopolitical actions through Iran's military support for Russia and other activities.

Using prospect theory to explain Iran's military support for Russia, we identify two elements. The first is the framing phase during which Iranian officials received and processed domestic and geopolitical developments in a way that created the perception of operating in the domain of losses. Viewing oneself in the domain of gains or losses, prospect theory suggests, is judged relative to a reference point usually defined as the status quo. For Iranian officials, this point was the signing of the JCPOA and the actual and perceptive gains that accompanied it during and after 2015. The third section of this chapter elaborates on why the JCPOA was viewed as a reference point for the Islamic Republic and how the combination of these three factors created the perception that Iran was subsequently situated in the domain of losses.

The second element is the evaluation phase. Prospect theory posits that actors tend to be risk-seeking when they see themselves as operating in the domain of losses, and risk-averse when being in the domain of gains.² As noted earlier, one manifestation of Iran's risk-seeking behavior was its military support for Russia during the Ukraine war. In the next two sections of this chapter, we argue that this support resulted from the loss framing of Iranian leaders and officials during the following geopolitical and domestic developments: the MPC against Iran that began in 2016 and culminated in the US withdrawal from the JCPOA in May 2018, the stalled negotiations between the United States and Iran to revive the JCPOA in April 2022, the cycle of popular protests that erupted in December 2017 and continued with the Woman, Life, Freedom ones that started in September 2022, and the prospect of an Arab–Israeli front against Iran in the Persian Gulf within the framework of the US-brokered Abraham Accords that was signed in September 2020 and could eventually contain Saudi Arabia.

The theoretical insights from prospect theory help us predict what is more likely to happen in the conflict between Iran and the United States and their respective allies and partners, given Iran's increasing risk-seeking behavior. This prediction is based on historical evidence from the period after the Green Movement of 2009. During this period, Iran became more hostile toward Israel, leading many analysts to believe that a US-backed military attack on Iran was exceedingly probable.³ The confrontation between Iran and the United States and its regional allies led to the harshest sanctions regime against the Islamic Republic in history which instigated more geopolitical adventurism by Iran. That episode ended with the signing of the JCPOA in 2015, reducing US–Iran tensions to their lowest point in a decade. We believe that the most recent confrontation between Iran and the United States, which resurfaced after the latter withdrew from the JCPOA, will also end with such a deal that would deescalate tensions between both sides. In the end, neither of them can afford to pursue their policies to the extreme, whether it is the United States' maximalist position of regime change in Iran or the latter's risky behavior in the form of military support for Russia, among other activities.

The rest of the chapter is organized as follows. The second section examines a wide range of explanations for Iran's military support for Russia. Without rejecting any of them, the third section develops a prospect theory framework for situating Iran's risky behavior. This section elaborates on why the JCPOA was viewed as a reference point for Tehran and how the three developments created the perception that it was now operating in the domain of losses. The fourth section briefly discusses our take on the possibilities that lie ahead, considering what the empirical evidence suggests. The fifth and final section concludes the chapter.

Alternative Explanations for Iran's Drone Transfers and Other Aid to Russia

Historical Inertia or Path Dependency

Military drones comprised one of the four pillars of Iran's security strategy and force structure, complementing its missile technology, proxy forces, and cyber warfare.[4] Iran began manufacturing, operating, and exporting drones well before the Russian invasion of Ukraine in February 2022. During the Iran–Iraq War (1980–88), beginning in 1986, Iran first produced and used a basic drone called the Mohajer-1—which contained limited reconnaissance and combat capabilities—to conduct surveillance over Iraqi lines.[5] Throughout the Afghan civil war in the 1990s, Iran used early models of the Mohajer in Afghanistan for reconnaissance missions. In the 2000s, the Islamic Revolutionary Guard Corps (IRGC) utilized the Mohajer-4 (which was first unveiled in 2011) and the Ababil-2 multipurpose drone to surveil US warships in the Persian Gulf and the Strait of Hormuz.[6]

The Islamic Republic has used surveillance and attack drones for domestic counterinsurgency and exported them to predominantly quasi- or nonstate partners and proxies in the region for use against American assets and allies, as well as extremist groups like al-Qaeda and ISIS.[7] Beyond the regional partners and proxies of Iran, it sought out government buyers for drones including Venezuela (Mohajer-2, Mohajer-6, and Shahed-171) during the 2000s, alongside Ethiopia (Mohajer-6) during the Tigray War (2020–22).[8] Iran's drone transfers or exports to Russia during the Ukraine war could be viewed as a natural outgrowth of its highly developed and sophisticated military drone complex, with over thirty-three models, as well as its rising ambitions in the global military drone market.[9]

Political Opportunities

Before the UN arms embargo against Iran expired in October 2020, Iran also exported drones to its partners and proxies.[10] Alongside the Bashar al-Assad regime since the Syrian civil war (2011–2025), one exception to this trend was Venezuela. After the embargo expired, the Islamic Republic's drone exports to Venezuela and other states increased. In November 2020, Tehran purportedly transferred to Caracas the technology for the Mohajer-6, which was sighted during a televised speech by Venezuelan President Nicolás Maduro (2013–present) that month.[11] In August 2021, and as previously indicated, Iran exported two Mohajer-6s to Ethiopia during the Tigray War. In the summer of 2022, it began exporting the Mohajer-6 and Shahed series of surveillance and attack drones to Russia during the Ukraine war. After a key provision of UN Security Council

(UNSC) resolution 2231 expired in October 2023, Iran could deliver to Russia longer-range and more lethal drones and missiles, like the Arash-2 suicide drone and the Fateh-1110 and Zolfaghar short-range ballistic missile (SRBM), without being subjected to snapback sanctions.[12]

Iran–US Tensions and Eastward-Leaning Policies

A third alternative explanation for Iran's delivery of military drones and other assistance to Russia during the Ukraine war were the geopolitical conditions created by the United States. These conditions forced the Islamic Republic to pursue an Eastward-leaning foreign policy despite the foundational principal and slogan of "neither East nor West" that had existed since the Iranian Revolution of 1979. After President Donald Trump (2016–20) unilaterally withdrew from the JCPOA, Iran pursued "strategic patience" or "heroic flexibility" to see if other signatories could salvage the JCPOA. After about a year, tensions between the Islamic Republic, the United States, and their allies and partners in the region increased in 2019. That year, these tensions manifested themselves in the form of Iran's targeting of regional oil tankers and facilities, its downing of a US drone in international waters, and its attack against the US embassy in Iraq through local partners and proxies. They culminated in the US assassination of IRGC Quds Force Major General Qasem Soleimani, and Iran's retaliatory missile strike against US troops at the al-Asad airbase in Iraq in January 2020, bringing both countries to the brink of war.[13]

During this period of heightened US–Iran tensions and throughout the remainder of his presidency, Hassan Rouhani (2013–21) pursued an Eastward-leaning foreign policy through greater rapprochement with China and Russia.[14] This policy was inherited and intensified by his successor, Ebrahim Raisi (2021–24). Raisi signed a Twenty-Five-Year Strategic Cooperation Agreement with Beijing in March 2022 and an energy agreement with Russia in July of that year, despite misgivings from some centrist Iranian officials on becoming too closely aligned with Russia.[15] Between June and July, Tehran invited Russian officials to visit Kashan airfield at least twice to view the Mohajer-6, Shahed-129, and Shahed-136, before first acquiring and deploying them in August and September.[16]

At the same time and during the presidency of Joe Biden (2021–24), he was unwilling and unable to deliver on his campaign promise to rejoin the JCPOA despite multiple rounds of indirect negotiations with Iran in Vienna through other members of the P5+1 (the five permanent members of the UN Security Council including Britain, China, France, Russia, and the United States, plus Germany, which had signed the JCPOA with Iran in 2015). As previously mentioned, and within the framework of prospect theory, Iran's risk-seeking behavior in the form of increased military operations and stronger Eastward relations during a period of escalating tensions and unmet expectations with the United States could be considered the consequence of operating in the domain of losses. Alternatively, this behavior could be construed as a last resort after all avenues toward constructive engagement with the United States were closed.

Security Alliances

Somewhat related to political opportunity structures, another alternative explanation was the state or status of Iran's security alliances or lack thereof as a structural opportunity or constraint to its transfers to Russia. In contrast to Turkey and the UAE, and without being a member of a regional security alliance, Iran became the obvious or natural supplier of military drones and other aid and technology to Russia in Ukraine, particularly after the United States withdrew from the JCPOA. Despite disagreements between the United States and Turkey over democratic backsliding, the Gülen movement, and the Kurdish issue, Ankara was a NATO ally and had been on the opposing side of conflicts against Russia. As in Syria, Libya, and Nagorno-Karabakh, and starting in February 2022, the Turkish–Russian rivalry most recently emerged in Ukraine, where the Turkish medium-altitude and long-endurance Bayraktar TB2 (which was first unveiled in 2014) featured prominently in the Ukrainian campaign, especially at the outset, to resist and repel the Russian invasion and occupation.[17]

Compared with Turkey and Iran, the UAE displayed less self-sufficiency by reportedly flying missions and launching airstrikes in conflict zones inside and outside of the Middle East (e.g., Libya and Ethiopia) using China's CAIG Wing Loong II drone. The UAE delivered drone technology to Russia and cooperated with it in conflict zones like Libya while seeking to balance relations with Washington and Moscow before and during the Ukraine war. For Abu Dhabi, supplying drones to Russia would disrupt that balance by alienating or antagonizing the United States and would be complicated by the fact that the UAE tended to export drones from China, which initially maintained a somewhat ambiguous stance on the Russian invasion of Ukraine, ranging from neutrality to support.[18]

Conflict Dynamics

Iran's drone transfers to Russia did not occur in a vacuum, but were rather in response to the Ukraine war's conflict dynamics or as part of them. Specifically, and as noted previously, Russia acquired military drones from Iran and deployed them in Ukraine after suffering setbacks related to personnel, equipment, territory, and prestige from Ukrainian counteroffensives using reconnaissance and combat drones and other capabilities supplied by the United States and its NATO allies, including Poland and Turkey, before and during the conflict.[19]

For Russia, such setbacks could be viewed both in terms of prospect theory's domain of losses and risk-seeking behavior, as well as the Ukraine war's conflict dynamics. In addition to Iran initially transferring drones to Russia while confronting protests at home, Moscow first deployed the drones against Ukraine's infrastructure and population after Kyiv had allegedly bombed the Crimea Bridge on October 8, 2022. Between October 10 and 17, Russia deployed hundreds of Shahed-136 or Geran-2, alongside dozens of missiles, that killed Ukrainian civilians, struck power stations, and caused extended blackouts in Kyiv and surrounding cities, towns, and villages. The drones and missiles crippled an estimated 30 percent of the country's energy infrastructure and capacity ahead of winter.[20]

As Russia sustained setbacks from Ukrainian counteroffensives in the east and south, even after deploying the Shahed-136 or Geran-2 there, it shifted its strategy toward continuing to lay siege to civilians around the country and depriving of them of electricity, water, and other necessities ahead of winter. In early November, Iranian and Russian defense officials reportedly finalized a deal for Tehran to transfer the designs and components of combat drones to Moscow. The deal allowed Russia to manufacture hundreds of the drones on its soil through its own assembly line and was a way for Iran to potentially avoid more sanctions.[21] Between November 15 and 17, and after withdrawing from Kherson (a launchpad for Iranian/Russian drones alongside Crimea), Russia deployed hundreds of missiles and drones, including the Shahed-136 or Geran-2, which caused considerable death and damage to Ukrainian civilians and infrastructure.[22] Combined with the previous Russian drone and missile attacks in October, the ones in mid-November and later that month crippled Ukraine's energy capacity and left millions of Ukrainians without power for days. They took place as temperatures dropped to freezing and below freezing levels, and fears rose of a difficult winter ahead.[23]

Iran's Military Support for Russia: A Risk-Seeking Response to a Perception of Loss

Prospect theory equips us with the necessary theoretical tools to situate Iran's transfer of drones and military aid to Russia during the Ukraine war within the broader context of its risk-seeking behavior. The latter's goal was to gain valuable returns mainly in the form of concessions from the United States and its allies and partners in the Persian Gulf. In this section, we examine the loss framing in which Iranian leaders and officials found themselves since the start of the MPC. Before that, they had adjusted to the returns of the JCPOA and its atmosphere that promised social and political stability, as the reference point relative to which they viewed Iran's losses or gains. It is necessary to clarify here that regardless of how insignificant the financial windfall from the JCPOA might have been, as some argue, it was perceived by Iranian officials as an outlier of the status quo that had existed since 1979 and brought nothing but isolation, tensions, and sanctions.[24]

These officials believed that Iran began to operate in the domain of losses due to the MPC, coupled with frequent domestic protests (which were viewed as an outcome of the MPC) and the prospect of an Arab–Israeli alliance within the framework of the US-brokered Abraham Accords. Within this framing, and because of it, they aspired to attain greater returns by taking more risks, such as providing military support to Russia in Ukraine. As such, this support made sense as an extension of a risk-seeking string of behavior by Iran at the geopolitical level.

Even before its military support for Russia, Iran's risk-seeking behavior had manifested itself in greater "terrorism"—as stated by the data from Trading Economics—and military expenditures, nuclear enrichment, and military support for the Houthis in Yemen. This data indicated there were meaningful changes in some indexes that showed an increase in Iran's level of risk-taking in 2018, when the United States withdrew from the Iran nuclear deal, compared to the deal period from 2015 to 2018. For example, Iran's Terrorism Index, which had fallen from 5.49 to 4.77 during the deal period, rose even higher than before to 5.74 in 2018. Also, Iran's military expenditures, which had decreased from $16,494 to $11,230 million between 2015 and 2018, rose to $15,825 million in 2018 (see table 9.1).

After 2017, Iran intensified its activities in Yemen following Saudi Arabia's support of President Trump's decision to decertify the deal. According to a report by the Center for Strategic and International Studies (CSIS), the number of Iranian-backed attacks by the Houthis against Saudi Arabia and the UAE more than doubled between 2019 and 2021, compared to the deal era.[25] Iran also resumed its uranium enrichment and increased its levels to between 60 and 80 percent. After the most recent protests began in mid-September 2022, Iran held security meetings with Russia and agreed to transfer more reconnaissance and combat drones, along with surface-to-air missiles (SAMs), on October 6.[26] Shortly afterward, between October 10 and October 17, Russia first deployed the drones against Ukraine's critical infrastructure and civilian population, with devasting localized effects.[27]

TABLE 9.1. Iran terrorism and military expenditure indexes

INDEX	BEFORE THE DEAL IN 2014	THE DEAL PERIOD 2015–18	AFTER THE DEAL'S TERMINATION IN 2018
Terrorism Index	5.49	4.77	5.74
Military expenditure (million)	$16,494	$11,230	$15,825

Source: "Iran," Trading Economics, https://tradingeconomics.com/iran/

The task of this section is to examine how the MPC, the protests in Iran, and the possibility of an Arab–Israeli alliance in the Persian Gulf and the Middle East and North Africa (MENA) created a framing of loss for Iranian leaders and officials. But before that, we need to establish why we believe that the Iran nuclear deal, in terms of both its objective and perceptive gains, was the reference point relative to which these leaders and officials processed the framing within which they were operating. We argue that, as the deal promised, at the very least, the prospect of a more economically and socially stable society, these leaders and officials quickly adopted the new condition as a reference point against which they calculated their gains and losses. With the start of the MPC, the frequency of domestic protests, and the possibility of an Arab–Israeli front in the region, these leaders and officials found themselves in the domain of losses and became increasingly risk-acceptant.

Reference dependence is the central analytic assumption of prospect theory. It assumes that actors are more sensitive to *changes* in assets, in the form of gains or losses, than to *net* asset levels.[28] For Iranian leaders and officials, this meant that the 2015 Iran nuclear deal created a reference point relative to which they evaluated their current situation. They believed that they had achieved something through the deal that was taken away later with the introduction and implementation of the MPC. At the same time, any explicit acknowledgment by these leaders and officials of this effect of the MPC would mean giving credit to it—which directly contradicted their rhetoric of resistance.

Beginning in early 2015, in anticipation of the signing of the nuclear deal, there were signs of improvement across a wide range of economic areas in Iran. As shown in table 9.2, with the negotiation, anticipation, and signing of the deal in July of that year, Iran witnessed a palpable increase in its gross domestic product (GDP) annual growth rate, GDP per capita, overall exports and oil exports, petroleum production, total imports, and gross official reserves, along with a significant decrease in its inflation rate. Iran's monetary freedom score (which measures price stability and controls) rose from 47.3 in 2014 to 60.1 in 2015, shifting its money from the "repressed" to the "moderately free" category. After

TABLE 9.2. Iran's economic indicators before, during, and after the signing of the nuclear deal

INDEX	BEFORE THE DEAL	THE DEAL PERIOD 2015–18	AFTER THE DEAL'S TERMINATION IN 2018
GDP Annual Growth Rate	−5%	15%	−11.4%
GDP per Capita	$4,990	$5,401	$5,017
Exports	$17,386 million	$29,336 million	$8,938 million
Oil Exports	$31,848 million	$65,818 million	$21,043 million
Oil Production	3 mbpd	4 mbpd	2 mbpd
Imports	$12,902 million	$22,836 million	$9,150 million
Inflation Rate	42%	8%	53%
Gross Official Reserves	$55 billion	$122.5 billion	$4 billion
Dollar to Rial	34,690 r	35,810 r (before Trump)	88,970 r
Monetary Freedom	47.3	60.1	40.6

Source: "Iran," Trading Economics.

a period of constant decline in the value of the Iranian rial against the US dollar from 1,204 rial in 2009 to 3,200 rial in 2014, the rial maintained its value after the signing of the deal and even witnessed an increase at some point in 2015. The Iranian currency exchange market, like the stock market, was more sensitive than other economic indexes to developments in the United States. Therefore, even before the MPC, the value of the rial started to decline after Trump, who was already known in Iran for his hostile approach to the country, won the presidency and came into office between 2016 and 2017.

While the Iran nuclear deal's objective economic gains might have been significant for the Iranian people in general, its subjective returns were far more valuable for the ruling elite. The deal brought about a sense of hope in the future and, with that sentiment, a sense of social and political stability that had not been felt for a long time. Previously, during the presidency of Mahmoud Ahmadinejad (2005–13) and his belligerent foreign policy, a barrage of sanctions came along that only made the prospect of coming out of isolation less likely for Iranians. The economic hardship and the international loss of prestige that he was perceived to have inflicted on Iranians finally ended with the developments in Geneva surrounding the signing of the deal in July 2015. The moment the deal was signed, millions of people, including the first author of this chapter, poured into the streets across the entire country. For a short period, these people thought that years of harsh restrictions and international isolation were finally over.

More importantly, the deal restored the trust of the people in the state in the sense that they viewed their leaders as competent in at least one area, namely foreign policy. The deal came to be seen as the Islamic Republic's greatest foreign policy achievement since President Mohammad Khatami's (1997–2005) "Dialogue Among Civilizations" by increasing, at least temporarily, Iran's international prestige. Suddenly, the foreign minister at the time of the deal, Mohammad Javad Zarif, became a national hero whose status or popularity was compared with Ahmad Qavam. The latter had served as prime minister five times from the Constitutional Revolution in 1909 to after World War II in 1952, during which time he saved northern Iran from Soviet annexation. According to a 2015 poll of 1,012 Iranians, 78 percent of the respondents liked Zarif, who led the team that had negotiated the deal.[29]

Maximum Pressure Campaign (MPC)

Due to the real and perceived benefits of the nuclear deal for the Iranian public and ruling elite, the atmosphere created by it quickly became the new adjusted reference point relative to which state officials viewed their gains and losses. Given the importance of the deal for domestic stability and state legitimacy and support, if not further consolidation, the MPC did not just aim to change the behavior of a so-called rogue state. It also intended to instigate political and social instability that would ostensibly lead to regime change, as advocated by a transnational investment bloc of businesses and governments that influenced US foreign policy in the Persian Gulf.[30] As shown in the rightmost column of table 9.2, all of Iran's economic indicators declined significantly after Trump's election in 2016 and his withdrawal from the deal in 2018. The fact that the official website of the US Department of State exhibited some of these declines as a sign of the MPC's effectiveness and victory made Iranian officials see the termination of the deal even more as further proof of US hostility toward them and the regime.[31]

Ever since he started his presidential campaign, Trump adopted an "anything-but-Obama" approach. Bashing the Iran nuclear deal, the signature achievement of Barack Obama's foreign policy, became the centerpiece of Trump's criticism of it. This criticism received support from Americans, particularly those who had lived through the Iran hostage crisis between 1979 and 1981.[32] Trump's rhetoric about the deal was littered with the threatening and confrontational language that most anti-Iran policy-planning organizations and think tanks had been using for decades. Suddenly, the future of the deal was going to be determined by the policy recommendations of institutions like the American Enterprise Institute (AEI), Heritage Foundation (HF), and Foundation for the Defense of Democracies (FDD).

To show how Trump's rhetoric reflected years of negative sentiment toward Iran, we examined hundreds of policy recommendations (containing over one million words) regarding the Iran deal or JCPOA on the official websites of the

AEI and HF between 2015 and 2018.³³ Using NVivo, we analyzed these recommendations against hundreds of pages (containing over 200,000 words) of Trump's statements about Iran since the start of his presidential campaign. It should be noted that these pages were cleaned to eliminate junk words and topics unrelated to Iran—which was by far the most time-consuming task of this section. The results showed a staggering correlation of 0.82 and 0.81 between Trump's language and that of AEI and HF, respectively. Our comparative analysis of the frequency of the most common themes in Trump's statements and the AEI and HF's publications about Iran supported these high correlations. These indisputable similarities clearly heralded the resurgence of a policy current that would reverse the outcomes of the deal for the Iranians.

During Trump's campaign and election in 2016, Iranian leaders and officials noticed that the loss of what they had gained through the nuclear deal with the United States and other great powers was becoming increasingly plausible. With the deal gone in 2018, so were its economic dividends and the hope it had precipitated.

Domestic Protests

Even before the US withdrawal from the nuclear deal and after Trump's election victory in 2017, a series of mass protests began in Iran that were equally, if not more, alarming, for Iranian leaders and officials than the loss of the deal, which was not even significant in terms of material dividends.³⁴ These leaders and officials, however, perceived the loss of the deal as being strongly tied to the protests or their main cause. Moreover, the termination of the deal made it easier for these leaders and officials to frame or portray the protests as plotted by "external enemies." The protests began in 2017–18, reemerged or resurfaced in 2019 and 2020, and culminated, most recently, in those of the Woman, Life, Freedom movement in 2022–23. They significantly increased social unrest in Iran and seriously threatened the survival of the regime in a way not seen since the Green Movement protests in 2009.

As these protests became more frequent and intense, the regime responded with greater brutality and further undermined state legitimacy, as evidenced by a cursory comparison between the mass protests in 2009 and 2022–23. Even though the exact death toll in either set of protests was unknown, sources reported one of around 150 in 2009 and approximately 500 in 2022–23. During the recent protests, seventy of those killed were children, though Iranian officials tried to justify these figures by claiming the average age of the protestors was fifteen.³⁵ Whereas the number of arrests in 2009 totaled 1,000 individuals, that figure in 2022–23 exceeded 20,000 people, 110 of whom were sentenced to death, according to the Human Rights Activists News Agency (HRANA).³⁶

Since 2017, several developments led to extraordinary mass protests that might not have existed or persisted if the Iranian economy and living standards had not deteriorated to such an extent. In 2017–18, protests erupted in response to the government's failure to revive the struggling economy, address high unemployment and inflation, and combat alleged corruption. These protests were triggered by Rouhani publicly disclosing the national budget with some irregularities related to parastatal foundations. In 2019, they started following a 50 to 200 percent increase in fuel prices in November. In 2020, people took to the streets to show they were outraged by the incompetence and opacity of the government after it announced that the military had accidentally shot down Ukraine International Airlines flight 752, which contained mostly Iranian passengers. And finally, in 2022–23, the largest and longest protests, by far, were triggered by the death of Amini while in the custody of the Iranian morality police.

All these protests posed a grave threat to what Iranian leaders and officials were most concerned about—the survival of the regime itself. Each protest was considered a heavy blow to the body of the regime and the legitimacy of the state. For the ruling elite and as indicated above, the threatening character of these protests was revealed by the fact that, since 2017, they were met with greater repression and blunt force. According to an article published in the *Guardian*, the latest protests in 2022–23 "evolved into the biggest challenge for the clerical leadership since the 1979 revolution," making the government's response even harsher than before.[37] As always, Iranian leaders and officials downplayed the gravity of the protests by calling the protestors "thugs," "looters," and "rioters," to delegitimize their dissent and demands. However, as the 1,255 protests spread to 164 cities across the country and lasted longer than previous protests for over one hundred days, according to data from HRANA, these leaders and officials did not hesitate to suppress them by any means possible.

Arab–Israeli Alliance

The last factor that contributed to the perception of loss for Iranian leaders and officials was the prospect of a unified American–Arab–Israeli front in the Persian Gulf against Iran. This prospect was somewhat mitigated by the Iran–UAE and Iran–Saudi Arabia talks that began in 2019 and by the China-brokered diplomatic agreement between Iran and Saudi Arabia that was reached in March 2023. The possibility of this front became increasingly plausible after the historical normalization agreement signed in August 2020 between Israel and the UAE that was officially known as the Abraham Accords. This agreement was the first of its kind between Israel and an Arab Gulf state, even if de facto bilateral relations had long existed between Israel and the UAE before the agreement. The last time

Israel had signed such an agreement with an Arab country was with Jordan in 1994—which had little, to any, geopolitical ramifications for Iran.

After the Israel–UAE agreement was reached and expanded to other Arab states (Bahrain, Morocco, and Sudan), the possibility of a far more geopolitically consequential agreement increased, this time between Israel and Saudi Arabia—the so-called deal of the century. As the Saudis' closest ally in the region, the UAE deciding to normalize relations with Israel significantly raised the prospect of an Israel–Saudi Arabia agreement. Since 2021, both sides signaled the possibility of a normalization agreement. For example, immediately after Trump had "made history with his [direct] flight" from Riyadh to Tel Aviv on May 22, 2017, Israeli Prime Minister Benjamin Netanyahu tweeted: "I hope one day an Israeli prime minister will be able to fly from Tel Aviv to Riyadh."[38] Echoing his position, Israel's defense minister, Avigdor Lieberman, called for "full diplomatic and economic relations" with Saudi Arabia.[39]

What presumably drew Israel and Saudi Arabia together was their shared antipathy for Iran. In January 2022, the two countries met at a secret US-brokered summit to discuss the "shared threat of Tehran's growing drone and missile capabilities." A week after the summit, Israel's defense minister, Benny Gantz, described what he called the "Middle East air defense alliance" as already operational.[40] After addressing the shared interests between Israel and Saudi Arabia in countering or containing Iran, Israel's intelligence and transportation minister, Yisrael Katz, said at a national strategy initiative conference that he would like the Saudis to extend their special treatment of Trump to Netanyahu, including inviting him to visit Riyadh, and make the "deal of the century."[41]

Perceiving the main target of these Arab–Israeli normalization agreements to be Iran, its leaders and officials considered them a large geopolitical loss for Iran. After the Israel–UAE agreement was reached in August 2020, Rouhani warned the UAE "not to open the doors of the region to Israel." He portrayed the agreement as "treachery" and its purpose "solely to cheer up the U.S." In a more scathing and threatening tone, IRGC officials warned the agreement would "foretell a dangerous future for the UAE's leaders."[42]

Since the Israel–UAE agreement was signed, Iranian leaders and officials used a more threatening tone as Israel and the UAE strengthened their relationship. One week after the signing of the agreement in August 2020, Israeli Prime Minister Naftali Bennett made a surprise visit to the UAE and met with its president, Sheikh Mohammed bin Zayed Al Nahyan, to display the strengthening alliance between both countries and the importance of forming a united front against Iran, especially in response to Tehran's recent increases in nuclear enrichment. During the meeting, Bennett and Al Nahyan reportedly discussed "advancing the regional architecture" and other regional affairs, with Iran as the top priority, according to the Associated Press. The speculation surrounding the prioritization of Iran during the discussion was based on a video statement that Bennett had issued before departing for Abu Dhabi. In the video, he commended countries at a recent International Atomic Energy Agency meeting in Vienna that had voted to censure Iran over its lack of transparency about nuclear activities at three undeclared sites.[43] Following the meeting between Bennett and Al Nahyan, Iran's foreign ministry spokesman, Saeed Khatibzadeh, expressed his concern and immediately issued a "serious warning" regarding any action that would consolidate Israel's presence in the region. Events like the meeting, he warned, would disrupt the region's security and violate or undermine Iran's interests.[44]

In sum, starting in 2016, Iranian leaders and officials saw a backsliding in what they had hoped would be a path to economic prosperity and further consolidation. As the MPC set in, the indexes that showed economic improvement during the Iran nuclear deal era began to regress, especially after the US withdrawal from the deal. The economic hardship and unmet expectations caused by the reimposition and intensification of sanctions put Iranian society on edge at every turn. Agitated people used every opportunity to show their dismay. Between 2017 and 2022, they leveraged or exploited such political opportunities as the government budget disclosure, gasoline price hike, downing of the Ukrainian airliner, and death of Amini to voice their dissent by coming to the streets. With each round of protests turning into nationwide unrest, the regime felt more threatened and became more repressive in suppressing the protests. While perceiving and portraying these protests as the plot of "external powers," Iranian leaders and officials developed the perception that they have been operating in the domain of losses since the MPC.

This perception was augmented by the prospect of an Arab–Israeli front against Iran in the Persian Gulf despite the China-brokered agreement between Tehran and Riyadh. As Aaron David Miller and Steven Simon pointed out in their *Foreign Policy* piece: "Saudi Arabia and Israel are tacit allies against Iran, even if the kingdom is currently pursuing détente with Tehran."[45] This was especially true if the agreement was viewed through the prism of the US–China geopolitical rivalry. That is, while the United States had assumed a leadership role in the Middle East after World War II and the Cold War, China positioned itself to do the same by attempting to end the conflict between Iran and Saudi Arabia, even if bilateral talks had transpired between both sides in countries like Iraq and Oman. From this perspective, the agreement appeared to be more of a Chinese geopolitical publicity stunt than the intention or result of resolving deep-seated problems between the Iranians and Saudis.

Altogether, the three trends of the MPC, domestic protests, and Arab–Israeli rapprochement led the Islamic Republic to become not only more repressive in dealing with the protests at home, but also more risk-acceptant in its geopolitical conduct abroad. Iran's military support for Russia, along with other recent provocative actions, can best be understood in this context. The next section examines this support in the form of drone transfers and other assistance from this perspective.

The Actual and Potential Gains from Iran's Risk-Seeking Behavior

Iran's drone transfers to Russia as a bold geopolitical move were expected to generate significant returns for the Iranians. In terms of actual gains, these transfers helped Iran improve its position within the ongoing and evolving arms race involving this technology between Iran and its regional rivals. Iran and other middle powers in the Middle East, such as Turkey and the UAE, competed in this race by manufacturing, operating, and exporting competitively priced and comparatively effective drones to countries inside and outside of the region.[46] In the process, Iran and its regional rivals projected power and earned profits, showcased technology and enhanced prestige, and strengthened alliances and influenced conflicts in the Middle East and other regions.

Before the UN arms embargo expired, Iran witnessed how the drones of its regional rivals, namely Turkey and the UAE, with first-mover advantage, turned the tide of nearby conflicts in Syria, Libya, and Nagorno-Karabakh, where the Islamic Republic was also involved on the same or opposing side. Consequently, and since 2021, Iran was more active and assertive in the global military drone market, as evidenced by Tehran's export of combat drones to the Ethiopian government during the Tigray War, alongside Ankara and Abu Dhabi, as well as its transfer of the technology to Russia to surveil and strike military and civilian targets in Ukraine.

In the domain of gains, drones increasingly offered an asymmetric advantage to Iran, with the understanding that it cannot compete with more modern air forces in the region. Iran used drones against the oil tankers and facilities of Israel, Saudi Arabia, and other rivals, culminating in the drone and missile strike on the Saudi oil processing facilities at Abqaiq and Khurais on September 14, 2019. At the same time and in a quid pro quo fashion, Iran provided drones, missiles, and other military aid to Russia to help it compensate for a depleted ballistic missile arsenal and a limited reconnaissance and combat drone capability to complement a dwindling supply of Orlan-10 surveillance drones in Ukraine. In exchange, Moscow may help Iran modernize its air force by delivering Sukhoi SU-35 multirole fighter jets.[47] Moreover, Iran sought to leverage the military drones and other assistance to Russia in exchange for energy investment, trade corridors, and other economic incentives.

Beyond strengthening the Iran–Russia alliance and extracting military and economic benefits from it, exporting drones to Russia enabled Iran to earn profits, enhance prestige, and influence conflict. During the Tigray War in August 2021, Iran exported two Mohajer-6 mid-range reconnaissance and combat drones to Ethiopia, a middle power in Africa and the Global South, amid a largely low-profile civil conflict against former rulers and local rebels. By contrast, since the summer of 2022, Iran allegedly exported hundreds of Shahed-129 surveillance and attack drones and Shahed-136 suicide or kamikaze drones, among other models like the Mohajer-6 and Shahed-191, to Russia, a major power in Europe and the international system, during an extremely high-profile, high-stakes interstate war against the United States and its NATO allies.[48] For this reason, on October 18, as Russia continued deploying the Shahed-136 (which it renamed the Geran-2 after making modifications and enhancements) against Ukraine's infrastructure and population, Major General Yahya Safava, a top military aide to Khamenei, claimed that twenty-two countries wanted to purchase Iranian drones.[49]

In terms of potential gains, Iranian leaders and officials were likely using the drone transfers to Russia and other high-risk behavior to pressure the United States and other Western countries to revive the nuclear deal or another agreement of that sort. Such an agreement would restore hope and stability to a deteriorating socioeconomic situation inside Iran. These leaders and officials learned from experience that having a chance to revive the deal or one like it required adopting a threatening rather than a congenial approach toward the United States and its allies and partners—which they perceived as being untrustworthy. What was happening now in terms of Iran's risky behavior was largely a reiteration of the developments that had unfolded after the 2009 Green Movement protests. The latter had posed an immense internal threat or challenge to the Iranian state, which perceived and portrayed the protests as a foreign conspiracy orchestrated by the United States and its allies and partners.

In terms of external pressure, it was during this period that the Obama administration started its oil war against Iran. This policy had been on the US agenda for years and was so bold that Congressional and Treasury Department officials privately referred to it as the "nuclear option" in any financial war. The United States had not taken such measures against an enemy's economy since the 1940s when Franklin Delano Roosevelt had imposed an embargo on all Japanese oil exports. In response, the imperial Japanese navy had attacked Pearl Harbor in 1941 and dragged the United States into World War II.[50]

Additionally, the White House dispatched its point man on Iran policy, Dennis Ross, to ask the Arab Gulf states—mainly Saudi Arabia, Kuwait, and the UAE—to once again adopt the old oil-offset strategy. They increased their petroleum production and exports to continue supplying the Asian economic powerhouses of China, Japan, South Korea, and India while they reduced imports of Iranian oil.[51] Shortly after Ross's trip, the Arab Gulf oil producers and exporters started to implement this strategy by replacing Iranian energy exports to Asian markets. In a private mission to Beijing in 2010, Emirate Crown Prince Al Nahyan communicated his government's willingness to quadruple its oil exports to China to offset any reduction of purchases from Iran. In a private gathering of American and British servicemen at an air base outside London in the spring of 2011, Prince Turki Al Faisal, the former head of Saudi intelligence, said: "Iran is very vulnerable in the oil sector and it is there that more could be done to squeeze the current government. . . . To put this into perspective, Saudi Arabia has so much [spare] production capacity—nearly 4 million barrels [per] day—that we could almost instantly replace all of Iran's oil production."[52]

The pressure coming from the new wave of crippling sanctions targeting Iran's oil exports and connection to the global financial system, coupled with the Arab Gulf states' oil-offset strategy, was compounded by the possible formation of an Arab–Israeli alliance against Iran. Although Arab governments constantly complained that strategy in the Persian Gulf was very much influenced and practically dictated by the American Israel Public Affairs Committee (AIPAC), they found its initiatives against Iran to be quite effective. In November 2011, AIPAC circulated a letter to Congress calling for sanctions against Bank Markazi. The letter was supported by ninety-seven out of one hundred US senators and placed major pressure on the White House to act. Arab Gulf states led by the UAE announced their support for this initiative and showed a willingness to target Iran's finances.[53]

At this point, Iranian leaders and officials realized that they were being pressured from every angle, internally and externally. Beginning in 2010, one year into the Green Movement protests, this perception was reinforced by a wave of assassinations against Iranian nuclear scientists that were seen as the work of Israel's Mossad and its internal collaborators. It was at this stage that Iran started to increase its threats against Israel and Saudi Arabia. On October 11, 2011, the United States claimed that it had stopped what became known as the "Iran assassination plot" against the personnel of the Israeli and Saudi embassies in Washington, DC, and Buenos Aires. This plot was proceeded by the targeting of Israeli embassy staff in Georgia and India in 2012. That year, the number of Iranian proxy attacks against Israeli citizens and cities significantly increased.[54] Iran also increased its support for Hezbollah and deployed troops to Syria during the Syrian civil war.[55]

After 2009, and in response to its internal and external pressures, Iran exhibited a riskier geopolitical conduct that, at the time, manifested itself in waging a proxy war against Israel, especially through Hezbollah by carrying out suicide bombings from South Lebanon.[56] The Obama administration viewed the situation as dangerously spiraling out of control and moving toward a direct military confrontation between Iran and Israel that would eventually drag the United States into it as well. The administration then realized that a deescalatory round of negotiations with Iran became necessary. The 2015 Iran nuclear deal was the result of these negotiations that started mainly because Iran had acted as risk-seeking actor rather than a risk-averse one.[57] This scenario complicated and contradicted the narrative that economic sanctions and enrichment rights had brought Iran to the negotiating table.

The current situation signaled similar developments that had been seen after 2009. As such, we believe that the current phase of the Iran–US conflict will probably end with another agreement resembling the Iran nuclear deal—which already appeared to be in the works.[58] Prospect theory enables us to draw this insight, which cannot be derived from the alternative explanations discussed earlier. We certainly do not mean to suggest that such an agreement would put an end to this decades-long conflict. Rather, it would likely stabilize the Islamic Republic's position domestically for several years until hardliners and hawks inside Iran, the United States, and elsewhere express dissatisfaction with or outrage over the agreement, seek to terminate it, and so forth. What happens between these cycles of escalation and deescalation is that the Iranian regime temporarily satisfies its constituents and ensures its short-term survival for several more years.

Since the start of the MPC rhetoric and policy in 2016, Iran engaged in risk-seeking behavior, culminating in military support for Russia during the Ukraine war. An assortment of alternative explanations offered valuable insights into the reasons behind this behavior. Though the latter can be better understood through the conceptual framework of prospect theory. From this perspective, Iran's support of Russia was only one in a series of risk-seeking behavior stemming from the perception of operating in the domain of losses. In this chapter, we argued that this perception or framing began with the onset of the MPC as a critical juncture. It caused Iran to lose the psychological and material dividends of the 2015 Iran nuclear deal, regardless of their significance from a financial standpoint. The perception of Iranian leaders and officials, some of whom had expended considerable political capital to consummate the deal, was that the MPC directly targeted and undermined the stability and survival of the state and placed it squarely within the domain of losses.

As of 2017, this perception was reinforced by more frequent and intense protests, including, most recently, the Woman, Life, Freedom ones of 2022–23. Each of these protest cycles dealt a severe blow to the legitimacy and stability of the state and caused it to respond with greater repression, creating a vicious cycle of sorts. Iranian leaders and officials perceived and portrayed the protests as a byproduct of the MPC and a plot by foreign enemies, namely the United States or "Great Satan" and its allies and partners in Western Europe and the Middle East. Further contributing to the perception of loss by Iranian leaders and officials was the prospect of a US–Arab–Israeli front against Iran in the Persian Gulf. This front gained added momentum in the aftermath of the Abraham Accords and the Israeli–Saudi talks between 2020 and 2022. For Iran, such a front was somewhat neutralized by bilateral talks with Saudi Arabia and the UAE since 2019, as well as the Chinese-brokered agreement between Tehran and Riyadh in 2023. However, it remained to be seen whether these developments could realistically overcome the deep-seated suspicion and historical hostility that existed between Iran and Arab Gulf states like Saudi Arabia and the UAE. For the time being, they continued to largely operate under the US security umbrella despite their increasing rapprochement with China and Russia.

Motivated by the perception of loss, Iran engaged in risk-seeking behavior to acquire an assortment of actual and potential gains. In the case of Iranian drone transfers and other military assistance to Russia in Ukraine, these gains included earning profit, enhancing prestige, and projecting power. Through this assistance and the adoption of other risk-acceptant behavior, such as enrichment, attacks, hostages, and proxies, Iran endeavored to extract concessions from the United States and Western Europe in the form of a new nuclear deal. As was the case during the Green Movement protests leading up to the signing of the JCPOA between 2009 and 2015, such a strategy delivered sanctions relief, social stability, and societal optimism, albeit short lived, that were conducive to the survival and sustainability of the state. Based on our analysis of the empirical evidence, we anticipate a similar outcome coming to fruition. As of this writing, reports surfaced that Washington and Tehran had negotiated an informal agreement for nuclear restrictions and prisoner releases in exchange for frozen assets.

As in the past, this prospective agreement presumably faced strong opposition on both sides, not to mention from their regional allies and partners. In the United States, Republicans and Democrats both had their fair share of Iran hawks, who fed off the low-hanging fruit of taking a hardline approach toward the Islamic Republic to score political points with donors and voters. For some Iranian elites, the status quo of persistent tensions with the United States created perverse incentives of rallying segments of the population around an external enemy, deflecting attention away from government mismanagement and corruption, and exploiting sanctions to minimize foreign competition, monopolize economic sectors, and strengthen smuggling networks. That said, this opposition could be overcome by agreement among the executives on both sides. On one side, the US president aimed to reduce regional tensions, as he confronted conventional conflicts in Europe and Asia and entered the next election cycle in America. On the other side, the Iranian supreme leader and president sought greater regional and domestic stability, with the power dynamics of the Middle East steadily shifting and the succession issue in Iran looming large. Time will tell whether the agreement can serve as a stepping stone to dialing down US–Iran tensions and those in the Middle East more broadly—an outcome bolstered by Chinese mediation efforts and greater regional engagement.

NOTES

1. Robbie Gramer, "Iran Doubles Down on Arms for Russia," *Foreign Policy*, March 3, 2023, https://bit.ly/47LmvPo.

2. Amos Tversky and Daniel Kahneman, "Rational Choice and the Framing of Decisions," *Journal of Business* 59, no. 4 (1986): 251–78.

3. Jim Zanotti, Kenneth Katzman, Jeremiah Gertler, and Steven A. Hildreth, "Israel: Possible Military Strike Against Iran's Nuclear Facilities," Congressional Research Service, September 28, 2012, https://bit.ly/49QsIf4.

This possibility was later mitigated by the launching of the Stuxnet attack on Iran's supervisory control and data acquisition systems related to its nuclear program.

4. Eric Lob and Edward Riehle, "The Difficulty of Disrupting Iranian Drones," *National Interest*, January 14, 2023, https://bit.ly/3unPASJ; and Eric Lob and Edward Riehle, "Assessing the Threat of Iran's Drone Carriers," Middle East Institute, March 7, 2023, https://bit.ly/40O44r8.

5. Hadi Ajili and Mahsa Rouhi, "Iran's Military Strategy," *Survival* 61, no. 6 (2019): 139–52; Michael Rubin, "Iran: Mohajer-6 UAV Strikes Targets in Iraq," *OE Watch Commentary/ APAN Community*, September 1, 2019, https://bit.ly/47AEyYG; and "Mohajer-6 dar bazar-e sadarat-e movafaq khohad bud?/ Pehpad-e chandmanzureh-e Irani ra bishtar beshnasid" [Will the Mohajer-6 be successful in the export market? / Learn more about the Iranian multipurpose drone], Tasnim News, September 7, 2021, https://bit.ly/3sUnXAa.

6. Mohammad Eslami, "Iran's Ballistic Missile Program and Its Foreign and Security Policy Towards the United States Under the Trump Administration," *Revista española de ciencia política* 55 (2021): 37–62; and "Kodam-e pehpad-e Irani dar Tajikistan tawlid mishavad?/Gozaresh-e Tasnim az pehpad-e Ababil ba ghabeliyat-e shenasayi, razmi va entehari" [Which Iranian drone is produced in Tajikistan? / Tasnim's report on the Ababil UAV with reconnaissance, combat and suicide capabilities], Tasnim News, May 18, 2022, https://acr.ps/1L9zRZZ.

7. Rubin, "Iran"; "Gozaresh/Mohajerha-ye Sepah bala-ye sar-e teroristha-ye Kurdistan/Avalin-e amaliyat-e boroonmarzi-e Mohajer-6 ba bombha-ye Qaem" [Report/IRGC migrants above the heads of Kurdistan terrorists/First overseas operation of Migrant-6 with Qaem bombs], Tasnim News, July 12, 2019, https://bit.ly/3MU1eeA; Gawdat Bahgat and Anoushiravan Ehteshami, *Defending Iran: From Revolutionary Guards to Ballistic Missiles* (Cambridge University Press, 2021), 82, 190–91; Mohammad Eslami, "Iran's Drone Supply to Russia and Changing Dynamics of the Ukraine War," *Journal for Peace and Nuclear Disarmament* 5, no. 2 (2022): 507–18: 511FN7; "Kodam-e pehpad-e Irani dar Tajikistan tawlid mishavad?"; and Euan Ward and Farnaz Fassihi, "Iran Ramps Up Drone Exports, Signaling Global Ambitions," *New York Times*, July 28, 2022, https://bit.ly/47ql6y1.

8. Robert Beckhusen, "Don't Freak Out, But Iran Is Helping Venezuela Build Drones," WIRED, March 8, 2012, https://www.wired.com/2012/03/iran-venezuela-drones/; Rubin, "Iran"; Wilder Alejandro Sanchez, "Venezuelan Technology Plan May Lean on Iran," Shephard Media, November 27, 2020, https://bit.ly/3sDnaDU; Robert Tollast, "Iran Ramps Up Arms Transfers to Venezuela and Plans Regional Strife," *National*, December 7, 2020, https://bit.ly/3Ra0apl; "Mohajer-6 dar bazar-e sadarat-e movafaq khohad bud?"; "Kodam-e pehpad-e Irani dar Tajikistan tawlid mishavad?"; and Ward and Fassihi, "Iran Ramps Up Drone Exports."

9. Lob and Riehle, "Difficulty of Disrupting."

10. Nasser Karimi, "UN Arms Embargoes on Iran Expire Despite US Objections," AP News, October 18, 2020, https://acr.ps/1L9zRoM.

11. Sanchez "Venezuelan Technology"; Tollast, "Iran Ramps Up Transfers"; and Ward and Fassihi, "Iran Ramps Up Drone Exports."

12. Lob and Riehle, "Difficulty of Disrupting."

13. For an analysis of the United States targeting Soleimani due to its framing of the IRGC and the Quds Force as terrorist organizations, see Seyed Milad Kashefi Pour Dezfuli, "Targeted Killings and the Erosion of International Norms Against Assassination," *Defense & Security Analysis* 39, no. 2 (2023): 191–206.

14. Reza Bagheri and Eric Lob, "Rouhani's Africa Policy: Disengagement, 2013–21," *Middle East Policy* 29, no. 1 (2022): 154–173.

15. Robbie Gramer and Amy Mackinnon, "Iran and Russia Are Closer Than Ever Before," *Foreign Policy*, January 5, 2023, https://bit.ly/4h5HIbC.

16. Natasha Bertrand, "Exclusive: Russians Have Visited Iran at Least Twice in Last Month to Examine Weapons-Capable Drones," CNN Politics, July 15, 2022, https://bit.ly/4fPTDt5; Kateryna Stepanenko, Layne Phillipson, Karolina Hird, Katherine Lawlor, Angela Howard, and Frederick W. Kagan, "Russian Offensive Campaign Assessment," Institute for the Study of War, August 5, 2022, https://bit.ly/4gSJg99; and Ashish Dangwal, "1st Evidence Of Russia-Operated Iranian Suicide Drone Emerges in Ukraine; Kiev Claims Downing Shahed-136 UAV," *EurAsian Times*, September 13, 2022, https://bit.ly/408onzx.

17. Amberin Zaman, "Turkish Drones Boost Ukrainian Spirits amid Fears of Russian Invasion," Al-Monitor, January 27, 2022, https://bit.ly/428P5L8; Valius Venckunas, "Ukraine Receives New Batch of Bayraktar TB-2 Drones from Turkey," *Aerotime Hub*, March 2, 2022, https://bit.ly/4gKmvEs; Matthew Gault, "Ukraine Has Written a Folk Song About Its Drone," Vice, April 4, 2022, https://bit.ly/4ae0lrO; Jomana Karadsheh and Isil Sariyuce, "Turkish Drones Have Become a Symbol of the Ukrainian Resistance," CNN, April 11, 2022, https://bit.ly/4gZ6kTo; and Ash Rossiter and Brendon J. Cannon, "Turkey's Rise as a Drone Power: Trial By Fire," *Defense and Security Analysis* 38, no. 2 (2022): 5, 10–11.

18. Patrick Wintour, "Ukraine: What Will China do? There Are Signs It Is Uneasy About Putin's Methods," *Guardian*, February 27, 2022, https://bit.ly/4h5ANit; Camille Bourgeois-Fortin, Darren Choi, and Sean Janke, "China and Russia's Invasion of Ukraine: Initial Responses and Implications," China Institute, March 7, 2022, https://bit.ly/4jaBF7y; Aglaya Snetkov and Marc Lanteigne, "Ukraine: Why China Is Not Yet Bailing Out Russia," Conversation, March 18, 2022, https://bit.ly/4j6KEGJ; and Austin Ramzy, "Russia Says That a Senior Chinese Official Expressed Support for the Invasion of Ukraine," *New York Times*, September 11, 2022, https://bit.ly/428DETQ.

19. "Turkey, Ukraine Sign Military Cooperation Agreements," VOA News, October 16, 2020, https://bit.ly/4gOt2Oc; Claire Mills, "Military Assistance to Ukraine 2014–2021," House of Commons Library, March 4, 2021, https://bit.ly/3C3wgOY; Keoni Everington, "Taiwan's Revolver 860 Combat Drones Being Used By Ukrainians on Battlefield," *Taiwan News*, August 18, 2022, https://bit.ly/4jbZdJ2; Lolita C. Baldor and Matthew Lee, "US to

Send $3 Billion in Aid to Ukraine as War Hits 6 Months," AP News, August 23, 2022, https://bit.ly/3WfbJ0K; David Brown and Tural Ahmedzade, "What Weapons Are Being Given to Ukraine By the UK?" BBC News, September 20, 2022, https://bit.ly/422D7Tl; Eslami, "Iran's Drone Supply," 509; and Isabelle Khurshudyan, Mary Ilyushina, and Kostiantyn Khudov, "Russia and Ukraine are Fighting the First Full-Scale Drone War," *Washington Post*, December 2, 2022, https://acr.ps/1L9zSpn.

20. Jared Malsin and Isabel Coles, "Russia Uses Iranian-Made Drones to Strike Military Base Deep Inside Ukraine," *Wall Street Journal*, October 5, 2022, https://bit.ly/40nJoaW; Douglas Barrie, "Explainer: Russia Deploys Iranian Drones," *Iran Primer*, October 12, 2022, https://bit.ly/3BOvKnW; and Isabelle Khurshudyan, Annabelle Timsit, and Kostiantyn Khudov, "Drones Hit Kyiv as Russia Aims to Destroy Ukraine Power Grid Before Winter," *Washington Post*, October 17, 2022, https://bit.ly/3WdHd7o.

21. Joby Warrick, Souad Mekhennet, and Ellen Nakashima, "Iran Will Help Russia Build Drones for Ukraine War, Western Officials Say," *Washington Post*, November 19, 2022, https://bit.ly/4gSL1mL.

22. David L. Stern and Robyn Dixon, "Russia Pummels Ukraine with Missiles and Drones, Injuring Civilians," *Washington Post*, November 17, 2022, https://bit.ly/4hbr0Yt.

23. Jack Guy, Yulia Kesaieva, Jo Shelley, Denis Lapin, and Tim Lister, "Russian Strikes Leave 10 Million Ukrainians Without Power as Temperatures Plummet," CNN, November 18, 2022, https://bit.ly/3Waixwk; and Jessica Parker and Phelan Chatterjee, "Ukraine War: Most of Kyiv Spends Night Without Power After Missiles," BBC News, November 24, 2022, https://bit.ly/3DPMTy7.

24. Neil Bhatiya and Edoardo Saravalle, "Iran's Post-Sanctions Financial Windfall Was Overstated. What Does That Mean for Policy?" *National Interest*, September 24, 2017, https://bit.ly/4gSLvt5.

25. Seth G. Jones, Jared Thompson, Danielle Ngo, Joseph S. Bermudez, Jr., and Brian McSorley, "The Iranian and Houthi War Against Saudi Arabia," Center for Strategic & International Studies, December 21, 2021, https://bit.ly/3DRyoKg.

26. "Iran Agrees to Ship Missiles, More Drones to Russia," Reuters, October 18, 2022, https://bit.ly/401TPzm.

27. Lob and Riehle, "Assessing the Threat."

28. Jack S. Levy, "Prospect Theory, Rational Choice, and International Relations," *International Studies Quarterly* 41, no. 1 (1997): 87–112.

29. Barbara Slavin, "New Poll Says Iranians Like Zarif, Dislike US," Al-Monitor, February 2, 2016, https://bit.ly/3C2V2P6.

30. Mazahar Koruzhde, "The Iranian Crisis of the 1970s–1980s and the Formation of the Transnational Investment Bloc," *Class, Race and Corporate Power* 10, no. 2 (2022): 1–10; Mazaher Koruzhde and Ronald W. Cox, "The Transnational Investment Bloc in U.S. Policy Toward Saudi Arabia and the Persian Gulf," *Class, Race and Corporate Power* 10, no. 1 (2022): 1.

31. See Office of the Spokesperson, "Maximum Pressure Campaign on the Regime in Iran," US Department of State, April 4, 2019, https://bit.ly/428p7Ym.

32. Mazaher Koruzhde and Valeriia Popova, "Americans Still Held Hostage: A Generational Analysis of American Public Opinion about the Iran Nuclear Deal," *Political Science Quarterly* 137, no. 3 (2022): 511–37.

33. See their respective websites: https://www.aei.org and https://www.heritage.org.

34. Bhativa and Saravalle, "Iran's Post-Sanctions Financial Windfall."

35. Sara Bazoobandi. "Iran's Uprising and the TikTok Generation," Carnegie Endowment for International Peace, January 2, 2023, https://bit.ly/4h4rW0D.

36. Simon Jeffery, "Iran Election Protests: The Dead, Jailed and Missing," *Guardian*, July 29, 2009, https://bit.ly/3DMeiRs; see also the homepage of Human Rights Activists in Iran: https://www.hra-iran.org/en/.

37. Agence France-Presse, "Fresh Protests Erupt in Iran's Universities and Kurdish Region," *Guardian*, November 6, 2022, https://bit.ly/3PrXQrY.

38. Colin Daileda, "Donald Trump Made History with His Flight from Saudi Arabia to Israel," Mashable, May 22, 2017, https://bit.ly/3We1ae9.

39. Emad Mekay, "Saudi Arabia and Israel Quietly Prepare 'Deal of the Century,'" International Bar Association, 2017, https://bit.ly/3WbT3io.

40. Bethan McKernan, "Israel and Saudi Arabia 'In Talks over Joint Defence Against Iran,'" *Guardian*, June 27, 2022, https://bit.ly/3BY11or.

41. Mekay, "Saudi Arabia and Israel Quietly Prepare."

42. Baran Abbasi, "Hoshdar-e tond-e Iran dar mowred-e rabeteh-e Emarat ba Esraeil" [Iran's sharp warning about the UAE's relationship with Israel], BBC News Farsi, August 15, 2020, https://www.bbc.com/persian/iran-53793535.

43. Tia Goldenberg, "Israeli PM Bennett in Snap UAE Visit amid Standoff with Iran," AP News, June 9, 2022, https://bit.ly/4acAxfF.

44. "'Hoshdar-e jedi-e' Iran darbareh-ye adisazi-ye menasebat ba Esraeil" [Iran's "serious warning" about normalizing relations with Israel], DW, December 14, 2021, https://acr.ps/1L9zSgW.

45. Aaron David Miller and Steven Simon, "Is Saudi-Israeli Normalization Worth It?" *Foreign Policy*, June 5, 2023, https://bit.ly/4fU1GFf.

46. Sebastien Roblin, "How Chinese Ballistic Missiles and Iranian Drones Popped Up In Ethiopia's Civil War in Tigray," *National Interest*, September 22, 2021, https://bit.ly/4fRosgM.

47. "Iran to Host Russian Trade Delegation amid Rumors of 'Su-35 Deliveries,'" Amwaj.media, November 14, 2022, https://bit.ly/4fLVoYl; Eslami, "Iran's Drone Supply," 507–11; and Lob and Riehle, "Difficulty of Disrupting."

48. Ellen Nakashima and Joby Warrick, "Iran Sends First Shipment of Drones to Russia for Use in Ukraine," *Washington Post*, August 29, 2022, https://bit.ly/40p2FJ3; Yaroslav Trofimov and Dion Nissenbaum, "Russia's Use of Iranian Kamikaze Drones Creates New Dangers for Ukrainian Troops," *Wall Street Journal*, September 17, 2022, https://bit.ly/428FaFw; and Peter Beaumont, "Russia Escalating Use of Iranian 'Kamikaze' Drones in Ukraine," *Guardian*, September 29, 2022, https://bit.ly/3BRs7gZ.

49. Eslami, "Iran's Drone Supply," 507–18; and Lob and Riehle, "Difficulty of Disrupting."

50. Jay Solomon, *The Iran Wars: Spy Games, Bank Battles, and the Secret Deals That Reshaped the Middle East* (Random House, 2016), 194.

51. Solomon, *Iran Wars*, 196.

52. Solomon, *Iran Wars*, 197. Those days seem to be gone with Saudi Arabia, as part of OPEC Plus, refusing to increase petroleum production against Russia and Iran by extension during the Ukraine war. However, one cannot downplay the Saudis' ongoing reliance on US security in the Persian Gulf.

53. Solomon, *Iran Wars*, 199.

54. Mark Hosenball, "Exclusive—New York Police Link Nine 2012 Plots to Iran, Proxies," Reuters, July 20, 2012, https://bit.ly/4a7ZAAp.

55. It is necessary to mention that Iran would have probably supported the al-Assad regime regardless, as the latter was Iran's only Arab ally. However, from the perspective developed in this chapter, we can view the potential demise of the al-Assad regime as another point of external pressure that involved the United States and its Arab Gulf allies and partners.

56. Hosenball, "New York Police Link Nine 2012 Plots."

57. Solomon, *Iran Wars*.

58. Laurence Norman and David S. Cloud, "U.S. Launches Quiet Diplomatic Push with Iran to Cool Tensions," *Wall Street Journal*, June 14, 2023, https://bit.ly/4h2Z1Kc.

10

THE DEFENSE SECTOR AND FOREIGN POLICY DECISIONS

The Case of Iran's Policy Toward Russia

Abdolrasool Divsallar

The small group effect on foreign policy decision making has been largely researched in international relations (IR). Previous studies have revealed that interaction among group members creates particular patterns of behavior that affect how the policy process will evolve and likely influence policy outcomes.[1] Concept such as military–industrial complex has been introduced to capture the effect of specific group of security actors by presenting a conceptual model to explain how a network of security apparatuses, the militaries, defense industries, and legislative bodies seek to influence state choices.[2] In particular and in the case of Iran, previous research has shown that different institutional roles and groups have substantial influence in shaping foreign policy outcomes.[3]

The perpetual state of existential threat against Islamic Republic and the primacy of adjustment with threat dynamics has given a powerful voice in foreign policy debates to those groups that have a bigger role in guaranteeing the survivability of the political system.[4] The defense sector is at the top of the list of such groups, and it includes a group of military–security institutions such as the Islamic Revolutionary Guards Corps (IRGC), the General Staff, Ministry of Defense (MOD), and military intelligence organizations. These institutions hold a critical responsibility to assess the level of which partnership with external actors can be helpful in insulating the Islamic Republic from hybrid threats—a logic that is becoming the core of Iranian foreign policy rationale.

It is believed that under the supervision of the supreme leader, Iran's key decisions about Russia is a result of debate among a closed network of defense and security sector, although it can be still checked to certain extent by public opinion and other government bodies. This important dynamic is often underappreciated in the studies of Russo–Iranian partnership and generally in understanding role of the defense sector in shaping and implementing Iran's Look East policy.

This chapter investigates this assumption by studying the narrative of Russia in Iran's defense sector and the impact of these narratives on country's foreign policy directions toward Russia. It argues that defense sector's strong voice has allowed it to strategically influence Tehran's decisions toward Moscow, probably making its narrative of Russia to be one of the most, if not the most, influential factor in the decision-making cycle. Although this is not a new phenomenon, its importance has been gradually raised by increasing risks of war and regional escalations, deterioration of Iran's relations with the West, and the war in Ukraine. Any analysis of Russia–Iran ties cannot be made without proper understanding of group influence and especially defense sector's view of Moscow.

On this backdrop, this chapter identifies five narratives about Russia in Iran's defense sector: Russia as an arms supplier, Russia as a technology provider, Russia as a source of doctrinal inspiration, Russia as a supporter of Iran's military strategy, and Russia as an unreliable partner. These narratives reflect an overall positive attitude toward Russia yet have a strong flavor of conservatism. This pattern is a departure from the views of other governmental institutions and public opinion, which have a stronger sentiment of historical suspicion toward Russia and seek more balanced ties with Moscow. This case study shows how the perceptions of small group of institutions can outweigh preferences of other stakeholders despite the overall frictions and costs that they may impose.

The Key Arms Supplier

The history of arms deals between Islamic Republic and Russia goes back to 1980s and during the Iran–Iraq war when the Soviet Union was a controversial actor. On one side, from the early stages of the war, Soviets emerged as a leading arms supplier to Iraq, providing Saddam Hussein with advanced weapons, including Tu-22 bombers and SCUD-B missiles with strategic impacts on the course of the conflict. But Moscow's green light was also essential for delivering Soviet-made weapons to Tehran from Libya, Syria, and North Korea.[5] Soviet weapons helped Iraq in the so-called War of the Cities, creating an adverse reaction toward the then-Soviet state inside Iranian leadership. Iraqi use of Soviet-made weapons, however, also raised the status of these weapons as an alternative to Western arms from which Tehran had been cut off post-1979. For example, Iranian air defense operators were impressed by the Tu-22 bombers' performance and how it was difficult to defend against them. These encounters with Soviet weapons and witnessing their effectiveness led those in the Iranian defense sector to become more interested in these products and officers positively recommended that they be purchased.[6] Ironically, Iraq's use of Soviet-made missiles highlighted the value of these weapons in future Iranian procurement plans.

Since the 1990s Russia has played a significant role in refurbishing Iran's depleting arsenal, effectively preventing the country's demise of conventional deterrence. This fact has impacted the perception of Russia inside the Iranian defense sector more than anything else. Tehran started a massive rearmament process by the end of the Iran–Iraq war to replenish its devasted arsenal. Soviet Foreign Minister Edouard Shevardnadze's February 1989 visit to Tehran and Ali Akbar Hashemi Rafsanjani's trip to Moscow in June 1989 led to an agreement with the Soviet Union to sell military hardware to Tehran. This diplomatic outreach culminated in Moscow's decision to sell its first ever large arms package to Tehran.

Between 1991 and 2000, the Russian list of sales to Iran included three Kilo-class diesel submarines, about twenty-five MiG-29 and twelve Su-24 combat aircraft, hundreds of R-73, R-60, and R-27 air-to-air missiles, up to 422 T-72 tanks, and 413 BMP-2s, about forty-two SA-5 and number of SA-6 air defense systems, dozens of torpedoes and mines, and 13,500 various antitank missiles, though not all of them were fully delivered.[7] Iran's purchase of Russian weapon systems resumed after the 2000s with Vladimir Putin's presidency. Between 2000 and 2016, Tehran received forty-four Mi-8MT/Mi-17, six Su-25 ground attack aircraft, twenty-nine Tor-M-1 units with 750 missiles, four S-300PMU2 units with 152 missiles, an unknown number of VA-111 Shkval torpedo, dozens of SA-16/18 Igla missiles, several important air search radars, including two units of 1L119 Nebo-SVU and two units of Kasta-2E2, and advanced electronic warfare (EW) systems such as 1L222 Avtobaza-M.[8] Russia also exported small arms such as AK-103 and towed guns to Iran during this period.

These acquisitions were essential in filling the gap of critical military capabilities, as Tehran lacked indigenous industrial and technological capacity to fill them. For example, Iranian anti-access/area denial capability substantially strengthened by Russian-made short- and long-range air defense systems, long-range early warning radars, and EW systems. Another example is the IRGC's close air support capability which was established based on only Russian-made jets. Also, the country's tactical airborne logistics strengthened by the newly purchased helicopter fleet from Russia.

Although reactions to arms imports from Russia were overall positive across the force, but there were some differences between the Artesh and IRGC too. It took a longer time for the Artesh air force and navy to put aside initial doubts about non-Western weapons systems and acknowledge their performance. The air force and navy were traditionally operating Western weapons; thus they had to make organizational and technical adjustments to switch to Russian systems. These adjustments were not always a straightforward process. Yet, as these systems entered into service, they gradually attracted attentions of their operators. For example, several Iranian pilots trained in Russia on the new aircraft were former F-14 pilots who had previously trained in the United States. These pilots expressed satisfaction with Russian jets' performance despite the Russian provision of analogue versions of MiG-29s that lacked modern electronics and aerial refueling pods.[9] The overall assessment was that MiG-29 and Su-24 provided a new capability, including strategic long-range bomb capability, that filled capability gaps in the air force after the war. Russian submarines, however, were probably the most important single asset that created a positive wave of assessment across the Artesh. The Kilo-class diesel submarines were advanced and formidable assets, and Iran had never had such a capability. Despite suffering from several shortcomings, the Iranian navy's operational review of Kilo submarines was positive.[10] These evaluations reflected themselves in the Armed Forces General Staff assessments and impacted future acquisition decisions.

The IRGC was even more satisfied with Russian deliveries from the very beginning. Its aerospace force benefited immensely from Russian assistance in acquiring aerial capability. It relies on Su-25 and Su-22 and thus owes the backbone of its airborne capability to the Russian systems. Despite whether these systems were imported from different sources, including indirect purchases, and fleeing from Iraq during the 2003 US invasion of Iraq, their Russian origin connects the IRGC's aerospace force with Russia in persistent ways. In fact, and opposite to Artesh, the IRGC's air force's organizational design and operational model were initially designed to host Russian systems.

As evidenced in the volume and quality of Russian arms sales, political issues such as the infamous Gore–Chernomyrdin agreement, through which Moscow agreed with Washington to limit its military assistance to Iran, had temporary impacts. Therefore, notwithstanding periods of disruptions in Russian sales due to international pressures, dynamics of US–Russia relations, and Russian defense industries' approaches to arms sales, the flow of Russian arms to the Iranian military continued over the last three decades. Russian motives for such exports, from attracting cash for their starved defense industry in the 1990s to anti-Americanism and attempts to remain relevant in the Middle East, seems to less important factors in the Iranian defense sector's assessment of Russia. What mattered is that the Russian-manufactured weapons became the only major foreign weapons available to the Iranian military in the post-1979 revolution, and Moscow remained the key state party to supply spare parts, provide trainings, and other services. This fact has not gone unnoticed by Iranian top military officers, especially when comparing other politically close states such as China. Despite China's warm relations with Iran and signature of the Twenty-Five-Year Cooperation Agreement, Beijing's arms exports to Iran remained substantially low.

Russia as a Technology Provider

Several critical Iranian defense programs, including the nuclear program, missile program, passive defense program, space program, and radar and optic advancements, remained dependent on Russian contributions at different stages of their development. No less prominent than direct arms sales, Russian provision of technology and know-how to Iran proved to be an effective approach that gave Moscow an endured presence and influence inside Iranian defense sector.

Russian technological influence on Iran's defense industries since the 1990s has manifested itself in at least three ways: technology transfer, exposure effects, and direct training. First, and at least since 1994, the Office of Presidential Cooperation (OPC) initiated a systematic effort to attract scientists, engineers, and agents in post-Soviet countries interested in selling and transferring critical sensitive technologies to Iran. The OPC benefited from President Ali Akbar Hashemi Rafsanjani and Mohamad Reza Khatami's support and, in a close link with the Ministry of Intelligence and Ministry of Defense, successfully transferred important missile, radar, optics, and jet engine technologies and sometimes complete systems to Iran. Second, Iran's state-to-state collaborations with Russia in the high-tech industry had a significant exposure effect. It gave Iran's defense industries unique access and working experience in sensitive fields. Through state-level contacts and formal visits to Russian industrial complexes, defense technicians and managers were exposed to designs, production lines, standards, and know-how for industrial-scale management in technological fields that they had little experience in before. Third, since the early 1990s, Russia has remained a critical source for the training and education of Iranian experts in high-tech fields.

This three-dimensional model of technological contacts played an essential role in the initial stages of establishing Iran's indigenous defense industry and its later evolution to a mature industry. While the early postrevolutionary scientific cooperation between Iran and Russia was under the shadow of the OPC and was heavily relied on covert operations and informal contacts, Putin's tenure was a new era for bilateral ties.[11] Technological contacts continued through more formal agreements between the two states in this era. In this way, low-profile, unofficial Russian transfer of defense technologies and know-how to Iran continued even during the 1995 Gore–Chernomyrdin agreement in which Russia promised the United States it would avoid selling arms to Iran.

Iran's missile program was among the first important sectors that received Russian technological assistance. Since 1994, Russian entities and individuals contacted by the OPC and Iran's Ministry of Intelligence have played a role in transferring missile technology to Tehran. While no official acknowledgment of these transfers was made, and some Russian sources claimed the unauthorized nature of these transfers, their sensitive nature and the fact that most Russian institutes involved in this matter were part of the Russian state-owned defense industry make such claims less reliable. By 1997 to 1998, US concerns over Russian missile technology leaks to Iran had become part of the bilateral US–Russia dialogues. Testifying at the Senate in 2000, then–CIA Director George Tenet claimed that "the transfer of ballistic missile technology from Russia to Iran was substantial and . . . will continue to accelerate Iranian efforts to develop new missiles and to become self-sufficient in production."[12] According to US observations reported to the Gore–Chernomyrdin Commission in 1997, Russian assistance was essential in shortening the time the Iranians would be able to develop, manufacture, and deploy their medium-range ballistic missiles (MRBMs).[13]

The assistance in question included material and know-how that may be used for parts of a ballistic missile, maybe for the warhead, maybe for the fuselage, provided to Iran by Russian entities, in some cases state institutes, universities, and for-profit organizations.[14] These transfers included propulsion and guidance technology training at Baltic State Technical University in St. Petersburg and perhaps at the Moscow Aviation Institute.[15] Transferring chemicals for fuel, high-strength steel for producing fuel tanks, special alloys and composites, wind tunnels, and measurement equipment for testing RD-214 (SS-4) rocket engines were also part of these transfers.[16] These connections later continued in the 2000s, including by training Iranians in long-range missile technologies and assistance for the Shahab-3 launchers.

Fast-forwarding to the era of war in Ukraine, Politico claimed in 2023 based on unknown diplomatic sources that Iran has been in talks with the state-owned Russian chemical maker FKP Anozit, to acquire large amounts of ammonium perchlorate, or AP, the main ingredient in solid propellants used to power missiles.[17] Western intelligence source have raised a possibility that Iran can seek Russian technological assistance for quality improvement of its missile program and access to new technologies, such as hypersonic missiles, in return for exporting arms to Russia amid the war in Ukraine.

The space program is another field influenced by collaboration with Russia. Contact on space issues between Tehran and Moscow goes back to the late 1990s. In one example, the Spurt Science and Production Center, known for its work on classified space programs, helped Iran to develop a national communications satellite.[18] Iran's space apparatus was initially developed in collaboration with the

Reutov Mashinostroyenie Science and Production Association, which has also been involved in developing Iran's ballistic and cruise missiles and military space systems. By the 2000s, Iranian students were sent to Russia, and Iranian military officials were granted access to several space facilities across Russia. All these exposures were essential to help Tehran shape its own domestic missile and space industry.

Later and on the sidelines of the MAX 2015 aviation show in Moscow, an initial agreement was signed on space cooperation. The discussion focused on Russian assistance to Iran's plan of sending humans to space, technical cooperation to develop satellites and control centers, launching Iranian satellites into orbit, and Russian aid for launcher program. The Khayyam satellite was one of the first results of this agreement. This satellite was designed by Iran and constructed by Russia under the supervision of Iranian teams. Iran's minster of communication and information technology claimed the agreement included technology transfer.[19] It has exposed Iranian technicians to Russian space industry procedures, standards, and industrial management. This process helped Tehran to boost its know-how of establishing its own space industry. The Khayyam satellite was put in orbit in July 2022 from Baikonur Space Station, where Iranian observers and technical teams were present.

While Iran can put satellites into orbit up to fifty kilograms, its attempt to launch 220- and 350-kilogram payloads failed. Thus, Russian assistance in launching heavier loads is critical in realizing Iran's ten-year space program. The head of Iran's Space Agency (ISA) announced in July 2022 that talks with Russia to assist country's human space program were undergoing. On this basis, in December 2022, Moscow and Tehran signed a new space agreement mainly focused on joint manufacturing and design of heavy remote sensing and communication satellites, developing satellite testing infrastructures, establishing joint laboratories and other infrastructures required for sustained launches, and launching Iranian satellites.[20]

Although not as large as the missile and nuclear programs, Russia also transferred critical radar, optics, bioscience, and material science technologies to Tehran under different modalities. For example, Russian industrial and technical assistance in the early 2000s were essential for producing special type of cement that are needed to build hardened bunkers and missile bases. Also, some of the main indigenously built radar systems, such as the Over the Horizon (OTH) Sepehr and Ghadir radars, seems to be revered-engineered versions of Russian Resonance-NE radars. While there is no hard evidence, it is not inconceivable that Iran received and reverse-engineered powerful EW and jamming systems, such as Krasukha-4, over the past decade. The Iranian version of the Krasukha-4 is now produced by Iranian defense industry under the name of Cobra V8.[21]

In other fields such as bioscience, collaboration since the early 2000s enjoyed extensive ties between state-owned universities that assisted Tehran to advance its national biological program. These collaborations, guided under the president's deputy for science and technology, helped Tehran in establishing critical laboratories and instruments needed for bioscience research.

Moscow contributed to the flourishing of Iran's defense industry by agreeing under the license production of Russian arms inside Iran and provision of needed spare parts. According to SIPRI, between 1993 and 2000, Russia sent 200 V-46-6 diesel engines to modernize T-54, T-55, and T-59 tanks to T-72Z standards. Later, between 2000 and 2012, Moscow sent 130 BMP-2 turrets for Boraq IFVs produced in Iran.[22] Also, Moscow provided spare parts for the maintenance and modernization of MiG-29s and Kilo-class submarines inside Iran. According to unconfirmed reports, Moscow provided additional spare parts for SU-22 jets that the IRGC operated. On light weapons, Russia agreed for domestic production of the AK-103 assault rifle in Iran. The production of the Iranian version of the AK-103 under the name of AK-133 started in 2017 with some modifications according to the IRGC's requests.[23]

More recently, and since the outbreak of the war in Ukraine, both sides have attempted to expand technological collaborations beyond the military sector. Putin's assistant for science and technology met the deputy for science and technology of Iran's president in Tehran in June 2023. They agreed to restore the Joint Committee on Science and Technology to lay out a roadmap and prioritize areas of cooperation. In previous years, the joint committee benefited from ten working groups on different science and technology domains. It has supported over one hundred Iranian researchers to receive grants and conduct research in Russia and funded fifty-eight joint projects. In parallel, another fifty-nine collaborative projects between Russian and Iranian scientists concluded by 2022 with the support of Iran's Fund for Support of Researchers and Innovators and the Russian Foundation for Basic Research. Yet the Iranian defense sector also values the spillover of these projects, especially on artificial intelligence, cyber security, and other dual-use technologies.

A Source of Doctrinal Inspirations

Often, nontechnological and nonweapon aspects of Russian influence in Iranian defense sector are underestimated. Russia is among the most organizationally, procedurally, and operationally advanced military powerhouses. This fact has put the Russian military on the spotlight of Iranian military studies, fascinated Iranian observers, and thus contributed to a narrative that perceived Russia as a unique source of learning on military strategy and doctrine. Military-to-military contacts, frequent visits to military facilities in Russian territory by top Iranian military leadership, and exchange of lessons learned in recent wars have helped position Russia as a major source of military thinking. This way, Tehran has constantly studied and learned from Russian doctrines, operational experiences, and institutional models.

Post-1979, and under the influence of revolutionary ideologies, the Iranian military used aspects of Soviet and Russian organizational models. Postrevolutionary military institutions noticed the importance of ideological training for their forces to preserve revolutionary values and objectives. Much like Soviet practices, since the revolution's early years, the Iranian military established "politico-ideological deputies" responsible for indoctrinating forces based on Islamic ideology. Even more controversial, the infamous Khomeini slogan of "army of twenty million," which referred to the mobilization of twenty million people to defend the revolution, resembles the Stalinist concept of mobilizing thirty million fighters. While it can be disputed if these similarities were deliberate imitations from the Soviet system, they mark an important diffusion of concepts and sympathy between ideologically driven military institutes.

Even though the Artesh was originally influenced by Western military institutions and organizational culture, the rising military-to-military contacts with Russia changed this course and transformed it into an organization with both Western and Russian elements. The Islamic Republic followed the Russian models of state-owned defense industries and centralized Russian defense procurement. Furthermore, Iranians carefully looked at Russian counterintelligence organizations' approaches. All of these possibly played an inspirational source for organizational revisions inside the Iranian security sector.

Impacts of Russian military thinking can be also traced in Iran's military doctrine. This influence is nowhere better seen than Iran's passive defense program. Iran's Passive Defense Organization was officially established in 2004. It envisions a mission of boosting the country's deterrence through nonkinetic measures that can minimize vulnerabilities and increase the resiliency of the country's national defense. While the initial conceptual source of the strategy was influenced by similar international practices, Tehran also used Russian concepts and designs in different phases of implementing its passive defense strategy. For example, the urban passive defense measures in Soviet cities attracted Iranian researchers and inspired the initial manuals on military and civilian passive defense measures.[24]

Iranian teams visiting Russian military bases in the 1990s and early 2000s noticed the extensive hardening, camouflage, and concealment measures, and use of underground facilities in Soviet designs. Between 2001 and 2003, IRGC research centers conducted extensive studies on the design, architecture, and typology of Russian military bases which highlighted passive defense measures' role in making sensitive military bases resistant to US first strikes. These ideas were inspirational for Iran's military strategists, and earnings from such measures assisted planners in Tehran in shaping their own unique approach in widespread use of hardened underground structures for nuclear and military purposes.

In recent years, however, a new domain of learning has intensified against the backdrop of two sides operational collaborations in both the Syrian and Ukrainian wars. Russian precision missile strikes proved a critical means to neutralize Ukrainian infrastructure and capabilities in areas where aerial bombing was risky. This observation seems to have reinforced Iran's earlier assessments about the battlefield value of mass firing short- and medium-range ballistic missiles and thus will likely impact the thinking about Iran's missile doctrine.[25] According to the *Washington Post* Russia shares assessments of these strikes against Ukraine's NATO-equipped forces with Iran in real time, which helps Tehran to improve the tactical and technical aspects of its missile forces.[26] The Russian experience also highlighted the importance of missile stockpile size. The war in Ukraine brought the direct link between qualitative factors associated with failure rates and the size of missile stockpiles to the Iranians' attention. Finally, the Russian experience entails important leaning on the operations procedures and concepts such as the best practices in complex coordinated hybrid missile–drone operations, evasion from enemy's countermeasures and antiair defense systems, and other tactical measures to raise the efficiency of missile and drone operations.

Russian Backing of Iran's Military Strategy

Russia's position toward Iran's defense strategy is unique among the great powers feeding a narrative that portrays Russia, in the eyes of Iranian military leadership, as the only major international actor that share military interests with Iran and is ready to support country's defense posture. Key elements of Iranian military strategy, including its large missile stockpile, network of nonstate actors, maritime asymmetrical capabilities in the Persian Gulf, and even nuclear latency, are not perceived by Moscow as a direct threat. Moscow's view is indeed in contrast to the United States, Europe, Arab states in the Persian Gulf, and Israel, who all see Iran's military strategy as destabilizing and threatening. As a result, Moscow stands out as the only major power that contributed to the advancement of Iran's military capabilities. What matters and feeds perception of Russia among Iran's defense sector is the fact that Moscow respects and actively supports Tehran's rights of building self-defense capabilities. In addition to pragmatic interest-based motives, Moscow's position is influenced by the two countries' persistent military-to-military dialogue, the minimum threat perception of Moscow from growth in Iranian capabilities, and occasional convergence of security interests that facilitates burden sharing.[27]

Multilayered and multiformat military-to-military dialogue has been a constant feature of both countries' relations in the last decades. Though these contacts experienced fluctuations and interruptions, decreasing during the Dmitry Medvedev presidency and increasing after the signing of the nuclear deal and the war in Ukraine, direct talks and visits between the two militaries never stopped. High-level meetings between ministers of defense and chiefs of general staff have been rising since 2015, leading to an agreement on military cooperation when the nuclear deal was imminent. These contacts reached its record high after the war in Ukraine when the two sides reached new levels of partnership.

The establishment of the Russia–Iran Joint Military Commission created a high-level platform to approve annual joint programs.[28] The commission regulates yearly visits among deputies of general staff and operational commanders, visits to military academies and headquarters, and a range of other visits to military facilities. At the same time, since 2013 and at the operational level, Iran's Quds Force and navy commanders have repeatedly visited Moscow. In return, commanders of the Russian air force and navy visited Tehran. The links at the unit level also continued to grow in the format of flagship visits to the ports, maritime drills, joint training, and military competitions.

The fact that Moscow does not perceive Iran's military capabilities as a threat also relates to the lack of geostrategic competition between the two states after the collapse of the Soviet Union. Competitions and disagreements are part of Iran–Russia relations, including competition in oil and gas markets, disagreements over the legal status of the Caspian Sea, pursuing conflicting interests in the Caucasus, and economic competitions in Syria. By the collapse of the Soviet Union, however, the two states have had minimum geostrategic competition, which may define them as potential threats and risks military confrontation.[29] The manifestation of this assessment can be seen in their force deployment. For example, Iran's missile forces are mainly positioned toward the south and the west of the country, where adversarial threats may form, implying Iran's no-threat perception from the north. In addition, their military-to-military links have facilitated discussions over Iranian missile and nuclear strategy, likely further reassuring Russia. Similarly, Iran's maritime activities in the Persian Gulf pose no threat to Russian interests, while Tehran's naval buildup in the Caspian Sea follows a close partnership with Moscow. Both countries reject the military presence of nonlittoral states in the Caspian Sea and oppose the US-led order in the Middle East, which reinforces their navies' cooperation in the Caspian Sea and Persian Gulf.

Finally, Moscow's view toward Iran's military strategy is impacted by the benefits Russia receives from it. Moscow and Tehran share a range of threat perceptions across the international system that has worked as a pillar of their security convergence.[30] Consequently, there is a common interest to cooperate in neutralizing shared threats, a fact that could be best seen in Syria, where Moscow and Tehran deemed joint intervention necessary to prevent the threat arising from the collapse of the Syrian regime, and later in Ukraine, when the two sides agreed on the need to neutralize the NATO threat. The Syrian and Ukrainian cases reveal how elements of Iranian military strategy might become strategically beneficial for Russia.

General Ghasem Soleimani, then–commander in chief of the IRGC Quds Force, traveled to Moscow in 2015 and 2016, which facilitated a long-term Russian collaboration with the Quds Force. The Iran-backed axis of resistance directed by Quds Forces was at the heart of the Russo–Iranian joint operation. Notwithstanding different visions about the future of Syria, disagreement about the penetration of Iran-backed militias into the Syrian army, and the extent of each side's influence, Moscow cooperated on the battlefield with these groups and had not found them troubling to its core interests. Even Moscow finds that improving its ties with Iran-backed militias is a valuable part of its coordination attempt with Iran and can help resolve possible disputes with Tehran and prevent escalations with Israel.[31] After February 2022, Moscow relinquished several key positions in central and eastern Syria to Iran-backed militias and to Hezbollah, while also ramping up intelligence sharing with Iran-backed militias and supplying Hezbollah with antiship missiles via Syria.[32]

Tehran's maritime strategy also seems to support the broader Russian objective of weakening the American-led regional order. Iran's naval doctrine shifted to an offensive strategy in the post-2016 period after the US military presence in the Persian Gulf intensified.[33] From the Russian perspective, this shift provides an opportunity through which Tehran can counterweight US presence at the regional level, thus accommodating a larger space for Russian Middle East policy. These examples indicate convergence in security interests has built multiple layers of motives for Moscow to back Iranian military strategy.

An Unreliable Partner

The last, but equally influential, narrative about Russia in the Iranian defense sector relates to the mistrust in long-term cooperation and dissatisfaction about the implementation of joint agreements. Lack of trust has contributed to Iran's push toward a model of defense cooperation that could eventually strengthen the domestic defense industry rather than simple arm import models. One explanation for Iran's arms export to Russia after the war in Ukraine is linked with this assessment, since Iran's perceives a new emerging Russian dependency as an opportunity to gain new leverage and form a more equal partnership.

This dissatisfaction can partly be attributed to Tehran's expectations to receive weapons systems that Moscow has refused to provide. Moscow's refusal is tied to a combination of factors such as nonproliferation concerns, constraints originating in partnerships with Persian Gulf states, regional stability considerations, and bureaucratic challenges. For example, top IRGC officials have expressed frustration about Russian refusal to sell ballistic missiles to Iran in early 2000s when the Iranian missile program was still in its preliminary phase. According to the Iranian view, the Russian refusals imply limits in the partnership with Moscow and risks embedded in reliance on Moscow as a long-term partner.

Another major source of Iran's dissatisfaction relates to Russia's disrespect of contractual commitments, resulting in delays, requests for additional payments, and even termination of the contract. In an interview, the IRGC aerospace forces commander in chief, General Amirali Hajizadeh, provided details of one of these incidents:

> we purchased seven radar systems from a friendly country [Russia] and paid the first sum of the money. The seller refused to deliver the purchased systems, demanding that we should introduce another end user for the systems due to licensing issue. We found a new end user. The seller refused again our proposed end user. This process prolonged in a way that eventually we remained with no other choice than to modify our initial order and purchase items which we had not requested.[34]

Delays in delivering the S-300 SAM systems is another classic example about Russian unreliability and Iran's role as a card in its great game with the United States.[35]

Besides, Iranian defense sector has been constantly criticizing complications in Russian implementation of its contractual obligations, especially provision of technical support and delivery of spare parts for purchased weapons systems. The memories of the Russian discrepancy in delivering spare parts for MiG-29s and the lack of airplane manuals are well-remembered among many Iranian officers. Russian demands for additional payments for delivering weapon manuals, which have been part of the initial deal, had made the Iranian side furious in various stages of their collaboration with Moscow. Similarly, the operationalization and maintenance of Kilo-class submarines were faced with challenges, leading submarines to be out of the service for a long time. In one case, frustrated Iranian officers doubted Russian intentions in insisting on conducting services of critical electrical components of submarines in Russia as a way for long-term grounding of the submarines.[36] Tehran struggled for years to fully operationalize these systems due to difficulties working with Russia, a lack of proper training, and problems with their spare parts.

Finally, doubts about Russian intentions increased after series of incidents that Moscow deliberately disclosed confidential interactions to gain immediate political interests. In one incident and during the Syrian civil war, Russia's disclosure of its use of Iran's Hamadan air base prompted severe criticism from military officials. Tehran in response, and due to public pressure, temporarily suspended Russian flights from it. A similar revelation by Moscow about Iran's drone export to Russia during the war in Ukraine raised criticism in Tehran. According to Iranian sources, Tehran made a formal complaint to Moscow and expressed its dissatisfaction to what was perceived as Russian attempt to gain political leverage notwithstanding the costs it can impose on Iran.[37]

Almost every arms deal signed between Iran and Russia experienced a delay, influenced by preferences of external factors, and caused Iranian public dissatisfaction. However, these negative insights are only one side of Iran and Russia's complex military–security ties. The other less discussed but more important side is that Russia remained consistent in arms export to Iran, provision of technology, and multilayered security assistance, thus strategically sympathized with Iran's defense posture and showed a level of convergence of core security interests.[38] The latter has most influenced Iran's defense sector's perception of Russia and has given Moscow an enduring influence on Iranian politics.

As this chapter has shown, Russian contributions to Iran's defense sector has not always been in the form of direct arms sales. Instead, it followed a more complex pattern. Giving inspiration for institutional designs; doctrinal learnings; weapon concept imitations; and technology transfer, training, and industrial-scale know-how have been all part of Russian assistance to the Iranian defense industry. Some more indirect and less publicized assistance has probably created long-lasting sympathy toward Russia in the Iranian defense sector. Indeed, a sense of technological and doctrinal fascination toward Russian weapons mixed with having access to part of these products, technology, and weapon designs facilitated the perception of Russia as an inspirational source. Indeed, Moscow has smartly benefited from its defense industry and security assistance to buy influence inside Iran and build allies at the core of the Islamic Republic's centers of power.

As far as Tehran is concerned, the military partnership with Russia directly matches its key military and defense objectives. It is one of the few paths of international defense cooperation for Islamic Republic that entails technology transfer and know-how, thus strengthening its indigenous defense industry and domestic arms production. At the same time, it provides the chance to improve the country's conventional deterrence by calculated and measured high-tech acquisitions that its domestic industry cannot produce. Eventually, it will give international recognition to Iran's military status and shield its asymmetrical deterrence model from external pressures. The combination of these factors feeds into an assessment that views military ties with Russia as beneficial and strategic for Iran's defense sector. While historical mistrust at the individual level remains a fixed character of the Iranian approach to Russia, pragmatically rooted positive narratives at the defense sector transcends case-by-case dissatisfactions and individual and public mistrust.

Finally, the lack of alternative sources to replace what Russia provides plays a pivotal role in shaping the narrative of Russia in Iranian defense sector. This factor probably plays the most significant role in the sustainability of Russo–Iranian military links. As long as the Islamic Republic remains in power and Tehran remains under international isolation, the Iranian alternative to substitute a military partnership with Russia will be limited if not nonexistent. This sense of dependency is coupled with an understanding about Moscow's pragmatic and opportunistic motives in supporting Tehran. Pragmatic character of Russian foreign policy has strengthened the view that Islamic Republic cannot rely on Russian assistance in critical moments, feeding a counterargument about the feasibility of strategic partnership with Russia. Efforts to boost leverage against Russia, however, can be seen in arms exports to Moscow after the war in Ukraine.

NOTES

1. The views expressed in this chapter are those of the author and are not an official policy or position of the UNIDIR (United Nations Institute for Disarmament Research) or the United Nations.
Jean A. Garrison, "Small Group Effects on Foreign Policy Decision Making," *Oxford Research Encyclopedia of International Studies*, December 22, 2017, https://bit.ly/3YcKOCW.
2. Charles C. Moskos, "The Concept of the Military-Industrial Complex: Radical Critique or Liberal Bogey?," *Social Problems* 21, no. 4 (1974): 498–512, https://doi.org/10.2307/799988.
3. Abdolrasool Divsallar, "The Foreign Policy Establishment in Iran," in *The Sacred Republic: Power and Institutions in Iran*, ed. Mehran Kamrava (Oxford University Press, 2023), 221–58, https://doi.org/10.1093/oso/9780197747711.003.0010.
4. Abdolrasool Divsallar, "Shifting Threats and Strategic Adjustment in Iran's Foreign Policy: The Case of the Strait of Hormuz," *British Journal of Middle Eastern Studies* 49, no. 5 (2022): 873–95.
5. "The Iraq-Iran War and the Arms Trade," SIPRI, March 1984, https://bit.ly/3QMlwb3.
6. Anonymous Iranian Hawk SAM system veteran, interview by author, March 2005.

7. "Transfers of Major Weapons to Iran: Deals with Deliveries or Orders Made for 1990 to 2022," SIPRI, accessed July 11, 2023, https://bit.ly/46GCzkR.
8. "Transfers of Major Weapons to Iran."
9. Anonymous Iranian F-14 pilots, interview by author, 2006.
10. Anonymous former submarine commander, interview by author, 2006.
11. Nikolay Kozhanov, "Understanding the Revitalization of Russian-Iranian Relations," Carnegie Moscow Center, May 2015, https://bit.ly/3C3obZZ.
12. Quoted in Michael Eisenstadt, "Russian Arms and Technology Transfers to Iran: Policy Challenges for the United States," *Arms Control Today*, March 1, 2001, https://www.armscontrol.org/act/2001-03/iran-nuclear-briefs/russian-arms-and-technology-transfers-iranpolicy-challenges-united.
13. Richard Speier, Robert Gallucci, Robbie Sabel, and Viktor Mizin, "Iran-Russia Missile Cooperation," in *Repairing the Regime: Preventing the Spread of Weapons of Mass Destruction*, ed. Joseph Cirincione (Routledge, 2000), 186–88.
14. Speier et al., "Iran-Russia Missile Cooperation."
15. Michael R. Gordon and Eric Schmitt, "Iran Nearly Got a Missile Alloy from Russians," *New York Times*, April 25, 1998, https://bit.ly/3A62lEJ.
16. Fred Wehling and Scott Parrish, "Russian Missile Exports to Iran—the 1998 Moscow Summit," James Martin Center for Nonproliferation Studies, August 31, 1998, https://bit.ly/3MWCYZg.
17. Matthew Karnitschig, "Iran in Secret Talks with China, Russia to Acquire Sanctioned Missile Fuel," Politico, April 12, 2023, https://www.politico.eu/article/vladimir-putin-ukraine-war-xi-jinping-china-russia-in-secret-talks-to-supply-iran-missile-propellant/.
18. Stephen J. Blank, "Russian Proliferation in the Middle East and Its Strategic Implications," *Defence Studies* 1, no. 3 (2001): 43 https://doi.org/10.1080/714000040.
19. "Zarepur: Gharardad kharid manpavareh khiam ra bah gharardad enteghal taknology tabadil kardim" [We changed the Khayyam satellite contract to technology transfer], IRNA, August 12, 2022, https://bit.ly/3MQSJAX.
20. "Iran va Russiah tfahim namih hmkeara shet Idaaa amda kerdnd + falm" [Iran and Russia signed a space cooperation MOU], IRNA, December 14, 2023, https://bit.ly/40NTfoS.
21. Hanna Notte and Jim Lamson, "Iran and Russia Defense Cooperation: Current Realities and Future Horizons," James Martin Center for Nonproliferation Studies, Middlebury Institute of International Studies at Monterey, August 2024, 15, https://acr.ps/1L9zSjs.
22. "Transfers of Major Weapons to Iran."
23. "Tolid-e Anboh-e Selah-haye Sabok dar Keshvar Motehavvel Shod" [Light weapons production is transforming in the country], Tasnim News Agency, June 2, 2017, https://bit.ly/3Uhqv5T.
24. See, for example: Behshid Hosseini and Mohsen Kameli, "M'eaarhaa pedafnd ghar'eaml dr traha m'emara sakhtman haa jm'ea shhra" [Passive defense measures in design of civilian complexes], *Journal of Architecture and City Building*, no. 15 (2015), https://bit.ly/3YH4OiB.
25. Abdolrasool Divsallar, "Iran Is Learning from Russia's Use of Missiles in Ukraine," Middle East Institute, May 2, 2022, https://bit.ly/3BPswAb.
26. Joby Warrick, "Russian Weapons Help Iran Harden Defenses Against Israeli Airstrike." *Washington Post*, April 15, 2015, https://bit.ly/3BRMjil.
27. This also includes conceiving Iran as a shield in its southern neighborhood against dominance of US-led order, ad hoc benefits of Iranian military power in regional conflicts, and the benefits Iran provides to implement Russian Middle Eastern policy. See Abdolrasool Divsallar and Pyotr Kortonuv, "The Fallout of the US-Iran Confrontation for Russia:

Revisiting Factors in Moscow's Calculus," European University Institute, December 22, 2020, https://acr.ps/1L9zRQ2.

28. "Sadfar-e Moaven-e Reis-e Setad-e Kolle Nirou-haye Mosallah-e Iran beh Rusiyeh" [Visit of deputy of armed forces general staff to Russia], Aran News Agency, December 11, 2019, https://bit.ly/3TawI4b.

29. Abdolrasool Divsallar, "Russia and Iran: A Continuity of the Past or a Historical Juncture?," in *Struggle for Alliance: Russia and Iran in the Era of War in Ukraine*, ed. Abdolrasool Divsallar (I. B. Tauris, 2024), 9.

30. Abdolrasool Divsallar, "The Pillars of Iranian-Russian Security Convergence," *The International Spectator* 54, no. 3 (2019): 107–22, https://doi.org/10.1080/03932729.2019.1586147.

31. Abdolrasool Divsallar and Julia Roknifard, "Iran, Russia, and the Militias: Seeds of Tactical Cooperation," ISPI, March 22, 2023, https://bit.ly/40RvhZT.

32. Notte and Lamson, "Iran and Russia Defense Cooperation," 16.

33. Ali Bagheri Dolatabadi and Mehran Kamrava, "Iran's Changing Naval Strategy in the Persian Gulf: Motives and Features," *British Journal of Middle Eastern Studies* 51, no. 1 (2024): 131–48, https://doi.org/10.1080/13530194.2022.2105815.

34. Amirali Hajizade, "Hajizadeh: Az Keshvar-e Doost Radar Kharidim, Tahvil Nadadand" [We bought a radar from a friendly country and they did not deliver], BBC Persian, October 5, 2024, https://bit.ly/3YgGVNi.

35. Mohsen Jalilvand, "Qodrat-e Bazdarandegi-e Moshak va Pahbad az Sukhoi-35 Bishtar Ast" [The deterrence power of missiles and drones are more than Sukhoi], *Shargh Daily*, October 10, 2022, https://bit.ly/3Gc8WNl.

36. General Abbas Zamini commented in "Salam-e Nezami-e Iran va Rusiyeh dar Rand-e Payani-e Mozakerat-e Hasteh-i" [Iran's military salute to Russia in the last round of the JCPOA talks], *Fars News*, June 13, 2015, https://bit.ly/3ulwxZ8.

37. Iranian diplomat, interview by author, April 11, 2024.

38. Abdolrasool Divsallar, "Authoritarian Alliance: The Systemic Factors that Bring Russia and Iran Together," in *Struggle for Alliance: Russia and Iran in the Era of War in Ukraine*, ed. Abdolrasool Divsallar (I. B. Tauris, 2024).

Part IV

IRAN'S RELATIONS WITH CENTRAL ASIA AND THE SOUTH CAUCASUS

11
IRAN AND THE SOUTH CAUCASUS

Gawdat Bahgat

Both academic literature and political discussions have been heavily focused on Iran's relations with its Arab neighbors on the other side of the Persian Gulf. Most of Tehran's hydrocarbon reserves and production are concentrated around this strategic waterway, where oil and natural gas exports pass every day. Iran and Iraq were engaged in a devastating war for eight years (1980–88), Tehran and Abu Dhabi fight over three islands, and Tehran and Doha share the largest natural gas structure in the world. For decades, the rivalry between Sunni Islam led by Saudi Arabia and Shiism championed by the Islamic Republic has shaped the entire Middle East. Outside the Gulf region, Iran has had strong military and political presence in Lebanon and Syria for decades.

This Sunni–Shiite/Arab–Persian rivalry and cooperation have been a major preoccupation of Iran's foreign, security, and economic policies for millennia. But they do not tell the whole story. Iran borders seven countries (Afghanistan, Armenia, Azerbaijan, Iraq, Pakistan, Turkey, and Turkmenistan). Relations with these neighboring countries, as well as with global powers, give a deeper and more comprehensive understanding of Tehran's policy. Indeed, some of these countries were parts of the Persian Empire for a long time. At the end of the Russo–Persian war (1826–28), the two sides signed the Treaty of Turkmenchay, in which the Qajar dynasty ceded a large part of the South Caucasus region. With the disintegration of the Soviet Union in the late 1980s and early 1990s, Armenia, Azerbaijan, and Georgia emerged as independent states.

Given these three countries' ethnic composition and the Soviet legacy, independence has brought neither political stability nor economic prosperity. The military confrontations between Armenian and Azerbaijan are a good example of these "frozen conflicts" that became "hot." The deep hostility and repeated clashes between Yerevan and Baku have provided incentives for foreign powers to intervene. Iran, with joint borders with both Armenia and Azerbaijan, cannot afford to be indifferent to growing instability in its backyard. As President Ebrahim Raisi stated, "The Caucasus region is a part of Iran's history, civilization and culture. Security and peace in the region are significant for Iran. The presence of outside forces can only exacerbate regional problems."[1]

This chapter examines Iran's relations with the major players in the South Caucasus, Armenia, Azerbaijan, Turkey, Israel, Russia, and Western powers (the United States and European Union). Having been under US economic sanctions since 1979 and currently in an intense strategic rivalry with some of its Arab neighbors for most of the last few decades, the Islamic Republic has ideological, strategic, and economic needs to "Look East." For a long time, Iranian leaders have argued that the United States is in decline and the international system is a multilateral one where other global powers such as China, Russia, India, and Japan (among others) play a significant role. Within this context, forging close relations with Asian and Eurasian powers can contribute to Tehran's national security and ease economic pressure. Two conclusions can be drawn from a close examination of Iran's policy in the South Caucasus region over the last few decades. First, the standoff with Western powers over the nuclear program and the extensive and harsh sanctions have limited the options Iran can pursue to advance its national interests in the South Caucasus (and elsewhere). Second, like almost every country in the world, Iranian foreign policy is driven by both ideology and perceived national interests. In the South Caucasus, Tehran has shown a remarkable degree of pragmatism.[2]

Iran–Armenia Relations

Iran and Armenia share very little in terms of ideology. Armenia prides itself on being the world's first Christian nation (early fourth century), while Shiism is a major driver of the Islamic Republic's domestic and foreign policies. Diplomatic relations between the two nations were established in February 1992. According to the Armenian Ministry of Foreign Affairs, there are about 200 international treaties, agreements, memorandums, and protocols covering almost all spheres of mutual relations between Tehran and Yerevan.[3] Almost all Iranian presidents visited Armenia and other senior officials visit each other capitals regularly.

Religious differences aside, the two nations have grown closer. Regional and international dynamics have highlighted and deepened the joint diplomatic, strategic, and economic interests between Tehran and Yerevan. Both countries push back against efforts by external powers to isolate them. Since the establishment of the Islamic Republic in 1979, the United States and some European countries have sought to isolate Iran from the international community. Similarly, Iran has had hostile relations with some of its Arab neighbors. To counter these efforts, Iranian leaders have sought to establish and strengthen relations with Russia, China, India, Latin America, Africa, and neighbors in the South Caucasus and Central Asia. Armenia, however, is a landlocked country with shared borders with Azerbaijan, Georgia, Iran, and Turkey. Ankara is a strong supporter of Baku and the two nations have been seen as enemies by the majority of Armenians. Since the early 1990s, borders between Turkey and Armenia have been mostly closed. Meanwhile Yerevan and Baku have engaged in large and small military clashes since independence, and until early 2025 the prospects for permanent peace seem dim. In short, in the last few decades both Iran and Armenia have been trying to push back against their adversaries' efforts to isolate them.

Armenia, Belarus, Kazakhstan, Kyrgyzstan, and Tajikistan are all members in the Russia-led Collective Security Treaty Organization (CSTO). According to Article Three, a major goal of the CSTO is to protect "territorial integrity and sovereignty of the member states."[4] Despite this clear, strong legal commitment, senior Armenian military officers believe Russia has not fulfilled its commitment and has not provided the military assistance Yerevan expected as a military ally during the 2020 war with Azerbaijan and in its aftermath.[5] Armenia needs military assistance from other sources. There are no credible reports that Iran has provided arms to Armenia. But in the last few decades Tehran has developed a relatively sophisticated military industry. Equally important, Tehran has the political will to assist Armenia. As will be discussed later in this chapter, the military alliance between Azerbaijan, Turkey, and Israel is a major national security threat to the Islamic Republic. Within this context, Supreme Leader Ayatollah Ali Khamenei warned, "If there is an effort to block the border between Iran and Armenia, the Islamic Republic will oppose it because this border has been a communication route for thousands of years."[6] Former Foreign Minister Amir-Abdollahian echoed these sentiments, "Iran considers the security of Armenia and the region to be its own security. Our policy is to respect territorial integrity as well as internationally recognized borders."[7]

These prospects of diplomatic and military cooperation are further reinforced by trade and economic relations. Iran is a major oil and gas producer and exporter. US economic sanctions have complicated, but have not stopped, Iranian efforts to find markets for its hydrocarbon exports. Lacking indigenous resources, however, Armenia imports most of its energy needs. Natural gas is largely imported from Russia via a pipeline through Georgia and from Iran through a barter agreement under which it exports electricity in exchange.[8]

Given these diplomatic, security and economic considerations, Iran has grown closer to Armenia in the last three decades. Officially, Tehran has always called for a diplomatic solution to the Armenian–Azerbaijan conflict and sought to mediate between the two sides. This official neutrality is not in line with demography. Ethnic Azeris in Iran make up a large share of the nation's total population while ethnic Armenians are a fraction. Azerbaijan's foreign and security alliances in the last three decades explain the growing tension between Tehran and Baku.

Iran–Azerbaijan Relations

For more than three decades Iran–Azerbaijan relations have been complicated, experiencing periodically escalating tensions, ethnic and territorial disputes, as well as mutually beneficial cooperation. Three main dynamics explain these overlapping cycles of conflict and cooperation—ethnicity and Shiism, energy resources in the Caspian Sea, and foreign policy orientation.

It may seem puzzling that Iran and Azerbaijan—two countries with Shiite-majority populations and home to millions of ethnic Azeris—are not close allies and occasionally see each other as adversaries. But a close examination of how the two countries have developed over the last several decades explain how coethnic populations and shared religion can fuel tension instead of promoting cooperation. The northwestern part of Iran is home to a large population of Azeri Iranians. Iran is predominantly Shia with small religious minorities (Sunnis, Christians, Jews, and Zoroastrians). The nation has much larger ethnic minorities, including the Azeris in the northwest, Kurds in the west, Lurs in the west, Baloch in the southeast, Arabs in the southwest, and Turkmen in the northeast.[9] Generally speaking religious minorities are more integrated than ethnic ones. There are more Azeris in Iran than in Azerbaijan and they are represented in the political–security establishment in Tehran. Despite having a strong national identity, Azeri pride has not completely faded away. At the end of Second World War the Azerbaijan People's Government was established as a separate state in northern Iran and lasted for thirteen months. In November 2022, President Ilham Aliyev complained that Iran does not allow ethnic Azeris to study in their native language.[10] He also stated that Iranian Azerbaijanis are "part of our nation."[11]

Iranian policy has always reflected the relative weight of two significant trends in the nation's psyche—nationalism and Shiism. Shiism has been the state religion of Iran since the sixteenth century and has been a major driver of the Islamic Republic's policy since it was established in 1979. The Iranian constitution accepts the doctrine of popular sovereignty and enshrines the principle of government of the jurist (*velayat-e faqih*). The first article states, "The form of government in Iran is that of an Islamic Republic, endorsed by the people of Iran on the basis of their longstanding belief in the sovereignty of truth and Qur'anic justice."[12] After 200 years of intense antireligious policy instituted in Russia and then the Soviet Union, however, Azerbaijan is largely a secular country where religion plays a minimum role in public life. The bases of Islam have been eroded in society and atheist feelings are more widespread than religious belief.[13] Azeri officials have occasionally accused Iran of trying to revive Shiism and support religious groups such as Muslim Unity Movement and Huseynyun.[14]

The Caspian Sea is located in northwest Asia. Azerbaijan, Iran, Kazakhstan, Russia, and Turkmenistan all share the Caspian Basin. The exploration and development of the region's hydrocarbon resources since the collapse of the Soviet Union in late 1991 have been major drivers of both conflict and cooperation between Iran and Azerbaijan (and other countries). The region's energy deposits have become more significant since Russia invaded Ukraine in February 2022 and Western powers imposed sanctions on Moscow's oil and gas exports.

Shortly after the collapse of the Soviet Union, the Caspian states became open to foreign investment and the region emerged as a potentially significant player in global energy policy. Uncertainty surrounding the legal regime that governs the oil and gas exploration and development operation in the Caspian Sea was a major risk that investors had to take into consideration in doing business in the region. Prior to the dissolution of the Soviet Union, Moscow and Tehran signed two agreements to govern the Caspian—the Friendship Treaty of 1921 and the Treaty of Commerce and Navigation of 1940.[15] These two treaties were replaced by the 2018 Convention, signed by the five littoral states during the Fifth Caspian Summit in the Kazakh city of Aktau in August 2018. The convention has not clearly defined the legal status of the Basin, but a de facto system has emerged.[16] Unlike the other four littoral states (Azerbaijan, Kazakhstan, Russia, and Turkmenistan) Iran has yet to ratify the agreement. Tehran's dissatisfaction with the de facto legal system is further complicated with its exclusion of the development and transportation of Baku's oil and gas reserves due to US economic sanctions. Most of these deposits and pipelines have been developed by Western companies.

Ethnic and religious challenges combined with deep disagreement over energy deposits in the Caspian Sea have been major reasons behind the significant deterioration of relations between Tehran and Baku in the last few decades. Azerbaijan's growing security ties with Israel have been seen by Iranian leaders as a major national security threat.

Israel in the South Caucasus

One of the biggest changes in Iranian foreign policy after the 1979 revolution is the perception and animosity toward Israel. Shortly after Israel was created, Iran granted it a de facto recognition. Under the shah, the two countries had close economic and security cooperation.[17] These warm ties were a main cause for public resentment and the eventual toppling of the Pahlavi dynasty. Since the establishment of the Islamic Republic both Tehran and Tel Aviv have seen each other as sworn enemies. Israel has been the world's leading opponent of Iran's nuclear program and in the last several years the two countries have been engaged in a "low-intensity" war, including assassinations, sabotage, cyberattacks, and missile, drone, and air attacks.

In this ongoing conflict, both Tehran and Tel Aviv have sought to prepare for and present the other side with a multifront war. Iran maintains close ties with proxies and allies in Gaza, Lebanon, and Syria. Similarly, Israel established security ties in some of the Gulf Cooperation Council (GCC) states and in Azerbaijan. Iran perceives the growing Israeli military presence in both the Persian Gulf and South Caucasus as a major national security threat.

Israel was one of the first countries in the world to recognize the independence of Azerbaijan in 1991 and inaugurated an embassy there in 1993. In March 2023, Azerbaijan opened its embassy in Israel, becoming the first Shiite-majority country to have a diplomatic mission in the Jewish state. These official diplomatic ties reflect growing cooperation in two main areas—energy and armament. Since the early 2000s, Israel has discovered and developed significant natural gas deposits in the Mediterranean Sea. These discoveries have positively altered the country's energy outlook. Since the creation of Israel in 1948 and for approximately half a century, the country produced very little oil and gas and was deeply dependent on foreign supplies. Since the early 1990s, Azerbaijan, along with some Central Asian countries, has provided a large share of Israel's oil, petroleum products, and natural gas needs.

Arms sales make up the other important area where Baku and Tel Aviv share mutual interests. Given the unresolved conflict with Armenia, Azerbaijan has been building its military capabilities since the mid-1990s in partnership with two strong allies—Israel and Turkey. Israel accounted for 27 percent of Azerbaijan's import of major arms over the decade 2011 to 2020. Most of these deliveries took place from 2016 to 2020, with Israel accounting for 69 percent of Azerbaijan's imports of major arms in that period.[18] This means Azerbaijan supplies Israel with oil and refined products and buys high-tech weapons, dual-use electronics, attack and reconnaissance drones, navigation and optic systems, and precision-guided munitions. Undoubtedly, these weapons have given Baku the upper hand in the military confrontations with Yerevan.

The strong and growing energy and security alliance between Baku and Tel Aviv is largely driven by the two nations' perception of Iran as common enemy. After eight rounds of negotiations between Joe Biden's administration and Iran to revive the nuclear deal, negotiations have reached a deadlock. Israeli leaders have repeatedly threatened to attack Iran's nuclear facilities. Tehran sees the Israeli presence in Azerbaijan as a base for gathering intelligence, recruiting spies and a staging ground for possible future attacks. The Israeli Foreign Minister Eli Cohen stated that Azerbaijan's strategic location "makes the relationship between us of great importance and great potential. Israel and Azerbaijan share the same perception of the Iranian threat. The Iranian regime threatens both our regions."[19] The Azeri Foreign Minister Jeyhun Bayramov echoed these sentiments, describing the opening of the embassy in Israel as "a new stage in strategic partnership" between the two states.[20] The Iranian Foreign Ministry responded by asserting that Tehran "cannot remain indifferent to the conspiracy of the Zionist regime against the country from the territory of the Republic of Azerbaijan."[21]

This strong Israel–Azerbaijan alliance has had a mild impact on Iranian–Armenian relations. Given the decade-long animosity between the United States and some European countries on one side and Iran on the other and the special US–Israeli relationship, Yerevan cannot afford to be an overtly anti-Jewish state or pro-Islamic Republic.[22] Armenia and Israel established diplomatic relations in 1992 but have had no embassies in each other's capitals until the early 2020s. The Armenian government decided to open embassy in Israel in late 2019, but the inauguration was delayed due to the pandemic. Iranian officials argued that the move will have a negative impact on stability and security in the region and urged their Armenian counterparts to reconsider their decision.[23] Armenian–Israeli relations have long been frosty. Opening a diplomatic mission in Tel Aviv and sending an ambassador in 2022 is not likely to substantially alter the relationship between the two countries.

Turkey in the South Caucasus

Given the intense hostility between the Islamic Republic and the Jewish state, Tehran is deeply concerned about Israel's strong ties with Azerbaijan and its growing presence in the South Caucasus region. Turkey is another major regional competitor. By building a strong alliance with Ankara, Baku is trying to neutralize the Iranian and Russian influence. In 2020, Azeri leaders thought to mediate between Ankara and Tel Aviv.[24] This mediation might have contributed to the rapprochement between Turkey and Israel.

Iran and Turkey share several similarities and major differences. Reza Shah Pahlavi, the founder of Iran's last ruling dynasty, admired Kemal Ataturk, the founder of the Turkish Republic and sought, unsuccessfully, to follow his modernization and secularization example. For many good reasons the experiment in Iran failed and in 1979 Mohammad Reza Pahlavi was toppled and the Islamic Republic was established.[25] Relations between the two nations have been less tense and occasionally warm since President Recep Tayyip Erdoğan and the Justice and Development Party (AKP) took office in 2002. Shahram Akbarzadeh and James Barry describe Iran and Turkey as "not quite enemies but less than friends."[26] Turkey is still secular, but with a strong Islamic tone. Despite the fact that Turkey is a NATO member, Ankara opposes sanctions on Iran. Tehran and Ankara share long borders and have extensive economic and trade relations. Both Iranian and Turkish leaders have repeatedly pledged to increase bilateral trade to $30 billion per year, but they still have long way to go in order to reach this level. Natural gas and petroleum products constitute a big part of this volume of trade. After Russia, Iran is the second-largest gas exporter to Turkey.

Faces with several regional crises in the last few decades, Tehran and Ankara have adopted different and sometimes conflicting policies. Syria is a clear example but not the only one. Both nations support the Palestinians, but Ankara has strong ties with Israel. In the South Caucasus, Iran is officially neutral, but has close ties to Armenia. Turkey, however, has been a strong supporter of Azerbaijan, which is based on many factors, including shared cultural heritage. Azerbaijan (along with Kazakhstan, Kyrgyzstan, and Turkmenistan) is a Turkic-speaking nation. It is little wonder that Turkey and Azerbaijan refer to themselves as one nation, two states.[27] Azerbaijan's decisive victory in the 2020 war with Armenia has significantly raised Turkey's influence in the South Caucasus and left Iran with little leverage. The main challenge to further expand Ankara's influence is the decade-long Russian presence, not Iran.

A strong alliance between Baku and Ankara means weak and confrontational relations between the latter and Yerevan. Turkey officially recognized the independence of Armenia in December 1991, but more than three decades later diplomatic relations have yet to be established. For most of these years, borders have been closed.[28] A major disagreement between the two nations is over the accusations that the Ottoman Empire committed genocide against more than a million Armenians at the end of the First World War. Turkey insists that "no authentic evidence exists to support such claim and that the Ottoman socio-cultural fabric did not harbor racist attitudes that would facilitate such a horrific crime."[29] Another complicating factor is the large and diverse Armenian diasporas. They are generally more militant and obstinate than their counterparts inside Armenia. The most important challenge to Ankara and Yerevan is the strong alliance between the former and Baku. Turkey is not and does not pretend to be a neutral player in the South Caucasus. Armenia's occupation of Nagorno-Karabakh, internationally recognized as Azerbaijani territory, in the early 1990s pushed Turkey and Azerbaijan closer. Baku's victory in the forty-four-day war in 2020 and restoring sovereignty over most of the land it lost in the last round have not weakened the Ankara–Baku alliance. Given the substantial economic challenges Ankara has faced in the last several years, President Erdoğan has sought to reduce tension with regional powers, including Israel, Saudi Arabia, the United Arab Emirates, and Egypt. A rapprochement between Ankara and Yerevan would help the two nation's economies, but there are no signs yet.

The Way Forward

The 2020 war between Armenia and Azerbaijan has drastically changed the balance of power in the South Caucasus and left Iran with limited strategic options to pursue its national interests. The Azeri forces, supported by Turkey and Israel, successfully pushed their Armenian foes out of Nagorno-Karabakh and the surrounding regions of Azerbaijan. A trilateral armistice was signed by Baku, Yerevan, and Moscow, and Russian peacekeeping forces were deployed. Enjoying a strong support from its Turkish and Israeli allies, and watching Russia being distracted and weakened by the war in Ukraine, Baku has frequently tested the trilateral armistice. Within this context, Armenian Prime Minister Nikol Pashinyan has argued that the only way to end the conflict with Azerbaijan is for his country to relinquish its claim to Nagorno-Karabakh.[30]

For Iran, the outcome of the 2020 war between Baku and Yerevan and its aftermath present two alarming developments. First is the emerging Azerbaijan–Israel–Turkey axis on its northwestern doorstop. Second, the risk of territorial changes and redrawing the political map that is certain to lead to expanding Azeri and Turkish leverage at the expense of Iran's strategic and economic interests. President Aliyev has been talking about building the Zangezur Corridor that would link Azerbaijan via Armenia's south province Syunik to its exclave Nakhichevan and on to Turkey. He claims that the corridor is a "historical necessity" and has threatened to use force to take it.[31] Such corridor would separate Iran from Armenia and would be a geopolitical catastrophe. There are two options for Iran to access European markets: open the border with Armenian to move exports to Georgia and the Black Sea, and via Turkey. Joint borders with Armenia also give Iran leverage over Turkey by offering access to Turkmenistan and other Asian countries.[32] In a warning to Azerbaijan, Major General Mohammad Bagheri, chief of staff of Iran's armed forces, said that Tehran "will not tolerate changes in the borders through war and will not remain silent."[33] Iran also opened a consulate in the city of Kapan, Syunik province, to single its opposition to the Zangezur Corridor.

To further underscore its strong opposition to the Azeri plan, Iran has conducted a number of large-scale military exercises that include setting up pontoon bridges and crossing the Aras River on the borders with Azerbaijan.[34] These diplomatic and military warnings highlight the change in Iran's stance on the South Caucasus. Officially, Tehran has maintained its neutrality between Baku and Yerevan and presents itself as a neutral arbiter, but it has increasingly moved closer to Armenia. Undoubtedly, Tehran strongly advocates for a successful diplomatic negotiation to end the ongoing fighting between its two neighbors.[35] This unresolved conflict and the rising tension and potential of regional war have prompted global powers to intensify their efforts and presence in the South Caucasus.

For several decades, Russia enjoyed a political–military hegemony in the South Caucasus. Iran and other regional and global powers, more or less, recognized the South Caucasus as part of Russia's sphere of influence.[36] The war in Ukraine has significantly eroded this hegemony. Russian leaders are understandably preoccupied by the war and lack the resources to maintain their political–military presence in other regions. Their failure to bring their invasion of Ukraine to a decisive and quick victory has raised serious questions about Russia's military superiority and power-projecting capabilities. The war in Ukraine has also pushed Moscow closer to the Ankara–Baku nexus. Azerbaijan has successfully managed to maintain good ties with both Russia and Western powers.[37] Two days before Russia invaded Ukraine, Moscow and Baku signed a Declaration on Allied Cooperation, further deepening their political and military partnership.[38]

Five conclusions can be drawn from the stalemate in Ukraine and its impact on security in South Caucasus. First, Russia is concerned about being pushed out of regional and global efforts to stabilize the Armenia–Azerbaijan conflict. Military clashes and rising tension do not seem to service Moscow's national interests. Second, the intense political–military confrontation between Russia and the West in Ukraine means little, if any, coordination between them in the South Caucasus. Third, Moscow's eroded credibility should not be overstated. Russia still maintains strong ties in the region and has the ability to spoil any outcome it deems against its national interests. Fourth, Russia's preoccupation with the war in Ukraine has left a security and geopolitical vacuum and uncertainty in the South Caucasus. Azerbaijan is trying to take advantage of this key change in the security landscape by consolidating its gains and pushing for a peace treaty on its own terms. Meanwhile both Washington and Brussels see an opportunity to assert their influence and take the lead in shaping the region strategic landscape. Finally, although Iranian and Russian interests in the South Caucasus are not identical, Moscow's shrinking leverage in the region is not viewed positively in Tehran. Iranian leaders are closely watching the growing US and EU presence.

The United States has important, but not vital, interest in the South Caucasus.[39] These include promoting democracy and free market economy, preventing war and containing Russia's influence. Both the US government and American oil companies have been interested in developing Baku's energy deposits. Given the rising tension with both Russia and Iran, Washington has been paying more attention to geopolitical developments in these former Soviet republics.[40] Both Azerbaijan and Armenia, however, have sought to deepen their ties with Washington without upsetting Moscow. In the last few decades, Baku has supported US policy around the world, including in Kosovo, Afghanistan, and Iraq, as well as in the war on terrorism. Meanwhile, the Armenian–American lobby enjoys significant influence in Washington. Nancy Pelosi, speaker of the House, visited Yerevan in September 2022, the highest level visit by a US official since the country gained its independence.

The European Union has been interested in the South Caucasus region for at least two reasons. First, the region provides important transport corridors linking the European Union with Asia. Second, for a long time European leaders have been aware of their deep energy dependence on Russia. The war in Ukraine has highlighted Europe's vulnerability to interruption of oil and gas supplies from Russia. Azerbaijan and other major producers can and indeed have contributed to energy diversification and security in Europe since Russia's invasion of Ukraine in February 2022.

The European Union has been indirectly involved in the global efforts to end the conflict between Armenia and Azerbaijan under the European Partnership for the Peaceful Settlement of the Conflict over Nagorno-Karabakh (EPNK) and the Organization for Security Cooperation in Europe (OSCE) and the Minsk Group, cochaired by France, the United States, and Russia.[41] After several clashes between the Armenian and Azeri forces, the credibility of both the CSTO and OSCE was eroded, and both Yerevan and Baku were not satisfied with the Russian peace mission. In order to fill this security vacuum, the European Union deployed a new monitoring mission early in 2023. It will take some time to assess the effectiveness of this mission. What is remarkable, however, is that Iran has not opposed the deployment of this EU monitoring mission. A main theme of Iran's foreign policy in the South Caucasus and elsewhere has been a strong opposition to the intervention of extraregional forces and support of a regional approach. Tehran has been disappointed at Moscow's unwillingness or inability to block Baku's efforts regarding the Zangezur Corridor and Iran–Armenia joint borders. Iran does not have a representative at the joint Russian–Turkish center for monitoring the ceasefire regime in Karabakh and opposes a unilateral or bilateral approach to the conflict. Rather, Tehran supports the 3+3 regional format, which includes Armenia, Azerbaijan, and Georgia plus Iran, Russia, and Turkey.[42]

The unresolved conflict between Armenia and Azerbaijan and the rising tension between the latter and Iran do not mean that war is imminent or unavoidable. A close examination of strategic developments in the last few years suggests two major uncertainties that might threaten regional peace and stability. First, for years Israeli leaders have warned that they might strike Iran's nuclear facilities and other targets. If such attack does happen and if it is initiated from Azerbaijan (with or without its consent) Iranian leaders have vowed to retaliate against both Israel and "the collaborator." Azeri leaders have repeatedly asserted that they would not allow any attack against neighboring Iran from their territory. Second, Iranian leaders have warned their Azeri counterparts that the Zangezur Corridor is a "red line." Tehran has vital strategic and economic interests in preventing any change in the political borders in the South Caucasus. If an emboldened Baku goes ahead with its plan for the corridor, Iran is certain to respond.

These two certainties aside, the South Caucasus region is likely to witness a combination of cooperation and competition between the major regional and international players in the coming few years. Iranian and Russian interests are not identical, but the two countries are united in their opposition to what they perceive as US global hegemony. Meanwhile, Iran and Western powers do not support opposite sides in the Caucasus. Tehran has closer ties to Yerevan than to Baku and both the United States and Europe are increasingly concerned about the Azeri leadership growing more belligerent and authoritarian.

Finally, shared economic interests might incentivize adversaries to make painful compromises and work together instead of against each other. These shared economic interests can alter the political dialogue from a zero-sum proposition to a win–win one. Iran has a free-trade agreement with the Eurasian Economic Union (Armenia, Belarus, Kazakhstan, Kyrgyzstan, and Russia). Meanwhile, Iran's volume of trade with Azerbaijan is roughly equivalent to that with Armenia and Georgia combined.[43] In May 2023, Iran and Russia signed a $1.6 billion agreement to build a 162-kilometer (one hundred miles) railway between the Iranian city of Rasht on the Caspian Sea and the Iranian city of Astara on the border with Azerbaijan. The agreement is part of the International North–South Transport Corridor (INSTC), a rail, road, and ship network linking Russia to India. The aim of the INSTC is to increase trade between all involved countries (Azerbaijan, India, Iran, Kazakhstan, Russia, and Turkmenistan).[44] These growing economic and trade ties and interdependence are likely to contribute to regional peace and stability.

NOTES

1. Ani Mejlumyan, "Iran and Armenia Agree to Double Gas Trade," *Eurasianet*, November 2, 2022, https://bit.ly/47IWtwp.
2. Khoshnood Arvin and Khoshnood Ardavan, "Iran's Quandary on Nagorno-Karabakh," *Middle East Quarterly* 28, no. 2 (Spring 2021): 1–9.
3. "Bilateral Relations: Iran," Ministry of Foreign Affairs of the Republic of Armenia, accessed March 27, 2025, https://bit.ly/3QIdbVL.
4. Collective Security Treaty Organization, "Charter of the Collective Security Treaty Organization, Dated October 07, 2002," April 27, 2012, https://bit.ly/3QIdgsx.
5. Major general, interview by author, Yerevan, March 28, 2023.
6. Gabriel Gavin, "Iran Is Filling Armenia's Power Vacuum," *Foreign Policy*, December 1, 2022, https://bit.ly/3Q92Hyu.
7. Fuad Shahbazov, "Will Azerbaijan-Iran Tensions Reach Point of No Return?," *Amwaj Media*, March 3, 2023, https://bit.ly/3G6zDTx.
8. "Armenia Energy Profile," International Energy Agency, March 31, 2023, https://bit.ly/47iOTZC.
9. "Iran," Central Intelligence Agency, March 27, 2025, https://bit.ly/47jUHC5.
10. "Iran Does Not Allow Ethnic Azerbaijanis to Study in Their Language, Unlike Armenians," Turna, November 25, 2022, https://bit.ly/3SNeyFm.
11. Chris Devonshire-Ellis, "Azerbaijan, Iran, Move Closer to Military Conflict," NEWS.am, February 2, 2023, https://bit.ly/46gRWQJ.
12. "Iran (Islamic Republic of)'s Constitution of 1979 with Amendments Through 1989," Constitute Project, March 2, 2025, https://bit.ly/3G4cLEa.
13. Nasib L. Nassibi, "Azerbaijan-Iran Relations: Challenges and Prospects," Belfer Center for Science and International Affairs, November 30, 1999, https://bit.ly/49TTUcO.
14. Omar Ahmed, "The Huseynyun: Iran's New IRGC-Backed Movement in Azerbaijan," Middle East Monitor, October 9, 2021, https://t.ly/AsFAc.
15. Gawdat Bahgat, *American Oil Diplomacy in the Persian Gulf and the Caspian Sea* (University Press of Florida, 2003), 160.
16. Michal Pietkiewicz, "Legal Status of Caspian Sea—Problem Solved?" *Marine Policy* 123, no. 1 (January 2021): 104321.
17. Gawdat Bahgat, *Israel and the Persian Gulf: Retrospect and Prospect* (University Press of Florida, 2006).
18. Pieter D. Wezeman, Alexandra Kuimova, and Jordan Smith, "Arms Transfers to Conflict Zones: The Case of Nagorno-Karabakh," SIPRI, April 30, 2021, https://t.ly/WhZG5.
19. "Azerbaijan to Open Embassy in Israel Today," Israeli Ministry of Foreign Affairs, March 29, 2023, https://t.ly/sgeEg.
20. "Iran Asks Azerbaijan for Explanation on 'Strategic Partnership' with Israel," Tasnim News Agency, March 31, 2023, https://t.ly/GiS1z.
21. Marzieh Rahmani, "Iran Warns Against Israeli Conspiracy in Azerbaijan Territory," Mehr News Agency, March 31, 2023, https://t.ly/aH0qC.
22. Benyamin Poghosyan, "Azerbaijan Becomes a New Battlefield for Iran-Israel Rivalry," *Armenian Weekly*, November 16, 2022, https://t.ly/Rr9Lc.
23. Emil Danielyan, "Armenia Reassures Iran over Embassy in Israel," Azatutyun, January 11, 2020, https://t.ly/kPGW4.
24. Barak Ravid, "Scoop: Azerbaijan Seeks to Mediate Between Turkey and Israel," Axios, December 23, 2020, https://t.ly/tLqfZ.
25. F. Stephen Larrabee and Alireza Nader, "Turkish-Iranian Relations in a Changing Middle East," RAND Corporation, 2013, https://t.ly/AsBhq.

26. Shahram Akbarzadeh and James Barry, "Iran and Turkey: Not Quite Enemies But Less than Friends," *Third World Quarterly* 38, no. 4 (2017): 980–95.

27. Nurbanu Kizil, "Turkey-Armenia Normalization May Foster Peace But Challenges Remain," *Daily Sabah*, May 1, 2022, https://t.ly/68ivA.

28. "Bilateral Relations: Türkiye," Ministry of Foreign Affairs of the Republic of Armenia, November 27, 2024, https://t.ly/hJWly.

29. "The Events of 1915 and the Turkish-Armenian Controversy over History: An Overview," Turkey Ministry of Foreign Affairs, accessed March 27, 2027, https://t.ly/vlsw0.

30. Kirill Krivosheev, "Armenia Is Ready to Relinquish Nagorno-Karabakh: What Next?," Carnegie Endowment for International Peace, April 28, 2023, https://t.ly/gjJRm.

31. "Realization of Zangezour Corridor Is Historical Necessity—President Ilham Aliyev," Trend, January 10, 2023, https://t.ly/kgsDN.

32. Devin Haas, "Explainer: Azerbaijan, Iran and the Crisis in the South Caucasus," Emerging Europe, February 2, 2023, https://t.ly/qeNnL.

33. Andrew Lumsden, "Media Guide: Iran and the Armenia-Azerbaijan Conflict," American Iranian Council, December 13, 2022, https://t.ly/QD5ic.

34. Amberin Zaman, "Turkey Rises, Russia Fades as Iran and Azerbaijan Clash over Armenia," Al-Monitor, January 31, 2023, https://t.ly/F_4v-.

35. Eleonora Tafuro Ambrosetti, "A New Regional Order in the Making: The Coming Geopolitics of the South Caucasus," ISPI, November 7, 2022, https://t.ly/B-QeX.

36. Vasif Huseynov, "Turbulent Times Ahead for South Caucasus as Russia's Regional Hegemony Erodes," *National Interest*, March 31, 2023, https://t.ly/oaWhx.

37. Ali Noureddine, "Iran-Azerbaijan Rift: Historical and Geopolitical Factors," Fanack, February 23, 2023, https://t.ly/u0lCN.

38. "Azerbaijan Signs Declaration on Allied Cooperation with Russia. What Does It Mean?," JAM News, February 22, 2022, https://t.ly/c1Yb_.

39. Eugene Rumer, Richard Sokolsky, and Paul Stronski, "U.S. Policy Toward the South Caucasus: Take Three," Carnegie Endowment for International Peace, May 31, 2017, https://t.ly/_f-t1.

40. Svante Cornell, "US Engagement in the Caucasus: Changing Gears," *Helsinki Monitor*, no. 2 (January 1, 2005): 111–19, https://t.ly/r_SHs.

41. Josep Borrell, "Why We Need More EU Engagement in the South Caucasus," European Union External Action, July 2, 2021, https://t.ly/rQJfx.

42. Vali Kaleji, "Iran Not Opposed to Deployment of EU Monitoring Mission Along Armenian-Azerbaijani Border," *Eurasia Daily Monitor* 20, no. 50, March 27, 2023, https://t.ly/aRdvD.

43. Vali Kaleji, "The Complex Web of Interdependence and Threat Balancing that Prevents War Between Iran and Azerbaijan," Middle East Institute, April 4, 2023, https://t.ly/jRdHY.

44. "Iran, Russia Ink $1.6 Billion Rail Deal to Rival Suez Canal," Al-Monitor, May 17, 2023, https://t.ly/rJ4x0.

12

CONFLICTS ALONG IRAN'S NORTHERN CORRIDORS

Implications for National Security, Regional Order, and the Look East Policy

Banafsheh Keynoush

The interplay of the war in Ukraine in Eurasia with the Armenian–Azerbaijani conflict in the smaller subregion of the South Caucasus profoundly affected Iran. With its northern borders increasingly fragmented due to conflicts, Iran aimed to retain influence over land corridors in the South Caucasus through Azerbaijan and Armenia, and in Eastern Europe through Georgia and Ukraine. Vital to expanding its trade in Asia, the land corridors offered Iran opportunities to also expand its Look East policy.

A key challenge to retaining its influence along its northern corridors, however, was Iran's failure to pay sufficient attention to complex conflict dynamics in the South Caucasus and Eurasia as the country tried to rebuild its ties with the major powers and especially the West following the breakdown of the 2015 Joint Comprehensive Plan of Action (JCPOA), otherwise known as the Iran nuclear deal. When the nuclear deal broke down in 2018, after the administration of President Donald J. Trump withdrew the United States from the JCPOA (other major powers including Russia, China, France, Germany, and the United Kingdom tried but failed to fully salvage the deal), Iran belatedly began advocating for a stronger Look East policy to advance its security by balancing ties with both East and West.

To avert risks emerging from its precarious interactions with the conflict-prone regions of the South Caucasus and Eurasia, Iran advocated for a nonalignment policy in the north, which constituted one of its first policy articulations for an emerging Look North policy. But as tensions broke out first between Armenia and Azerbaijan by 2019, and after the outbreak of war in Ukraine in 2022, the unfolding geopolitical landscape along Iran's northern corridors increased world power competition on its doorsteps, and challenged Tehran in its ability to uphold a fully nonaligned policy.

Hence, despite its proclaimed nonalignment, Iran's foreign policy behavior and its political identity frequently clashed with other policies and identities conceived by its neighbors to the north, as well as other regional and world powers to build influence in the South Caucasus and Eurasia while forces of a larger order seemed to be reshaping the area. Consequently, Iran's Look East policy suffered, and the country failed to articulate a clear Look North policy, despite it enjoying a symbiotic relationship with Armenia, an indispensable partnership with Russia, economic and ideational links with the predominantly Shia state of Azerbaijan, and diplomatic ties with Ukraine.

Contextual Theorization of Iran's Approach to Conflicts in the South Caucasus and Eurasia

Iran lacked a well-articulated "Look North" policy to complement its "Look East" policy once conflicts broke out in the South Caucasus and in Eurasia. A Look North policy would have involved building better ties with Iran's northern neighbors which failed to materialize due to the outbreak of fresh border tensions between the Republic of Azerbaijan and the Republic of Armenia over Nagorno-Karabakh in 2021, and the Russian war in Ukraine in 2022.

Responding to the festering conflicts to its north, Tehran's nonaligned policy projected impartiality albeit with mixed results due to misleading and ad hoc foreign policy decisions and nonneutral Iranian policy formulation and implementation that aimed above all to exercise influence with its northern neighbors and contain the northern conflicts from spreading. Nevertheless, Iran managed to engage in "metarelational exchanges" with these neighbors. These exchanges involved multiple actors, and they were rationally driven by realpolitik calculations to advance Iranian interests against the backdrop of a Russian-dominated regional order in the South Caucasus and Eurasia, and Western encroachment on that order. Furthermore, the policies facilitating such exchanges involved a host of complex diplomatic, security, economic, and ideational challenges and initiatives.[1]

However, containing Iranian power and influence in the South Caucasus and Eurasia was part and parcel of the Russian-dominated regional order, as well as a goal that other rival international and regional powers such as the United States, Israel, Turkey, and Saudi Arabia pursued. This in turn challenged the diplomatic, security, economic, and ideational aspects of Iranian foreign policy toward its northern neighbors. Furthermore, it strained Iranian–Russian ties in light of Moscow's aversion to Iran's ideological policies.

Consequently, Iran failed to formulate a strong proactive foreign policy in response to the Nagorno-Karabakh conflict and the war in Ukraine. This led to the systemic degradation of the Iranian ability to reshape conflicts to its north without blurring diplomatic, security, economic, and ideational interests, and confusing neighbors. Iran's officially declared nonalignment policy, which was designed to remain independent from belligerence, and which might have helped the country formulate an effective Look North policy, fluctuated too. In practice, Iran was unable to stay neutral and lacked steady objectivity about what neutrality constitutes in handling the conflicts in the South Caucasus and Eurasia.

To overcome challenges with its northern neighbors, Iran projected policies of passive and positive neutrality. The policies represented Iran's proclaimed attempt to remain directly uninvolved in the conflicts in the north. By adopting a passively neutral stance, however, Tehran hoped that it could benefit from dividends resulting from conflict fatigue in the South Caucasus and in Eurasia, mindful of unresolved nature of the tensions between Armenia and Azerbaijan, and Ukraine and Russia. In other words, Tehran calculated that conflict fatigue could eventually grant opportunities to direct policies in its favor when dealing with its norther neighbors. Through the exercise of positive neutrality (i.e., an external manifestation of its desire to observe a "neutral" right to somehow affect the outcome of those conflicts), Iran proactively averted instability along its northern borders by adopting diplomatic, security, economic, and ideationally driven policies to contain the spread of war from the north.[2]

This posturing between passive and positive neutrality undoubtedly spared Iran the trouble of needing to directly entangle itself in the conflicts to its north, and left room for Tehran to develop realpolitik responses that ensured it could remain a distant player in these conflicts. It further enabled Iran to lead a flexible foreign policy agenda in handling the tensions between Armenia and Azerbaijan, and Russia and Ukraine. The flexible metarelational contacts and exchanges that Iran forged with multiple actors along its northern corridors secured its northern borders, despite opposing foreign government interests in the two conflicts.

Iranian policies, however, fueled suspicions. The Pentagon declared Iran to be a major global challenge in 2023, mindful of the role it played in supplying Russia with military equipment. Russia, meanwhile, viewed its neighborly rivalries with Iran as a hindrance to advancing Moscow's interests in the South Caucasus and Eurasia. In response, Iran explained that its policy choices could lead to collective regional determination to localize, contain and affect conflicts and military strategy, in a manner that would preclude foreign actors such as the United States from intervening in the South Caucasus and Eurasia. Iran's dialogue with its neighbors to the north further encouraged policy determination through diplomacy, aversion to conflict and promotion of peace, and the embrace of regional governance initiatives and collective security guarantees.[3]

Iran further aimed to transform the regional structure peacefully, to help advance its Look East policy. By evaluating and motivating its policy through metarelational exchanges, it kept its northern neighbors engaged to highlight the imperatives of cooperation and the cost of noncooperation. It discouraged Israel's close ties with Azerbaijan and Ukraine, and stressed that Tehran would rather avoid conflicts than move in the direction of war. This relationality, in other words relating to its northern neighbors' conflict problems and interests to build peace, helped Tehran stress the need to engage with regional political and economic communities of which it was a part. The plurality that Iran aimed to highlight in this process reinforced its Look East policy, despite being fraught with disagreements with its northern neighbors.

Iran's Metarelational Exchanges Along Its Northern Corridors

Regional transformations in the South Caucasus and Eurasia due to conflicts were linked with the decentering of Eurocentrism and the transatlantic alliance between the United States and Europe, in favor of regional solutions to war and peace to avert potential Western encroachment. At the very least, this was the perspective that Iran held in terms of how it viewed the conflicts along its northern corridors.

Unsurprisingly, this perspective contributed to Iran's situationally relational foreign policy agenda with its northern neighbors. By tolerating the 2019 Ukrainian constitutional amendment to join NATO, and Azerbaijan's NATO bid and irredentist claims over both Armenian and Iranian territories, Tehran quickly came to terms with the diversity and contradictions evident in its ties with its northern neighbors.[4]

Simultaneously, it recognized that regional transformation would likely be marked by perpetual conflict and war fatigue in the South Caucasus and Eurasia. This demanded that Iran cross-engage with multiple actors in conflict zones to its north to navigate emerging challenges through a series of diplomatic, security, economic and ideational exchanges outlined below.

Iran's Diplomatic Challenges and Initiatives

Iran's contacts with its northern neighbors in the South Caucasus and Eurasia represented a continuum of interstate exchanges that involved several actors, including Russia, Ukraine, Azerbaijan, and Armenia, against the backdrop of global geopolitical influences. As the South Caucasus and Eurasia regions struggled to transform peacefully, Iran promoted regional mechanisms to foster peaceful transformations. But its relational interactions with neighbors in the face of regional conflicts to its north forced its shift from passive neutrality toward a more robust foreign policy, in order to ensure survival and stability.

Iran frequently offered to mediate an end to tensions in the South Caucasus and Eurasia, throughout the period 2020 to 2022. It repeatedly stressed that its northern borders could be secure only by negotiations, while insisting that they were inviolable.[5] When Yerevan objected to an Azerbaijani-backed border change through the Zangezur Corridor in southern Armenia, on grounds that this change could restrict Iran's land access to the South Caucasus, an Armenian member of the Iranian parliament Ara Shaverdian also warned against Azerbaijan using the corridor to the landlocked enclave of Azerbaijan known as the Nakhchavan Autonomous Republic and Turkey at Iran's expense.[6] Meanwhile, Tehran officially warned against NATO expansion eastward through Azerbaijan or Ukraine, and it called it a "serious threat."[7]

Unwilling to assume that its northern neighbors had limitless power to engage in perpetual conflict or shun regional or international mediation efforts, Iran further advanced its diplomatic goals by recognizing that while it lacked power to deal with all the conflicts to its north, it could at least affect their course through diplomacy. Iran therefore frequently made public statements to denounce what it termed as "interference of foreigners in the region."[8] In principle, Iran also continued to uphold a neutral position. Ukraine and Azerbaijan, being mainly in the Western camp, Tehran was warned by Iranian policymakers not to get engaged in the two conflicts directly, which in turn helped advance its declared neutrality.

But broader calculations constantly shaped Iran's diplomatic interactions in response to conflicts along its northern corridors. As Israel expanded its diplomatic outreach in the South Caucasus and in Eurasia, in December 2022, Iran opened a new consulate in the southeastern Armenian city of Kapan, two miles away from the border with Azerbaijan, and days before Tehran conducted war games along the border, designed to send a message of "peace and friendship." Moscow's refusal to directly intervene in the Nagorno-Karabakh conflict, meanwhile, despite Armenian membership in a 2002 Moscow-led Collective Security Treaty Organization (i.e., a military bloc, including Armenia, Belarus, Kazakhstan, Kyrgyzstan, Russia, and Tajikistan), paved the way for Yerevan's embrace of an enhanced Iranian diplomatic presence in Armenian territory.[9] Iran further warned that it would offer a "proportional" response to Ukraine's decision to significantly reduce the Iranian embassy staff in Kyiv in September 2022, while insisting that it would prevent the destruction of diplomatic ties.[10]

The interrelational dynamics of Iran's exchanges with its neighbors to the north, however, delayed Iranian ability to fully interact with regional and international bodies to help end the conflicts in the South Caucasus and Eurasia. Policy experts in Iran warned that even the Presidential Office led by Ebrahim Raisi lacked strong subject matter expertise on the South Caucasus and Eurasia, and hardly sought advisory opinion from academics despite Iran's potentially high capacity as a neighbor to help resolve the conflicts with Azerbaijan and Ukraine. Rather, Tehran frequently reacted to these conflicts by offering piecemeal policy to handle tensions with its northern neighbors, without gaining influence over them compared to other rival countries, including Turkey, Russia, Israel, Saudi Arabia, and the United States.

Unable to formulate a strong Look North strategy or offer conflict mitigation solutions, Iran took sides with Armenia and Russia despite its desire to remain a neutral party in the Nagorno-Karabakh conflict and the war in Ukraine. The opening of the Israeli embassy in Azerbaijan in March 2023, making it the first majority Shia-populated country in the region to embrace formal ties with the Jewish state, came after Iran opened a consulate in Kapan. Israel's simultaneous measures to expand its diplomatic presence in other Central Asian capitals along Iran's borders, and close ties with Kyiv, countered Iranian regional diplomatic initiatives, casting serious doubts over Tehran's diplomacy in advancing an effective Look East policy across Asia in the face of tensions to its north.

Iran's Security Challenges and Initiatives

Festering conflicts between the republics of Azerbaijan and Armenia and the war in Ukraine fueled instability along Iran's northern borders in less than two years. Tehran's security response to those conflicts was multifold. Above all, Iran aimed to ensure stability, by expanding border security and agreements with Russia. Additionally, it ensured that its tensions with Azerbaijan and Ukraine remained confined within its neighbors' borders, to avoid conflict spillover into Iran. Tehran also combined defensive posturing with offensive capabilities in the form of military drills and arms supplies to some of its northern neighbors, in order to deter and preempt threats from Azerbaijan and Ukraine.

Despite its proclaimed nonalignment, in diplomatic circles, Tehran argued that it had the right to sell arms to its neighbors, which it did not see as interfering with its declared neutral position toward the conflicts along its northern corridors. Although Tehran rejected that it supplied arms to the war in Ukraine, Iranian drone and ammunition supplies to Russia reportedly picked up by 2022.[11] Iran reportedly gave Yerevan 500 units of the Iranian Dehlavieh antitank missile system and another one hundred units of the Almas system in October 2022.[12]

While supporting Armenia materially, Iran's positive positions on Azerbaijan, which were initially ambivalent between the first and second Nagorno-Karabakh wars from 1994 to 2020, slowly formed after the formation of the Organization for Security and Co-operation in Europe (OSCE) Minsk Group cochaired by Russia, France, and the United States in 1992. At this time, the Nagorno-Karabakh enclave (also referred to by Armenians as Artsakh) had declared independence as a new republic the year before, at which point Iran decided to support United Nations resolutions stipulating that the enclave was Azerbaijani territory. Internally, Iran maintained a delicate balancing act, mindful that it was home to an Armenian population, as well as a large ethnic Azeri community. A small number of Azeri Iranians had supported Azerbaijan's claims over Nagorno-Karabakh. This balancing act, aiming to maintain an equilibrium in ties with Armenia and Azerbaijan, reassured its northern neighbors that Tehran recognized the inviolability of their territorial integrity which under UN resolutions also meant that Armenia occupied Azerbaijani land that had to be returned.[13] Finally, in a meeting between Iranian President Hassan Rouhani and Azerbaijan's President Ilham Aliyev in Tehran in early November 2017, Tehran and Baku were able ease tensions between them over Iranian backing for Armenia.

But Iran's publicly declared proactive neutrality over the tensions between Baku and Yerevan continued to shift in response to US engagements with Azerbaijan. In February 2019, Armenian Prime Minister Nikol Pashinyan was in Tehran to seal a partnership deal in the event that another major conflict broke out with Azerbaijan. Despite technically having to remain in compliance with a UN monitoring system that tracked Iranian conventional weapons inflows and sales, Iran said it was entitled to selling arms and it reportedly transferred military equipment to Armenia through the Nordooz border terminal using Russian Kamaz trucks, amid heavy fighting in Nagorno-Karabakh in October 2020.[14]

When the forty-four-day fall war of 2020 between Armenia and Azerbaijan broke out, Tehran adopted the position that it could not afford to take sides, but only to trigger events circumstantially in its favor. This meant backing Armenia materially, but adhering to international and regional decisions to build a ceasefire between Yerevan and Baku. As the Iranian proactive policy of neutrality took shape, to ensure the security of its borders by backing Armenian border interests, Tehran continued to resort to regional diplomacy to retain open channels of communication with Azerbaijan.

However, Iran's limited political capabilities to address the conflicts in the north meant that it could not play a prominent role in fixing tensions between Yerevan and Baku.[15] Adding to this challenge was the issue of arms sales to Baku by Turkey and Israel, including drones, which threatened to disrupt the Nagorno-Karabakh conflict against Armenia. The landing of missiles from the conflict on Iranian soil triggered a harsher Iranian response by late 2020, at which time Baku and Yerevan signed a Russian-backed ceasefire agreement in November. Armenia handed over some territory to Azerbaijan, and made commitments to ensuring the safety of transport communication in the South Caucasus along its land corridors with Azerbaijan, which sought to control the "Zangezur Corridor" and build a territorial divide between Armenia and Iran.

This overt and rapid securitization of Iran's northern borders became an immediate threat to the country. The reciprocal danger to the security of Iran and Azerbaijan was obvious, if tensions between them persisted. Azerbaijan was a recipient of massive material support from the United States, Israel, and Turkey, as well as Saudi Arabia, adding to Iranian fears of encirclement by rival or hostile powers.

In response, in October 2021, Iran's army conducted the "Conquerors of Kheibar" military drill. The military exercise displayed superior Iranian ground force capabilities compared to Azerbaijan, along borders with Nackchavan. Iran's "Lashkar Ashura" military units, led by the Iran–Iraq war veteran Commander Mehdi Bakeri and involving an entire unit of Azeris recruited from the Republic of Azerbaijan, served in the drill to warn Azerbaijan of the threat to its internal security if it challenged Iran.[16] Pointedly, the drill arrived on the heels of another military exercise led by Azerbaijan in September 2021, along with Turkey and Pakistan, dubbed "Three-Brothers—2021."[17]

The resumption of conflict between Armenia and Azerbaijan in 2022, along with Azerbaijan's stated interest to join NATO, and participation in NATO-led activities in Afghanistan, had Iran even more concerned and it pushed the country to cooperate with Russia. A meeting between President Vladimir Putin and Prime Minister Pashinyan in Moscow in April 2022 reaffirmed Moscow's close ties with Yerevan, and Tehran's support, despite US efforts later in the year to stir Yerevan away from this Russian–Iranian camp.[18]

But Iran's partnership with Russia over the conflict with Azerbaijan soon backfired. To forestall NATO expansion, Russia accused Baku of violating the November 2020 Moscow-brokered ceasefire deal by allowing Azeri troops to cross over a set demarcated line in March 2023.[19] By allowing Azerbaijan to reclaim territory, Russia abandoned its historic backing of Armenia in favor of avoiding a protracted battle. It was also able to station Russian forces in Azerbaijan to monitor borders, including those borders that previously directly linked Iran with Armenia.

Nonetheless, Azerbaijan's takeover of Karabakh territories after the ceasefire meant that Armenia lost the war but was saved the brunt of a long battle. Peace along Armenia's borders was what Iran aimed to establish as well. The peace settlement, however, did not mean that Tehran could expand its influence in the South Caucasus unless it fixed its ties with Azerbaijan first.

Tehran's policy calculations toward Baku, however, involved understanding what Russia might need first in terms of containing Azerbaijan and the war in Ukraine, while ensuring that Tehran would not get embroiled in either conflict unnecessarily. This made Iranian policies piecemeal and beholden to complex Russian interests, and with little impact on a grand scale, but sufficient to advance Iranian deterrence and preemption capabilities. It also invited paradiplomacy by Iranian-backed substate or nonstate actors. According to some reports, for example, Iran was using nonstate actors to influence the outcome of conflicts in the north. These reports pointed that the Lebanese Hezbollah may have fortified its strongholds on the border with Israel using Russian air defense systems, just as Israel expanded its ties with Azerbaijan.[20] Other reports pointed that Hezbollah may have offered its assistance to Russia to contain the war in Ukraine, shortly after Moscow asked Baku to sign a declaration on allied cooperation in February 2022.[21] In addition, Iran shipped drones to Russia, although it claimed the unmanned aerial vehicles (UAVs) were delivered prior to the outbreak of the war in Ukraine.[22] Despite other reports pointing to Iran's supply of other military advisory services to Russia, including advanced precision-guided missiles and material to build a drone manufacturing plant east of Moscow, Tehran said it remained committed to bringing peace in Ukraine.[23] But Tehran's supply of military equipment to Russia worsened Iran's tensions with Ukraine.

Iran's alliance with Russia over Ukraine proved costly. By upholding its official neutral stance, Tehran hoped to deflect international criticism. Even when Kyiv insisted that Tehran was complicit in the Russian war campaign, and that it had shot down more than 250 Iranian UAVs, and Washington vowed to penalize Iran over it, Tehran proceeded to ask Kyiv to supply evidence that Iranian drones were supplied directly to the warfront.[24] Yet, unprecedented levels of technical and military cooperation between Iran and Russia had the West worried, securitized Iran's ties with Western countries and Ukraine, increased Baku's and Kiev's hostility toward Tehran, prolonged the tensions along Iran's northern corridors, and increased US and Israeli efforts to stall Iran's Look East policy.

The increased securitization of Iran's northern borders also fueled immediate tensions with Azerbaijan and even pushed Russia to contain Iranian power. In July 2022, Azerbaijan closed its land borders with Iran in the Julfa area and along three cross-border posts shared by the two countries with Turkey, citing COVID-19 concerns.[25] By August, the Azeri president had built an inspection unit in Lachin city to replace Russian peacekeepers stationed there after the ceasefire with Armenia was established in 2020. The sealing of the Lachin Corridor, which had earlier linked Armenians to Nagorno-Karabakh for the purpose of the transfer of munition and military equipment, was combined with increased support for Baku from countries such as Pakistan, Turkey, and Saudi Arabia. Then, in August 2022, Russian military inspection units were stationed along the borders between Armenia and Iran, to address rising regional tensions. Azerbaijan hoped to use the area and a railway link through it with Nakhchavan. Moscow cited increased drug trafficking from Iran to Armenia as reason to control the border, and concerns over the violation of the border by radical and terrorist groups coming from Iran.[26]

In response, Iran's Islamic Revolutionary Guards Corps (IRGC) launched large-scale military drills dubbed the "Mighty Iran" in the Aras region along the borders with Armenia in October 2022. Shortly before the drill, Iran's armed forces Chief Mohammad Hossein Bagheri and Azeri Defense Minister Zakir Hasanov discussed holding a joint drill of their own, but to no avail. The IRGC drill was the third of its kind in two years, and took place along Iran's entire northwestern border.[27] To deescalate tensions, however, the IRGC proceeded to reject that Iran had any major tensions in its ties with President Aliyev. But Iran's Quds Force Commander Esmail Ghaani insisted that Tehran would not be indifferent if Israel were to plot against Iran inside the Republic of Azerbaijan, a warning that arrived publicly in March 2023.[28]

A May 2023 peace deal between Armenia and Azerbaijan was finally brokered by Moscow, which also monitored the conflict in Azerbaijan's breakaway, mainly ethnic Armenian region of Nagorno-Karabakh. But as of the time of this writing, tensions in the area had once again broken out between Baku and Yerevan. Meanwhile, the Organization for Security and Cooperation in Europe had previously stationed British army officers in Donetsk, Ukraine. These moves along Iran's northern borders made Tehran realize how little influence it had along its northern corridors.

In July 2023, in the face of warnings that a new Karabakh deal might fail again and that Washington would forge a new historic mediation process in the South Caucasus, Iran and Russia signed a new policing agreement to address instability in a host of security arenas, and to protect government infrastructure.[29] The Russian–Iranian security partnership challenged efforts by Azerbaijan, Armenia, and Ukraine to forge strong partnerships with the West or with Israel in a manner that could irreversibly harm security for Moscow and Tehran. In turn, Iran displayed modest signs of an elevation of its Look East policy in the security arena through its strengthening security partnership with Moscow. But Tehran struggled to maintain a balanced dialogue with the West, or over its nuclear program, and its policies toward the conflicts to its north remained increasingly overshadowed by Russian interests, making Iran's international standing more precarious in light of the fact that Washington seemed to be keen to contain both Moscow and Tehran in the South Caucasus and Eurasia. This, in turn, cast doubt on whether the Russian-Iranian security partnership might not fall prey to the bigger negotiations that Moscow would plan to have with the West over Ukraine, in the event of which, Iranian access corridors to its north could remain sealed and its Look East policy could suffer further setbacks.

Iran's Economic Challenges and Initiatives

Without easy access to its vital northern corridors, Iran's potential starvation was in the making, mindful that the country's other land corridors to its east bordering Pakistan and Afghanistan, and to the south bordering hostile Gulf waters, were also unremarkably slow in offering new trade routes for Tehran. The only main land corridor open to Iran was through Iraq, which itself faced constant conflict. Consequently, Iran's policy to serve as a trade corridor linking the Global South to Central Asia, and the Caucasus to East Asia, was derailed by the redrawing of the maps by Armenia and Azerbaijan, and Western efforts to expand economic interests in Eurasia through Ukraine. Western sanctions due to the unresolved status of the Iran nuclear deal, meanwhile, exacerbated Iran's economic vulnerability and its prospects for food security and trade.

Aiming to open trade routes linking Syria to Iraq through Iran to the South Caucasus and Eurasia, and using the same routes to then connect to Europe and the Mediterranean, Tehran had long hoped that its northern borders were peaceful and ripe with trade opportunities. But Iranian northern transit routes narrowed as a result of the 2020 Nagorno-Karabakh war. Iranian experts meanwhile argued that it was Azerbaijan's goal to make this happen, and to isolate Iran with help from the West and Israel, although the conflict over Karabakh triggered the war and provided the excuse.[30]

On a more positive note for Iran, in August 2022, according to Iranian news sources, Russia confirmed that it supported Iran's membership in the 2015 Eurasian Economic Union bloc.[31] Iran's trade with this bloc began by 2019; however, it struggled to build new tariff regimes with the bloc in the first two years, which in turn slowed down its trade volume, and led to increased imports from Iran from the bloc members. Even so, the total volume of trade between Iran and the bloc stood at US$3.3 billion in 2022.[32] Also in mid-September 2022, Iran signed a Memorandum of Obligations during the Shanghai Cooperation Organization (SCO) summit in Uzbekistan to become a permanent member of the body, which would serve also to better align Iranian economic interests with those of the two founding members of the body (i.e., Russia, as well as China).[33] Iran's trade with the SCO in the nonoil sector reportedly reached US$38.8 billion in the 2022 to 2023 Iranian calendar year, despite Western sanctions on Iran.[34] In October 2022, Russia and Iran agreed to set up a free-trade zone to enhance ties with the Eurasian Economic Union.[35] The North–South Transport Corridor (INSTC) extending from India to Russia through Iran opened new areas of cooperation.

In April 2022, Moscow and Tehran had signed a transportation agreement to operationalize a trade corridor by late 2022.[36] President Putin also referred to the North–South corridor as one of several main pathways to expanding Russian trade in Iranian markets, and predicted the volume of this trade could increase by 60 percent by 2030.[37]

But in May 2023, Ukraine imposed sectoral economic sanctions against Iran that prohibited trade in military and dual-use goods, restricted exchanges in the transportation fields, suspended financial obligations and electronic payment transfers, and prohibited the transfer of technology.[38] A year earlier, Iran's meager trade volume with Ukraine of less than US$3 million dropped by 90 percent, forcing Tehran to turn to Moscow to meet its food needs. Over a decade ago, this trade volume stood at US$500 million.[39]

Meanwhile, US sanctions against Armenian entities trading with Iran, and the lifeline connection between the Armenian and Iranian business communities and financial institutions, restricted Tehran from expanding trade, although it exchanged trade delegations with Yerevan. By March 2023, the volume of trade between Iran and Armenia stood at around US$300. Previously, this trade volume reached US$700 million in 2021, which also increased by 40 percent in 2022.[40]

The forty-four-day war between Armenia and Azerbaijan overhauled Iran's trade routes. The Zangezur tunnel linking Azerbaijan to Nakhchavan through Armenia, and to Russia and Turkey from thereon, enabled Azerbaijan's access to Asia, the Middle East, and Europe, and shortened the land transit route for trade for Baku. But the tunnel restricted Iran's land corridors with Armenia, which were already quite short. It further bypassed Iran for trade routing purposes, but enabled Turkey to reach the Caspian Sea and Central Asia and China far quicker, thus connecting by land and sea the regions of the Black Sea, Caucasus, Central Asia, India, and China.[41]

A day after Turkish Foreign Minister Molod Cavoshoglu traveled to Tehran to build a roadmap for cooperation in November 2021, and allay some of Iran's fears over these unfolding events, Azerbaijan had advanced into Armenian-held Kalbajar, causing a diplomatic stir. Russia intervened to force the Azeri forces to retreat. But the Azeri advancement pointed to Baku's desire by that time to remain centerstage in evolving trade corridors for the region. Additionally, Iran stood to entirely lose control over its border crossings with Azerbaijan. In fact, the Zangezur tunnel project could be useless to Iran, mindful that Azeri papers went as far as to openly dismiss Iranian claims over their border rights with Armenia, and suggest that Armenia would receive no rights to monitor the crossing per the ceasefire agreement of November 2020.[42]

The Zangezur Corridor could in effect potentially disconnect Iran's access to the South Caucasus, and from there to Europe. Russia was keen to use the corridor to maintain control over routes between the South Caucasus, Turkey, and Europe, pushing Armenia to comply despite ensuing blockages in its borders with Iran which itself remained heavily dependent on exports to the Black Sea region and to Armenia. Furthermore, in exchange for Iranian exports reaching Europe via Turkey, Tehran had granted Ankara land access to Turkmenistan and Asia, and could lose this connection as well. The blockage, therefore, threatened Iran's national security and had experts in the country warn of the potential economic starvation of the country in the long-haul. But the strong trade between Iran and Azerbaijan delayed a full blockage, and trade volumes steadily increased by almost 100 percent between 2021 and 2022. The two countries' preferential trade agreement which was being finalized, talks to advance a railway connection, and construct bridge and land transportation and transit projects offered Baku repeated incentives to work with Tehran on the trade front.[43]

President Aliyev's vision for a greater Eurasia geopolitical landscape, however, and a conference which he presided over on this theme, and pointedly held in Karabakh in May 2023, delegated Azerbaijan's trade ties with Iran to a secondary position, despite Iranian policy of using its northern borders to expand trade. Instead, Azerbaijan explored partnerships with the Organization of Turkic States (OTS), advanced a Western-backed Middle Corridor trade route between Asia and Europe and the Baku-based Alat Free Economic Zone, placing Baku at the epicenter of North–South and East–West Corridors in the region of the South Caucasus.[44]

These Azeri trade advancements, on a grander scale, affected emerging Iranian trade corridors with Latin America. At a meeting exploring trade partnerships with the Americas, Tehran invited the ambassadors of Russia, China, Kazakhstan, Armenia, and Pakistan to attend, along with those from Syria, Oman, Lebanon, Iraq, Venezuela, Bolivia, Nicaragua, and Cuba. The Armenian ambassador did not participate in sessions where the Pakistani diplomats were present, mindful that Pakistan had led military drills with Azerbaijan. Pakistan in turn encouraged a railway from Iran through Pakistan to China, over which at least five rounds of talks were already held to no avail. Also aiming to add Turkey to the railway system, Iran stressed the need to engage in free trade with the Caspian Sea littoral states, not to circumvent sanctions, but to seek solutions for sanctions which Tehran said was the right thing to do.[45]

But vital Azerbaijani oil supplies to Israel, and Azerbaijan and Ukraine being at the center of foreign power economic competitions, consequently meant that US energy investments in the Caspian Sea, along with Israeli economic and energy interests, could strangulate Iran's ability to export oil and gas along its northern corridors. It could further prevent Iran from engaging in global trade, as well as in Asia, where competing Saudi investments barred Tehran from advancing its economic interests. Consequently, the Look East policy that Iran embraced failed to fully help the country advance its desired trade routes in the South Caucasus and Eurasia.

Iran's Ideational Challenges and Initiatives

President Aliyev's public statements in support of the Iranian–Azeri community and their grievances as an ethnic minority group, along with Iranian responses in the form of reprimands over the provocations, intensified the ideological tensions between Baku and Tehran. Iran's ethnic Azerbaijani community of roughly fifteen million, which remained by and large loyal to its Iranian identity despite historic grievances with the Persians, was well positioned economically in the fabric of Iranian society, culture, and polity. But antigovernment protests in Iran in 2022 affected the marginalized Azeri and other ethnic communities such as the Kurds, and heavy security crackdown against the Kurds in this period led to unrest in areas where disenfranchised communities lived along Iran's northwestern borders with Azerbaijan.

In January 2023, after a fatal shooting at the Azerbaijan embassy in Tehran, led by an Iranian citizen by the name of Yaseen Husseinzadeh, Baku and Tehran took steps to ease tensions. Despite Iranian parliamentary objections, two dissident citizens of Azerbaijan were reportedly arrested in the city of Qom and extradited. The two, identified as Orkhan Mamedov and Tohid Ebrahim Beighli, were the leaders of the Hosseiniun Brigade (Hosseinchiler), the Islamic Resistance Movement of Azerbaijan. The entity was formed in 2015 to fight the Islamic State, or ISIS, recruited student fighters from Azerbaijan studying in Iran's seminary cities, and sent Azeri refugees in Iran for training with the Hashd al-Shaabi in Iraq. According to Baku, it carried out espionage on Azeri soil and attempted to influence the Islamic Party of Azerbaijan established in 1991 with Iran's help. Party members would later form the Hezbollah Azerbaijan in 1993.[46]

Mutual ideational provocations, however, remained a motivator of the Iranian–Azerbaijani foreign policy behavior but not the primary driver of their security interests toward each other. This enabled Baku and Tehran to deal pragmatically with their identity-driven threats without engaging in direct conflict, despite mutual provocations. Azerbaijan, for example, arrested dozens charged with spying for Iran. Tehran warned Baku to not harbor a separatist agenda for the Iranian Turks or Azeris. When Baku supported irredentist claims by Iranian Azerbaijanis, Iranians, including members of the Iranian–Azeri community, called for war with Azerbaijan, or referred to the country as the Republic of Baku, thereby implying that any territory controlled by President Aliyev in the name of Azerbaijan belonged only to Iran.

Even so, the ideological undertones of the tensions between Baku and Tehran remained a source of concern. According to Iranian parliament member, Ahmad Naderi, former IRGC Quds Force Commander Qasem Soleimani who was killed by US forces in Iraq in January 2020 had forewarned that after the civil war in Syria that broke out in 2011, tensions would spread to the South Caucasus to endanger Iran's security, as a result of which Soleimani had formed prior to his death, the Azeri Hosseiniun Statute, to build a new axis of resistance, despite the fact that the Republic of Azerbaijan at the time did not constitute part of the Iranian resistance axis.[47] The internal Azeri opposition in Iran, meanwhile, was far more muted than the opposition in the Republic of Azerbaijan against President Aliyev. Azerbaijan's internal conflict with its Shias enabled Iran to use this to address festering tensions with Baku on a quid pro quo basis when it provoked the local Iranian–Azeri community.[48]

Iran's relatively large local Armenian community, and Armenia's refusal to abandon its friendly relations with Tehran, along with a significantly pro-Ukrainian Iranian population, helped keep identity-driven politics out of Iranian calculations on how to manage ideational tensions with Yerevan and Kyiv. But Tehran encouraged Iranian population movement into Armenia, and previously to Ukraine, in part to counter the Turkish influence in the South Caucasus and Eurasia. Furthermore, the downing of a Ukrainian passenger plane by Iran in January 2020 stirred new identity politics connecting the plight of victims and families of the deceased in Iran and Ukraine against Tehran and the conduct of its foreign policy.

This emerging political identity formation, which garnered Western support for victims of the downed plane, provided a new frame of reference from which the pressure by foreign governments on Iran mounted and which in turn cast a heavy shadow over Tehran's ability to make a peaceful pivot in its Look East policy. In response, Iran failed to provide a strong collective elite identity that manifested sufficient accountability to the downing of the plane, as a result of which its status as a member of the international community was severely tarnished.[49]

But as Iran's proxy strategy evolved toward the two regions of the South Caucasus and Eurasia, its axis of resistance was set to expand into Armenia and Ukraine. Tellingly, Iranian clerics warned that the war between Armenia and Azerbaijan was designed to engage, wear out, and defeat the axis of resistance in the South Caucasus, and eventually contain Iran.[50] In response, Iran's media insisted that the country's axis of resistance had already shifted global geopolitical calculations, despite sanctions, and would land on the top as a victor, especially when it came to managing conflicts that linked the Middle East to Europe via Turkey.[51] This was a stark reminder that Iran may have set its eyes on the

South Caucasus and Eurasia in order to build new axes of resistance along its northern corridors.

In an emerging new regional security architecture along its northern borders with the South Caucasus and Eurasia, Iran was economically and ideologically overstretched in handling a series of conflicts with its neighbors, had a lingering nuclear file to resolve with the world powers, and faced immediate threats emanating from the Ukraine war and the Azerbaijan–Armenia conflict. Tehran said it did not see itself a party to either conflict, mindful of important Russian interests and efforts by the collective West to address them, and that it aimed only to build a positive experience interacting with its northern neighbors. But its actions were not readily matched with strong diplomacy or the ability to deescalate tensions, and Iran was by and large sidelined in the face of shifting regional power imbalances.

Operating as a sidelined member of the small regional subsystems of the South Caucasus and Eurasia to which it belonged, Iran was encouraged to employ relationality in its foreign policy behavior through complex interactions with the conflicts to its north. This required Iran to recognize that it could not expect to exist in peace as a mere observer of those conflicts.[52] Rather, Iran recognized that those conflicts would impact its own security. There were no great emotional divides between the Azeris living in Iran and those in the Republic of Azerbaijan, nor between the Armenians of Iran and those in the Republic of Armenia. With regard to Ukraine, relationality occurred over the need to contain the conflict in order to prevent Western encroachment in Eurasia along Iran's borders to its north.

While logic also demanded that Iran identify with the pain and suffering of the people of Ukraine and the Republic of Azerbaijan over their territorial losses, the overriding need for survival and stability forced Tehran into action to shape the conflicts its neighbors faced in its own favor. This reinforced Iran's Look East policy by ensuring constant engagement with Russia, Ukraine, Azerbaijan, and Armenia, through the exploration of mutual interests in diplomatic, security, economic and ideational spheres. It, however, hindered Iran's Look East policy by increasing tensions between Tehran and its northern neighbors. Consequently, Tehran was unprepared to manage these frequent tensions.

Despite frictions, the goal of achieving a plurality of views to transform the region of the South Caucasus and Eurasia through a complex and emergent mesh of agency, structure and order helped shed light on how Iran saw its relations with its northern neighbors and aimed to reorient them. Realpolitik was predicated in Iran's case on important insights about its foreign policy considerations, and prioritized state-centric policies that were pursued through an officially declared neutral policy in the South Caucasus and Eurasia. The fact that tensions between

Armenia and Azerbaijan were ethnically based, and also driven by religious disagreements, meant that Iran could expect to work with its two main partners (i.e., Russia and China) to defuse sectarian tensions in the South Caucasus, as part and parcel of building up a Look East policy. But Ukraine remained a constant challenge for Iran, who failed to rebuild ties with Kyiv. In this context, turning the northern corridor conflicts into opportunities needed further strategic calculations that Iran had yet to develop. Thus, in the absence of a much-needed Look North doctrine, the Iranian Look East policy was bound to suffer some setbacks as other foreign actors stepped in to contain Tehran's regional influence in the South Caucasus and Eurasia.

NOTES

1. For realpolitik concepts, see Brian Rathbun, "The Rarity of Realpolitik: What Bismark's Rationality Reveals About International Politics," *International Security* 43, no. 1 (Summer 2018): 7–55. Iran officially supports a neutral policy in the South Caucasus; see for example, "Yek sal pas az tahajom-e nezami rosiyeh be Ukraine; iran "bitaraf" ya "Ukraine-e doshman'?" [A year into the Russian military invasion of Ukraine; Iran "neutral" or "Ukraine's enemy?"], Radio Farda, February 22, 2023, https://bit.ly/3SdLNBk; "Akhareen khabar dar mored-e vaziyat-e mozakerat-e farjam be goftey-e bagheri kani" [Latest on the situation regarding JCPOA negotiations according to Bagheri Kani/Iran is neutral in Ukraine war], Khabar Online, February 12, 2023, https://bit.ly/474SEky; and "Vezarat kharejeh-ye iran: Ma amadeh miyanghari miyan-e armanestan va azarbaijan hasteem" [Iran Foreign Ministry: We are ready to mediate between Armenia and Azerbaijan], BBC Farsi, September 28, 2020, https://bit.ly/46FHByA.

2. For theoretical debates on neutrality and metarelational models see Pascal Lottaz, "Neutrality Studies," *Oxford Research Encyclopedia of International Studies*, March 2022, https://bit.ly/46JN5ID; see also Alan Page Fiske, "Metarelational Models: Configurations of Social Relationships," *European Journal of Social Psychology* 42, no. 1 (February 2012): 2–18.

3. See also Tamara Trownsell, Amaya Querejazu Escobari, Giorgio Shani, Navnita Chadha Behera, Jarrad Reddekop, and Arlene Tickner, "Recrafting International Relations Through Relationality," E-International Relations, January 8, 2019, https://bit.ly/3QuFW9t.

4. See also Emilian Kavalski, "Relational Theories in International Relations," *Oxford Research Encyclopedia of International Studies*, January 31, 2023, https://bit.ly/476pWA7.

5. "Iran Says Ready to Mediate Between Azerbaijan and Armenia," *Tehran Times*, July 17, 2020, https://bit.ly/3Qsl5Ua; "Iran Renews Call to Mediate Between Russia and Ukraine," *Tehran Times*, May 20, 2022, https://bit.ly/3Q2orvC; and "Tehran baray-e tavagof-e darghiriye gharebagh tarhi ra amadeh kardeh" [Tehran has prepared plan to halt Karabakh conflict], Hezbollah Analytical News Agency, October 5, 2020, https://bit.ly/46Y3hq5.

6. Sadeq Dehqan, "Tehran Should Be More Assertive on Northern Borders: Iran MP," *Iran Daily*, June 19, 2023, https://bit.ly/4709cKH.

7. Tuqa Khalid, "Iran Raisi Tells Putin NATO Expansion a 'Serious Threat' as Russia Invades Ukraine," AlArabiya, February 24, 2022, https://bit.ly/3tLTXXo.

8. See Yeghia Tashjian, "Is Iran Making a Comeback to the South Caucuses?," *Armenian Weekly*, October 20, 2021, https://bit.ly/406WR5b; and Joel Abrams, "Nagorno-Karabakh:

Why Iran Is Trying to Remain Neutral Over the Conflict on its Doorstep," Conversation, October 7, 2020, https://bit.ly/3tJTF3t.

9. Gabriel Gavin, "Iran Is Filling Armenia's Power Vacuum," *Foreign Policy*, December 1, 2022, https://bit.ly/3Q92Hyu.

10. "Iran Will Make 'Proportional' Response to Ukraine Reducing Ties," Reuters, September 24, 2022, https://bit.ly/494kcsj.

11. Deborah Haynes, "Arms Contract Shows Iran Has Sold Russia Ammunition for Ukraine War, Says Security Source," Sky News, June 5, 2023, https://bit.ly/407kfj5.

12. Vasid Huseynov, "Armenia and Iran Combine Forces Against Azerbaijan," Modern Diplomacy, December 11, 2022, https://bit.ly/494Visy.

13. Maziar Motamedi, "Iran's Delicate Balancing Act in the Nagorno-Karabakh Conflict," Al Jazeera, October 5, 2020, https://bit.ly/3Q94WSm.

14. Motamedi, "Iran's Delicate Balancing Act."

15. "Iran bayad dar masala-ye ghafghaz bitaraf-e fa'al bashad" [Iran should be an actively neutral actor on issue of Caucasus], *Shargh Daily*, September 22, 2022, https://bit.ly/3MCRl4X.

16. "Ekhtelaf-e iran va jomhuri-ye azarbaijan bar sar-e chist?" [What is the difference between Iran and Azerbaijan province about?], Roudad24, January 27, 2023, https://bit.ly/3s8OKZh.

17. "Turkey, Azerbaijan, Pakistan Launch 'Three Brothers' Joint Military Exercises," Arab News, September 14, 2021, https://bit.ly/3SdCGAO.

18. "Dalil-e huzoor-e nezami-ye rosiyeh posht-e marz-e iran va armanestan chist?" [What are the reasons for Russian military presence behind borders of Iran and Armenia?], BBC Farsi, August 10, 2022, https://bit.ly/3Q92POu.

19. "Russia Claims Azerbaijan Violated Cease-Fire with Armenia," Radio Free Europe, March 25, 2023, https://bit.ly/3Qv4OOt.

20. "Israel Concerned over Hezbollah's Possession of Russian Air Defense Systems," Asharq Al Awsat, July 1, 2023, https://bit.ly/3S9K6ET.

21. "Iran-Backed Hezbollah Reportedly Plans to Fight for Russia in Ukraine," Iran International, March 27, 2022, https://bit.ly/49anoCW; and "Lebanon's Hezbollah Chief Denies Sending Fighters to Support Russia in Ukraine," Reuters, March 18, 2022, https://bit.ly/3tNs1m7.

22. "US Reacts to Iran FM Comments on Drones Shipped to Russia," IRNA, November 6, 2022, https://bit.ly/3Qt4UGi.

23. "Amir-Abdollahian: Siyasat-e gheir-e ghabel-e taqir-e iran payan dadan be jangh dar Ukraine ast" [Amir Abdollahian: Iran's unchangeable policy is to end war in Ukraine], Fars News Agency, November 9, 2022, https://bit.ly/46Y8Unq; Aamer Madhani, "White House Says Iran Is Helping Russia Build a Drone Factory East of Moscow for the War in Ukraine," Washington News, June 9, 2023, https://bit.ly/40c6Fen; and Kylie Atwood, "Iran is Preparing to Send Additional Weapons Including Ballistic Missiles to Russia to Use in Ukraine, Western Officials Say," CNN, November 1, 2022, https://bit.ly/477Qgdb.

24. "Ukraine Foreign Minister Tells Iran Counterpart: Stop Sending Arms to Russia," Reuters, October 28, 2022, https://bit.ly/3S6t6j0; and Barak Ravid, "Ukraine Says It Has Shot Down Over 250 Iranian-Made Drones Used by Russia," Axios, October 27, 2022, https://bit.ly/49aB1lh.

25. "Jumhori-ye azarbaijan marzha-ye zamini khod bai ran va torkiyeh ra bast" [Republic Of Azerbaijan closed its land Borders with Iran and Turkey], Fars News Agency, July 2, 2022, https://bit.ly/494q1pJ.

26. "Dalil-e huzoor-e nezami-ye rosiyeh."

27. Joshua Kucera, "Iran's Military Starts 'Massive' Drills on Azerbaijani Border," Eurasianet, October 20, 2022, https://bit.ly/3Q8hnh7; and "Iran, Azerbaijan Welcome Idea to Hold Joint Drill," *Tehran Times*, October 5, 2022, https://bit.ly/3Qv4YW5.

28. "Iran Says 'Won't Be Indifferent' to Israel's 'United Front' with Azerbaijan," Assahifa, March 31, 2023, https://bit.ly/3Qc77nZ.

29. "Dastavard safar-e farmand=ye Faraja be rusiyeh" [Achievement of trip by FARAJA commander to Russia], Shahid News, July 2, 2023, https://bit.ly/3s4nrPI.

30. "Ekhtelaf-e iran va jomhuri-ye azarbaijan bar sar-e chist?"

31. "Rusiyeh: az ozviyat-e iran dar etehadye-ye eqtesadi orasia hemayat mikonim" [Russia: We support Iran's membership in Eurasian Economic Union], Fars News Agency, August 31, 2022, https://bit.ly/477N3KB.

"Putin be donbal-e forsatha-ye jadid bara-ye vorood be bazarhay-e iran va khavar miyaneh ast" [Putin seeks new opportunities to enter markets in Iran and Middle East], BBC Farsi, September 7, 2022, https://bit.ly/3Qw4XBh.

32. "Tejarat-e 10 Miliyard Dolari-e Iran va Urasia ta Kamtar az Do Sal-e Digar" [Iran's 10 billion–dollar trade with Eurasia in less than two years], *Iran Newspaper*, April 30, 2023, https://acr.ps/1L9GPlh.

33. "Iran Signs Memorandum to Join Shanghai Cooperation Organisation," Al Jazeera, September 15, 2022, https://bit.ly/3tJhB74.

34. "Tejarat-e si-o-noh milliard dollari iran ba a'aza-ye shanghai dar yazdah mah-e hezar-o-charsad-o-yek" [Iran's 39 billion–dollar trade with Shanghai members in the 11 months of 1401], IRNA, March 11, 2023, https://bit.ly/3QdsBRF.

35. "Tavafoq-e beyn-e rusiyeh va iran bara-ye ijad-e mantaghe-ye azad-e tejari ba etehadiy-e eqtesadi-ye orasiya" [Agreement between Russia and Iran to create free-trade zone with Eurasia Economic Union], Tasnim News Agency, November 1, 2022, https://bit.ly/3QibHl0.

36. "Iranian Minister in Moscow for Transportation Agreements," Iran Chamber of Commerce, Industries, Mines and Agriculture, April 27, 2022, https://bit.ly/3Q6ucIZ.

37. "Putin be donbal-e forsatha-ye jadid."

38. Hanna Shtepa, "Ukraine Imposes Sectoral Sanctions Against the Islamic Republic of Iran," Sanctions News, May 30, 2023, https://bit.ly/3Q2rsvW.

39. "Kahesh-e tejarat miyan-e iran va Ukraine va afzayesh-e varedat az rusiyeh" [0% reduction in trade between Iran and Ukraine and increase of imports from Russia], Otagh Iran Online, May 14, 2022, https://bit.ly/40bqCSl; and "Afzayesh-e tabadol-e tejarati-ye iran va Ukraine ta panj o yek milliard dollar" [Increase of trade Exchange between Iran and Ukraine up to US$5.1 billion], Kayhan, October 20, 2011, https://bit.ly/3SdMtXo.

40. "chehel darsad roshd-e tejarat-e iran va armanestan" [40% growth in trade volume between Iran and Armenia], Student News Network, March 22, 2023, https://bit.ly/3Mgdt4y.

41. "Ekhtelaf-e iran va jomhuri-ye azarbaijan bar sar-e chist?"

42. "Ekhtelaf-e iran va jomhuri-ye azarbaijan bar sar-e chist?"

43. "Tasir-e eqtesad bar pishgiri az tanesh-e miyan-e tehran va baku" [Impact of economy on avoiding escalation of tensions between Tehran and Baku], Tahlil Bazaar, April 29, 2023, https://bit.ly/3QaELL9.

44. See "Azerbaijani President Attends International Conference 'Shaping the Geopolitics of Greater Eurasia: From Past to Present to Future' in Shusha," Azer News, May 3, 2023, https://bit.ly/3SgT8Qz.

45. "Darkhast az keshvarha-ye amrika-ye latin be hamkari bai ran" [Request by Latin American countries to cooperate with Iran], Quds Online, March 1, 2023, https://bit.ly/45K74Wf.

46. Ebrahim Ramezani, "Group Leaders Sought by Azerbaijan 'Arrested' in Iran," Iran Wire, May 2, 2023, https://bit.ly/45KBszR.

47. "Dou mokhalef-e eslamgara-ye jomhuri-ye azarbaijan dastghir shodand" [Two Islamist Azerbaijan republic dissidents "arrested in Qom"], BBC Farsi, April 28, 2023, https://bit.ly/3tLbejz.

48. "Ekhtelaf-e iran va jomhuri-ye azarbaijan bar sar-e chist?"

49. See also Ursula Stark Urrestarazu, "'Identity' in International Relations and Foreign Policy Theory," in *Theorizing Foreign Policy in a Globalized World*, ed. Gunther Hellmann and Knud Erik Jørgensen (Palgrave Macmillan, 2015), 126–49.

50. "Hadaf-e jang-e azarbaijan va iran darghir kardan-e mehvar-e moghavemat bood" [Purpose of war of Azerbaijan and Armenia was to get the axis of resistance involved], Mehr News Agency, October 16, 2020, https://bit.ly/406yd4N.

51. "Chegoneh mehvar-e moghavemat naghshe-ye geopolitik-e jahan ra taqir dad?" [How did the resistance axis change the world geopolitical map?], Fars News Agency, December 31, 2022, https://bit.ly/46VuoBK.

52. See also Emilian Kavalski, "The Guanxi of Relational International Theory," *Journal of Asian Security and International Affairs* 6, no. 2 (2018): 221.

13
IRAN–TURKMENISTAN RELATIONS
Geostrategic Dynamics Under the
New Regional Order

Hessam Habibi Doroh

The complex relations between Iran and Turkmenistan have been characterized by cooperation and competition. An analysis of the geostrategic aspect of these relations, in the context of Iran's "Look East" policy, provides a comprehensive picture of Tehran's approaches toward its eastern neighbors and the "East" in general. This chapter traces the evolution of Iran's relations with Turkmenistan, providing an assessment of their strategic objectives. It outlines the main geopolitical and geoeconomic elements of Iran–Turkmenistan relations. The chapter also looks at the geosecurity dimension, mainly border security-related issues such as drug trafficking, organized crime, and terrorism. The long-shared border of these two countries has created the need for close cooperation for Iran's regional geopolitical objectives, particularly concerns about foreign influence in Turkmenistan.

It focuses on the changing regional dynamics in the aftermath of the US withdrawal from Afghanistan, Iran's increasing cooperation with Russia and China, and the renewal of Iran's relations with the Gulf countries, especially after the deal with Saudi Arabia. The chapter argues that significant regional and global geopolitical changes provide opportunities for Iran to increase its cooperation with Turkmenistan. Nonetheless, the challenge of transforming this relationship into a deeper partnership depends on the security imperatives that have formed the basis of their close relationship. In order to determine the broader scope of Iran's security strategy in the "Look East" policy, the chapter examines state behavior and Iran's security policy toward Turkmenistan.

The chapter uses sources written by Iranian social scientists and published in Iranian scientific journals and books related to the topic published over the last two decades. These primary sources help us to look at the way in which Iran–Turkmenistan relations are perceived, assessed, and debated within Iran. By looking at diverse multidisciplinary sources, this chapter presents a broad framework and analytical evaluation of contemporary interactions between two countries.[1]

Looking at the academic debate within Iran, almost all analysts discuss Iran–Turkmenistan relations through the prisms of geopolitics and geoeconomics. The two concepts are often used together without any differentiation. The majority of analyses in this framework provide a definition of "geopolitical" similar to Zbigniew Brzezinski, who claimed that the term "reflects the combination of geographic and political factors determining the condition of a state or region and emphasizing the influence of geography on politics."[2] Moreover, scholars in Iran use the American geographer Saul Cohen's framework for geopolitical analysis, emphasizing the geographical settings related to political power.[3] By pointing to Cohen's spatial frameworks,[4] scholars such as Mohammadreza Hafeznia[5] and Dorre Mirheidar[6] consider interacting political power units in their geopolitical analysis. In line with this logic, Ezzatollah Ezzati presents geopolitics as "understanding realities of geographic space to achieve power and in order to enter world game (system)."[7]

In the context of Iran, scholars such as Ezzati categorize the geopolitical elements as follows: invariable (geographic elements and topography of the country) and variable (population, natural resources, and societal aspects).[8] This categorization was used and modified by other scholars,[9] including Yaadollah Karimipur,[10] who delineates seven geopolitical elements which create possibilities and limitations: 1) spatial position such as proximity to the sea or ports; 2) economic attractions; 3) border and border-related issues; 4) heterogenous factors as language, religious denomination, ethnicity and minority groups; 5) domestic politics; 6) population; and 7) natural elements. A similar categorization was also adopted by a comprehensive study of Iran–Turkmenistan relations published by Iran's Defense Academy, which also added the military and security elements of geopolitical analysis.[11] This study uses five concepts, which were applied in the analysis of Iran's relations with Turkmenistan: geopolitical weight, balance, challenge, crisis, and dependency.[12]

On a theoretical level, it is also interesting to see how Central Asia in general was seen within the geostrategic analyses in Iran. For instance, Seyyed Jalal Dehqani Firuzabadi, who was the chief editor of *Foreign Relations Quarterly* under President Hassan Rouhani and published many works on international relations for the Ministry of Foreign Affairs, described as early as 2005 the foreign policy patterns of the Islamic Republic in Central Asia: first, playing a mediatory role to present a new image of Iran and gain regional trust, and second, expanding relations with Russia in order to neutralize the influence of the United States, Turkey, and Israel.[13] Moreover, in the case of Turkmenistan, scholars pay attention to the numerous opportunities it presents to Iran. Studies claim that due to the geographical aspects, Iran and Turkmenistan have geopolitically complementary relations that can explain the rationality of their affairs.[14] However, they also indicate a problematic aspect by pointing to the "potential node" in their relations in the context of Central Asia, which the chapter attempts to expand from different angles.[15]

Iran–Turkmenistan Relations: Opportunities and Challenges

Historically, Iran and Turkmenistan have shared long cultural and social ties for over 1,000 years. Both countries, through the historical region of Khorasan, were part of a vast geographical and cultural territory. The "historical and cultural commonalities" are still visible in many analyses, which emphasize the advantages of this cultural connection for both countries after the independence of Turkmenistan on October 27, 1991.[16]

Iran's foreign policy interests in the region and in Turkmenistan existed before the collapse of the Soviet Union. Shortly before the end of Mikhail Gorbachev's presidency in late 1991, the Iranian minister of foreign affairs, Ali Akbar Velayati, in coordination with Moscow, traveled to all the Muslim Soviet republics, including Turkmenistan. Following independence, Iran was one of the first countries to recognize the newly established Republic of Turkmenistan. Five months later, relations officially started as Iran sent its first ambassador to the embassy in Ashgabat.[17] Soon after, Turkmenistan's president at the time, Saparmurat Niyazov, traveled to Tehran to participate in the Economic Cooperation Organization (ECO), of which Turkmenistan became a member. This was an important element of relations in the multilateral context. Iran was also among the first countries to send its senior officials to Turkmenistan. In May 1992, President Ali Akbar Hashemi Rafsanjani went to Ashgabat to open a trade center along with a suboffice of Iran's trade bank. Indeed, under Rafsanjani and his close ties to Niyazov, relations between the two countries evolved very positively and Iran became Turkmenistan's strategic partner in maintaining its independence from Russia. The frequency of bilateral meetings between high officials between 1992 and 1995 shows the level of interest that led to a variety of memorandums of understanding covering oil, gas, and security-related aspects.[18] On an international dimension,

Tehran welcomed Turkmenistan's recognized status of permanent neutrality on December 12, 1995.[19]

The positive relations continued during the presidency of Mohammad Khatami, who assumed office in 1997. The energy sector was the main area of cooperation. An important development at that time was the building of the Iran–Turkmenistan Friendship Dam (known as Doosti Dam), which was built on the Hari River (Hariroud) and officially opened on April 12, 2005 by President Khatami and Niyazov.[20] Three years later, President Mahmoud Ahmadinejad implemented the transfer of water from the Friendship Dam to Mashhad. Currently this dam is one of the four dams that supply Mashhad's water resources and plays a key role in Iran's hydropolitics. In the early 2000s, and especially after the construction of the Friendship Dam, the Iranians repeatedly stated the success of relations with Turkmenistan in the economic, security, and cultural areas.[21] Similar to the Friendship Dam, another notable event was the Bajgiran border station, with a border market, which was opened by President Ahmadinejad and President Niyazov in 2006.[22] After the Niyazov era, his successor Gurbanguly Berdimuhamedow emphasized the continuation of good relations with Iran, and, in one of his first visits to Iran, he met with Supreme Leader Ali Khamenei.

Relations between the two countries, however, were not always without challenges. In 2007 and 2008, Iran was concerned about Turkmenistan's active bilateral relations with other countries such as the United States, and Ashgabat's practical cooperation with NATO.[23] This resulted in doubts in Tehran about Turkmenistan's neutrality, especially after Berdimuhamedow's participation in a NATO summit in Bucharest.[24] A notable issue was the cold winter of 2007 to 2008 when Turkmenistan stopped its gas exports to Iran, causing major shortages in Iran's northern regions. Despite this, the authorities in Iran communicated rationally and avoided any escalatory moves. Thus, the actions of Turkmenistan were interpreted as a protest against the low energy prices and, as the then-CEO of the National Iranian Oil Company, Reza Kasaizade, opined, "as an energy exporting country, Iran understands the position of Turkmenistan."[25] Both countries managed to expand their cooperation in the energy sector.

During the presidency of Hassan Rouhani, the country's diplomacy was more focused on resolving the nuclear agreement issue and improving Iran's relations with the West, while remaining disagreements and challenges with Turkmenistan continued unanswered.[26] The hopes of opening up the country and removing the sanctions after the JCPOA (Joint Comprehensive Plan of Action) were supposed to ease relations with neighbors such as Turkmenistan. The issue of clearing Iran's debts to Turkmenistan strained their relations and led to the cessation of gas exports. The US withdrawal from the JCPOA and Tehran's further regional issues, especially with Saudi Arabia, intensified the already existing problems. In that era, trade exchanges between Iran and Turkmenistan decreased to nearly one-tenth, and political relations witnessed a certain amount of disruption. Turkmenistan's sudden cancelation of the bilateral economic exchange exhibition in Ashgabat at that time was an example thereof. In another incident, Turkmenistan border guards killed two Iranian fishermen in the Caspian Sea.[27] This was criticized by Iran; however, authorities kept it low-key to avoid any potential escalation.

Geopolitical and Geoeconomic Importance

As discussed earlier, despite some ups and downs, especially after the presidency of Berdimuhamedow, relations between the two countries have remained consistent. This is because both are aware of the strategic value of their relations and are committed to maintaining them. Due to the geostrategic importance, countries' policies toward one another are shaped by interdependence.

Considering the geopolitical factors behind Iran–Turkmenistan relations, Iranian sources mainly emphasize several elements which make Iran important for Turkmenistan:[28] 1) Iran is the shortest way to reach free seas; 2) through relations with Iran, Turkmenistan can balance its regional policies—or as some sources exaggeratedly suggest, Iran can help Turkmenistan to adopt an "independent policy";[29] 3) maintaining its borders and security requires close cooperation with Iran; 4) Turkmenistan is a downstream country and highly dependent on shared water sources with Iran (after Tajikistan), as the main rivers flowing in Turkmenistan go through Iran; and 5) the ethno-sectarian aspect of the relations is important for Turkmenistan, considering the fact that over one million Turkmen live in Iran around the border area with ties to their kin in Turkmenistan.

Relations with Turkmenistan are also essential for Iran, however, which is reflected in the majority of sources.[30] Turkmenistan is de facto the *only* gateway to Central Asia. With respect to the legal regime of the Caspian Sea, Iran needs Turkmenistan as an important partner. As Iran and Turkmenistan share two important rivers, Turkmenistan cannot be ignored in terms of managing water resources. Iran also needs close cooperation with Turkmenistan when it comes to the border and security aspects. Cooperation with Turkmenistan and wider Central Asia is part of Iran's geostrategic plan of becoming a regional transportation hub, which is closely related to Iran's "Look East" policy. Due to the long historical connection, Iran can exercise geocultural soft power in the region through Turkmenistan. Lastly, the location of Iranian Turkmen around the border with Turkmenistan makes the ethno-sectarian aspect an important consideration.

Water and Sea Diplomacy

Due to the competitive aspect of border rivers, shared water resources have created an essential element of cooperation but also tension between Iran and Turkmenistan. The high consumption of water sources in both countries combined with continued drought in the region made the issue of shared rivers more problematic.[31] Two important rivers are shared between the two countries. First, Atrek (535 kilometer–long), which begins in the mountains of northeastern Iran, forms the border between the two countries. Second is the Harirud (1,124 kilometer–long), originating in Afghanistan, which forms sections of the Afghanistan–Iran and Iran–Turkmenistan border and counts as an essential water source for all three countries.

The "hydropolitical security complex" of the Harirud river is an essential element of the relations with upstream Afghanistan and downstream Iran and Turkmenistan.[32] In this regard, the hydro-hegemony of Iran and Turkmenistan by the bilateral development of the Doosti Dam to control the water resources could become a critical issue in regional geopolitical competitions.[33] The Doosti Dam, with a capacity of 1,250 million cubic meters (MCM), is shared equally by Iran and Turkmenistan. This dam supplies over 50 percent of the city's total domestic water to Mashhad.[34] Afghanistan and India have also tried to challenge this power relation by the construction of the Salma Dam, renamed later to the Afghan–India Friendship Dam, with an estimated cost of USD 275 million and a capacity of 633 MCM,[35] Although this dam is not a major challenge for downstream countries, further development of other dams on the Harirud in Afghanistan (such as the Kabgan, Tirpol, and Pishdan Dams) remains a major concern for Iran and Turkmenistan in the issue of water discharge.[36] The continuous instability in Afghanistan and the lack of trilateral cooperation over the Harirud (despite attempts made by Iran and Turkmenistan in 2006 and 2010), combined with the increasing effects of climate change, create great potential for cooperation but also tensions in this complex geopolitical environment.[37]

The other important river to consider is the Atrek, which begins in the Shah Jahan mountains of Iran and flows 535 kilometers into the Caspian Sea. This river forms part of the border between Iran and Turkmenistan, where the Atrek's tributary, the Sumbar, joins it. Historically, since the Treaty of Akhal, an agreement between Iran and Imperial Russia in 1881, the Atrek River has been important. It became the new boundary between the two powers, who shared equal rights to 50 percent of the frontier parts of the river. More precise elements were included in another treaty between Iran and the Soviet Union in August 1957.[38] Despite the importance of cooperation in the management of the river, both countries only cooperate on surface water management and border-related issues, while no major investment has been done in the hydro-economy of the river.[39] In addition to the Atrek, several other seasonal rivers such as the Shurluq, Chehel Kaman, Chehcheh, and Qara Takan flow from the heights of Hezar Masjed to Turkmenistan.[40] In this regard, it is critical to mention that in the eastern and northeastern parts of Iran, rapid population growth, as well as urbanization on the one hand, and inefficient agriculture and industrialization on the other, have led to an alarming overuse of underground waters.[41] Considering these factors, the dependency of both countries on their shared rivers will play an essential role in the future of Iran–Turkmenistan relations.

The legal regime of the Caspian Sea is another issue impacting Iran and Turkmenistan relations bilaterally and multilaterally.[42] In 1732, Russia and Iran first defined freedom of commerce and navigation on the Caspian Sea based on the Reshtsky Agreement.[43] The famous Treaties of Gulistan (1813) and Turkmenchay (1828) also addressed the issue of trading on the Caspian Sea.[44] Based on the Russo–Persian Treaty of Friendship (1921), both Russia and Iran had full and equal shipping rights in the Caspian Sea. The Soviet–Iran treaty of 1940 recognized previous agreements while emphasizing that only ships belonging to the two coastal countries have the right to sail across the Caspian Sea.[45] After the dissolution of the Soviet Union, different perspectives and issues emerged among the littoral states. In 1998, Russia and Kazakhstan, and later in 2001 Azerbaijan, supported on a bilateral basis the idea that the Caspian Sea is a sea and should be divided by the principle of a median line. Turkmenistan tried to maintain a neutral position in this regard. Nonetheless, in 2002 President Niyazov enunciated a position closer to Moscow than Tehran.[46] The issue with the median line from Tehran's perspective is that Iran's share of Caspian Sea would be less than 13 percent, reducing its access to oil and gas fields. Tehran claims that 20 percent of the water territory of the Caspian Sea belongs to it and the other 80 percent to the other littoral states, a position that the other states, including Turkmenistan, have not agreed upon.[47]

The uncertainty around the water territories of the Caspian Sea is still unresolved. The latest convention, agreed in the fifth summit in 2018, emphasized that negotiations in this regard are ongoing.[48] However, Iran's security apparatuses still claim the country's 20 percent territorial rights in the Caspian Sea.[49] Thus, there is a possibility that issues related to the legal regime of the Caspian Sea will persist despite the common agreement among the five Caspian littoral states. Regarding oil and gas fields and other minerals, the geopolitical interests of Tehran and Ashgabat and their bilateral coordination is especially essential. While Azerbaijan bilaterally made agreements with Russia and Kazakhstan since the 2018 convention, a similar agreement does not exist between Iran and Turkmenistan.[50] Although there are unanswered questions after the latest convention, positive cooperation between Turkmenistan and Iran has great economic and political significance for Iranian national security and the wider perspectives of the "Look East" policy.

Energy and Road Nexus

Turkmenistan's economic potential in the field of energy is highlighted by many scholars and analysts in Iran. These analysts emphasize that Turkmenistan is Iran's gateway to Central Asia, and the attraction of Iran to Turkmenistan is that, as a landlock country, the fastest, cheapest, and most secure way to access the open sea is through Iran.[51] In this regard, the Bafq–Bandar Abbas and Mashhad–Sarakhs–Tajan railways, which were completed in 1994 and 1996, respectively, connected the Iranian port city of Bandar Abbas on the Persian Gulf to the Central Asian countries.[52] Another important project to consider here is the 1,500 kilometer-long Kazakhstan-Turkmenistan-Iran (KTI) pipeline, with a capacity of 1 million barrels per day, which links the oil fields of northwestern Kazakhstan to the Persian Gulf and to the international market via the western region of Turkmenistan. It should be noted that this project was affected by the United States, as they supported the Baku–Tbilisi–Ceyhan (BTC) pipeline, bringing Caspian oil from the Azerbaijani port of Baku through the Georgian capital, Tbilisi, to the Turkish port of Ceyhan on the Mediterranean Sea.[53] Iran explicitly emphasizes on the role of US geopolitical pressure to isolate the country and hinder its energy cooperation with Turkmenistan.[54]

The importance of the energy cooperation between Iran and Turkmenistan was in fact twofold. Turkmenistan could reduce its dependence on Russia in energy exports and diversify its export routes. Iran, through energy swaps, however, could supply the northern regions in the country through Turkmenistan, Kazakhstan, and Azerbaijan, while delivering an equal volume of energy to the Persian Gulf.[55] As outlined earlier in this chapter, Ashgabat's decision in stopping the gas transfer to the northern part of Iran not only created insecurity and suspicions in foreign relations, but it also created uncertainty for Iran's energy exports.[56] In this regard, another problematic issue was Iran's debt to Turkmenistan, which had already become $2 billion in 2016.[57] The struggle continued as Turkmenistan brought its claim to the International Criminal Court (ICC), something that politically depicted Tehran as a weak and passive actor.[58] This issue became one of the main criticisms of Ebrahim Raisi's government toward his predecessor. Javad Owji, Iran's minister of oil, stated after his latest meeting with his counterpart Batyr Amanov that past debts have been paid and future agreements between the two countries are on the agenda.[59]

Apart from energy cooperation, Iran's place in the economy of Turkmenistan is minimal and limited. Nevertheless, the economic interactions between the two countries exhibit a unique dynamism primarily rooted in individual-level engagements, a characteristic that distinguishes relations with Turkmenistan. It is worth noting that this particular trait, played a pivotal role in assisting Iran during harsh economic sanctions, offering a viable avenue to circumvent sanctions.[60] Furthermore, many projects, such as the establishment of the third electricity line from Sarakhs to Merv and other transportation construction projects, remained nonoperational and only at the agreement level.[61] In 2008, Iran was considered after Russia to be the second-largest economic partner of Turkmenistan. However, this role has decreased over time, with Turkey, Russia, and China playing far more active roles in Turkmenistan's economy than Iran by 2021.[62] More important for Tehran are the corridors and becoming the regional transportation hub. In addition to the Bafq–Bandar Abbas and Mashhad–Sarakhs–Tajan railways, in the middle of 2014, the KTI railway opened new opportunities for Iran and Central Asia. On the importance of the interconnectedness of this railway, the president of Kazakhstan, Kassym-Jomart Tokayev, said: "Railway has a serious potential, which opens the shortest route from East Asia to the countries of the Persian Gulf."[63] More recent talks are about the Uzbekistan–Turkmenistan–Iran–Oman corridor, which was discussed in the Ashgabat agreement of 2016.[64]

The Geosecurity Dimensions

Turkmenistan's importance to Iran, however, goes beyond energy and economics. Security and the perception of threats are an essential part of geosecurity of Iran–Turkmenistan relations, so much so that some scholars have even emphasized the "security" element of the relations rather than the "opportunity."[65] Examination of the analyses within Iran reveals that Tehran has three core priorities in its geosecurity approach to Turkmenistan: First, there is an ethno-sectarian aspect to the relations; second, there are issues related to border security; and, third, the presence of other countries such as the United States and Israel is a major issue for Iran.

The Ethno-Sectarian Element

In one of the early studies on the Iran–Turkmenistan border, Abbasi Semnani analyzed the security elements of the border.[66] As a strategic recommendation, he highlighted avoiding the socio-political decentralization of the Turkmen communities in Iran. This community, which consists of Sunnis following Hanafi

Islam, is located on the border regions in the north and northeast Iran. In certain areas such as Gamishan and Aq Qala over 90 percent of the population are Turkmen. Adding to the complexity of this area, there is a growing number of Baluch people living in the province of Golestan due to environmental issues and drought.[67] The presence of other Sunni groups, close to the Turkmen Sunni community, created a sectarian awareness, causing concerns for the authorities in Iran.[68] This issue became a wider geosecurity question as Iran's relations with Saudi Arabia intensified in the shadow of regional tensions in the Middle East. In this connection, some security studies warned about the potential expansion of Wahhabism in the Turkmen populated regions in Iran.[69]

While the large Turkmen community in Iran and their ethnic and denominational ties with Turkmenistan can be seen as an issue by the state, there is also an opportunity from a soft power perspective. Magtymguly Pyragy, the Turkmen spiritual leader, poet, and Sufi guide, is one example. His mausoleum, located in Aq Taqeh-ye Qadim in Golestan Province, created a platform for sociocultural interaction. Every year, cultural events in memorial of Magtymguly bring many Turkmen from both Iran and Turkmenistan together, strengthening the relations of Turkmenistan with the provinces of Golestan, Mazandaran, and Gilan.[70] Furthermore, the influence of Sunni madrasas and Sunni clerics from the Turkmen community in Iran on Sunnis in Turkmenistan should be noted. This impact dates back to before the independence of Turkmenistan.[71] In the cultural domain, further exchanges are also organized between universities and other institutions in Iran to highlight the common history.[72] In general, there is a strong connection between Turkmen people in Iran and Turkmenistan. However, living in Turkmenistan is not appealing for Iranian Turkmen, as many have found it more appealing to migrate to Turkey in recent years and expand their connection there instead of Turkmenistan. This is one of the reasons that many Iranian experts emphasize better investment in cultural convergence between the two countries, which will play an important role in establishing "sustainable security" and "regional convergence," which are part of Iran's national security agenda.[73]

In a broader context, owing to the authoritarian nature of Turkmenistan's political system and the absence of substantial social and political organizations in both Iran and Turkmenistan, I believe that concerns over ethnic consciousness and related matters from the Iranian perspective may be overstated.[74] Furthermore, with regards to sectarianism, it is worth emphasizing that the Sunni Turkmen communities in both Iran and Turkmenistan are, to a significant extent, isolated and lack extensive interactions with other Sunni groups within Iran. Thus, the challenges posed by sectarianism, as highlighted in certain research studies, do not appear to be a substantial concern for either country.

Border Security and Counterterrorism

Historically, the border between the two countries was first established under Imperial Russia following the Treaty of Akhal in 1881 and later in 1893. The question of border was briefly discussed in another treaty between Iran and the Soviet Union in 1921. Based on this treaty a certain old part of Sarakhs (Sarahs), which was historically part of the ancient Silk Road, remained under the control of the Soviets, whereas Russia agreed to return Ashurdare, which is the only island on the Iranian coast of the Caspian Sea, and Firuze (Firjuza in Turkmen language) to Iran. While Iran obtained control over Ashurdare, Firuze has not been returned to Iran.[75] The importance of Firuze and other areas close to the border are related to the small Shia Kurdish minority group who share a similar culture with other (Kurmanji) Kurds on the Iranian side located in north Khorasan. Although there is an awareness in this regard among the Iranian Kurds in Khorasan, any interaction with the other Kurds on the other sides, is highly restricted by authorities in Turkmenistan, according to eyewitnesses.

Despite several bilateral agreements between Tehran and Ashgabat regarding border management, issues such as drugs and human trafficking remain the main security concerns for both countries.[76] The tri-border area of Zulfaqar, where the boundaries of Afghanistan, Iran and Turkmenistan meet, is one such example. In addition, both countries share a common concern about extremism and terrorist activities emerging from Afghanistan.[77] In the case of combating drug trafficking, Iran and Turkmenistan signed their first agreement in 1999, which was then renewed two years later. Since then, there has been ongoing cooperation on this issue between the two in bilateral and multilateral forms together with other countries in Central Asia. In the framework of bilateral cooperation, there are intelligence exchanges, joint operations, and research, as well as joint workshops and events.[78] The necessity of security cooperation between the two countries has been emphasized by all Iranian presidents, and especially during the presidency of Rouhani, when the rise of extremist groups became a continuous regional concern.[79]

Concern over Foreign Influence

From Iran's strategic defense–security perspective, while Turkmenistan is a neutral country, it has relations, or is exaggeratedly suggested in some analyses to have "an alliance" with the US and Israel.[80] In this regard, and similar to all the other border regions in Iran, the security apparatuses see the border as a potential entry point for foreign intelligence services, adding more suspicion to the borderlands.[81] In addition, Turkmenistan participated as the first Central Asian country in NATO's Partnership for Peace program in 1994. In the post-9/11 era this partnership became more important as the air bases in Turkmenistan were used for transport from the West to Afghanistan. Reportedly, US military aircrafts have been using Turkmen airspace and facilities since 2002, which did not remain unnoticed in Tehran.[82] In the case of the Israeli presence, Iranian analysts have warned about Israel's soft power in Central Asia and the Caucasus in general and in Turkmenistan in particular. The establishment of Israel's permanent embassy in Ashgabat in March 2023 increased the already existing concerns over further cooperation between Israel and Turkmenistan, undermining Iran's security.[83]

To overcome these challenges, Tehran has to maintain close relations with Ashgabat in intelligence exchange, joint border control and operations, and also adopt new technologies.[84] Moreover, on the ethnic dimension, Iran will continue to maintain a limited cultural exchange with Turkmenistan, while also using the Turkmen community as a means of soft power to influence Turkmenistan and wider Central Asia. In general terms, Tehran sees Turkmen ethnic groups in Iran and their relationship with the people of Turkmenistan as a potential threat to a certain extent.[85] Nonetheless, from a strategic view, Tehran does not see the country in a passive position especially in the absence of strong socio-political organization in Turkmenistan, which can impact the Turkmen society in Iran. The Iranians also believe that Turkmenistan authorities do not care about the Turkmen in Iran.[86] From the geostrategic perspective, studies in Iran have indicated that Turkmenistan's natural border with Iran and the closeness of Ashgabat to Iran's border (which is about sixty kilometers away from Bajgiran) are not in Turkmenistan's advantage and place it strategically in a weaker position, lacking strategic depth.[87] In order to overcome the security challenges around the border with Turkmenistan, Iranian defense studies suggest maintaining and enhancing Iran's intelligence dominance by using better technologies and including the local communities around the border. Moreover, they also recommend encouraging the use of ethnic and cultural commonalities between the two countries as part of security cooperation.[88]

Indeed, the situation around the border of Iran and Turkmenistan has been quite stable compared to other border regions, such as Sistan-Baluchistan in the east and Kurdistan in the west. In light of Tehran's "Look East" policy, maintaining this stability is even more important, demanding closer cooperation between the two countries in order to become a reliable security partner and to achieve a regional security order in Central Asia.

Changing Regional Realities

During Raisi's tenure in office, the "Look East" and "Neighborhood" policies became part of the country's foreign policy approach. In this regard, relations with Turkmenistan were strengthened again. In June 2022, in addition to the presidents of Tajikistan and Kazakhstan, Serdar Berdimuhamedov, the third and current president of Turkmenistan, visited Iran, meeting with President Raisi and Supreme Leader Khamenei. A year later, by the end of May 2023, Berdimuhamedow, the former president and the current chairman of the Halk Maslahaty (People's Council), also visited Tehran.[89] Although in his visit he met with high officials including the president, head of parliament and expediency discernment council, and the supreme leader, which sent a clear signal of better relations, there was no sign of a major project as had been the case in the past with opening the Friendship Dam or Bajgiran border customs.

Apart from Tehran's emphasis on the "Look East" and "Neighbor First" policies, there are important geopolitical factors that have to be considered in terms of relations with Turkmenistan. First, there is a systemic shift to the East,[90] which is very much focused on by the authorities in Iran.[91] Regardless of the theoretical background of the belief in an emerging world order, policymakers in Tehran are convinced of these changes. In the words of Iran's former foreign minister and current head of Strategic Council of Foreign Affairs, Kamal Kharazi:

> We are waiting for a new order regionally and internationally. The new order comes with the change in the balance of power. Every country that has power tries to stabilize its position and play a higher role in coming changes.... Today, a maturity is shaping in the region to cooperate and distance ourselves from the differences and work together to create structures in the region without the interference of foreign powers (in that sense the Western powers) so that the region moves towards development and progress and promoting its independence.[92]

Tehran views the declining power of the United States in the region and the rise of China and Russia as forming a multipolar international system in which Iran is geopolitically in the middle. In this regard, in cooperation with China, Iran is eager for Central Asia to become an emerging economic and cultural space. In light of China's Silk Road plan, with which Iran is engaged, Central Asian countries, including Turkmenistan, are becoming part of a geostrategic setting, leading the way in geopolitical and geoeconomic opportunities.[93]

As discussed earlier in the chapter, Tehran, considers US influence as one of the main obstacles to energy cooperation with Turkmenistan. The onset of US "maximum pressure" and unilateral sanctions on Tehran further pushed policymakers to strengthen their relations with Russia and China. In this regard, China and Russia, in cooperation with Iran, have demonstrated an open challenge to US policy in Asia.[94] While the United States is losing its authority and power in the region with this new systematic shift, there is hope in Tehran that under a Sino-centric region together with Russia, Iran can revitalize its geostrategic plans with Turkmenistan and wider Central Asia. In this context, Tehran is keen to strengthen its position in commitment with the Shanghai Cooperation Organization (SCO), as well as its active engagement with the ECO, of which Turkmenistan is also a member.[95] Furthermore, the effort is to be linked with the Eurasian Economic Union (EAEU) and International North–South Transport Corridor (INSTC) with China's Belt and Road Initiative (BRI). This reflects Tehran's view of its position as an international transit hub connecting Eurasia to the Persian Gulf and South Asia.

The Sino–Russian factor in Iran–Turkmenistan relations, thus, should be closely observed within the context of Tehran's general effort to establish itself in the new emerging international order and build stronger ties with other like-minded states to challenge the liberal world order.[96] Finally, one should also mention the China-brokered agreement between Iran and Saudi Arabia in March 2023, which, to some extent, and in line with China and Russia, is about excluding the United States from the region. The importance of the deal is the normalization process of the relations between Iran and the Gulf countries. In this context, improved regional relations after the deal can create a more favorable environment for cooperation. Enhanced economic ties between Iran and the Persian Gulf countries might increase the chances of the realization of economic opportunities and trade between Iran and Turkmenistan and Central Asia in general.

In addition, under the current regional order, it appears that Tehran's concern about Western military presence in Turkmenistan has become less important, creating the possibility of desecuritizing bilateral relations with Turkmenistan. Nonetheless, Afghanistan following the Taliban's takeover presents a common challenge for Iran, Turkmenistan, and the wider region. As previously discussed, Tehran is trying to benefit from the new situation by seizing the opportunity to advance relations and strengthen its position as a regional actor in Central Asia. In the context of Iran's full membership in the SCO, Tehran is much closer to achieving its "Look East" foreign policy approach.[97] By emphasizing its active contribution to regional security through combating regional challenges such as extremism, Tehran has positioned itself as an important partner for Central Asia, especially Turkmenistan, which has an 804-kilometer border with Afghanistan. This assessment, which has been part of Tehran's ambition since 2004, when it submitted its application for observer status in the SCO, was strongly highlighted at the fourth Meeting of the Foreign Ministers of Neighboring Countries of Afghanistan in Samarkand on April 13, 2023.[98]

This chapter has discussed the fundamental logic driving Tehran–Ashgabat geostrategic relations. Through an analysis of the different geopolitics, geoeconomics, and geosecurity elements, it is clear that Iran and Turkmenistan have complementary relations, which have created an interdependency between them. Shared challenges and newly emerging opportunities cannot be managed and facilitated without profound collaboration. These will be related, but not limited, to water security and sea diplomacy, energy (gas, oil, and electricity), transit and transportation roads, joint technical projects, multilateral regional cooperation (through the ECO, Caspian Summit, and Conference of Countries Neighboring Afghanistan), and also border security–related issues such as extremism.

The chapter discussed Iran's cooperation with Turkmenistan in the context of its engagement with both China and Russia amid stalled nuclear talks, the Taliban takeover of Afghanistan, and the systemic shift in the international order. On one hand, the Sino–Russian factor in Iran–Turkmenistan relations has created converging visions for regional cooperation and commitment. On the other hand, from the security aspect, the new situation in Afghanistan has provided Iran, Turkmenistan, and the wider region a common ground for closer cooperation focused on shared security approaches. The future of Tehran–Ashgabat relations will depend to a great extent on other issues, such as the future of the Russia–Ukraine war and China's path to greater power. The importance of bilateral ties between Iran and Turkmenistan will remain at the strategic level. Despite deep commonalities between Tehran and Ashgabat, the remaining unanswered differences and diverging competitions can hinder the realization of a cohesive alliance in light of the "Look East" policy.

In his meeting with Berdimuhamedov in Iran in June 2022, Raisi pointed out some of the aspects of Iran and Turkmenistan relations. On that occasion he emphasized that both countries are not just neighbors, but brothers, sharing common civilization and culture—a common perspective that Iran has toward Central Asia. Most important, Raisi described the two countries as having a "family relation."[99] This might describe the very nature of this relation, in which both sides will work to maintain their ties and harmonies, despite existing struggles, from exogenous and endogenous factors.

NOTES

1. These are materials mainly published in the field of defense policy, published by the Defense Academy of the Defense Ministry (Danishgah-i Defa'-i Milli), but also in strategic studies, security studies, border studies, as well as international relations.

2. Zbigniew Brzezinski, *Game Plan: How to Conduct the US-Soviet Contest* (Atlantic Monthly Press, 1986), xiv.

3. Saul B. Cohen, *Geography and Politics in a World Divided* (Random House, 1963).

4. Cohen, *Geography and Politics*, 25.

5. Mohammadreza Hafeznia, *Usul va mafahim-i zhiupulitik* [Principles and concepts of geopolitics] (Papoli, 2006). In his definition (p. 37), geopolitics is the combination of

three elements: geography, power, and politics. This concept was also redefined and used in another work published by Iran's Defense Academy: Shahram Noruzani Kuhestani, *Nigarishi nu bar naqshafarini-i avamil-i zhiupulitik-i Afghanistan* [A new perspective on the role of geopolitical factors in Afghanistan] (Danishgah va Pazhuhushgah-u 'Ali-yi Defa'-i Milli va Tahghighat-i Rahburdi [Supreme National Defense University], 1398), 53.

6. Dorre Mirheidar, "Zhiupulitik, ira'i-yi tarifi jadid" [Geopolitics, Providing a New Concept], *Tahqiqat-i Joghrafiyai* 13 (1998): 22. Mirheidar brings also the factor of power to the core aspect of his definition, which is then followed by: Mojtaba Sharbati and Amirhossein Rashidi, "Zhiupulitik-i Turkamanistan va tasir-i an bar amniyat-i melli" [Turkmenistan's geopolitics and its impact on the political security of the Islamic Republic of Iran], *Mudiriyat va Pazhuheshha-yi Defa'I* 79 (2015): 160.

7. Ezzatollah Ezzati, *Zhiupulitik* [Geopolitics] (Samt, 1992), 7. See also Ehsan Yari and Marziyye Abedi, "Tahlil va arzyabi-i gereh-i Turkamanistan dar shabaki-yi mantaqi-yi Iran; Forsatha va chalishha-yi zhiupulitik-i va zhiuikonomiki-yi hamkari-yi Iran va Turkmanistan" [Analysis and evaluation of Turkmenistan in Iran's regional network; geopolitical and geoeconomic opportunities and challenges of Iran–Turkmenistan cooperation], *Mutaliat-i Siyasi-yi Jahan-i Islam* 15 (2015): 197–98.

8. Ezzati, *Zhiupulitik*, 75.

9. For instance see Hasan Chagini, *Nizam-i mudiriyat-i istiratizhik-i defa'i* [Strategic defense management system] (Aja, 2005), 171; Gudarz Tafte, "Avamil-i zhiupulitiki-yi fursatafarin-i kishvar-i Turkamanistan mu'asir bar tadvin-i rahburd-i difai-yi jumhuri-yi Islami-i Iran" [The impact of Turkmenistan's geopolitical opportunities on the development of the Islamic Republic of Iran's defense strategy], *Mutalia-yi Difayi Isteratizhik* 66 (2016): 249; and Gholamali Rashid, *Juzvi-yi darsi zhiupulitik* [Geopolitics handbook] (Difa'-i Ali-yi Milli, 2010), 81.

10. Yadollah Karimipur, *Zhiupulitik, juzvi-yi darsi* [Geopolitics, a handbook] (Farmandihi va Sepahi Pasdaran, 1996), 54–56; see also Tafte, "Avamil-i zhiupulitiki," 249–50.

11. Davud Golkarian, *Rahburdha-yi hamkari-yi difa'i-amniyati jumhuri-i Islami-i Iran ba kishvar-i Turkamanistan* [The Islamic Republic of Iran's defense–security cooperation strategies with Turkmenistan] (Danishgah va Pazhuhishgah-i 'Ali-yi Difa'-i Milli va Tahghighat-i Rahburdi, 2019), 51.

12. For a detailed definition of each concept see Golkarian, *Rahburdha-yi hamkari-yi difa'i-amniyati*, 44–45. See also Hafeznia, *Usul va mafahim-i zhiupulitik*, 109–10, 119–21, and 126–30.

13. Seyyed Jalal Dehqani Firuzabadi, "Guftiman-i siyasat-i khariji-i Iran dar asiya-i markazi va qafqaz" [Iran's foreign policy discourse in Central Asia and the Caucasus], *IRAS* 1 (2006): 122. See also Yari and Abedi, "Tahlil va arzyabi-i gereh-i Turkamanistan," 196.

14. Reza Mokhtari and Mohammad Zohdi Goharpur, "Manabi'-i tanish va tahdid-i marz-i Iran va Turkamanistan va asar-i an bar amniyat-i dakhili va ravabit-i zhiupolitiki du kishvar" [Sources of tension and threat to the Iran–Turkmenistan border and their impact on the two countries' domestic security and geopolitical relations], *Danishkadi-yi ulum va funun-I marz* 4 (2013): 55.

15. Yari and Abedi, "Tahlil va arzyabi-i gereh-i Turkamanistan," 197.

16. For instance: Barat Shamsa, "Daramadi bar munasibat-i jumhuri Islami-i Iran ba Turkamanistan" [An introduction to Iran–Turkmenistan relations], *IRAS* 28 (2010): 16; Reza Joneidi, "Rafter-i zheupolitiki Turkamanistan dar barabar-i Iran, takhtan-i asb ru-yi labi-yi tigh" [Turkmenistan's geopolitical behavior toward Iran, riding a horse on sharp edge], *Siyasat-i Defa'yi* 77 (2011); and also Golkarian, *Rahburdha-yi hamkari-yi difa'i-amniyati*, 310.

17. Shamsa, "Daramadi bar munasibat-i jumhuri," 15.

18. Araz Mohammad Sarli, *Turkamanistan* [Turkmenistan] (Vezarat-i umur-i khariji, 2001), 122.

19. Amirmohammad Hajiyusofi and Azam Rabbani, "Iran va Turkamanistan: Vaz'iyat-i kununi, chashmandaz-i ayandi"]Iran and Turkmenistan: Current state of relations and future prospects], *Mutaliat-i Baynulmilali* 42 (2014): 173–74; see also Mehdi Sanai, "Nigahi be ravabit-i siyasi Iran ba jumhuriha-yi Asiya-yi markazi" [A look at Iran's political relations with the Central Asian Republics], *Mutaliat-i Asiya-yi Markazi va Ghafghaz*, 66 (2009): 1–22.

20. Sarli, *Turkamanistan*, 123–24, 130; Hajiyusofi and Rabbani, "Iran va Turkamanistan," 173–74.

21. "Negah-i ijmali bi ravabit-i Iran va Turkamanistan" [An overview of Iran–Turkmenistan relations during Khatami's presidency], IRNA, August 20, 2005, https://bit.ly/45NTi57.

22. "Payan-i marzi-yi Bajgiran ba huzur-i ruasa-yi jumhuri Iran va Turkamanistan iftitah mishavad" [Bajgiran border station will be opened with the presence of the presidents of Iran and Turkmenistan], IRNA, July 23, 2006, https://bit.ly/409aa52.

23. It is important to mention that Turkmenistan was the first of the five Central Asian states to join NATO's Partnership for Peace program in 1994.

24. Farhad Ataei and Hamidreza Azizi, "Naqsh-i 'amil-i inirgi dar ravabit-i Iran va Turkamanistan" [The role of the energy factor in Iran–Turkmenistan relations], *Tahqiqat-i Siyasi va Baynulmilali* 2 (2010): 108–9.

25. Joneidi, "Rafter-i zheupolitiki Turkamanistan," 149–50.

26. "Turkamanistan, hamsayi-yi faramush shude" [Turkmenistan, a forgotten neighbor], Jame Jam Daily, November 29, 2021, https://bit.ly/3Se8AwS.

27. "Vakunish-i rasmi Iran be ghatl-i sayyadan-i Irani tavasut-i marzbanan-i Turkamanistan" [Iran's official response to the killing of Iranian fishermen by Turkmenistan's border guards], Mashregh News, March 22, 2018, https://bit.ly/3Qv8u2D.

28. See Sharbati and Rashidi, "Zhiupulitik-i Turkamanistan," 174–75; Alireza Kuhkan and Yusof Momenifard, "Barresi-yi zaminiha-yi hamgarayi Iran va Turkamanistan" [Examining areas of cooperation between Iran and Turkmenistan], *Tafsir-i Siyasi* 4 (2020): 136–37; and Tafte, "Avamil-i zhiupulitiki-yi fursatafarin-i," 259.

29. Shamsa, "Daramadi bar munasibat-i jumhuri," 19.

30. See for instance: Sharbati and Rashidi, "Zhiupulitik-i Turkamanistan," 175; Kuhkan and Momenifard, "Barresi-yi zaminiha-yi hamgarayi," 137–38; and Seyedmohammad Seyedi Asl and Ataollah Bahremani, "The Impact of Geopolitical Borders Factors on Iran-Turkmenistan," *Uluslararası Kriz ve Siyaset Araştırmaları Dergisi* 5 (2021): 680.

31. Zahra Pishgahifard, Kamal Ranjbari, "Tahlil-i zheupulitik-i ravabit-i Iran va Turkamanistan ba takid bar diplomasi-yi ab va intiqal-i inirzhi" [A geopolitical analysis of Iran-Turkmenistan relations with a focus on water diplomacy and energy transfer], *Mutaliat-i Urasiya-yi Markayi* 13 (2020–21): 405; and Seyyed Hadi Zarqani, Malihe Akhbari, Neda Charei, and Najme Mahmoudi, "Tahlil-i tangnaha-yi hidrupulitik-i Turkamanistan dar rabita ba hamsayigan" [Analysis of Turkmenistan's hydropolitical challenges to its neighbors], *Pazhuhishha-yi Jughrafiya-yi Siyasi* 14 (2019): 1–32.

32. Mohsen Nagheeby and Jeroen Warner, "The Geopolitical Overlay of the Hydropolitics of the Harirud River Basin," *International Environmental Agreements: Politics, Law and Economics* 18 (2018): 839–60.

33. Mohsen Nagheeby, "Analysis of the Hydro-Political Impacts of Dam Development in Transboundary River Basins: A Case Study of the Harirud River Basin" (master's thesis, UNESCO-IHE Institute for Water Education, 2014). See also Nagheeby and Warner, "Geopolitical Overlay," 842.

34. *Second Assessment of Transboundary Rivers, Lakes and Groundwaters* (United Nations, 2011), https://acr.ps/1L9zRts.
35. "Modi, Ghani Inaugurate Long-Awaited Salma Dam Project," *Afghanistan Times*, June 4, 2016, https://bit.ly/46Ku88O.
36. Nagheeby, "Analysis of the Hydro-Political Impacts," 86.
37. Zarqani et al., "Tahlil-i tangnaha-yi hidrupulitik-i Turkamanistan," 21–22.
38. "Russian–Iranian Treaty of August 11, 1957," *Middle East Journal* 13 (1959): 193–95.
39. Pishgahifard and Ranjbari, "Tahlil-i zheupulitik-i ravabit-i Iran va Turkamanistan," 405.
40. Zarqani et al., "Tahlil-i tangnaha-yi hidrupulitik-i Turkamanistan," 25.
41. David Michel, "Iran's Impending Water Crisis," in *Water, Security and US Foreign Policy*, ed. David Reed (Routledge, 2017), 168–88. See also Joneidi, "Rafter-i zheupolitiki Turkamanistan," 140; and Zarqani et al., "Tahlil-i tangnaha-yi hidrupulitik-i Turkamanistan," 25–27.
42. Regarding the academic discussion around the declaring the term "lake" or "sea" see: Witt Raczka, "A Sea or a Lake? The Caspian's Long Odyssey," *Central Asian Survey* 19 (2000): 189–221; and Barbara Janusz-Pawletta, *The Legal Status of the Caspian Sea: Current Challenges and Prospects for Future Development* (Springer, 2021).
43. Ardak Kapyshev, "Legal Status of the Caspian Sea: History and Present," *European Journal of Business and Economics* 6 (2012): 719–20.
44. For more details on the historical developments see: Janusz-Pawletta, *Legal Status of the Caspian Sea*, 17–20.
45. Kapyshev "Legal Status of the Caspian Sea," 719; and Joneidi, "Rafter-i zheupolitiki Turkamanistan," 136–37.
46. Joneidi, "Rafter-i zheupolitiki Turkamanistan," 137.
47. Kapyshev, "Legal Status of the Caspian Sea," 721.
48. Aleksej Kalmikov, "'Ni more, ni ozero': Kaspiy podelili na pyaterykh. Na eto ushlo 22 goda" ["Neither the sea nor the lake": The Caspian was divided into five], BBC, August 12, 2018, https://bit.ly/479gHz7.
49. See, for instance, the report after the national army's military exercise in the Caspian Sea: "Razmayish-i amniyat-i paydar 1400 artish dar darya-yi Khazar Aghaz Shud" [Sustainable security 1400 of the naval force launched in the Caspian Sea], Tasnim News, June 30, 2021, https://bit.ly/49c6unp; or the statement from Amir Habibollah Sayyari, the former commander of the Islamic Republic of Iran Navy, declaring "20% Khazar ra taht-i kunturul darim" [We have the control of the 20% of the Caspian Sea], Jahan News, August 20, 2017, https://bit.ly/3tKT1Tc.
50. Michał Pietkiewicz, "Legal Status of Caspian Sea—Problem Solved?," *Marine Policy* 123 (2021): 7.
51. The other options for access to open water for Turkmenistan are the Afghanistan–Pakistan route, Russia route, China route, and Caspian Sea route (Baku–Ceyhan).
52. Farhad Atai and Hamidreza Azizi, "The Energy Factor in Iran–Turkmenistan Relations," *Iranian Studies* 45 (2012): 746; and Pishgahifard and Ranjbari, "Tahlil-i zheupulitik-i ravabit-i Iran va Turkamanistan," 409.
53. Atai and Azizi "Energy Factor," 751.
54. Joneidi, "Rafter-i zheupolitiki Turkamanistan," 133; and Pishgahifard and Ranjbari, "Tahlil-i zheupulitik-i ravabit-i Iran va Turkamanistan," 412.
55. Atai and Azizi "Energy Factor," 748; Oksan Bayulgen, "Caspian Energy Wealth; Social Impacts and Implications for Regional Stability," in *The Politics of Transition in Central Asia and the Caucasus*, ed. Amanda E. Wooden and Christoph H. Stefes (Routledge, 2009), 168; and Hajiyusofi and Rabbani, "Iran va Turkamanistan," 178.

56. Mohammad Hossein Ahadi, "Mahkumiyat-i Iran dar chalish-i gazi ba Turkamanistan va mulahizat-i amniyat-i inirzhi" [Iran's conviction in the gas dispute with Turkmenistan and energy security concerns], *Amniyat-i Iqtisadi* 12 (2020): 61.

57. "Mahkumiyat-i sangin-i gazi Iran babat-i shikayat-i Turkaman Gaz" [Harsh conviction of Iran gas in response to Turkmengaz's complaint], Farda News, June 29, 2020, https://bit.ly/3s6Ft3X.

58. For instance see the statement from a conservative parliament member in Iran: "Chira vazir-i naft az Turkmanistan be dadgah-i Lahi Shikayat Nakard" [Why didn't the oil minister file a complaint against Turkmenistan to the International Criminal Court?], Mashregh News, June 1, 2017, https://bit.ly/40aZ3IN.

59. "Majara-yi bidihi-yi milyardi Iran bi Turkamanistan chi bud?" [What was the story behind Iran's billion debt to Turkmenistan?], Fardaye Eghtesad, May 30, 2023, https://bit.ly/409IsFs.

60. In conversation with Dr. Hannes Meissner, an expert on political risk analysis and management with specialized expertise in Turkmenistan.

61. Amin Navakhti Moghada and Qasem Osuli, "Fursatha va chalishha-yi hamkari zheuikunumik Iran va Turkamanistan" [Opportunities and challenges of Iran–Turkmenistan geoeconomic cooperation], *Siyasat-i Baynulmilal* 9 (2021): 339.

62. Joneidi, "Rafter-i zheupolitiki Turkamanistan," 148; and Navakhti Moghada and Osuli, "Fursatha va chalishha-yi hamkari zheuikunumik," 342.

63. "Kazakhstan-Turkmenistan-Iran Railway Has Great Potential," Azer News, September 16, 2022, https://bit.ly/3Qay1Nk.

64. "Iran-Oman-Turkmenistan-Uzbekistan Corridor to Be Launched," *Shargh Daily*, May 30, 2023, https://bit.ly/3FQSL89. See also Navakhti Moghada and Osuli, "Fursatha va chalishha-yi hamkari zheuikunumik," 353.

65. See for instance: Sharbati and Rashidi, "Zhiupulitik-i Turkamanistan," 156–57.

66. The study was first published in 2007 as thesis and later on published by Iran's Border Guard Command as a book: Hossein Zolfaqari and Alireza Abbasi Semnani, *Tahlil-i zheupulitiki-yi marz-i Iran va Turkamanistan va naqsh-i an dar amniyat-i milli jumhuri-yi Islami-i Iran* [A geopolitical analysis of the Iran–Turkmenistan border and its role in the national security of the Islamic Republic of Iran] (Marzbanan, 2019).

67. Alireza Abbasi Semnani and Nematollah Moini, "Barrasi-yi amniyati-yi gusalha-yi mazhabi dar marz-i Iran va Turkmanistan" [A security analysis of religious challenges to the Iran–Turkmenistan border], *Amniyatpazhuhi* 11 (2012): 118.

68. Turkman Sunni cleric, personal communication with author, March 2023.

69. Abbasi Semnani and Moini, "Barrasi-yi amniyati-yi gusalha-yi mazhabi," 130, 136.

70. Joneidi, "Rafter-i zheupolitiki Turkamanistan," 148.

71. Regarding Sunnis in contemporary Iran see: Hessam Habibi Doroh, *Sunni Communities in the Islamic Republic of Iran 2013–2021, Securitization, Secularization and Privatization* (Brill, 2023), 42–62.

On Iranian Turkmen and their relations with Turkmenistan see Araz Mohammad Sarli, *Turkmenistan dar tarikh* [Turkmenistan in history] (Amirkabir, 1996), 80–82. More details on the Sunni communities of Turkmen in Iran, in the province of Golestan, can be found in: Araz Mohammad Sarli, *Madaris-i Dini Ahl-i Sunnat-i Turkmansahra* [Religious schools of Sunnis in Turkmen-Sahra] (Makhtumquli, 2019).

72. Shamsa, "Daramadi bar munasibat-i jumhuri," 1–2.

73. Seyyed Mahmudreza Shams Dolatabadi and Davud Golkarian, "Rahburdha-yi hamkari-yi difa'i-amniyati jumhuri-i Islami-i Iran ba kishvar-i Turkmanistan" [The Islamic Republic of Iran's defense–security cooperation strategies with Turkmenistan], *Mutaliat-i Defa'i Istiratizhik* 77 (2019): 320; and Kuhkan and Momenifard, "Barresi-yi zaminiha-yi hamgarayi," 134.

74. The author is also thankful to Dr. Hannes Meissner for sharing his expertise on this topic.

75. Mokhtari and Zohdi Goharpur, "Manabi'-i tanish va tahdid-i," 67; and Joneidi, "Rafter-i zheupolitiki Turkamanistan," 143.

76. Mokhtari and Zohdi Goharpur, "Manabi'-i tanish va tahdid-i," 68; and Seyedi Asl and Bahremani, "Impact of Geopolitical Borders Factors," 683, 688.

77. Kuhkan and Momenifard, "Barresi-yi zaminiha-yi hamgarayi," 145.

78. "Tosi'-i Hamkariha-yi Iran va Turkamanistan dar Mubarizi ba Mavad-i Mukhaddir" [Development of Iran–Turkmenistan cooperation against drugs], Iranpak, May 29, 2012, 30–32, http://magiran.com/p1012586.

79. "Turkamanistan sharik-i amniyati-yi Iran ast?" [Is Turkmenistan Iran's security partner in Central Asia?], IR Diplomacy, May 21, 2016, https://bit.ly/3s976ti.

80. Regarding one of the common definitions of defense strategy see: Shams Dolatabadi and Golkarian, "Rahburdha-yi hamkari-yi difa'i-amniyati," 300, 297.

81. Joneidi, "Rafter-i zheupolitiki Turkamanistan," 143; Mokhtari and Zohdi Goharpur, "Manabi'-i tanish," 70; and Shams Dolatabadi and Golkarian, "Rahburdha-yi hamkari-yi difa'i-amniyati," 85–87.

82. Deirdre Tynan, "Turkmenistan: Ashgabat Playing Key US/NATO Support Role in Afghan War," Eurasianet, January 10, 2011, https://bit.ly/3QzjMDb.

83. This potential scenario is discussed in the following: Hajiyusofi and Rabbani, "Iran va Turkamanistan: Vaz'iyat-i Kununi, Chashmandaz-i Ayandi" [Current state of relations and future prospects], 183.

84. For more details on the security recommendations see: Kuhkan and Momenifard, "Barresi-yi Zaminiha-yi Hamgarayi Iran va Turkamanistan" [Examining areas of cooperation between Iran and Turkmenistan], p. 148.

85. Joneidi, "Rafter-i zheupolitiki Turkamanistan," 143.

86. For instance after a flood in north Iran which impacted dramatically the lives of many Iranian Turkmen in 2019, the Iranian hardliner news agency Tasnim reacted surprisingly about the fact that Ashgabat remained silent after this natural catastrophe: "Chira turkamanistan ba Turkamanha-yi Iran Hamdardi Nakard?" [Why did Turkmenistan not sympathize with Iranian Turkmens?], Tasnim News, April 13, 2019, https://bit.ly/3tLspl9. In this regard see also: Mohammadreza Hafeznia, Mohammad Hossein Afshordi, and Goodarz Tafteh, "Muhimtarin A'vamil-i Zhiupulitiki Kishvar-i Turkamanistan Muasir bar Tadvin-i Rahburdi Difa'i Jumhuri-i Islami Iran" [The most significant geopolitical factors of Turkmenistan affecting the development of the Islamic Republic of Iran's defense strategies], *Mutaliat-i Difa'i Istiratizhik* 61 (2015): 149–72.

87. Joneidi, "Rafter-i zheupolitiki Turkamanistan," 141; and Golkarian, *Rahburdha-yi hamkari-yi difa'i-amniyati*, 118–19.

88. Golkarian, *Rahburdha-yi hamkari-yi difa'i-amniyati*, 200–205.

89. "Comprehensive Report: Arkadag Berdimuhamedov and Iranian President Ebrahim Raisi Held Talks in Tehran – Five Documents Signed – Joint Declaration Adopted," News Central Asia, May 31, 2023, https://bit.ly/3QcV0XX.

90. Regarding the core argument of a systemic shift in the context of Iran-China relations see: Anoushiravan Ehteshami, "Asianisation of Asia: Chinese-Iranian Relations in Perspective," *Asian Affairs* 53 (2022): 8–27.

91. Among different events one of the latest was the International Conference on New World Order Geometry, which was organized at the Defense Academy of the Defense Ministry.

92. "Sukhanrani-yi rai's-i shura-yi rahburdi ravabit-i khariji" [Speech of the head of the Strategic Council on Foreign Relations], Markaze Gofteman, May 14, 2023, https://bit.ly/3s3J9DF. See also the essay by Ali Baqeri titled "Chashmandaz-i siyasat-i khariji dar

partu-i nazm-i nuvin-i jahani" [The perspective of foreign policy in light of the new world order], Islamic Republic of Iran's Ministry of Foreign Affairs, May 20, 2023, https://bit.ly/474yS93.

93. Ehteshami, "Asianisation of Asia," 16.

94. For more recent publications on this topic see: Nicole Grajewski, "An Illusory Entente: The Myth of a Russia-China-Iran 'Axis,'" *Asian Affairs* 53, no. 1 (2022): 164–83; and Alam Saleh and Zakiyeh Yazdanshenas, "China-Iran Strategic Partnership and the Future of US Hegemony in the Persian Gulf Region," *British Journal of Middle Eastern Studies* 51, no. 2 (2024): 377–400.

95. For detailed discussion on this see: Grajewski, "An Illusory Entente," 172–75.

96. Grajewski, "An Illusory Entente," 178. Regarding this discussion from the scholarly works in Iran see: Navakhti Moghada and Osuli, "Fursatha va chalishha-yi hamkari zheuikunumik," 351–52.

97. Hessam Habibi Doroh, "Iran Facing Two Taliban: Iran-Taliban changing relations" in *The Taliban's Takeover in Afghanistan* (Counter Extremism Project Germany and Konrad Adenauer Stiftung, 2022), https://acr.ps/1L9zRDm.

98. For the final declaration see: "Samarkand Declaration of the Fourth Meeting of Foreign Ministers of Afghanistan's Neighboring States," Ministry of Foreign Affairs of the People's Republic of China, April 14, 2023, https://acr.ps/1L9zSmh. And for the statement from Iran's foreign minister see: "Statement by His Excellency Hussein Amir-Abdollahian," Islamic Republic of Iran's Ministry of Foreign Affairs, April 13, 2023, https://bit.ly/3Md1Ziv.

99. "Musammam bi imza-yi sanad-i hamkari-yi 20 sali ba Turkamanistan hastim" [We are committed to signing a 20-year cooperation agreement with Turkmenistan], Mashregh News, June 15, 2022, https://bit.ly/3tNyNIy.

Part V
IRAN'S RELATIONS WITH MALAYSIA AND INDONESIA

14
CONSISTENCY THROUGH INSTABILITY
Malaysian–Iranian Relations

Rowena Abdul Razak

Engaged in a devastating war with Iraq, Iranian Foreign Minister Ali Akbar Vilayati paid an official visit to Malaysia in the early 1980s. Isolated internationally, Iran could rely on only a few countries for recognition and partnership. It quickly looked to Malaysia, a postcolonial, neutral, and developing nation, under the leadership of upcoming Asian powerhouse Mahathir Mohamad. Building on relations established during the Mohammad Reza Pahlavi era, this symbolic visit to the Southeast Asian country revealed Iran's reliance on smaller nations during times of crisis. While attention has been given to Iran's relations with more prominent Asian nations such as China, India, and Pakistan, Tehran's diplomatic ties with Malaysia is less known, but offers important insights into Iran's realist approach to foreign relations. This chapter seeks to understand the paradoxes in this relationship, which on the surface should not work as well as it does. Malaysia has close relations with the West and Arab countries and, most strikingly, has banned Shiism as a form of Islamic practice for its citizens. However, ties have remained relatively stable with strong diplomatic relations, open trade, and interest in cultural ties, despite global Shia–Sunni tensions and Western pressure. This chapter explores the consistencies in bilateral ties and offers a historical perspective to Malaysian Iranian relations while exploring the enduring nature of the political relationship.

A day after Anwar Ibrahim was confirmed to be Malaysia's tenth prime minister, the late Iranian President Ebrahim Raisi made a courtesy phone call to congratulate the new leader of the Southeast Asian country.[1] In the midst of nationwide protests following the death of a Kurdish-Iranian woman Mahsa

Amir-Abdollahian, in custody, Raisi and his government were under immense pressure. The incident not only caused outcry domestically but also saw international condemnation against the Islamic Republic. In addition, the country faced economic pressures stemming from continuing sanctions, high inflation, rising living costs, and governmental mismanagement of basic resources. Iran has been facing a lot of international pressures as well. Since the outbreak of the war on Gaza since October 7, 2023, Iran has increased its presence in the region and its support for its key allies, Hamas and Hezbollah. Israel has retaliated by invading Lebanon and assassinating important figures, including Hezbollah leader Hassan Nasrallah. Iran and Israel have also escalated tensions by launching missiles at each other. Furthermore, in the last year, there was a change of leadership after Raisi's sudden death in a helicopter accident with the election of Masoud Pezeshkian. During times of crisis and chaos, Iran has relied on its few friends to seek some sense of stability and normalcy. Historically, scholars and Iran observers have looked at its relations with powerful and prominent nations such as Russia, China, and Pakistan. But what can its relationship with smaller nations tell us about its international psyche?

This chapter attempts to provide some answers to a deceptively simple question. Tehran's approach to smaller nations is underresearched and may not seem as relevant as compared to more powerful nations such as China or India, so it is easy to dismiss further inquiry as unnecessary or irrelevant. But the interest in Iran's historical and political relations with smaller nations is gaining wider traction. Robert Steele, for example, has examined Iran's engagement with sub-Saharan Africa through Muhammad Reza Shah's relationship with Haile Selassie of Ethiopia. He examined how the shah was driven by concerns of Soviet infiltration of the Persian Gulf region to pursue the relationship and envision the African continent as part of Iran's foreign policy vision.[2]

Iran's relations with Malaysia offer an interesting case study. Both are Muslim nations but have pursued different political paths. Politically and historically, Malaysia has pursued relations with Sunni nations of the Middle East, such as Turkey and Saudi Arabia. Apart from the 1980s when Malaysian Prime Minister Mahathir pursued his "Look East" policy, Malaysian governments have taken pro-Western stances, even when it came to Iran, which included the adoption of sanctions against Iran. Furthermore, Malaysia is a majority Sunni country where Shiism is illegal. However, despite this, Iran has maintained positive relations and attitudes toward Malaysia and its leaders. Indeed, Malaysia has often shown international solidarity with Iran. When Israel launched missiles against Iranian targets in April and October 2024, Malaysia condemned the attacks and reinforced Iran's sovereignty.[3] Furthermore, since the start of the October 7 conflict, Malaysia, especially under Ibrahim, is aligned with Iran's stand with Palestine and its allies in the Levant, such as Hamas and Hezbollah. Furthermore, despite concerns within society about the spread of Iranian Shiism, Malaysia retains diplomatic relations with Iran and shows enormous respect for Persian culture. No Malaysian home is complete without the presence of a Persian carpet, while shopping malls in the capital, Kuala Lumpur, are filled with shops selling Persian nuts and dried fruits. In addition, Persian is frequently heard among the small but significant Iranian population, who call the Malaysian capital home.

Diplomatic relations were established in 1970 after the shah and his wife Farah Diba made an official visit to the country a year before. Despite the 1979 revolution, ties have remained unbroken and through the unstable 1980s with the Iran–Iraq war, Malaysia proved to be a constant and steadfast ally. During this decade, they collaborated on Palestinian solidarity, and Malaysia received a few ministerial visits from Tehran. In October 1994, Iranian President Ali Akbar Hashemi Rafsanjani became the first leader of the Islamic Republic to visit Malaysia officially. Since then, every Iranian president has visited Malaysia (except for Raisi). Why has this Southeast Asian nation featured on Iran's radar? On the surface, diplomatic relations appear steady and perhaps even monotonous. But, as this chapter will demonstrate, ties are complex but no less crucial to Iran's international standing. Bilateral relations and cooperation with Malaysia bring a sense of normalcy for the Islamic Republic's foreign relations.

There is still a paradox to address, however: How is this the case despite conflicting policies when it comes to religion and the approach to the West? There are three parts to this answer. First, current bilateral relations rely on historical continuity. The Islamic Republic built on foundations laid during the Pahlavi era and found common grounds to develop a strong relationship with Malaysia throughout the late twentieth and early twenty-first centuries. Second, the Iranian Republic operates within complex realism. Raymond Hinnebusch and Anoushiravan Ehteshami pointed out how environmental pressures often pulled countries in contradictory directions, which led to prioritization of certain policies at the expense of other values.[4] As will be demonstrated here, it overlooks Malaysia's domestic policies toward Shiism to prioritize its strategic interests in the region and improve its trade relations. Third, by applying a pericentric approach to Malaysia, we might be able to understand how smaller members in the international system applied their agency to further their needs. While Tony Smith used this theory with regards to junior states in the Cold War, it does help us understand how Malaysia was able to pursue an independent path with regard to its relations with Iran.[5] Thus, by looking at Iran's relations with Malaysia, we are able to move away from the prevailing narrative that Iran is in constant confrontation with the world and offers an example of Iranian pragmatism in action.

This chapter has made use of archival material from the Malaysian and Singaporean national archives, in addition to speeches and newspaper articles. It begins by examining the evolution of foreign policies of both Iran and Malaysia. It then goes into the history of the relationship since the Pahlavi era, highlighting the reasons why this relationship was pursued and to show the various crossing points between Iranian and Malaysian approaches to the world. It will demonstrate how Malaysia featured in Iran's foreign policy with regards to its global position, its geostrategic interests and trade position.

Iranian Foreign Policy from the Pahlavis to the Islamic Republic

Iranian foreign policy in the twentieth and twenty-first centuries underwent several changes. It is worth to examine this evolution to understand how Iran has participated internationally, which helps to place its relationship with Malaysia. Although 1979 marked an important break in Iran's worldview from alignment with the West to a radical anti-Western stance, there were several consistencies. For many years, the shah had aligned himself and his country with US policies.[6] Emblematic of this relationship, and apparent subservience, was the shah's adoption of policies that brought Iran in line with American vision for Iran, mainly as a key partner in the region that looked out for US interests. Such a pattern of policy alignment with the United States arguably began earlier on in the shah's reign. A British–US-sponsored coup in August 1953 overthrew Muhammad Mossadeq, the popular leader who nationalized the Iranian oil a few years before. In Ali Rahnema's assessment of the events of Mordad 28 (the Persian calendar date of the coup), the coup "interrupted Iran's attempt to assert its right of self-determination over its polity and economy as well as over its future," which resulted in the submission to the political and economic will of the United States.[7] Indeed, the shah came to rely on US aid and backing to consolidate his regime to the point that Iran was regarded as a client state.[8]

From Dwight D. Eisenhower to Jimmy Carter, each US president developed their own policies to support Iran. Aid was varied and came in the form of financial packages and knowledge exchange. The CIA trained Iran's intelligence, which helped stave out any threats, especially from any communist elements in the country.[9] Indeed, from the start, the United States saw Iran as a key ally in the Cold War and therefore at the frontline of the United States' regional perimeter defense strategy. This was probably expressed most clearly when Iran became an important focus for the Richard Nixon doctrine.[10] During the Carter administration, when human rights became a policy priority, the shah relaxed laws, released political prisoners, and adopted liberal policies. This contributed in part to the empowerment of the opposition against the shah, which had taken an anti-imperial tone in light of Iran's alignment to the United States. This is not to say that Iran under the shah completely lacked agency, nor did he entirely lack independence, however. He pursued relations with the Soviet Union and explored relations with African and Asian countries to suit his own designs for Iran. Indeed, this Eastward perspective continued into the postrevolutionary period.

The 1979 revolution disrupted the internal system of Iran and saw the replacement of the pro-Western monarchy of the shah with an Islamic Republic. Ayatollah Ruhollah Khomeini became the leader of the opposition movement after many years in exile, first in Iraq and then in France. Making alliances with democrats and socialists, from the international student unions to the Tudeh Party, he brought together the different anti-shah threads. After months of consistent protests and demonstrations, the shah left Iran in early 1979. In his place, Khomeini returned from exile to oversee the transfer of power first to the democratic governments of Mehdi Bazargan and Abolhassan Banisadr and then finally to the Islamists. Khomeini pursued an approach that was radically different from the shah, especially with regards to attitudes toward the West. This was probably symbolized best by the break in diplomatic relations with the United States, following the hostage crisis that saw radical Iranian students take over the US embassy in Tehran for months. Unable to reach a solution, the crisis cost Democratic President Carter another term in office and saw a permanent pause between Washington and Tehran.

After the establishment of the Islamic Republic, Iranian foreign policy went through some important identity changes. The most obvious and pertinent one was the incorporation of Islam and anti-imperialism as key pillars. Khomeini established the novel notion of "Neither East nor West, but the Islamic Republic."[11] Iran, unlike before, was now venturing forth on its own. Iran's new self-identification affected foreign outlook and international relations. The triumph of Khomeini sparked the need to export the revolution beyond its borders, driven by the notion that the Islamic Republic would play the role of a vanguard state that could lead oppressed nations to liberation. Idealistic to an extent, confrontation with the United States and the war with neighboring Iraq only served to radicalize Khomeini's worldview.[12] As noted by Ray Takeyh, Iran's "ideological crusade" went beyond the region. During the 1980s, Khomeini led Iran on an inflexible path which prolonged the war with Saddam Hussein and saw Iran become heavily involved in the Levant. Because of this path, Iran became more isolated throughout this period. The hostage crisis irreparably broke relations with the United States, while the fatwa against British writer Salman Rushdie only showed Iran to be extremist and difficult.[13] This saw a break in diplomatic relations with the United Kingdom and Iran remained in its difficult period in its relationship with the West. However, as will be shown in more detail in this chapter, Iran grew closer to Malaysia during this period when Mahathir implemented his "Look East" policy that rejected close alignment with the United States and the United Kingdom.

After Khomeini's death, subsequent presidents have tried to navigate Iran out of its isolation. President Rafsanjani led this new path and introduced more pragmatic policies that prioritized national interests, which included improving Iran's postwar economy. He sought cooperation and a more liberal approach to foreign policy.[14] Since then, every Iranian president has implemented their own policies and visions. Iranian politics is roughly divided between three factions: the Conservatives, the Pragmatists, and the Reformists. Each faction has vied for power and have all been able to assert their worldview on policymaking. They each have their own approach to domestic and foreign issues but do contain overlaps. For instance, they all agree that internationally, Iran needs to remain independent, strive for equality, and to occupy a prominent role.[15] But the tensions between the different factions have nonetheless affected policymaking, which, unsurprisingly, has resulted in contradictions in policy and outlook. The constant struggle between pragmatism and ideology is present and has obstructed Tehran from making realistic or rational choices, especially when it comes to relations with the West.[16]

However, different observations can be made when we examine Iran's relations with the non-Western world, especially East Asia and Southeast Asia. During the Pahlavi era, relations with Asian countries were also prioritized. Relations with China go back thousands of years, with a long history of cultural interactions and trade relations. In the modern era, Sino–Iranian relations were built in the 1960s through trade treaties, but the shah was cautious of the reach of Chinese communism in Asia and in Iran itself with the emergence of a Maoist movement. Nonetheless, Iran responded to China's overtures with culture and trade at the heart of their relationship.[17] These foundations laid during this era allowed for the Islamic Republic to continue developing ties Eastward.

Indeed, as will be shown here, relations with Malaysia allowed Iran to appear less isolated, especially during the 1980s, when the country faced a devastating war with Iraq and was at the height of Khomeini's radicalism. This was true for the rest of Iran's relations with Asia. In his study of Iran's economic ties with Southeast Asia, Mohammad Soltaninejad highlighted how they helped to "reduce political pressures from the West" and improve its international standing.[18] Iran's Eastward policy became more pronounced following Khomeini's death, with Rafsanjani making official visits to Malaysia and Indonesia in the early 1990s. Since then, Iran has pursued policies that saw a massive improvement in trade and increased cooperation with Southeast Asia.

The importance of religion in its foreign policy is never that far from policy considerations. Islam occupies an important role to build ties with other Muslim nations. Since Khomeini came to power, religion has not been separated from the nation and this is true domestically, as well as internationally.[19] Eva Rakel deepened the question to understand how Shiism specifically played a role in Iranian foreign policy. Shiism has had a long place in Iranian polity, since the Safavid ruler Shah Ismail I declared Twelver Shiism to be the official religion of his new state. This decision came with concerns about how it would be received by its Sunni citizens and neighbors.[20] Nonetheless, this path was followed and saw the clergy gaining considerable power and influence.[21] The 1979 revolution resulted in the end of monarchical rule and the implementation of the *velayet-e faqih* (guardianship of the jurist), which saw the concentration of decision making in the hands of the supreme leader and the religious elite.

Despite some fundamental changes in outlook, the country's Iranian identity under the Islamic Republic has remained as important as it did during the Pahlavi era. This strong sense of Iran's place in history and as part of an ancient civilization has permeated different presidencies as a way in which they present Iran to the world. Shahram Akbarzadeh and James Barry, in their study, noted how Iran has played on its identity to engage with those in its "cultural sphere" and to build connections with countries that share similar traditions, such as the celebration of Nowrouz, the Persian new year.[22] Furthermore, this strong sense of the national has infused with the religious tenets of its foreign policymaking, resulting in a distinctly Iranian rendition of political Shiism. In this way, Iran can present itself as a Muslim powerhouse that is distinct from its Arab brethren. During the presidency of Mahmoud Ahmadinejad, this was promoted extensively to the point of inciting sectarian tensions. His government frequently described Shiism as moderate and portrayed itself as a good balance against extremist groups such as the Salafis, Islamic State, and al-Qaeda.[23] This attitude indicates a pragmatic streak within foreign policy and an ability to play down dogma to assimilate or even assert influence beyond Iran.

Malaysia therefore presents a particular challenge as a pro-Western, Sunni country that is hostile to Shiism. Here, are we able to note the inherent tension between ideology and pragmatism. The tension between them in foreign policymaking has been present for a long time. Ruhollah Ramazani traced this struggle back to pre-Islamic times from the Achaemenid Empire. In the twentieth century, the shah merged his dynastic ambitions with a desire to turn Iran into a "Great Civilization." The Pahlavi monarch's ideological drive goes through a few phases and was driven by pre-Islamic notions of Iran's prominence. He saw the means of purchasing American arms to make Iran well-armed as an end to his vision. However, his agreements with the United States made him appear to be

Washington's lackey, which added to his downfall.[24] With the Islamic Republic, pragmatism becomes a way in which Iranian leaders can navigate difficulties and overcome ideological constraints. As Takeyh notes, "Iran's international orientation has been shaped by its internal evolutions."[25]

In some ways, the formal incorporation of "Looking East" into Iranian foreign policy has been a way in which Iran can exercise its ability to be pragmatic without compromising on its key pillars. President Ahmadinejad formally launched the country's Look East policy during his term. Facing sanctions and another difficult period of relations with the West, Ahmadinejad sought cooperation with powers in the Eastern hemisphere, particularly Russia, China, and India. This was continued under the Hassan Rouhani presidency in light of US President Donald Trump's belligerent stance against Iran.[26] Relations with Asia therefore present Iran in a different light and show the extent of its ability to be pragmatic and forward-looking, while still retaining its identity and ideology.

Malaysia's Foreign Policy: From the Cold War to Looking East

To fully appreciate Iran's Eastward policy toward Malaysia, it will be shown here that the approach has been reciprocal. After all, one of the key reasons why Iran has been able to establish ties with this Southeast Asian nation is because of Malaysia's own interests and reasons. Since its independence, it has gone through several phases of its attitude toward the world. As a middle power, it has played an important role regionally and has maintained a balance between West and East. In recent years, there has been the steady corporation of Islam in its politics.[27] As will be seen here, Malaysia's foreign policy throughout the years has been conducive to relations with Iran. During the colonial period, when the Malayan peninsula was under British rule, the Malay states were limited to pursue independent paths of connection with Persia. Most of the Malay states were forced to accept British advisers and like the Persian Gulf states of Qatar, Oman, the Trucial States, and Bahrain, were not allowed to have their own foreign policy.

When Malaya gained independence from the British in 1957, it developed its own place in a world dictated by Cold War tensions.[28] There were points of neutrality and profession for less extreme positionality. During the Cold War, Malaysia started by aligning itself strongly with the West and relied on British armed support to counter its local communist movement. Unsurprisingly, in the early years of Malaysia's independence, the country pursued alignment with the West in the Cold War to preserve its territory and internal security.[29] However, by the 1960s, it made a concerted effort to move toward nonalignment. Wanting to be in line with the emerging trend of postcolonial states, Malaysia pursued "peaceful coexistence" and diluted its original Western orientation by diversifying its international outlook.[30] Throughout this decade, Malaysian politicians debated about what stance the country would take in the ongoing confrontation between East and West. Johan Saravanmuttu pinpoints the Vietnam War as a key turning point for Malaysian policymakers to move toward outward solidarity with its neighbors and toward nonalignment in the Cold War.[31]

This turn toward neutralism allowed for Kuala Lumpur to pursue relations with the communist bloc, establishing relations with Moscow in 1968 and normalizing relations with China in 1974.[32] Similar trends can be observed within the Pahlavi government, who also pursued relations with the Eastern bloc. Malaysia institutionalized neutrality within the region by pushing for the Kuala Lumpur Declaration for the Neutralization of Southeast Asia, which came to be known as the Zone of Peace, Freedom, and Neutrality Declaration (ZOPFAN) and was signed by Indonesia, the Philippines, Singapore, and Thailand.[33] As seen here, nonalignment was an important component of Malaysia's foreign policy, which allowed for it to take a route independent of US and Soviet interests.

Since this recalibration, Malaysia has been able to emerge as a stable developing nation with strong links to the international system while maintaining a position of nonalignment, even beyond the Cold War. This is in part aided by its domestic politics with its delicate balance of power sharing between the three main races: the Malays, the Chinese, and the Indians. Although there have been moments of racial and political tension, Malaysia has been able to avoid any major disruption to its political and economic trajectory.[34]

This independent stance in Malaysia's foreign policy was best expressed when Mahathir became prime minister for the first time in 1981. Throughout the 1980s, he shaped Malaysian foreign policy according to his own vision and appraisal of the country's political and economic needs.[35] His desire to improve economic development and to also make a stand against British policy saw the implementation of the Look East policy. Just six months into his premiership, he launched a "Buy British Last" initiative as a response to an increase in fees for UK universities, which were popular with government-sponsored Malaysian students, and a deterioration of economic cooperation between London and Kuala Lumpur.[36] Such a stance toward the West resonated with Iran during its period of isolation under Khomeini. Their similar stance vis-à-vis the West manifested in cooperation and solidarity platforms.

Although Malaysia's Look East policy began as a reaction to Britain, it soon became a framework in which the country emulated successful Eastern nations, particularly Japan. This included improving economic ties with the region and presenting Malaysia as a forward-looking Asian nation that had the potential to surpass the West.[37] Such rhetoric resonated in Iran and a few members of the Islamic Republic government visited Malaysia during the 1980s. Mahathir's stance went on to define Malaysian foreign policy during this period and became an important model for Asian development. For the country, it was also an important impetus for the "Vision 2020" campaign that was launched by Mahathir to put Malaysia on a path to become a developed country by the start of the new millennium.[38] The campaign also called for closer relations with ASEAN and to improve economic cooperation with Malaysia's neighbors.[39]

ASEAN proved to be an important platform of Iran's interest in Malaysia, and indeed, the region in general. This South–South aspect of Iranian foreign policy had echoes in Malaysia's policies. When Malaysia turned toward neutralism in the Cold War, ties with the Third World were strengthened, especially within organizations such as the Non-Aligned Movement (NAM). After the end of the Cold War, Malaysia, particularly under Mahathir, championed for the NAM to take on a new global role, especially in conflicts involving Muslim-majority countries and regionally to improve its relations with ASEAN and Asia.[40] As can be ascertained here, the years under Mahathir gave Malaysia a distinctive identity when it came to international outlook. Appearing as provocative, different, and even polarizing, he brought an uncompromising stance for Malaysia, which drew detractors from the West but made him a hero of the East.[41] To do so, he was assertive and employed what Jörn Dosch describes as Mahathir's "trademark megaphone diplomacy." His vision for Malaysia's foreign policy stems from his personal experiences growing up under British colonial rule and formed a polarizing view of East against West and north against south.[42] As already noted with Ahmadinejad's own Look East initiative, Malaysia laid an important template for Iran and normalized this kind of confrontational leadership style.

In the last thirty years, the Malaysian government has gradually incorporated Islamism into its domestic and foreign policies. Already under Mahathir, Malaysia endeavored to play a more prominent role in global Muslim politics. Since the early 1980s, Palestine has been a mainstay of Malaysia's foreign policy. It has consistently criticized the West's treatment of the conflict and its support of Israel.[43] Indeed, the Palestinian cause served as a common platform for Malaysia and Iran to collaborate on, and served as an important binding force in bilateral ties. Under Mahathir, Malaysia played a more involved role in conflicts involving Muslim countries, which saw a strong stand on Bosnia in its war with Serbia.[44] This religious expression in foreign policy became more embedded within national ideology when Abdullah Badawi replaced Mahathir as prime minister in October 2003. Turning away from his predecessor's more confrontational attitude toward the West, he wanted to introduce a more modernist and moderate approach through his concept of "Islam Hadhari" (civilizational Islam).[45] He saw this as part of a global response to America's "war against terrorism," and in many ways echoed Khatami's own "Dialogue Among Civilizations" campaign. Badawi used his campaign to strengthen his government's ideological foundation, especially against the Islamic party, Parti Islam Se-Malaysia (PAS). The "Islamic race" between PAS and the ruling party showed the value of religion in domestic politics, which very quickly infused foreign policy.[46]

Internationally, Badawi articulated his version of moderate Islam in several ways. The same year he took office, Malaysia hosted the 10th Summit Conference of the Organization of Islamic Cooperation (OIC), which gave Malaysia an important platform to assert its Islamic drive among Muslim nations. Regarding Palestine, Malaysia did not change its stance and remained firm, but relations with the West were improved with the toning down of rhetoric and more emphasis on dialogue.[47] Badawi's successor Najib Razak further developed and deepened the role of Islam in Malaysia's international outlook. Much like his predecessors, he saw the importance of using regional and international conflicts involving Muslims as a way in which Malaysia can fulfill a leadership role of the Islamic world.[48] In this sense, Malaysia shared a similar vision with Iran in terms of its place among the *ummah*.

Iran Looks East to Malaysia: Crossing Points

In Iran's outlook toward Malaysia, there are several discerning and fascinating crossing points, especially with regard to the Muslim world, Asian geopolitics, and the importance of religion in international outlook. Cooperation between Kuala Lumpur and Tehran have survived a revolution, radicalization, and the entrenchment of extreme Sunni values in Malaysia. This section examines why the bilateral relationship has endured. Drawing upon the historical building blocks and their approaches to foreign policy, it will be seen here that Iran's pragmatism and Malaysia's neutrality and determination to steer its own path have allowed for bilateral ties to flourish, despite the obvious obstacles.

While relations were only formalized in 1970, Iranian interaction with Malaysia goes back centuries. Situated on a major route connecting the Persian Gulf and China, the Malacca straits between the Malay peninsula and island of Sumatra have historically played a major role for trade. Its prime location invited the interest of the Portuguese, Dutch, and British, who all controlled it at different points from the sixteenth to the twentieth century. During the Safavid era, trade increased with this part of the world. While trade and commerce played an important role in connecting Iran with the Malay peninsula, this also resulted in an increase in cultural and religious exchanges.[49]

In the twentieth century, Iran seriously started developing a relationship with Malaysia as part of a general move of the shah to look Eastward. After his official visit to Thailand in January 1968, he paid a visit to Malaysia, traveling across the country. He visited the sites of ongoing agricultural projects, which seemed in line with his own land reforms back in Iran. His visit carried a lot of weight, and the Malaysian government showered him with all kinds of honors, including an honorary degree from the University of Malaya.[50] This visit was followed up by an exchange of ambassadors and the opening of embassies in Tehran and Kuala Lumpur. Since then, Malaysia has remained an important mainstay of Iranian foreign policy.

Relations with Malaysia were an important way in which Iran avoided political isolation. After the revolution, with the hostage crisis and the war with Iraq, Iran underwent a period of remoteness. During the early 1980s, Tehran sought to maintain relations with Malaysia and to continue the rapport it had under the Pahlavis. However, the relationship clearly entered a new phase with new considerations and platforms of collaboration. Under Mahathir, Malaysia looked eastwards, prioritizing relations with its neighbors and the Muslim world. To an extent, this was fortuitous timing for the Islamic Republic, who was able to tap in and build ties easily with a ready and willing Malaysia.

Several high-profile visits between Malaysia and Iran have helped keep Iran relevant and prevent isolation. Since diplomatic relations were established in 1971, Malaysian politicians and kings have visited Iran and vice versa. During the twenty-five hundredth anniversary commemoration of the Persian monarchy in 1971, the Malaysian Agong and Permaisuri Agong attended as royal guests of honor.[51] After the shah's visit to Malaysia in 1968, his half-brother Gholam Reza Pahlavi and sister-in-law Manijeh Jahanbani visited Kuala Lumpur in 1973 to show a continued interest in the country where he met with the Agong and visited other cultural sites, focusing on batik factories and sports stadiums.[52] These royal visits were important and helped to strengthen ties between the two, reinforcing the importance of high-level visits. These types of visits continued into the revolutionary period. During the Iran–Iraq war, Malaysian Foreign Minister Ghazali Shafie was sent to Iran in 1983 to strengthen political and economic ties.[53] Rafsanjani was the first president to pay an official visit to Malaysia in 1994, followed by Khatami in 2002, Ahmadinejad in 2006, and Rouhani in 2016. While these visits may appear superficial and functionary, they are indicative of the importance of Malaysia as a nation with which Iran can do business with.

Malaysia features extensively within Iran's interests in the wider Asian region. Within it, Southeast Asia has long been an area of importance for Iran since the Pahlavis. Iran established diplomatic relations with Indonesia in 1950 soon after it attained its independence from the Dutch. In 1958, Iran attended the United

Nations Seminar on Regional Planning held in Tokyo, one of the first international meetings that looked at decolonization and development. It was also the first time that Iran officially interacted with Malaysia, where they discussed common issues such as development, economic, social, and administrative planning, as well as the need for regional cooperation.[54] Malaysia has a long history with the region, being one of the first members of the Association of Southeast Asia when it was formed in 1961 with Thailand and the Philippines. When ASEAN was formed in 1967 with the inclusion of Singapore and Indonesia, the region became more collective and the decision-making process was characterized by consultation and agreement, while adhering to an informal, nonconfrontational attitude.[55] Known as the "ASEAN way," such an approach to diplomacy and foreign policy in part explains why interactions with Iran have remained consistent before and after the revolution.

The foundations laid by the shah were continued after 1979. Diplomatic relations were gradually established with each of the member states. When the shah made his trip to Malaysia in 1968, he also made a point to visit Thailand and Singapore. The timing was not incidental and formed part of the shah's global projection of Iran's power and reach. Cyrus Schayegh charted the shift in Iran's persona in pursuing an independent national and international status during this period, especially with the apparent overreliance on the relationship with the United States. To promote this, the shah established relations with countries, both big and small, including China, Yugoslavia, the German Democratic Republic, and North Korea.[56] Around this time, Iran was also exploring relations and interactions with the African continent. Establishing relations with Ethiopia in the 1960s, Iran regarded sub-Saharan Africa as a pathway to balance out the radicalism of Nasserism and the revolutionary fervor that was sweeping the continent. Indeed, Iran at the time saw East Africa as a gateway in which it could extend its influence and explore economic opportunities with the newly independent states of Africa.[57]

After the revolution and the establishment of the Islamic Republic, Iran's attitude toward the ASEAN region did not change much. At the beginning, Khomeini emphasized the importance of Islam in Iran's international outlook, which implicitly advocated the export of the revolution to the rest of the world. However, with regard to ASEAN, Iran pursued close relations equally with both Muslim and non-Muslim Southeast Asian nations. Iran has continued to play an important role in regional politics. Relations with Thailand and Singapore in particular have been warm and have seen areas of cooperation. Within Iran's foreign ministry, there is an assigned deputy for Asia and Pacific affairs, who is tasked with attending to issues related to Southeast Asia. This role is active in establishing ties and exploring opportunities within the region. The Islamic

Republic has regarded its involvement with the region, and Malaysia, within its commitments to other organizations such as the NAM and the D-8 Organization for Economic Cooperation. In addition, it is a member of the Asia Cooperation Dialogue, an organization that promotes cooperation and integration with other regions, including the Middle East. In 1993, Iran hosted the 13th Conference of Asian and Pacific Labor Ministers in Tehran, which was attended by ASEAN members.[58] More recently, in 2018, Iran became a signatory to the Treaty of Amity and Cooperation (TAC), an international agreement that upholds the integrity of ASEAN.[59] Iran has used such platforms to promote its foreign relations with non-Western states, and clearly regards Southeast Asia as key to ensuring it remains active and has a wider reach. Indeed, Ahmadinejad prioritized this relationship during his revival of revolutionary and idealist discourse, which corresponded with a decline in relations with the West.[60] Thus, Malaysia can be viewed within Iran's Southeast Asian policy. It serves as a key partner within the overall relationship.

At the heart of the Islamic Republic's relations with Southeast Asia is commerce. Under US-imposed sanctions, especially in the last thirty years, Iran has few trading partners in the world and the relative neutrality and independence of the region has been an attractive market for Iranian business. Despite being a close US ally, Singapore since the mid-2000s has actively encouraged better economic relations with Iran, even seeing the potential to extend.[61] Similarly, Iran has sought trade ties with Vietnam, first by exporting petroleum, petrochemical products, and agricultural goods in exchange for coffee, tea, and spices.[62] In 2016, Iranian businesses signed an agreement to purchase 10,000 tons of rubber every year from a Laotian company, in addition to an oil and gas deal with Cambodia in 2015.[63]

As such, Iran's political, commercial, and trading ties with Malaysia forms an important part of its policies toward Southeast Asia in general. Malaysia has been particularly crucial in the distribution of Iranian oil, especially in the era of sanctions. Despite officially adhering to sanctions, Malaysia has had a strong economic connection with Iran since the 1990s. In 1994, during Mahathir's official visit to Iran, he signed several treaties that were all concerned with the expansion of economic and commercial ties between the two countries.[64] This has seen the emergence of plenty of Iranian businesses in Malaysia, especially for fruits and nuts and Persian carpets, which are regarded as status symbols within Malaysian society. But the oil industry has been the most significant area of commerce between Kuala Lumpur and Tehran. In the 1990s, Malaysia's national oil company, PETRONAS, signed a contract to extract oil from the Iranian Sirri oil field, which saw the Malaysian oil enterprise gain 30 percent of stakes.[65] Recently, there have been significant developments that may see Malaysia and Iran drawing closer together economically as well. In November 2024, Malaysia, together with Indonesia, Vietnam, and Thailand, became a partner country of BRICS, of which Iran is a member state. The expansion of this economic bloc has the potential to intensify the East–West rivalry and competition.

Economics aside, religion has played an important role in the bilateral relationship between Malaysia and Iran, especially after the 1979 revolution. On the one hand, both being Muslim countries has served as an area of cooperation, unity, and solidarity. On the other, hailing from different sects has been a source of contradiction and tension. Regardless, both countries appear committed to the relationship by either dealing with these issues head-on or by ignoring them. Before the revolution, religion did not appear as an important pillar of the shah's foreign policy. Nonetheless, while not as prominent as his relations with the United States, he did develop relations with the Muslim world. During his visit to Kuala Lumpur in 1968, he made a point to perform Friday prayers with the Agong prime minister and deputy prime minister.[66] This was an important display of standing side by side with other Muslim leaders. In the prerevolutionary era, religion continued to unite the two countries. In October 1973, Malaysia hosted an international Quran recitation competition and welcomed a delegation from Iran.[67]

After the revolution, Islam became an even more palpable force in the relationship, not only at a government-to-government level but also within Malaysian society. The rise of Khomeini and toppling of the pro-Western shah was regarded as a triumph of Islam and added to a growing movement of Islamic revivalism that was sweeping Indonesia and Malaysia.[68] Even before the revolution, people in the Malay–Indonesia world were already exposed to the writings of Ali Shariati. In Malaysia, his works were published and distributed widely throughout the 1980s in both English and Malay.[69] Malaysians were drawn to the revolution itself and to Iran, especially in the first decade. A delegation of politicians and ordinary observers traveled to Iran to witness the building of the new Islamic Republic. Malaysians were fascinated by the Iran–Iraq war and while many Arab Sunni countries sided with Hussein, Malaysia displayed sympathy for Iran, which was symbolized by a Malaysian delegation visiting a war field and meeting with commanders in Qom in 1981. Even in the public sphere, the war received plenty of attention. In the popular magazine *Mastika*, the conflict became front-page news with an article detailing the war. The writer highlighted the nationalistic fervor of the Iranian Shias and spoke of Hussein's aggression.[70] Malaysian and Indonesian Islamists also engaged with Iranian revolutionary thought, and some even went on to study in Iranian Islamic seminaries.[71] Although the revolution clearly inspired the Muslim societies of Southeast Asia, particularly Malaysia and Indonesia, the new Iranian government concentrated on exporting the revolution to the Middle East.[72] Furthermore, the while there was a noticeable spread of Shia religiosity in the region, this never bubbled into a revolutionary movement.[73]

Despite this apparent openness toward Iran, and indeed Shiism, Malaysia underwent a shift toward a more extreme position. It declared Shiism to be deviationist and illegal for Malaysians to practice Shiism when a fatwa was issued by Malaysia's religious council in 1996.[74] This did not halt bilateral relations, and despite this, Iran has taken a pragmatic approach to its ties with Malaysia. This seems contradictory when we observe Iran's historically tense relations with other Sunni nations, such as Saudi Arabia and the other Arab Gulf states.[75] However, as it has been noted by scholars, Iran has the ability to focus on nonreligious matters in its foreign policy.[76] Indeed, it has been easier to ignore Malaysia's policies as it has strictly applied its anti-Shia policies to its citizens and not to the thousands of Iranians who make Malaysia their home.[77]

Indeed, Malaysia and Iran have been able to collaborate closely on issues pertaining to the Muslim world. This is particularly the case with Palestine, which has been an important area of campaigning for both countries, especially in the post-1979 era. In 1983, Mahathir hosted a conference on Palestine to discuss how Muslim countries could best show up and support the cause. Iran sent at the head of its delegation, the Deputy Foreign Minister Hussein Sheikholeslam.[78] Both countries have kept a strong stance on Palestine, fiercely refusing diplomatic ties with Israel. Furthermore, Ahmadinejad and Mahathir were known for their strong comments about Israel. Both countries have also pursued close relations with Palestinian leaders, from Yasser Arafat to Mahmoud Abbas, which has continued since the outbreak of the Israel–Gaza war since October 7, 2023. Both countries have reinforced their support of Palestine, and this will lead to further alignment as well. In November 2024, Ibrahim called to expel Israel from the United Nations.[79] This forms part of Malaysia and Iran's efforts to discredit Israel, which also included the publication of a book written jointly by the Malaysian Consultative Council of Islamic Organization and the Cultural Attaché of the Islamic Republic of Iran's Embassy in Kuala Lumpur.[80] This bond over Palestine thus serves as a consistent crossing point for Malaysian–Iranian relations.

These crossing points and areas of cooperation have served Iran well, especially in the postrevolutionary period. As has been demonstrated here, there are plenty of overlaps in terms of policy, which suggests consistency and the enduring importance of certain pillars—such as the need to protect Iran's strategic position, the centrality of Asia in its global outlook and its flexibility in international matters. Iran's Look East policy, although only formalized in Ahmadinejad's presidency, has clearly origins from before, as seen in its relations with Malaysia, from the Pahlavi era to Khomeini's early years. Building on the foundations laid out during the Pahlavi era, Iran deepened its ties with Malaysia within its policies toward Southeast Asia and the Muslim world. Relations with Malaysia thus have important implications for Iran's international standing and economy. For instance, it is still able to trade and Malaysia has taken significant steps to circumvent those sanctions. In June 2023, Malaysia increased its purchases of Iranian oil and avoided attraction by the elaborate switching consignments and ships.[81] On the other side, Iran's pragmatism has proven pertinent with regards to its relations with Malaysia, with a significant diaspora, although this number is dwindling.[82] The year 2024 has proven to be significant for their bilateral ties, with renewed alignment over Palestine and more common grounds for collaboration through BRICS.

Malaysian foreign policy contains many components that appear conducive to this relationship: the influence of its domestic makeup, its regional position, and its connection to Islam. Since the country's independence, it evolved from a pro-Western stance in the Cold War to nonalignment, and in the last thirty years, to the adoption of Islamic posturing in foreign policy. Furthermore, its own Look East policy, in place since the 1980s, has been an important platform for collaboration with Iran, even during its most isolated years. This historical neutrality has helped Malaysian pursue a middle path toward Iran, allowing both close ties with the West and warm attitudes toward Iran. There is a sense of defiance as well, born out of the Mahathir era, which saw this neutral stance emerge into activity, with collaborative efforts and gestures of acceptance toward Iran. Indeed, the disconnection between the domestic and the international is rooted in this very neutrality. Malaysia continues relations with Iran to maintain that outward neutrality and to present a united front in the Islamic world. This is also supported by Iranian pragmatism and reliance on smaller nations for a sense of global participation and to avoid isolation. Both countries therefore operate at a supra level to prioritize the symbolic nature of the relationship.

NOTES

1. Kalbana Perimbanayagam, "Iran Keen to Work with Malaysia Under New Prime Minister," *News Straits Times*, November 26, 2022, https://www.nst.com.my/news/nation/2022/11/855190/iran-keen-work-malaysia-under-new-prime-minister.

2. Robert Steele, "Two Kings of Kings: Iran-Ethiopia Relations under Mohammad Reza Pahlavi and Haile Selassie," *International History Review* 43, no. 6 (2021): 1375–92.

3. Embassy of Malaysia in Tehran, Iran, "Malaysian Condemns the Zionist Israeli Regime's Attack on the Sovereign State of the Islamic Republic of Iran," Embassy of Malaysia, Tehran, October 26, 2024, https://www.kln.gov.my/web/irn_tehran/news-from-mission/-/blogs/malaysian-condemns-the-zionist-israeli-regime-s-attack-on-the-sovereign-state-of-the-islamic-republic-of-iran.

4. Raymond Hinnebusch and Anoushiravan Eheteshami, "Foreign Policymaking in the Middle East: Complex Realism," in *International Relations of the Middle East*, ed. Louise Facett, 4th ed. (Oxford University Press, 2013), 241.

5. Tony Smith, "New Bottles for New Wine: A Pericentric Framework for the Study of the Cold War," *Diplomatic History* 24, no. 4 (2000): 568.

6. Shahram Akbarzadeh and James Barry, "State Identity in Iranian Foreign Policy," *British Journal of Middle Eastern Studies* 43, no. 4 (2016): 616–17.

7. Ali Rahnema, *Behind the 1953 Coup in Iran: Thugs, Turncoats, Soldiers and Spooks* (Cambridge University Press, 2015), 2.

8. However, this international client relationship was not one-sided. They both benefited and were aligned on issues such as security, economics, and worldview. As Gasiorowski explains, the patron state provided the client with economic aid such as loans, grants, technical advice, and so on, while the client would provide services to enhance the patron's security. In the case of the United States and Iran, Iran served as Washington's regional policeman and carried out military and intelligence operations. Mark J Gasiorowski, *US Foreign Policy and the Shah: Building a Client State in Iran* (Cornell University Press, 1991), 1–3.

9. Gasiorowski, *US Foreign Policy and the Shah*, 91–92.

10. During the Nixon presidency, the US found itself stretched with the Vietnam War.

11. Rakel, "Iranian Foreign Policy," 167.

12. Ray Takeyh, *Guardians of the Revolution: Iran and the World in the Age of the Ayatollahs* (Oxford University Press, 2009), 2–3.

13. Takeyh, *Guardians of the Revolution*, 58.

14. Rakel, "Iranian Foreign Policy," 170–71.

15. Rakel, "Iranian Foreign Policy," 166.

16. Takeyh, *Guardians of the Revolution*, 4.

17. William Figueroa, "China and the Iranian Revolution: New Perspectives on Sino-Iranian Relations, 1965–1979," *Asian Affairs* 53, no. 1 (2022): 110–19.

18. Mohammad Soltaninejad, "Iran and Southeast Asia: An Analysis of Iran's Policy of 'Look to the East,'" *International Journal of Asia Pacific Studies*, 13, no. 1 (2017): 30.

19. Akbarzadeh and Barry, "State Identity in Iranian Foreign Policy," 618–19.

20. Roger Savory, *Iran Under the Safavids* (Cambridge University Press, 1980), 27–29.

21. It is not within the scope of this article to go into the development of political Shiism and the long journey of how the Shia clergy gained power and influence in Iran. Roy Mottahedeh's study of religion and politics in 20th century Iran remains one of the best studies on the subject. Roy Mottahedeh, *The Mantle of the Prophet: Religion and Politics in Iran* (Oneworld, 1985); see also Eva Patricia Rakel, "Iranian Foreign Policy since the Iranian Islamic Revolution: 1976–2006," *Perspectives on Global Development and Technology* 6 (2007): 161–63, for a succinct explanation of the implementation of this new style of government in Iran under Khomeini.

22. Akbarzadeh and Barry, "State Identity in Iranian Foreign Policy," 617.

23. Akbarzadeh and Barry, however, also note that the prejudice against Iran remains a barrier while its ideological strand of political Islam makes it impossible to be viewed as moderate by others in the West, and even in the Muslim world. Akbarzadeh and Barry, "State Identity in Iranian Foreign Policy," 627.

24. R. K. Ramazani, *Independence Without Freedom: Iran's Foreign Policy* (University of Virginia Press, 2013), 188–89.

25. Takeyh, *Guardians of the Revolution*, 111.

26. Hongda Fan, "China-Iran Relations from the Perspective of Tehran's Look East Approach" in *Asian Affairs* 53, no. 1 (2022): 52.

27. Prashant Waikar, Mohamed Nawab Mohamed Osman, and Rashaad Ali, "Dancing with the Ummah: Islam in Malaysia's Foreign Policy Under Najib Razak," *The Pacific Review* 34, no. 2 (2021): 232.

28. Malaya became Malaysia when Singapore Sabah and Sarawak joined in 1963. Singapore was expelled two years later.

29. Johan Saravanmuttu, *Malaysia's Foreign Policy, the First Fifty Years: Alignment, Neutralism, Islamism* (ISEAS Publishing, 2010), 54.

30. Saravanmuttu, *Malaysia's Foreign Policy, the First Fifty Years*, 91.

31. Saravanmuttu, *Malaysia's Foreign Policy, the First Fifty Years*, 90.

32. Abdul Razak Baginda, *China-Malaysia Relations and Foreign Policy* (Routledge, 2016), 23–24.

33. Chandran Jeshurun, *Malaysia: Fifty Years of Diplomacy, 1957–2007* (Talisman Publishing, 2008), 120–30.

34. Baginda, *China-Malaysia Relations*, 14–15.

35. Saravanmuttu, *Malaysia's Foreign Policy, the First Fifty Years*, 184.

36. His anti-British stance has a long history and would extend to his relations with the Commonwealth, which saw Malaysia withdraw from two general meetings during the 1980s. Johan Saravanmuttu, "Malaysia's Foreign Policy in the Mahathir Period, 1981–1985: An Iconoclast Come to Rule," *Asian Journal of Political Science* 4, no. 1 (2008), 2.

37. Saravanmuttu, "Malaysia's Foreign Policy," 4.

38. This vision was never realized. He stepped down from the office of prime minister in 2003. But the campaign was an important symbol and rallying point for the country.

39. The grand ambition of creating an ASEAN economic corridor was at the heart of this but became too difficult to achieve. Saravanmuttu, "Malaysia's Foreign Policy," 6.

40. Saravanmuttu, "Malaysia's Foreign Policy," 7.

41. Jörn Dosch, "Mahathirism and Its Legacy in Malaysia's Foreign Policy," *European Journal of East Asian Studies* 13 (2014): 10–11.

42. Dosch, "Mahathirism and Its Legacy," 12–14.

43. Saravanmuttu, *Malaysia's Foreign Policy, the First Fifty Years*, 194.

44. This was expressed through public condemnations of the conflict and saw Malaysia take several thousands of Bosnians (Muslim, as well as non-Muslim) refugees throughout the 1990s. Hamza Karcic, "'One-Way Ticket to Kuala Lumpur': Bosnian Muslims in Malaysia in the Early 1990s," *Indonesia and the Malay World* 42, no. 124 (2014): 400–404.

45. Saravanmuttu, *Malaysia's Foreign Policy, the First Fifty Years*, 235.

46. Waikar, Osman, and Ali, "Dancing with the Ummah," 237.

47. Saravanmuttu, *Malaysia's Foreign Policy, the First Fifty Years*, 244.

48. Waikar, Osman, and Ali, "Dancing with the Ummah," 231.

49. Arash Khazeni, *The City and the Wilderness: Indo-Persian Encounters in Southeast Asia* (University of California Press, 2020).

50. "Universiti Malaya, Tunku Abdul Rahman menyampaikan ijazah kepada Shahanshah di Dewan Tunku Abdul Rahman," January 18, 1968, 2001/0036515W, Arkib Negara Malaysia, Kuala Lumpur.

51. "Yang di Pertuan Agong dan isteri berlepas ke Iran, Kuala Lumpur, Jabatan Penerangan Malaysia," 12 October 1971, 2001/00405073, Arkib Negara Malaysia, Kuala Lumpur.

52. "Santapan tengahari, Yang Di-Pertuan Agong dan Raja Permaisuri Agong meraikan putera dan puteri dari Iran, Istana Negara," August 27, 1973, 2001/10042229W, Arkib Negara Malaysia, Kuala Lumpur; "Puteri Manigeh Pahlavi, Lawakan ke kilang batik, Selangor Baru, Kuala Lumpur," August 28, 1973, 2001/0042233W, Arkib Negara Malaysia, Kuala Lumpur; and "Iran, Putera Gholam Reza Pahlavi, Lawatan ke Stadium Merdeka, Kuala Lumpur," August 27, 1973, 2001/0042231W, Arkib Negara Malaysia, Kuala Lumpur.

53. M. Reza Bayat, "The Malaysia–Iran Relationship," in *Malaysia and the Islamic World*, ed. Abdul Razak Baginda (ASEAN Academic Press, 2004), 166.

54. "Asian Countries Consider Regional Planning," Singapore Government Press Statement, August 19, 1958, YMC/INFS.Au.58/52, National Archives of Singapore.

55. Tobias Ingo Nischalke, "Insights from ASEAN's Foreign Policy Co-Operation: The 'ASEAN Way', a Real Spirit or a Phantom?," *Contemporary Southeast Asia* 22, no. 1 (April 2000): 90.

56. Cyrus Schayegh, "Iran's Global Long 1970s: An Empire Project, Civilisational Developmentalism, and the Crisis of the Global North," in *The Age of Aryamehr: Late Pahlavi Iran and Its Global Entanglements,* Edited by Roham Alvandi (Gingko Library, 2018), 260–62.

57. Robert Steele, "Two Kings of Kings: Iran-Ethiopia Relations Under Mohammad Reza Pahlavi and Haile Selassie," *International History Review* 43, no. 6 (2021): 1376–79.

58. Speech by Dr. Ong Chit Chung, Parliamentary Secretary for Labour, Republic of Singapore, at the 13th Conference of Asian and Pacific Labour Ministers, Tehran, April 21, 1993, Ministry of Information and the Arts, occ19930421s, National Archives of Singapore.

59. "Iran Joins Amity, Coop. Treaty of ASEAN," *Mehr News Agency*, July 7, 2018, https://en.mehrnews.com/news/135469/Iran-joins-amity-coop-treaty-of-ASEAN.

60. Soltaninejad, "Iran and Southeast Asia," 32.

61. Speech by Mr. Lim Hng Kiang, Minister for Trade and Industry at the Iran Business Seminar, December 9, 2004, Singapore, Ministry of Information, Communications and the Arts, 2004120997, National Archives of Singapore.

62. Saleh Adibi, "Vietnam–Iran Relations Developing Comprehensively," World and Viet Nam Report, August 8, 2018, https://acr.ps/1L9zSkB.

63. "Laos-Iran: Signature d'un contrat d'achat-de vende de caoutchouc," [Laos-Iran: Signing of a trade contract for coatchouc] *Agence de Presse Lao*, April 18, 2016, https://acr.ps/1L9zS76; and Pav Suy and Ban Sokrith, "Cambodia, Iran Set to Sign Oil and Gas Deal," *Khmer Times*, September 14, 2015, https://www.khmertimeskh.com/59411/cambodia-iran-set-to-sign-oil-and-gas-deal/.

64. Soltaninejad, "Iran and Southeast Asia," 35.

65. Soltaninejad, "Iran and Southeast Asia," 35.

66. "Shahanshah Iran menunaikan fardhu Jumaat di Masjid Negara, Kuala Lumpur, Jabatan Penerangan Malaysia," 19 January 1968, 2001/0042226W, Arkib Negara Malaysia, Kuala Lumpur.

67. Pertandingan membaca Al-Quran peringkat antarabangsa, perasmian oleh Yang Di-Pertuan Agong, Baginda berramah mesra dengan peserta dari Iran, Stadium Merdeka, Kuala Lumpur, October 15, 1973, 2001/0042323W, Arkib Negara Malaysia.

68. Soltaninejad, "Iran and Southeast Asia."

69. Majid Daneshgar, "The Images of Shah and Khomeini in Indonesia and Malaysia: Honoured or Hated?," *Asian Journal of Middle Eastern and Islamic Studies* 14, no. 2 (2020): 253.

70. Zainal Fakir, "Iran–Iraq berperang: Khomeini–Saddam Hussein buru pengaruh di Teluk Parsi," [Iran-Iraq at war: Khomeini-Saddam Hussein fight for influence in the Persian Gulf] *Mastika*, November 1980, 5–15.

71. Daneshgar, " Images of Shah and Khomeini in Indonesia and Malaysia," 253–54.

72. This can be seen with the establishment of the Supreme Assembly of the Islamic Revolution of Iraq, the Islamic Republic Movement of the Arabian Peninsula, the Islamic Front for the Liberation of Bahrain, and similar groups for Syria and Lebanon. Ramazani, *Independence Without Freedom*, 132.

73. R. Michael Feener and Chiara Formichi, "Debating Shi'ism in the History of Muslim Southeast Asia," in *Shi'ism in Southeast Asia: Alid Piety and Sectarian Constructions*, ed. R. Michael Feener and Chiara Formichi (Oxford University Press, 2015), 12–13.

74. Rodger Shahanan, "Malaysia and Its Shi'a 'Problem,'" Middle East Institute, July 25, 2014, https://www.mei.edu/publications/malaysia-and-its-shia-problem.

75. Toby Matthiesen, *The Caliph and the Imam: The Making of Sunnism and Shiism* (Oxford University Press, 2023).

76. Akbarzadeh and Barry, "State Identity in Iranian Foreign Policy," 628.

77. They are restricted and are unable to open an independent Shi'a mosque or school.

78. "Persidangan antarabangsa mengenai isu Palestin, Perdana Mentreri mengalukan ketibaan timbalan menteri luar negara Hussain Sheikholeslam, Kuala Lumpur," May 5, 1983, 2001/0048236W, Arkib Negara Malaysia, Kuala Lumpur.

79. "National Statement By the Honourable Dato' Seri Anwar Ibrahim Prime Minister of Malaysia at the Extraordinary Arab and Islamic Sumit 11 November 2024 (Monday) Riyadh, Saudi Arabia," Ministry of Foreign Affairs Malaysia, November 11, 2024, https://www.kln.gov.my/web/guest/-/national-statement-by-the-honourable-dato-seri-anwar-ibrahim-prime-minister-of-malaysia-at-the-extraordinary-arab-and-islamic-summit-11-november-202-1.

80. "Iran, Malaysia Jointly Publish Book on Israel's Decline," Bernama–IRNA News, November 25, 2024, https://www.bernama.com/en/world/news.php?id=2367285.

81. Grant Smith and Anthony Di Paola, "Iranian Oil Is Quietly Flooding the Global Market Again," Bloomberg, June 16, 2023, https://www.bloomberg.com/news/articles/2023-06-16/iranian-oil-is-quietly-flooding-into-the-global-market-again.

82. The Iranian diaspora has been the subject of some study. See Navid Fozi, "A Fragmented and Polarized Diaspora: The Making of an Iranian Pluralist Consciousness in Malaysia," *Diaspora: A Journal of Transnational Studies* 21, no. 2 (2021), 231–258.

15

LOOKING BEYOND BEIJING
Iranian Overtures to Indonesia

Fred H. Lawson

November 2022 saw the arrival in Indonesia of two of Iran's most formidable warships. The Islamic Republic of Iran Navy Ship (IRINS) *Makran* and the IRINS *Dena*, an expeditionary force operations vessel and a missile-carrying light frigate, called at the port of Jakarta during the course of an extended familiarization tour of the eastern Indian and southern Pacific oceans.[1] The ships' commanders reportedly met with senior Indonesian naval officers to discuss emerging threats to the security of the surrounding sea lanes and the possibility of setting up a cooperative training program for cadets.

Six months later, President Ebrahim Raisi traveled to Jakarta to confer with Indonesian President Joko Widodo (Jokowi) about a wide range of economic, diplomatic, and cultural matters. The visit resulted in the signing of a dozen bilateral agreements, including a comprehensive preferential trade agreement (PTA) and a wide-ranging memorandum of understanding that committed the two countries to increase collaboration in biomedical research, facilitate technology transfer, and promote joint ventures among public sector enterprises. In addition, the two leaders announced plans for Iranian companies to play a major role in the construction and outfitting of Indonesia's new administrative capital at East Kalimantan on the island of Borneo.[2]

This burst of enthusiasm for forging closer ties to Indonesia reflects Iran's general turn toward the East, as well as its persistent search for attractive commercial and financial opportunities.[3] More specifically, though, it grows out of a convergence of two recent geopolitical developments. First, it constitutes a strategic riposte to a spate of initiatives throughout Southeast Asia on the part of the

Arab Gulf states, in particular Saudi Arabia and the United Arab Emirates (UAE). Second, it lays the foundation for sustained engagement in the heart of the Indo–Pacific arena at a moment when the contest among India, the People's Republic of China (PRC), Australia, Japan, and the United States of America for influence in this extensive region has intensified. Taken together, these trends generated a surge in the level and scope of Iran's Eastward activism during 2022–23.

Iranian Relations with Indonesia Prior to 2022–23

Economic and cultural ties between Iran and Indonesia have existed for more than a millennium. A vibrant community of Iranian merchants resided in the commercial center of Srivijaya as early as the ninth century CE. Trade between the northern Gulf and Southeast Asia flourished during the Safavid era, and became more direct after one of the primary intermediaries in Indian Ocean commerce, the Qutb Shahi principality of southern India, was overrun by the Mughal Empire in the late seventeenth century, prompting most of that principality's Shiite inhabitants to decamp to the territories that now make up Thailand.[4]

Contemporary connections can be traced to the years immediately following the 1980 to 1988 war between Iraq and the newly consolidated Islamic Republic of Iran.[5] The Iranian armed forces tried shortly after the fighting ended to purchase warships manufactured by the Indonesian shipbuilding company PT Penataran Angkatan Laut (PT PAL), but found the sale "blocked by the country which owned the rights to the weapons system that would have been fitted on the vessels."[6] Several attempts by Jakarta to pay for imports of Iranian oil with Indonesian-made dual-use helicopters and transport airplanes were scuttled as well. In June 1993, Indonesia's minister of state for research and technology—who also headed PT PAL and the state-affiliated aircraft company Industri Pesawat Terbang Nusantara (IPTN)—was reported to have offered to supply the Islamic Republic with military boats and Super Puma helicopters, but the deal had been scotched by US officials. A month later, the US Department of State rejected a plan by the Jordanian air force to sell a half-dozen aging F-5 fighter–bombers to the Indonesian air force, at least partly due to Washington's "worries about Indonesia's attempts to sell arms overseas."[7]

Iran's President Ali Akbar Hashemi Rafsanjani journeyed to Indonesia in August 1992 to attend a commemorative gathering of the leaders of the Non-Aligned Movement (NAM) in Bandung. Indonesia's President Suharto returned the favor by stopping in Tehran in November 1993 on his way to the summit of the Asia-Pacific Economic Cooperation in Seattle.[8] Eleven months later, Rafsanjani led a delegation of senior Iranian officials on an official trip to Jakarta and Bandung, whose schedule included a tour of the IPTN assembly plant.[9] At the conclusion of the visit, the two presidents agreed to set up a permanent commission to promote economic cooperation. The two countries subsequently became founding members of the Developing Eight Organization for Economic Cooperation (D-8), which took shape in June 1997 at the instigation of Turkey's Prime Minister Necmettin Erbakan.

It was not, however, until the initial years in office of Iranian President Mahmoud Ahmadinejad that relations started to pick up momentum. Ahmadinejad traveled to Indonesia in May 2006 to attend a D-8 summit meeting in Bali and took the opportunity to give several public addresses. In these speeches, he charged that US opposition to Iran's nuclear research program was part of a broader campaign to keep poorer countries at a disadvantage by preventing them from making technological advances. The events elicited public acclaim and prompted Indonesian President Susilo Bambang Yudhoyono to suggest that the D-8 take steps to investigate US policy toward technological initiatives undertaken by the organization's member states.[10]

Following the visit, the level and value of bilateral trade registered sharp increases.[11] Much of this trade consisted of Iranian exports of hydrocarbons, although manufactured goods made up a substantial proportion of Iran's total contribution as well. In January 2010, a group of Indonesian fishing companies agreed to supply the Islamic Republic with 2,000 tons of tuna as the first step toward augmenting shipments of locally caught fish to the Iranian market. That same year, officials in Tehran finalized plans to design and construct a large-scale oil refinery for Indonesia's national petroleum company, whose eventual output was projected to supply 14 percent of the host country's domestic fuel requirements.[12]

Burgeoning economic relations accompanied closer diplomatic affinity. Even before Ahmadinejad's visit, Jakarta had refused to join Washington's campaign to persuade the United Nations Security Council (UNSC) to punish Tehran for resuming its nuclear research program. Indonesia pointedly abstained in a February 2006 vote to place the matter on the council's agenda. A year later, Jakarta as a recently elected nonpermanent member of the UNSC did its best to modify the provisions of the US-drafted Resolution 1747, which threatened to impose a strict arms embargo and other punitive measures on the Islamic Republic. Indonesian representatives offered amendments to the draft that "affirm[ed] that all parties to the [Non-Proliferation Treaty], including Iran, have the right to develop nuclear technologies for peaceful purposes" and stipulated "that all international sanctions would be removed if Iran complied with the provisions provided in the UNSC resolution," among other things.[13] After the amendments were adopted, Indonesia voted in favor of the resolution.

Jakarta's support for Resolution 1747 provoked a firestorm of criticism at home.[14] President Yudhoyono quickly changed course and openly questioned the UNSC's authority to deal with the matter, making a point of calling Iran's nuclear program "peaceful." When the United States in March 2008 introduced Security Council Resolution 1803, which included even more severe punitive measures on the Islamic Republic, Indonesia voiced strong opposition to the practice of imposing sanctions as a means of changing Iranian policy; it then abstained when the resolution came up for a vote.[15] Jakarta once again objected when the UNSC augmented sanctions against Iran in June 2010, and called for the dispute over the nuclear program to be resolved "through dialogue and negotiations."[16]

Relations between Iran and Indonesia nevertheless plummeted after mid-2010. That February, Indonesian officials had arrested an Iranian citizen for taking part in a scheme to smuggle USD two million worth of methamphetamine into the country; the arrest came on the heels of three dozen earlier arrests of Iranian nationals for drug-related offenses.[17] Meanwhile, Washington was exerting intense pressure on the governments of Southeast Asia to sever ties to the Islamic Republic and comply with the dictates of the UN-mandated sanctions regime. More concretely, the United States placed an assortment of obstacles in the way of routine commercial and financial transactions between Iran and Indonesia. One of the most impactful was the expulsion of Iranian banks from the Society for the Worldwide Interbank Financial Telecommunication (SWIFT) network, the primary mechanism whereby currency is transferred among financial institutions. US officials also managed to block Indonesian producers from exporting one of the country's most profitable agricultural goods (palm oil) to the Iranian market during the winter of 2011–12.[18] The plunge in economic activity between the two countries bolstered Tehran's interest in cultivating more resilient commercial and financial connections with the PRC.[19]

Prospects brightened when Washington accepted the Joint Comprehensive Plan of Action (JCPOA) in the summer of 2015, thereby rescinding most of the sanctions that had been imposed on the Islamic Republic. And they brightened further in the wake of Iranian President Hassan Rouhani's October 2016 tour of Southeast Asia, which included stops in Vietnam, Malaysia, and Thailand.[20] Trade between Iran and Indonesia began to rebound during 2017.[21] At the same time, the two countries' state-affiliated petroleum companies initiated a cluster of joint ventures. A memorandum of understanding between their respective energy ministries opened the door to Iranian projects aimed at renovating and expanding Indonesia's network of electricity generating plants. Some of the refreshed facilities would make use of renewable sources of energy, while others would be reengineered to run on liquefied petroleum gas imported from the Islamic Republic.[22] Bilateral agreements concerning banking practices, the extradition of criminals, and regulations governing private businesses quickly followed.[23]

Relations stagnated again after the United States abruptly abrogated the JCPOA in May 2018, effectively reversing the lifting of economic sanctions on Iran. Excitement at the prospect of attracting investments from Saudi Arabia tempered Jakarta's willingness to strengthen links to the Islamic Republic over the next two years.[24] The Indonesian navy seized an Iranian tanker off the island of Batam in January 2021, and charged that it had been transferring crude oil to smaller ships in order to circumvent UN strictures. For Tehran, however, the termination of the JCPOA heightened the importance of Indonesia as a potential market for Iranian exports and prospective partner in the effort to combat US hegemonism. Iranian officials and cultural institutions found themselves compelled to play down the religious dimensions of their dealings with the country after 2018, as the Saudi presence had generated a rise in anti-Shiite sentiment among local Sunnis.

Iranian Foreign Minister Mohammad Javad Zarif traveled to Jakarta in April 2021 in a bid to reenergize bilateral relations, in particular discussions concerning the PTA.[25] Commercial exchanges between the two countries recovered in the aftermath of the visit.[26] More important, negotiations over the precise terms of the PTA accelerated. A delegation consisting of high-level Indonesian officials traveled to Tehran in May 2022 to hammer out the details of the agreement.[27] Iranian Minister of Industry, Mines and Trade Seyyed Reza Fatemi Amin invited the visitors to make use of the new port at Chabahar as a "regional hub" for Indonesia's future exports to Central Asia and the Caucasus.[28] Iranian officials also proposed transacting business either in national currencies or by means of barter arrangements as a way to bolster trade.[29] That October it was announced that the two governments were just about to put the finishing touches on the PTA by way of online communications.[30]

Relations between Iran and Indonesia therefore exhibited a generally ascending trajectory over the past three decades, despite sporadic plateaus and downturns. Two moments nevertheless stand out as occasions when Tehran exerted an extraordinary amount of energy to forge closer connections with Jakarta. The first came during the early years of the Ahmadinejad presidency, and the second occurred in the winter and spring of 2022–23. In both instances, the Islamic Republic found itself subjected to severe threats from the United States, the UNSC, and the West as a whole. What sets the latter episode apart are concurrent developments in the foreign policies of the Arab Gulf states and in the geopolitics of the Asia–Pacific region, which together bolstered Iran's determination to solidify a strategic alignment with Southeast Asia's largest country.

Arab Gulf States' Initiatives Toward Indonesia

Indonesia has attracted the attention of Saudi Arabia ever since it finally succeeded in detaching itself from the Netherlands in December 1949. Interactions between the two states remained tenuous throughout the decades of the Suharto presidency, however, largely due to Riyadh's links with religious activists who charged the authorities in Jakarta with implementing policies that favored the members of minority Christian communities over the Muslim majority.[31] Not until the turn of the twenty-first century did bilateral relations start to pick up momentum, stimulated by Saudi purchases of large tracts of productive farmland on the islands and Indonesia's sudden transformation from an exporter to an importer of hydrocarbons.

A delegation of senior officials from the Indonesian Ministry of Defense journeyed to Riyadh in March 2011 to explore possibilities for enhanced cooperation in security affairs. The visitors brought with them samples of small arms produced by Indonesian companies, as well as a model of the CN-235 military transport plane that was under development by the state-affiliated aircraft manufacturer PT Dirgantara.[32] The trip laid the foundation for a January 2014 visit to Jakarta by Saudi Arabia's Deputy Minister of Defense Salman bin Sultan bin 'Abd al-'Aziz Al Sa'ud, which was billed as a mission to explore collaborative measures to deal with continuing threats from Islamist militants. The talks eventuated in the signing of a formal agreement that authorized joint "counterterrorism" operations by the two countries' special forces and laid the groundwork for Saudi purchases of various kinds of Indonesian-made weaponry, including the next-generation CN-295 transport plane.[33]

In September 2015, President Jokowi led a delegation of senior Indonesian officials to Riyadh, and then went on to the UAE. During the stop in Abu Dhabi, the delegation worked out an arrangement whereby armaments produced by the Indonesian company PT Pindad would be distributed by the UAE-based military logistics enterprise Continental Aviation Services (CAS), which would facilitate technology transfers to PT Pindad from arms manufacturers in Europe and North America.[34] At the same time, negotiations got underway regarding the UAE navy's purchase of artillery-carrying warships manufactured by PT Pindad. These developments prompted Saudi Minister of Foreign Affairs Adel Al Jubair to hurry to Jakarta to signal Riyadh's commitment to cultivating closer relations. The Saudi and Indonesian governments subsequently pledged to augment bilateral trade by 100 per cent from 2015 to 2020.[35]

In February 2017, two UAE-based defense companies, Abu Dhabi Shipbuilding and International Global Group, signed a contract with PT PAL to work together to design and build frigates and fast patrol boats for the UAE navy, as well as to construct a new military shipyard on the island of Java to handle future orders.[36] This agreement set the stage for the arrival in Jakarta a month later of Saudi King Salman bin 'Abd al-'Aziz, accompanied by 1,500 senior officials, advisers, managers of public sector enterprises, and private businesspeople. The ruler's visit culminated with the promulgation of eleven memorandums of understanding, which dealt with trade, the pilgrimage to Mecca, tourism, scientific and educational cooperation, internal security, and national defense.[37] At the same time, representatives of Saudi public enterprises and private companies agreed to step up investments in construction, medical services, electricity, and tourism, and the Saudi government pledged USD 8.8 billion in official development assistance.[38] King Salman took special care during the trip to dispel deeply entrenched anti-Saudi attitudes among the Indonesian populace by displaying tolerance for women and Christians at ceremonial venues.[39]

Relations between Saudi Arabia and Indonesia stagnated in the wake of Salman's visit. Saudi investments in Indonesia lagged behind its investments in Malaysia and Singapore. Complaints about pervasive mistreatment of and withholding of pay from Indonesian laborers working in the kingdom threw a spanner into the works that caused serious internal damage to the relationship.[40] Not until the autumn of 2018 did the two governments reach an understanding that convinced Jakarta to rescind a moratorium on labor migration to Saudi Arabia. Jokowi conferred with Crown Prince Muhammad bin Salman during the Group of Twenty summit conference in Osaka in June 2019, and the two leaders agreed to revive the moribund Higher Consultative Committee that had been set up a decade earlier to oversee joint economic endeavors.[41] Bilateral trade started to recover in the wake of this decision: Exports of Indonesian rice, coffee, and fish products poured into the Saudi market during 2020–21. Meanwhile, Saudi officials announced plans to increase investments in infrastructural projects on the islands, particularly with respect to the electrical grid and the new administrative capital at Kalimantan.

As relations between Saudi Arabia and Indonesia sagged, the UAE swooped in. UAE Crown Prince Mohamed bin Zayed Al Nahyan visited Jakarta in July 2019 and supervised the awarding of just under USD ten billion in contracts to local companies. Six months later, the two governments signed contracts for goods and services worth almost USD twenty-three billion, including purchases of Indonesian-made weaponry and equipment for the UAE armed forces.[42] Two months after that, they signed a memorandum of understanding to further collaboration in the development of military technology and officer training.[43] March 2021 brought news that the UAE was going to inject USD ten billion into the Indonesia Investment Authority, the state's sovereign wealth fund; the Abu Dhabi Investment Authority then invested another USD 400 million in an

Indonesian state-affiliated enterprise that provided financial backing for local technology start-ups.[44] There were reports as well that a UAE-based defense company had arranged to design and build unmanned aerial vehicles (UAVs) in association with PTT Pindad.

Yet another set of substantial investments by the UAE, this time worth just under USD thirty-three billion, was announced after Jokowi's November 2021 trip to the UAE. The UAE-based seaports management giant DP World agreed to a thirty-year arrangement to upgrade and operate several Indonesian cargo facilities.[45] By the spring of 2022, the UAE had contributed USD ten billion to finance the construction of the new administrative capital, and Crown Prince Mohamed had been appointed chair of the committee supervising the project.[46] The two states concluded a comprehensive economic partnership agreement that July, which UAE officials boasted would triple nonhydrocarbon trade over the next five years.[47]

Competition between Saudi Arabia and the UAE over economic and security connections with Indonesia does not in principle work to the disadvantage of either one. The underlying dynamic is not inherently "zero-sum."[48] In practice, however, the jockeying between these two Arab Gulf states that escalated after 2020 had two important consequences. First, it cracked the united front that had earlier enabled the Arab Gulf states to bargain with the states of Southeast Asia from a position of strength and had dissuaded other extraregional states from challenging their actions in this part of the world. As differences in priorities and conflicts of interest between Saudi Arabia and the UAE became evident, potent rivals—most notably the Islamic Republic of Iran—found opportunities to augment their engagement with the region at the Arab Gulf states' expense.

More important, the peculiar character of the contest between Saudi Arabia and the UAE for ties to Indonesia gave Iran a compelling reason to involve itself more deeply in Southeast Asia. From the outset, the Saudi government emphasized the commercial and financial dimensions of its dealings with Jakarta; the UAE, by contrast, highlighted military connections, even as it devoted substantial amounts of energy and resources to expanding its domestic armaments industry. This difference in concentration left Riyadh's connections with Jakarta subject to the vagaries of the international economy, while putting the UAE on a path that converged with policies favored by the Indonesian authorities.[49] As a result, Saudi relations with Indonesia languished, while the alignment between the UAE and Indonesia quickened.

Because the UAE focused on the production of armaments and the development of new weapons systems in its dealings with Indonesia, the burgeoning partnership posed a serious threat to the security of the Islamic Republic.

Warships, military aircraft, and UAVs manufactured by joint ventures of UAE-based and Indonesia-based companies constituted the type of weaponry that could inflict damage on Iranian territory, whether in retaliation for an attack launched by Tehran or as part of an operation initiated by the UAE. By 2022–23, Iranian policymakers confronted an unpalatable choice between ignoring the consequences of collaborative military–industrial projects that enhanced the capabilities of one of its adversaries or taking steps to counterbalance that adversary's actions. Tehran's incentive to strengthen its security relations with Jakarta soared after Riyadh belatedly announced plans to match the UAE by acquiring Indonesian-built warships.[50]

Geopolitical Developments in the Indo–Pacific

Interstate contention in the oceanic arena that stretches from the Maldive Islands to the East China Sea is structured in several overlapping ways. Most obviously, it entails the responses of the ten member states of the Association of Southeast Asian Nations (ASEAN) and Japan to sustained efforts by the PRC to extend its control over the scattered islands, atolls, and reefs that command the sea lanes of the South China Sea. At the same time, it involves the reactions of the ASEAN states, Japan, Australia, India, and Pakistan to the PRC's ambitious infrastructural project called the Belt and Road Initiative (BRI).[51] It includes as well the countermeasures adopted by the ASEAN states, Australia, the PRC, and the United States to India's push to take a more direct and active part in shaping the affairs of Southeast Asia.[52] And it incorporates the initiatives undertaken by the PRC, the ASEAN states, and Pakistan to the campaign by the United States, Japan, and Australia to preserve the existing order by collaborating more closely with India through the mechanism of the Quadrilateral Security Dialogue, commonly known as the Quad.[53]

Confronted with these overlapping structures of contention, the ASEAN states adopted markedly divergent foreign policies. Vietnam firmly resisted the PRC's territorial ambitions in the South China Sea, while cultivating amicable relations with Beijing regarding the BRI and opening the door to strategic collaboration with New Delhi and Washington;[54] Cambodia allowed the People's Liberation Army Navy (PLAN) to set up a forward base at the port of Ream on the Gulf of Thailand, even as it kept India, the United States, Japan, and Australia at arm's length. It has become commonplace to characterize the policies of the ASEAN states as instances of "hedging," that is, pragmatic admixtures of conciliation and antagonism toward Beijing and Washington, and perhaps vis-à-vis New Delhi, Canberra, and Tokyo as well.[55]

At the very heart of the structures of contention that constitute the Indo-Pacific rests Indonesia. This long-slumbering protagonist in world politics showed signs of reawakening when rivalry between the PRC and the United States heated up during 2017–18. As the growing antagonism between Beijing and Washington threatened to engulf Southeast Asia, policymakers in Jakarta resuscitated the activist conception of nonalignment that had propelled Indonesian foreign policy throughout the 1950s and early 1960s. Nonalignment in this sense entails the notion that Indonesia will take "a proactive role in constructing a more inclusive multipolar regional architecture in the Asia-Pacific region, with the aim of promoting confidence-building measures, preventive diplomacy and cooperative security, and focusing on the development of friendship rather than the identification of enemies." The current version includes an important new twist—the idea "of establishing Indonesia, an archipelagic state, as a global maritime fulcrum (GMF), leveraging its location at the intersection between the Indian and Pacific oceans into something greater than a mere physical presence."[56]

President Jokowi and Foreign Minister Retno Marsudi pushed hard for the other ASEAN states to sign on to Indonesia's vision for the future. These efforts paid off in June 2019, when the organization adopted a manifesto called *ASEAN Outlook on the Indo-Pacific*, which implicitly affirmed Indonesia's leadership in restoring the "centrality" of ASEAN in regional politics.[57] The manifesto went on to call for the inculcation of "the habit of dialogue, of resolving disputes peacefully, and of avoiding the use of force."[58] The program laid out in this document was widely expected to gain traction as soon as Cambodia handed the Chair of ASEAN over to Indonesia in November 2022. US Secretary of Defense Lloyd Austin made a point of meeting with Jokowi two weeks after the transfer took place, and cajoled him to reaffirm Jakarta's security ties with Washington.[59]

Contrary to Washington's expectations, however, Jakarta implemented the GMF doctrine in ways that conformed to its underlying posture of active, multilateral nonalignment. After assuming the presidency in October 2014, Jokowi paid primary attention to projects designed to enhance the infrastructure that could make Indonesia the nexus of transportation and trade in the Indo–Pacific; to support this ambition, he solicited substantial financial and technical assistance from Beijing.[60] Courting PRC investment capital and expertise accompanied a muting of long-standing complaints about PLAN activities in Indonesian territorial waters, as well as in the South China Sea as a whole.[61]

When PLAN warships nevertheless intruded into the disputed area around the Natuna Islands, Jokowi boarded an Indonesian naval vessel and went in person to the area to convene a special meeting of the council of ministers.[62] Indonesian commanders quickly announced plans to augment army, navy, and air force units stationed in the frontier zone.[63] At the same time, however, the president issued "a series of conciliatory statements meant to ensure that the conflict did not escalate. Jokowi himself stated that Indonesia was still hoping to build a strong diplomatic relationship" with the PRC. Minister of Maritime Affairs Luhut Binsar Pandjaitan added that "there were no hostile intentions against China." Luhut's reassurances were echoed by the commander in chief of the armed forces, who pointed out that "all efforts to strengthen defense in Natuna were not a direct action to Beijing, since similar actions were taken in areas throughout Indonesia, such as Biak, Morotai, Sumlaki, and Marauke."[64] Emirza Syailendra describes Jakarta's nuanced response to Beijing's provocative incursions as "an explicit attempt to distinguish between promoting regional stability and not balancing against China."[65]

Jakarta reacted in a similarly nuanced fashion to US initiatives that infringed on Indonesian strategic interests. President Jokowi and Foreign Minister Marsudi both expressed deep misgivings over the reemergence of the Quad at the end of 2017.[66] Three years later, Indonesian officials refused to grant the US Air Force permission for its long-range surveillance planes to use airfields in Indonesia for refueling operations.[67] And Jakarta consistently criticized Washington's conception of "a free and open Indo-Pacific" as being inherently "noninclusive" and skewed in favor of US allies.[68] Meanwhile, Indonesia sharply increased its purchases of US-made armaments and stepped up its collaboration with the United States in the fields of maritime security and cybersecurity. The two states agreed in the spring of 2021 to expand the interoperability of their armed forces, and February 2022 saw Washington authorize the sale of three dozen F-15 fighter-bombers to the Indonesian Air Force.[69]

New Delhi showed a strong affinity to Jakarta's posture of activist, multilateral nonalignment. Indian President Narendra Modi journeyed to Jakarta in May 2018; the two governments took the opportunity to "lay out a joint maritime vision for the Indo-Pacific, in addition to announcing the elevation of the bilateral relationship to a 'comprehensive strategic partnership,' which included the signing of a defense cooperation agreement."[70] Modi's visit set the stage for an unprecedented granting of permission for Indian warships to use the Indonesian naval base on Sabang Island as a forward staging facility.[71] This was followed by the creation of a joint task force to promote economic and security collaboration in the adjacent areas around the (Indian) Andaman-Nicobar Islands and (Indonesian) Aceh.[72]

Strategic collaboration between Indonesia and India accelerated after 2020. The two militaries took steps to improve the interoperability of their weapons and communications systems; joint naval exercises took place on several occasions, including one in the Arabian Sea. In early June 2023, Indian warships took part in the Indonesia-sponsored naval maneuvers designated "Komodo," alongside warships from the PRC, the United States, Japan, Russia, Pakistan, the Republic of Korea, and the Democratic People's Republic of Korea.[73]

Closer ties between New Delhi and Jakarta accompanied a marked deterioration in relations between New Delhi and Tehran. Iranian officials bridled at India's pursuit of commercial, financial, and diplomatic initiatives toward the Arab Gulf states and Israel. The reinstatement of UN-sponsored economic sanctions in late 2018 severely disrupted the flow of Iranian hydrocarbons to the Indian market, and by the spring of 2019 Indian officials reported that the country was no longer receiving shipments of oil from the Islamic Republic.[74] Iran's supreme leader took the extraordinary step of criticizing an aspect of India's domestic politics that summer, when he denounced the Modi government's decision to limit the autonomy of Kashmir. The collapse of bilateral relations led in July 2020 to news that the authorities in Tehran would take over the construction of the railway linking the port at Chabahar to the city of Zahedan from the Indian consortium that had contracted to carry out the project.[75]

Growing estrangement between Iran and India gave policymakers in Tehran an added incentive to pursue closer ties to Indonesia. As New Delhi showed signs of gravitating into the synchronous orbits of the Arab Gulf states and the Quad, Jakarta found its policy of active nonalignment increasingly imperiled. An isolated Indonesia stood little chance of resisting pressure to align itself with one camp or the other in the escalating struggle for influence in the Indo–Pacific. To the extent that the Islamic Republic could encourage the Jokowi government to stay on an independent path, it might be possible to block external powers from exerting control over this newly integrated strategic arena.

Iran's Look to the East policy entails more than just the strengthening of economic and security relations with the People's Republic of China. It even involves more than building connections to Japan and the Republic of Korea, or to Russia and the post-Soviet republics of Central Asia and the Caucasus. The Islamic Republic recognizes the ascendence of the Indo–Pacific as a crucial arena of current and future geopolitical contention, which threatens to attract greater direct involvement on the part of the United States and its allies.

Policymakers in Tehran took steps to meet the twin threats of heightened US activism and escalating great power rivalry in the Indo–Pacific by forging closer links to Indonesia, arguably the one state in the region that championed a consistent policy of active nonalignment. Notable overtures to Jakarta during the winter and spring of 2022–23 were prompted by the consolidation of military connections between Indonesia and the UAE, which appeared likely to enhance the UAE's ability to carry out attacks against Iranian territory. They also reflected broad trends in the geopolitics of the region, which seemed likely to jeopardize

Indonesia's ability to maintain its nonaligned posture. Taken together, these developments gave Iran a strong incentive to boost its efforts to construct a strategic partnership with Indonesia, and thereby buttress a conception of stability in regional affairs that stands in sharp contrast to the notion of "freedom and openness" advanced by the West.

NOTES

1. Patrick Dupont, "Why Was the Iranian Navy in Jakarta?," *Diplomat*, November 18, 2022, https://bit.ly/4kWpqMQ; and Clément Therme, "The Ambitions of the Islamic Republic of Iran in the Pacific," *Lettre du Centre Asie*, no. 104, April 5, 2023, https://bit.ly/4c0iiuO.

2. Achmad Ibrahim and Niniek Karmini, "Iranian Leader Visits Indonesia to Deepen Economic Ties," Associated Press, May 23, 2023, https://acr.ps/1L9zQRH; and Muhammad Zulfikar Rakhmat and Yeta Purnama, "Iran's Growing Ties with Indonesia," Stratsea, June 27, 2023, https://acr.ps/1L9zQkM.

3. See, among many other studies, Anoushiravan Ehteshami and Gawdat Bahgat, "Iran's Asianisation Strategy," in *Iran Looking East: An Alternative to the EU?*, ed. Annalisa Perteghella (ISPI, 2019).

4. Mohammad Soltaninejad, "Iran and Southeast Asia: A Historical Overview of Relations," *International Journal of Asia Pacific Studies* 13, no. 1 (2017): 33–34.

5. On the consolidation of the Islamic Republic, see Mehran Kamrava, *Triumph and Despair: In Search of Iran's Islamic Republic* (Oxford University Press, 2022), especially chapters 2 and 3.

6. Susumu Awanohara, "Weapons of Discord: US Displeased with Jakarta's Arms Transfers," *Far Eastern Economic Review*, August 26, 1993, 24–25.

7. Awanohara, "Weapons of Discord."

8. "Suharto to Attend APEC Summit in Seattle Next Week," United Press International, November 10, 1993, https://acr.ps/1L9zRiN.

9. "Iranian President to Visit Indonesia," United Press International, October 10, 1994, https://acr.ps/1L9zR4w.

10. Maaike Warnaar, *Iranian Foreign Policy During Ahmadinejad: Ideology and Actions* (Palgrave Macmillan, 2013), 128.

11. Soltaninejad, "Iran and Southeast Asia," 37.

12. Soltaninejad, "Iran and Southeast Asia," 39.

13. Iis Gindarsah, "Democracy and Foreign Policy-Making in Indonesia: A Case Study of the Iranian Nuclear Issue, 20087–08," *Contemporary Southeast Asia* 34, no. 3 (December 2012): 421.

14. Gindarsah, "Democracy and Foreign Policy-Making in Indonesia," 417.

15. Soltaninejad, "Iran and Southeast Asia," 40.

16. Mustaqum Adamrha, "RI Calls UN Security Council Sanctions on Iran Ineffective," *Jakarta Post*, June 12, 2010, https://acr.ps/1L9zQJW.

17. Ariel Farrar-Wellman, "Indonesia-Iran Foreign Relations," *Current Threats*, June 28, 2010, https://acr.ps/1L9zQWl.

18. Niluksi Koswanage, "Malaysian Exporters Halt Palm Oil Supply to Iran," Reuters, February 8, 2012, https://acr.ps/1L9zQAq.

19. Soltaninejad, "Iran and Southeast Asia," 42–43.

20. John Calabrese, "Iran's Economic Outreach to Southeast Asia," Middle East Institute, November 15, 2016, https://acr.ps/1L9zQQN.

21. T. M. Kibtiah, A. Rahmasari, D. Novikrisna, S. C. Debora, and C. Raifanda, "Analysis of the Iran-SEA Cooperation (Indonesia-Malaysia-Thailand) in Facing US Economic Sanctions," *IOP Conference Series: Earth and Environmental Science* 729, no. 1 (2021): 4.

22. Kibtiah et al., "Analysis of the Iran-SEA Cooperation," 5.

23. Muhammad Ravi, "The Foreign Policy Objectives of Saudi Arabia and Iran in Indonesia" (master's thesis, Sakarya University, April 2019), 55–56.

24. Maxwell Lowe, "Khomeini in the Archipelago: Iranian Interests and Influence in Indonesia," *Diplomat*, February 15, 2021, https://acr.ps/1L9zQA3.

25. "Indonesia, Iran Discuss Expansion of Ties," *Kayhan*, April 19, 2021, https://acr.ps/1L9zR65.

26. "TPO: Iran Exports to ASEAN Rise 50%," *Kayhan*, September 8, 2021, https://acr.ps/1L9zQNS.

27. Rizwan Rafi Togoo, "Iran's 'Look to the East' Policy: Case Study of Indonesia," *Journal for Iranian Studies* 6, no. 16 (October 2022): 108.

28. "Minister Calls Indonesia to Use Chabahar Port for Exports," *Kayhan*, May 7, 2022, https://acr.ps/1L9zQW3.

29. "Tehran, Jakarta Weigh Plans to Boost Trade Ties," *Kayhan*, May 8, 2022, https://acr.ps/1L9zQY0.

30. "Indonesia and Iran Are in the Final Stages of Completing the PTA Negotiations," IDN Financials, October 6, 2022, https://acr.ps/1L9zQGJ.

31. Yon Machmudi, "Saudi Arabia's Relations with Indonesia," in *Saudi Arabian Foreign Policy: Conflict and Cooperation*, ed. Neil Patrick (I. B. Tauris, 2016); and Sumanto Al Qurtuby and Shafi Aldamer, "Saudi-Indonesian Relations: Historical Dynamics and Contemporary Development," *Asian Perspective* 42, no. 1 (2018): 128–29.

32. Ahmad Zainal Mustofa, "Defense Diplomacy of Indonesian [sic] and Saudi Arabia as a Development of Indonesian Military Strength," *Jurnal Diplomasi Pertahanan* 8, no. 2 (2022): 36.

33. Ankit Panda, "Indonesia and Saudi Arabia Sign Defense Cooperation Agreement," *Diplomat*, January 25, 2014, https://acr.ps/1L9zQo6; and Mustofa, "Defense Diplomacy," 37.

34. Prashanth Parameswaran, "Indonesia Weapons Firm Inks New Defense Deal with UAE," *Diplomat*, September 18, 2015, https://acr.ps/1L9zQkB.

35. Al Qurtuby and Aldamer, "Saudi-Indonesian Relations," 136.

36. Prashanth Parameswaran, "Indonesia, UAE Ink New Naval Shipbuilding Deals," *Diplomat*, February 25, 2017, https://acr.ps/1L9zQrL.

37. Mohammad Amin Fauzi, Obsatar Sinaga, Arry Bainus, and R. Widya Setiabudi Sumadinata, "Indonesian Foreign Relations with Saudi Arabia during the Joko Widodo Government," *Journal of Pharmaceutical Negative Results* 13, no. 1 (2022): 1709; Sumanto Al Qurtuby, "King Salman's Historic Visit to Indonesia: Mirror of a Changing Saudi Arabia," Middle East Institute, January 16, 2018, https://acr.ps/1L9zRlt; and Siwage Dharma Negara, "The Impact of Saudi King's Vitis to Indonesia," *ISEAS Perspective*, no. 16 (2017), https://acr.ps/1L9zRd8.

38. Nivell Rayda, "Joko moans over 'only $8.8bn,'" *Australian*, April 15, 2017, https://acr.ps/1L9zQXl.

39. Al Qurtuby, "King Salman's Historic Visit"; and Al Qurtuby and Aldamer, "Saudi-Indonesian Relations," 139.

40. Muhammad Zulfikar Rakhmat, "Developments in Indonesian-Saudi Relations Under President Joko 'Jokowi' Widodo," King Faisal Center for Research and Islamic Studies, June 2022, 10, https://acr.ps/1L9zQAk.

41. Rakhmat, "Developments in Indonesian-Saudi Relations," 14.

42. "Indonesia, UAE Sign Business Deals Worth About $23 Billion: Widodo," Reuters, January 13, 2020, https://acr.ps/1L9zQDL; and Muhammad Zulfikar Rakhmat and Yeta Purnama, "Indonesia Looks to the UAE for Military Cooperation," *Diplomat*, March 31, 2022, https://acr.ps/1L9zRcw.

43. Rakhmat and Purnama, "Indonesia Looks to the UAE."

44. Robert Mason, "Revitalized Interactions Between the Gulf and Indonesia," Middle East Institute, February 10, 2022, https://acr.ps/1L9zQK8.

45. Narayanappa Janardhan, "Thriving UAE-Indonesia Ties Highlight Potential in Southeast Asia," Arab Gulf States Institute in Washington, July 2022, https://acr.ps/1L9zQpN.

46. Janardhan, "Thriving UAE-Indonesia Ties"; and Muhammad Zulfikar Rakhmat and Yeta Purnama, "The Growing China-Indonesia-UAE Trilateral Relations," *Diplomat*, February 22, 2022, https://acr.ps/1L9zQns.

47. Alexander Cornwell, "Indonesia and United Arab Emirates Reach Trade Pact," Reuters, July 1, 2022, https://acr.ps/1L9zRgv; and Janardhan, "Thriving UAE-Indonesia Ties."

48. Timothy Bettis, "The Emerging Contours of Saudi-Emirati Competition in Southeast Asia," *Diplomat*, June 27, 2023, https://acr.ps/1L9zQsI.

49. Prashanth Parameswaran, "An Indonesian Defense Revolution Under Jokowi?" *Diplomat*, January 30, 2015, https://acr.ps/1L9zQAs; and Prashanth Parameswaran, "Indonesia Spotlights Defense Industry Challenge Under Jokowi," *Diplomat*, March 10, 2018, https://acr.ps/1L9zQPl.

50. Muhammad Zulfikar Rakhmat, "The China-Brokered Iran-Saudi Peace Deal: Implications for Indonesia," *Diplomat*, April 17, 2023, https://acr.ps/1L9zQw4.

51. See, for example, Jean-Marc F. Blanchard, ed., *China's Maritime Silk Road Initiative and Southeast Asia: Dilemmas, Doubts, and Determination* (Palgrave Macmillan, 2019).

52. See Amitava Acharya, "India's 'Look East' Policy," in *The Oxford Handbook of Indian Foreign Policy*, ed. David M. Malone, C. Raja Mohan, and Srinath Raghavan (Oxford University Press, 2015); and Frederic Grare, *India Turns East: International Engagement and US-China Rivalry* (Oxford University Press, 2017).

53. T. M. Hui and N. Hussain, "Quad 2.0: Sense and Sensibilities," *Diplomat*, February 23, 2018, https://acr.ps/1L9zQpQ.

54. David Brewster, "India's Strategic Partnership with Vietnam: The Search for a Diamond on the South China Sea?," *Asian Security* 5, no. 1 (2009): 24–44.

55. Among a very large number of studies, see See Seng Tan, "Consigned to Hedge: South-East Asia and America's 'Free and Open Indo-Pacific' Strategy," *International Affairs* 96, no. 1 (January 2020): 131–48; and Hunter S. Marston, "Navigating Great Power Competition: A Neoclassical Realist View of Hedging," *International Relations of the Asia-Pacific* 24, no. 1 (2024): 29–63.

56. Dewi Fortuna Anwar, "Indonesia and the ASEAN Outlook on the Indo-Pacific," *International Affairs* 96, no. 1 (January 2020): 113. See also Edna Caroline, "Indonesia's Global Maritime Forum: From Hedging to Underbalancing," *Journal of Asian Security and International Affairs* 8, no. 3 (2021): 413–32.

57. Irfan Ardhani, Randy W. Nandyatama, and Rizky Alif Alvian, "Middle Power Legitimation Strategies: The Case of Indonesia and the ASEAN Outlook on the Indo-Pacific," *Australian Journal of International Affairs* 77, no. 4 (2023): 359–79.

58. Anwar, "Indonesia and the ASEAN Outlook," 125.

59. Laura Southgate, "Indonesia's ASEAN Chairmanship: Promoting ASEAN Relevance in 2023?" *Diplomat*, January 19, 2023, https://acr.ps/1L9zQpa.

60. Emirza Adi Syailendra, "A Nonbalancing Act: Explaining Indonesia's Failure to Balance Against the Chinese Threat," *Asian Security* 13, no. 3 (2017): 242–43. See also

Tirta Nugraha Mursitama and Yi Ying, "Indonesia's Perception and Strategy Toward China's OBOR Expansion: Hedging with Balanging," *The Chinese Economy* 54, no. 1 (2021): 35–47; and "Indonesia, China Sign US$23.3 Billion Cooperation Contracts Under Belt and Road," Antara News, April 14, 2018, https://acr.ps/1L9zR1g.

61. Syailendra, "A Nonbalancing Act," 243.
62. Syailendra, "A Nonbalancing Act," 247.
63. Patrik Kirsthope Meyer, Achmad Nurmandi, and Agustiyara Agustiyara, "Indonesia's Swift Securitization of the Natuna Islands: How Jakarta Countered China's Claims in the South China Sea," *Asian Journal of Political Science* 27, no. 1 (2019): 70–87.
64. Syailendra, "A Nonbalancing Act," 247.
65. Syailendra, "A Nonbalancing Act," 248.
66. Vibhanshu Shekhar, "Indonesia's Great-Power Management in the Indo-Pacific: The Balancing Behavior of a 'Dove State,'" *Asia Policy* 17, no. 4 (October 2022): 127–28.
67. Sebastian Strangio, "Indonesia Rebuffs US Request to Host Spy Planes: Report," *Diplomat*, October 20, 2020, https://acr.ps/1L9zQwd.
68. Shekhar, "Indonesia's Great-Power Management," 140.
69. Shekhar, "Indonesia's Great-Power Management," 138.
70. Geoffrey F. Gresh, "The New Great Game at Sea," War on the Rocks, December 8, 2020, https://acr.ps/1L9zRgw; and Mustafa Izzudin and Ankush Ajay Wagle, "India and Indonesia: Constructing a Maritime Partnership," Institute of South Asian Studies, April 9, 2019, https://acr.ps/1L9zRa3.
71. Fahlesa Munabari, Diandri Filani Buani, Rizky Ihsan, and Nadia Utami Larasati, "Hedging Against Giants: Indonesia's Strategy Towards India and China in the Indian Ocean," *Politik Indonesia* 6, no. 3 (December 2021): 295.
72. Vibhanshu Shekhar, "The Sabang and Aceh-Andamans Initiatives: Beyond Base Access and Balancing," National Maritime Foundation, August 20, 2020, https://acr.ps/1L9zQVe.
73. Frega Wenas Inkiriwang, "Multilateral Naval Exercise Komodo: Enhancing Indonesia's Multilateral Defence Diplomacy?," *Journal of Current Southeast Asian Affairs* 40, no. 3 (2021): 418–35.
74. Nicolas Blarel, "Modi Looks West? Assessing Change and Continuity in India's Middle East Policy Since 2014," *International Politics* 59, no. 1 (2022): 105.
75. Blarel, "Modi Looks West?"

Part VI
IRAN AND A NEW WORLD ORDER?

16

IRAN'S LOOK EAST POLICY AND THE EMERGING NEW WORLD ORDER

Diana Galeeva

The fundamental transformations of the world order that have been kick-started by the Ukraine war, including the rebalancing of power, alignments, and policies, have also strengthened the significance of the widespread "Look East" policy among various states. It has been captured by Iran's Supreme Leader Ayatollah Ali Khamenei as "preferring East over West." It has been repeatedly restated in anticipation of the US withdrawal from the Joint Comprehensive Plan of Action (JCPOA) and following the election of President Ebrahim Raisi in 2021. Iran's attitude has been echoed by announcements from China and Russia that they will "set an example of a responsible world power and play a leading role," which is often interpreted as seeking to reduce economic interdependence with the West, and specifically to redirect energy deals from the West toward the East.[1] Politically, the policy has contributed to the expansion of bloc-to-bloc cooperation among non-Western countries, especially between the BRICS countries and the member states of the Shanghai Cooperation Organization (SCO). This chapter addresses a difficult but crucial analysis: Under the auspices of the "Look East" policy, how does Iran's collaboration with China and Russia challenge the "liberal world order," and how a new world order may be emerging from these alliances? The chapter will approach these questions by discussing the emergence of current and probable Eastern alignments through commonalities in politics, economics, and governance. Within this context, the role and influence of Iran is particularly important, and we must understand what "Looking East" means—and will mean—for a key regional power.

From an interpretivist methodological position, this chapter's originality lies in its attempt to offer a picture of what is undeniably a factor in the emerging world order, built by the triangle of Iran, China, and Russia. These states are united in their "Oriental" civilization, and their cooperation is strengthened under Iran's declared policy of favoring the East. To achieve these objectives, the data collected includes structured interviews with political stakeholders, in addition to a broad secondary literature in both Russian and English. To outline key features of this emerging world order, based on analyses of the policies of Iran's alignment with Russia and China, the chapter first discusses the key elements of the idea of a "liberal world order." It then evaluates the existing critique of this order in the literature alongside practical examples taken primarily from the "Look East" policies between Iran, China, and Russia. Second, the chapter evaluates the roles of both China and Russia in Iran's policy in order to outline the broad contours of an emerging nexus around an alternative world order. Finally, it underlines the elements on which these countries rely in appears to be a shared vision. These elements, the chapter argues, are largely reactions to the challenges presented by well-established elements of the liberal world order—democracy, international institutions, and economic interdependence—rather than real and substantive alternatives.

The "Liberal Order": The Concept and Its Critique

The post–Cold War world lives under a "liberal world order," a process of globalization dominated by Western and especially American practices and values, among the most prominent of which are democracy, market capitalism, and multilateralism.[2] In *Liberal Leviathan*, John Ikenberry connects the philosophical underpinnings of the liberal order to the ideas of Adam Smith, Immanuel Kant, and John Locke.[3] According to Ikenberry, the first component of the liberal world order is commercial liberalism, which dates back to Adam Smith. Capitalism and markets establish economic interdependence, shared interests, joint gains, and enticements for global cooperation. The second element of liberal order emerges from Kant's view of democratic peace theory. A third dimension is based on Lockean ideas of rights and the rule of law, which were largely responsible for the development of what is often called "liberal institutionalism." Institutions and international law are consequences of liberal communities that build rule-based obligations and expectations between them.[4]

These three elements, Ikenberry maintains, reinforce each other, as liberal democracies are able to overcome the insecurities generated by anarchical order.

Trade and other forms of exchange are equally valuable across the liberal democratic world. These and other similar interconnections establish incentives and stakeholders for the extension of a stable global order. International institutions, in sum, contribute to cooperation and exchange.[5]

Ikenberry also poses the possibility of a breakdown of this liberal world order. This might occur if the order were to become significantly less open and rule-based. The system of multilateral trade could collapse into a 1930s-style world of regional blocs, mercantilism, and bilateral pacts.[6] Security and political institutions, and rules of the US-led hegemonic internationalism, could also fragment into competing geopolitical blocks. Ikenberry maintains that:

> Such a breakdown does not necessarily need to entail a complete collapse of order—it simply means there is an end to its open, rule-based, multilateral character. The American hegemonic order could simply yield to an international system where several leading states or centers of power—for example, China, the United States, and the European Union—establish their own economic and security spheres.

He further clarifies:

> The global order would become a less unified and coherent system of rules and institutions, while regional orders emerge as relatively distinct, divided, and competitive geopolitical spheres.[7]

Ikenberry concludes that "some observers describe a coming fragmentation of the American-centered unipolar order as a 'return to multipolarity' ... The unipolar distribution of power could shift toward a system in which two or three states become peers. Or power could diffuse even more widely into the hands of many states—perhaps a dozen or more—that possess similar shares of world material capabilities."[8] In other words, an open and rule-based world order might survive this shift in power, and "it might be reinforced by the return of a group of leading states."[9]

A further step, a shift from unipolarity to rival poles, is what many observers mean by a return to multipolarity.[10] The final step in this process would be the emergence of a balance-of-power and security competition between these poles. "This is the classic system of rival great powers dividing the world into competing spheres and geopolitical blocks. The great powers are not just rival poles but also competing for security."[11] Simply put, Ikenberry's relevant contribution can be summarized as follows: "We are witnessing a passing of the American era, a return to multipolarity, and the rise of rival non-liberal order-building projects."[12]

"Rival poles" may have already emerged at the state level and increasingly interconnected relations between them, as in those that have developed between

Iran and other "Eastern" countries such as China. To this add Russia, which, even prior to the Ukraine war, had claimed that the current liberal global order is in a state of systematic crisis. Russia had earlier announced, in 2016, that the era of "pax Americana" had come to an end.[13] Further, Anne L. Clunan believes that narrowing the conduits of existing neoliberal globalization. It appears consistent with boosting the interests of "Russia First," "Nigeria First," "Japan First," "Iran First," "India First," "France First," "China First," "Britain First," "Brazil First," "Arabia First," or "America First" over and against "the existing liberal order." While Ikenberry clearly identifies the components of the liberal world order, he does not explain the development of each element either theoretically or practically.

As an example, he maintains that "The interconnected relations between the three states of Iran, China and the United States cannot be fully explained by the two contemporary dominant schools of international relations, that is, neorealism and neoliberalism."[14] This argument is common in discussions of an emerging alternative world order, as, for example, Robert Kaplan's argument that the vital characteristics of the new world (dis)order include a "coming anarchy." Based on this view, Georg Sorensen summaries that "the present world order is more liberal than it ever was, but this has opened up tensions in liberalism that were much less pronounced in earlier periods."[15] Similarly, since the collapse of the Soviet Union, "Russian elites have struggled to find an alternative to liberal triumphalism—some kind of international architecture that places them within the West, yet allows them the distinctiveness of their long history as a global rule-maker."[16] This invites the question, even if the liberal world order has been in decline, what kind of an alternative order is emerging, and what components is it based on? How, in the context of this discussion, does Iran's Look East policy fit into this alternative order?

Sorensen also focuses on this question, stating that limited agreement on the key features of (any) world order has contributed to a substantial extent of misperception among intellectuals and politicians. Sorensen raises very timely questions:

> What kind of order is emerging now? Is it the "liberal moment" a multipolar balance of power and a new round of potentially hostile competition between states; a "clash of civilizations"; "Jihad vs. McWorld"; "the coming anarchy"; the "return of history"; or some combination of all this, or perhaps something entirely different, even a really "New world order". The diversity of propositions demonstrates the confusion regarding the issue of world order. On the other hand, there are a significant number of radically diverging views about the makeup of the present order; on the other hand there are people who think that lack of order is what characterises the present period.[17]

From all these interpretations, Iran's Look East policy aligns closely with—or perhaps responds most deeply to—Samuel Huntington's "the West and the Rest" argument.[18] Huntington's thesis[19] about a "clash of civilizations" is often understood by non-Westerners as a conceptual shorthand.[20] It is ultimately a theoretical paradigm that has been transformed into a tool for particular ideological goals.[21] It applies mostly to a Western perspective serving Western interests.[22] Amitav Acharya believes that global international relations should surpass "the divide between the West and the Rest" to understand many methods of agency that hold local constructions of global order and respect diversity. Similarly, Andrew Phillips, Christian Reus-Smit, and Samir Saran question the idea of international order as mainly "Western." Instead, they stress a global approach to history, historical interpretations, and cultural diversity in international politics. They argue that relations within a liberal world have not primarily emphasized the agency of "non-West," and/or Global South in their contributions to the world order, and they also have problems with categories such as the "West."[23] In other words, there are many prevailing perspectives that suggest the world order should also be understood from "non-Western" points of view, in the face of mainstream theoretical assumptions. This is relevant to the notion of an emerging world order based on Iran's perspectives as a case study, accounting for its dialogues with other countries that follow a similar course toward the "East"; the "clash of civilizations," whatever its original positionality, has been harnessed in multiple ways to this narrative of shift.

Massimo Buscema, Guido Ferilli, and Pier Luigi Sacco argue that the clash of civilizations theory is not a primarily convincing method to systematically deal with world order matters.[24] It has, however, shown itself to be a powerful political myth, that is, it has become a political agenda rather than a logical hypothesis with particular empirical correlates and solid scientific goals.[25] Huntington's original argument is as follows:

> The fundamental source of conflict . . . will not be primarily ideological or primarily economic. The great divisions among humankind and the dominating source of conflict will be cultural. Nation states will remain the most powerful actors in world affairs, but the principal conflicts of global politics will occur between nations and groups of different civilizations. The clash of civilizations will dominate global politics. The fault lines between civilizations will be battle lines of the future.[26]

In Huntington's analysis, a civilization is viewed as "the broader cultural entity." He suggests "seven or eight" main civilizations. Critics questions these divisions, most especially because Huntington cherry-picked common cultural forms within a variety of communities. Moreover, he is "himself in doubt as to whether there is an African civilization, perhaps because he considers religion a central defining characteristic of civilizations and there is not a religion shared by all Africans. Such identities are much more diverse, and religion is not necessarily their primary core, whether in Europe, Africa, or China."[27] This might suggest some limitations to the theory, but, within the context of this chapter, the essential point about existing groups of countries certainly has mileage. Considering collaborations emerge between "Oriental" powers, including Russia, China and India—which are to some degree based on a shared identity unified through "Look East" policies—an alternative order might be needed in analyses on their foreign policies. For this reason, the next section will particularly focus on the nexus of China, Iran, and Russia to view the foundations of the emergence of this "Oriental pole."[28]

China–Iran–Russia Nexus: Part of Tehran's "Look East" Approach

Following the Iranian revolution, a policy of "neither East nor West" was adopted as part of the state's diplomacy. Based on Khamenei's interpretation, Iran should thus protect itself from entering into a relationship of dependence with any superpowers, specifically at a time of intense competition between the United States and the former Soviet Union.[29] But the collapse of the Soviet Union and changing global alignments eventually necessitated a change in Iranian foreign policy orientation.[30] The Mahmoud Ahmadinejad administration, in office from 2005 to 2013, initially introduced the "Look East" policy. The rationale for the policy was to counter the pressure of Western sanctions on the country by forging closer ties with "Oriental powers," especially Russia, China, and India. Its main goal was to deal with pressure from the Western powers and the United States.[31] When the Donald Trump administration formally launched a "maximum pressure campaign" against Iran, Tehran formally codified the Look East policy.

A broader shift of world power toward the East, especially through China's economic weight, and its importance in the world energy market, has continued. As Hongda Fan argues: "the look East approach is no longer just seen by Tehran as a tool to counter US sanctions, but also as an opportunity for Iran to participate in reshaping the regional and even global structure."[32]

China gradually came to play a central role in Iran's Look East policy.[33] Seyed Shamseddin Sadeghi and Kamran Lotfi argue that in the face of European and American sanctions, the Look East policy has emerged as a key concept in Iran's foreign policy, and one that encouraged increasing Eastward-looking thinking. First, Iran's "Look to the East" and China's "march West" seem to be congruent and mutually beneficial moves.[34] A second factor has been the growing role of China, versus declining Western powers. Chinese military, political, and economic weight is now able to rival, and arguably undermine Western power and influence. Barry Buzan describes this as a "post-western international order."[35] Regarding this "Westless world," Buzan argues:

> We are quite radically entering a new phase in which the West is no longer going to be the completely dominant power center behind international society. In some ways, we might look at this as a return to the world that once existed before modernity, global interdependence and the shrunken planet. Before the 19th century, in particular before the 16th century, the world was fairly loosely connected. And yet, amongst those connections, the distribution of power was fairly equal. So China, India and the Islamic world were all centers of power in their own right. We are now returning to something like that more equal world, but now with all of these centers of power closely connected and highly interdependent. This is really big change. I now use the label "deep pluralism" to describe this emerging world order.[36]

Within this context, Iran's choice of China as a close friend was calculated move. It also fits the general thrust of the "Look East" policy.

The Iranian leadership's interest also includes Russia in this policy, through a combination of Orientalizing narratives and timely connections. For example, in a letter sent to President Vladimir Putin on February 8, 2021, Khamenei said:

> Undoubtedly, the 21st century is the century of Asia. The Islamic Republic has always paid attention to Asia. There are many important and still untapped capacities in Asian countries such as Russia, China, India, Malaysia, Indonesia and subcontinental countries and as a result, we could exploit them due to our common interests with such countries in Asia... We should prefer the east to the west and neighbouring countries to distant countries in order to safeguard the national interests of our country.[37]

Russia and Iran share anti-Western sentiment, which has further united them toward an "East" policy. Ghoncheh Tazmini argues that the current Iranian–Russian alliance has revealed tensions between their overlapping cultural–civilizational identities and the drive to "catch up with the West."[38] She also reminds us of historic resistance in both Iran and Russia to the adoption of Western institutions. For example, Slavophiles have often believed that Russia was destined to preserve the purity of Christianity, to bring the various Christian churches together, and to usher in the thousand-year global Kingdom of God. This special sense of destiny was based on the "Russian idea" that openly espoused a rejection of Western culture, political systems, and models of modernization. Tazmini concludes that the Russian idea, especially the notions of Russian uniqueness (*samobytnost'*), statehood (*gosudarstvennost*), and community (*sobornost*), form the basis of Putin's discourse of the Russian state. She compares this Slavophile Russian position—which argues that Russia's future depends on a return to native principles for "Overcoming the Western disease"—with the emergence in the 1960s of Third World postcolonial narratives introduced by Iranian intellectuals such as Jalal al-Ahmad, who theorized about widespread "Westoxication" of Iranian politics and society because of imperialism.

The same distaste for Westoxication can be seen in the current leadership's view. In January 2022, in the shadow of the buildup of the Ukraine crisis, the late President Raisi visited Moscow and met with Putin, calling for closer collaboration to counter pressure from the United States. Raisi told the Russian president, "Just like you, we have also stood up against US sanctions from 40 years ago. . . . Today's exceptional circumstances require significant synergy between our two countries against US unilateralism."[39] Raisi viewed NATO with similar disdain. In his address to State Duma members, Raisi claimed that he expected Western states to continue following an expansionary policy. "NATO penetrates into different countries using various pretexts and covers. NATO's agenda includes imposition of the Western model and opposition to independent democracies, rejection of identity of the nations, culture and traditions."[40] This closely reflects the view of the Russian leadership. Putin once called the collapse of the Soviet Union as "the greatest geopolitical disaster of the 20th century." As one observer has noted, "he was going to bring all of Ukraine back into Russia's fold; he was going to expand Russia's influence throughout Eastern and Central Europe; he was going to fracture, if not force the collapse of NATO."[41] In September 2022, Putin also blasted what he called American attempts to preserve its worldwide domination, stating that "the objective development toward a multipolar world faces resistance from those who try to preserve their hegemony in global affairs and control everything—Latin America, Europe, Asia and Africa. . . . the hegemony has succeeded in doing so for quite a long time, but it can't go on forever . . . regardless of the developments in Ukraine."[42] The very similar discourses of both leadership between Russia and Iran based on common assumptions of Western imperial design can be seen as a basis on which alliances can be built, drawing on shared identities.

Expert analysis also demonstrates this view, as Sanam Vakil of Chatham House shared with the author:[43]

> Despite historical tensions, the shared experience of Western sanctions and isolation coupled with their paranoid worldview brings Russian

and Iranian policy elites together in more determined anti-Western security-based cooperation. Both states are deeply focused on pushing back against Western pressure and motivated by this shared concept of resistance. Their mutual experience affords Moscow and Tehran with an opportunity to deepen economic and security-based exchanges.[44]

While this can lead to enlarged economic and security-based relations, "leaders in Tehran and Moscow see the Iran-Russia partnership as increasingly necessary to advance Iranian and Russian interests amid a period of accelerating East-West bifurcation."[45] In other words, stressing Western imperial designs and expansionism helps to build an alternative view of the East. The Ukraine war marks a crucial and highly visible moment in this rejection of Western interdependence. As one expert has reflected on Iran and Russia, "two counties have invested efforts into strategizing ways to circumvent US- and EU-imposed sanctions in a bilateral capacity while working to establish an antihegemonic geopolitical order in which the US is a far weaker country."[46] These efforts can be seen particularly in the growing number of regular personal visits. In 2022, Putin met with Raisi on a number of occasions, as part of both multilateral and bilateral relations.

The Iranian–Russian alliance is emerging as a crucial dimension of a developing challenge the existing liberal world order. As we have seen, however, rather than suggesting any new, concrete steps, for now this and other similar partnerships have been largely based on only an expressed desire to challenge the well-established elements of liberal order as outlined by Ikenberry.

An Emerging World Order as Challenger to the Liberal World Order

The "Look East" policy puts Iran, along with Russia and China, on a course that implicitly challenges some of the cornerstones of the liberal world order. The first agenda then is opposing democracy with autocracy. In her analyses of the myth of a Russia–China–Iran "axis," Nicole Grajewski argues that development of the alternative world order for these three countries is based on the rejection of the validity of ostensible "liberal" norms via "civilizational essentialization" and counter-norm entrepreneurship.[47] Scholars agree that among the components through which Russia and Iran have been countering the US-led order is the promotion of autocracy versus democracy. This is also one of the key foundations of their bilateral relations, which Abdolrasool Divsallar calls "standing back-to-back for regime security."[48] He explains that:

> Russia has no agenda for regime change in Iran, but like the Iranian leadership, it sees the expansion of Western values and political structure as

a threat. Both states perceive Western values like freedom of speech and human rights as a security threat, endangering their state identity, civilizational narratives, and regime stability. In addition, elites on both sides view internal order as the state's top priority and share a similar view on means of fighting Western intervention.

Secondly, among the key features of the liberal order is international organizations. In this regard, the ongoing expansion of bloc-to-bloc cooperation among non-Western countries aims to become a counterweight to the influence of the United States and well-established, powerful blocs such as NATO or the European Union. Iran applied to join China and Russia in BRICS in June 2022, in addition to the SCO (Kazakhstan, China, Kyrgyzstan, Russia, Tajikistan, Uzbekistan, India, and Pakistan).[49] At the last SCO summit in Samarkand, Iran signed a memorandum of obligation to join the organization. As Grajewski explains, "Iran's full accession to the SCO—a process that could take up to two years once formally set in motion—should be viewed in the context of Tehran's efforts to expand its ties to both Russia and China rather than the realization of an alliance."[50] The Ukraine war has thus brought bilateral collaborations to "new levels."[51] While Elvira Nabiullina traveled to Iran, Russian Prime Minister Mikhail Mishustin signed a series of bilateral agreements to deepen investment in trade, promote agricultural exports, and boost sports cooperation as an immediate response to the new wave of sanctions.[52]

Finally, the most striking efforts to oppose the liberal world order are those linked with severing economic connections with the West. This can be discussed in the context of the "Eastern excursion," as the most sanctioned states—Iran and Russia—have had to overcome limitations. In the process, they have had to overcome the weight and the global reach of the US economy. Ongoing sanctions are also a key driver for closer cooperation between the two countries. Iran and Russia have sought to more closely link their banking and financial systems, and have begun to use both their national currencies for energy and trade payments. In December, Russia's second-largest bank, VTB, became the first Russian bank to offer money transfers in Iranian rials.[53] According to Russia's *Kommersant* newspaper, the bank will charge a 1 percent commission for moving up to $300,000 USD (twenty million rubles) to an Iranian bank account, with the transfer completed in one business day. The speaker of the State Duma, Vycheslav Volodin, noted in January 2023 that the share of the ruble and the real value of mutual settlements in national currencies with Iran already exceeds 60 percent.[54] This move is not surprising, since Russia and China have strategically deployed "dedollarization" and since 2014 have been shifting away from relying on the US dollar as the primary currency for financial transactions.[55]

Iran has become instrumental in this process of dedollarization, as it also seeks to avoid stringent sanctions imposed by the West. In 2021, before the Ukraine war started, Irina Khominich and Samira Alikhani of the Plekhanov Russian University of Economics argued that since both Iran and Russia are under sanctions, they could support each other's development by pursuing strategies such as reducing dependency on the dollar, developing bilateral economic relations, and avoiding trade barriers.[56] The recent wave of sanctions by the Group of Seven countries resulted in Nabiullina making an exceptional, urgent visit to Tehran to meet with the governor of the Central Bank of Iran.[57] The two discussed bilateral trade, banking cooperation, and expanding currency transactions between Russia and Iran. This meeting deserves closer attention for several reasons. This was the first time that the head of Russia's Central Bank visited Iran. Nabiullina's involvement was also notable as a rare instance of a Russian woman's involvement in diplomacy. Furthermore, as a Tatar Muslim, Nabiullina chose to wear the hijab during the meeting out of respect and as part of her Muslim identity. This focus on shared Muslim identity has also proven to be an effective tool in Russia–Iran relations.[58]

Examining Iran's "Look East" policy seems particularly valuable not solely in understanding the course of its foreign policy objectives, but also in seeing how and why it attempts to challenge well-established elements of the liberal world order. Within the theoretical context, this fits a shift toward the "old" debate—no one seems to have created a better debate—on liberalism versus constructivism, or an amplification of a "clash of civilizations" theory to contrast with liberal underpinnings of homogeneity. In this regard, the so-called Oriental narrative that for now seems to have united the trio of Iran, Russia, and China further contributes to their respective (and not identical) challenges to the well-established liberal world order, along with its key components, namely democracy, international institution, market capitalism, and economic interdependence with the West. Democracy has been challenged by autocracy; liberal international institutions have been challenged by regional bodies such as the SCO and BRICS, in which Russia and China play crucial roles; and economic interdependence with the West has become a necessity, hugely emphasized by the fallout from the Ukraine war. These countries have become each other's key partners in developing policies of dedollarizations, building alternative financial systems, and increasing economic collaborations that are not open to the traditionally dominant West. It is an ongoing process that combines political and cultural narratives as well as economic opportunism. "Look East" provides a common thread between the policies, and fuels a vision of an emerging world order to challenge a declining liberal hegemony. However, rather than creating something genuinely new, it is notable that the messaging is largely reactionary against facets of liberality. This reveals to a degree that looking East is to a large extent pragmatic rather than an aspirational alternative. Consequently, despite these complex dynamics and important shifts, in the short and even medium terms, the international power structure will likely remain based on a liberal world order. To imagine a longer-lasting, more transformative change would require these disparate challenges and collaborations to distill into something more coherent and assertive. It remains to be seen whether current priorities can cohere, over time, into a genuine alternative world order.

This chapter was written prior to October 7, 2023, which marked the beginning of the current Israel–Hamas war (Gaza war), as well as the further escalation of the conflict in the Middle East by the 2024 Israeli invasion of Lebanon. Ongoing developments have provoked concerted discussions about a shifting regional order, not least the assassination of the long-standing Hezbollah leader Hassan Nasrallah by the Israel Defense Forces on September 27, 2024, following Iran's missile attack on Israel, and Israel's subsequent targeting of the new Hezbollah leader in massive strikes in Beirut on October 4. Even in this contested arena, the scale of actions and reactions seems a profound alteration to an order in the Middle East that has been largely preserved over the last fifty years. As for the first anniversary of the start of the Gaza war, it is unclear which balance of power in the region prevails. Israel—supported by the United States and some European Union member states—may emerge stronger and as a result weaken Iran's strength in the region, or either may suffer both local turmoil and damaged global standing. It is also unclear the extent to which the war will challenge the role of Russia in the region, which seems more occupied with the Ukraine war, with less of an active "voice" in comparison to its key counterparts—the West—which Russia and Iran (and China), as this chapter demonstrated, have aimed to challenge. However, what *is* clear is that the regional dynamics will have a sustained impact on the further conceptualization of the emerging new world order, globally and regionally, including on Iran's "Look East" policy within it; there remains much need for future research to predict and understand coming developments in global and regional matters affected by these events.

Acknowledgment: The author would like to express gratitude to Professor Mehran Kamrava for kind invitation to participate at Iranian Studies Unit Third Annual Conference "Iran's Look East Policy" (September, 6–7, 2023), and for offering valuable and useful comments over the review process.

NOTES

1. Ken Bredemeir, "Putin Says He Understands China Has 'Concerns' About Ukriane 'Crisis,'" VOA, September 15, 2022, https://bit.ly/47cTcFO.

2. Jennifer Sterling-Folker, "All Hail to the Chief: Liberal IR Theory in the New World Order," *International Studies Perspectives* 16, no. 1 (2015): 40–49.

3. G. John Ikenberry, *Liberal Leviathan: The Origins, Crisis and Transformation of the American World Order* (Princeton University Press, 2011), 62–63.

4. Michael Doyle, *The Ways of War and Peace: Realism, Liberalism and Socialism* (W. W. Norton, 1997).

5. Ikenberry, *Liberal Leviathan*, 64–65.

6. Ikenberry, *Liberal Leviathan*, 310.

7. Ikenberry, *Liberal Leviathan*, 310.

8. Ikenberry, *Liberal Leviathan*, 310.

9. Ikenberry, *Liberal Leviathan*, 310.

10. Emma Ashford and Evan Cooper, "Yes, the World Is Multipoalr. And That Isn't Bad News for the United States," *Foreign Policy*, October 5, 2023, https://bit.ly/3G5uFpW.

11. Ikenberry, *Liberal Leviathan*, 310.

12. Ikenberry, *Liberal Leviathan*, 310.

13. Anne L. Clunan, "Russia and the Liberal World Order," *Ethics and International Affairs* 32, no. 1 (2018): 45–59.

14. Tony Tai-Ting Liu and Sahand E. P. Faez, "The Role of the United States in the Relation Between Iran and China as Two Key Members of the Asian Global Supply Chain," *Discrete Dynamics in Nature and Society* 2023 (2023): 1.

15. Georg Sorensen, *A Liberal World Order in Crisis: Choosing Between Imposition and Restraint* (Cornell University Press, 2011), 7–8.

16. Clunan, "Russia and the Liberal World Order," 45.

17. Sorensen, *A Liberal World Order in Crisis*, 7.

18. Sorensen, *A Liberal World Order in Crisis*, 8.

19. Samuel P. Huntington, *The Clash of Civilizations and the Remaking of World Order* (Simon & Schuster, 2002).

20. Tang Yije, "On the Clash and Coexistence of Human Civilizations," *Procedia—Social Behavioural Sciences* 2, no. 5 (2010): 7381–91.

21. Arshin Adib-Moghaddam, "A (Short) History of the Clash of Civilizations," *Cambridge Review of International Affairs* 21, no. 2 (2008): 217–34.

22. Jonathan Fox, "Two Civilizations and Ethnic Conflict: Islam and the West," *Journal of Peace Research* 38, no. 4 (2001): 459–72.

23. Shabham J. Holliday, "Beyond Hegemony, World Order as Domination: Iran's Green Movement and the Nuclear Sanctions Regimes," *International Relations* (2023): 7.

24. Massimo Buscema, Guido Ferilli, and Pier Luigi Sacco, "What Kind of 'World Order'? An Artificial Neural Networks Approach to Intensive Data Mining," *Technological Forecasting and Social Change* 117 (2017): 47.

25. Manfred Henningsen, "The Death of Civilizations: Huntington, Toynbee, and Vogelin—Three Variations on a Theme," *European Journal of Social Theory* 17, no. 2 (2014): 147–64.

26. Huntington, *Clash of Civilizations*, 24.

27. Sorensen, *A Liberal World Order in Crisis*, 21.

28. Hongda Fan, "China-Iran Relations from the Perspective of Tehran's Look East Approach," *Asian Affairs* 53, no. 1 (2022): 52.

29. "Only Those Who Believe in the People and Youth and Who Pursue Justice Should Hold Executive Power," Khamenei.ir, May 15, 2021, https://bit.ly/3ssyPFx.

30. Fan, "China-Iran Relations," 52.

31. Fan, "China-Iran Relations," 52.

32. Fan, "China-Iran Relations," 53.

33. Fan, "China-Iran Relations," 54.

34. Alam Saleh and Zakiyeh Yazdanshenas, "China-Iran Strategic Partnership and the Future of US Hegemony in the Persian Gulf Region," *British Journal of Middle Eastern Studies* 51, no. 2 (2024): 377–400.

35. Barry Buzan, "The Transformation of Global International Society and the Security Agenda: Interview with Professor Barry Buzan," *Security and Defence Quarterly* 30, no. 3 (2020): 7–8.

36. Buzan, "Transformation of Global International Society," 7–8.

37. Quoted in Fan, "China-Iran Relations," 53.

38. Ghoncheh Tazmini, "Parallel Discursive Fields in Pre-Revolutionary Russia and Iran: The West as a Model or an Anti-Model," *British Journal of Middle Eastern Studies* 50, no. 2 (2023): 465–85.

39. Brett Cohen, "Raisi in Russia," Iran Primer, January 21, 2022, https://bit.ly/3SIMVNB.

40. Cohen, "Raisi in Russia."

41. Ivo Daalder, "Putin's NATO Bungle," Politico, September 16, 2022, https://bit.ly/3unDOHP.

42. Vladimir Isachenkov, "Putin Blasts US Attempts to Preserve Global Domination," AP, September 20, 2022, https://bit.ly/47esUmu.

43. Sanam Vakil, interview by author, December 3, 2022.

44. Mark Katz reminds us that the list of Iranian historical grievances against Russia is long, including: the loss of territory to the Russian empire in the early 19th century; tsarist Russian military intervention against the Iranian Constitutional Revolution in the early twentieth century; Soviet support for secessionist movements in northwestern Iran at the end of both World Wars; the Soviet occupation of Iran during World War II; Moscow's support for the Tudeh (the Iranian Communist Party); and Soviet support for Baghdad during the Iraq–Iran war (1980–88). See Mark N. Katz, "Russia and Iran," *Middle East Policy* 19, no. 3 (Fall 2012): 54–64.

45. Giorgio Cafiero, interview by author, December 3, 2022.

46. Anonymous, interview by author, December 12, 2022.

47. Nicole Grajewski, "An Illusory Entente: The Myth of a Russia-China-Iran 'Axis,'" *Asian Affairs* 53, no. 1 (2022): 167.

48. Abdolrasool Divsallar, "Rising Interdependence: How Russo-Iranian Relations Have Evolved with the War in Ukraine," Trends Research & Advisory, December 12, 2022, https://bit.ly/47B5BTy.

49. Parisa Hafezi and Guy Faulconbridge, "Iran Applies to Join China and Russia in BRICS Club," Reuters, June 28, 2022, https://bit.ly/3G2yjRM.

50. Grajewski, "An Illusory Entente," 175

51. Gregrio Sorgi, "Putin Hails 'New Levels of Cooperation' with China," Politico, February 22, 2023, https://bit.ly/3SBbhJ8.

52. Amy Hawkins, "Russia and China Deepen Economic Ties amid Surge in Trade Since Ukraine Invasion," *Guardian*, May 24, 2023, https://bit.ly/47tNhM6.

53. "VTB zapustil transgranichnye perevody v Irane" [VTB made cross-border transfers to Iran], *Kommersant*, November 19, 2022, https://bit.ly/3uibcA5.

54. "CB Rossii i Irana zakluchili soglashenie o sotrudnichestve" [The Centrral Bank of Russia and Iran concluded agreement on cooperation], TASS, January 29, 2023, https://bit.ly/3QYeRMe.

55. Diana Galeeva, "The Art of Currencies in the Ukraine War," Arab News, May 25, 2022, https://bit.ly/46gDVlK.

56. Irina P. Khominich and S. Alikhani, ["Rosiiya i Iran v usloviyah ekonomicheskih sankciy: antisankcionnaya politika I ekonomika soprotivleniya" [Russia and Iran in

conditions of economic sanctions: Anti-sanction policy and resistance economy], *Vestnik of the Plekhanov Russian University of Economics* 18, no. 2 (2021): 5–12, https://bit.ly/47wfYYQ.

57. "Bank of Russia Chief Visits Iran in Rare Trip Abroad Since War," Bloomberg, May 24, 2023, https://bit.ly/47cVhS9.

58. See: Bulat Nizameev, "Rustam Minikhanov vstretilsya s poslom Irana v Rossii Kazemom Djalali" [Rustam Minnnikhanov met with the Iran's ambassador in Russia Kazem Jalali], Official Tatarstan, March 10, 2022, https://bit.ly/40CefPv; and Lubov Shebalova, "Strana interesna kak alternativnyi partner: Zachem Minnikhanov poehal i Iran?" [The country is interesting as an alternative partner: Why did Minnikhanov travel to Iran?], Tatar Inform, September 19, 2022, https://bit.ly/40IIBA2.

Acknowledgments

All books are collective endeavors, and edited volumes benefit from the insights of multiple contributors and subject matter experts. In working on this volume, I was fortunate to work with a number of superb contributors and colleagues. My sincere thanks to the contributors for their original contributions and for the trust they bestowed in me to publish their work. The project also benefited from the input of a number of other colleagues who generously shared their thoughts on the subject and their advice at various stages of work on the project. I am especially grateful to Cyrus Ashayeri, Omar Ashour, Aicha Elbasri, Mohamad Hamas ElMasry, Jonathan Fulton, Olivia Glombitza, Ayat Hamdan, Harith Hasan, Shireen Hunter, Marwan Kabalan, Emad Kaddorah, Nikolay Kozhanov, Si Liu, Kadhim Hashim Niama, Huda Raouf, Seyed Mohammad Kazem Sajjadpour, Li-Chen Sim, Bayram Sinkaya, Steven Wright, and Chuchu Zhang. Special thanks go to Hamideh Dorzadeh for her editorial work on earlier drafts of several of the chapters. Grateful acknowledgment also goes to the Arab Center for Research and Policy Studies for the opportunity to engage in in-depth study of this and other topics related to Iran.

Contributors

Rowena Abdul Razak is a lecturer at Queen Mary University of London. She holds a DPhil in Oriental studies from the University of Oxford, where she explored the British–Soviet occupation of Iran during the Second World War. She has written on Arab nationalism in Bahrain, the Iranian left, and the Iranian oil industry. She is working on her first book on the early Cold War in Iran.

Niloufar Baghernia is a PhD candidate in international relations at the Centre for Arab and Islamic Studies, Australian National University (ANU). Her research focuses on international relations, with a particular emphasis on case studies involving Iran and China, and their dynamics in the Middle East. Baghernia has contributed to peer-reviewed journals, including an article titled "China's Marginal Involvement in the 2023 Iran-Saudi Arabia Reconciliation," published in *Asian Affairs*. She currently serves as a sessional tutor at the Centre for Arab and Islamic Studies and the ANU College of Arts and Social Sciences.

Gawdat Bahgat is a professor of national security at the Near East South Asia Center for Strategic Studies, National Defense University, Washington, DC. He is the author of twelve books on the Middle East, US foreign policy, and energy security.

Abdolrasool (Farzam) Divsallar is a senior researcher at the UN Institute for Disarmament Research (UNIDIR) and an adjunct professor at the Universita' Cattolica del Sacro Cuore in Milan. His area of research lies at the intersection of security studies and regional studies. Divsallar's interests include regional security, civil–military relations, security assistance, WMD proliferation, GCC, and Iran's military–security strategies. Prior to joining UNIDIR, Divsallar co-led the Regional Security Initiative at the European University Institute (EUI) in Florence (2020–22), and worked as a policy leader fellow at the EUI School of Transnational Governance (2019–20). Between 2005 and 2018 he worked in Tehran in various positions, including at the Center for Strategic Studies and Defense Industries Training and Research Institute.

Karim Eslamloueyan is a professor of economics at Shiraz University. He received his PhD in economics from the University of Ottawa. His research interests include macroeconomics, international economics, and energy economics. Eslamloueyan focuses mainly on energy-rich countries and the Middle East and Asian economies. He has published extensively on macroeconomics, with over seventy-five research articles in peer-reviewed journals such as *Energy Policy*, *Economic Modelling*, *Emerging Markets Finance and Trade*, *Economic Analysis and Policy*, and *China Economic Review*.

Diana Galeeva is a visiting scholar to the Centre of Islamic Studies at the University of Cambridge. She has previously been an academic visitor to OSGA, University of Oxford (2022–23), a visiting fellow at Oxford Centre for Islamic Studies (2021, 2023), and an academic visitor to St. Antony's College, University of Oxford (2019–22). Galeeva is the author of four books: *Islam in Russia: Coexistence Formations* (Routledge, 2024), *Russia and the GCC: The Case of Tatarstan's Paradiplomacy* (I. B. Tauris, 2023), *Qatar: The Practice of Rented Power* (Routledge, 2022), and *Encyclopedia of Islam in Russia* (forthcoming with Mohamed Bin Zayed University for Humanities, 2025). She is also a coeditor of the collection *Post-Brexit Europe and UK: Policy Challenges Towards Iran and the GCC States* (Palgrave Macmillan, 2021).

Hessam Habibi Doroh is the author of *Sunni Communities in the Islamic Republic of Iran, 2013–2021* (Brill, 2023). He teaches courses on international relations and intercultural and interreligious studies. He is currently working on his PhD project at the University of Public Service in Budapest. His fields of interest are borders and borderlands in contemporary Iran and the international relations of the Middle East.

Jianwei Han is an associate professor and director of the Iranian studies program at the Middle East Studies Institute, Shanghai International Studies University. Her research interests include the modernization process of Iran, the digital economy in the Middle East, and China's diplomacy on the Middle East. She has published more than twenty articles in Chinese and English journals. Han has presided over and finished one of China's National Social Science Projects and published a book titled *The Economic Modernization of the Islamic Republic of Iran* (World Affairs Press, 2019).

Javad Heiran-Nia is the director of the Persian Gulf Studies Group at the Center for Scientific Research and Middle East Strategic Studies in Iran and has a PhD in international relations. He was the current affairs analyst at Cambridge Middle East and North Africa Forum. His articles have appeared in the Atlantic Council,

Stimson Center, *National Interest, Middle East Policy, Cambridge Middle East and North Africa Forum, Insight Turkey, Iran and the Caucasus Journal, Contemporary Review of the Middle East, Strategic Analysis,* and *LobeLog.* His book is titled *Iran and the Security Order in the Persian Gulf* (Routledge, 2024).

Mehran Kamrava is a professor of government at Georgetown University in Qatar. He also directs the Iranian Studies Unit at the Arab Center for Research and Policy Studies. Kamrava's most recent publications include *How Islam Rules in Iran: Theology and Theocracy in the Islamic Republic* (2024); *Righteous Politics: Power and Resilience in Iran* (2023); *A Dynastic History of Iran: From the Qajars to the Pahlavis* (2022); *Triumph and Despair: In Search of Iran's Islamic Republic* (2022); *A Concise History of Revolution* (2020); *Troubled Waters: Insecurity in the Persian Gulf* (2018); *Inside the Arab State* (2018); and *The Impossibility of Palestine: History, Geography, and the Road Ahead* (2016).

Zahra Karimi is an associate professor at the University of Mazandaran, Iran. Her areas of expertise include development economics, institutional economics, and the labor market. Karimi has taught at the University of Sunderland, UK, and National Chung Hsing University, Taiwan. She is a member of Economists for Full Employment, Global Labour University, and the Gender and Macroeconomics Working Group. Her publications include articles on the topics of "The Effects of International Trade on Gender Inequality in Iran"; "The Effects of Afghan Immigrants on the Iranian Labour Market"; "The Role of Credit in Women's Employment"; "The Case of Women's Cooperatives in Iran"; and "Iran's Labour Market Under the Sanctions."

Banafsheh Keynoush is a scholar in residence at the Kroc Institute for International Peace Studies, the University of Notre Dame. She is the coauthor of *The Abraham Accords: National Security, Regional Order, and Popular Representation* and the author of *The World Powers and Iran: Before, During and After the Nuclear Deal.* She received her PhD from Tufts University and completed coursework at Harvard University.

Sarvenaz Khanmohammadi is a lecturer and researcher based in Guangzhou, China. She holds a bachelor's degree in business from Shahid Beheshti University, and a master's in international relations from Shanghai International Studies University. Currently, she works as a Persian teacher in Guangdong University of Foreign Studies, China, and her main focus of research includes Sino–Iranian relations and international politics.

Mazaher Koruzhde is a lecturer of international relations at Howard University. He uses a critical political economy perspective to analyze US foreign policy in the Gulf. His recent article published in *Class, Race and Corporate Power* titled "The Iranian Crisis of the 1970s–1980s and the Formation of the Transnational Investment Bloc" examines the contribution of the Iranian revolution, hostage crisis, and war with Iraq to the formation of the US–Saudi Transnational Investment Bloc in the late 1970s.

Fred H. Lawson is a professor of government emeritus of Mills College at Northeastern University and adjunct professor of international relations at Universitas Brawijaya in Indonesia. His publications include *Constructing International Relations in the Arab World* (Stanford University Press, 2006) and the four-volume compendium *International Relations of the Middle East* (Sage, 2015). He currently edits the Syracuse University Press series Intellectual and Political History of the Modern Middle East.

Eric Lob is an associate professor of politics and international relations at Florida International University. He is the author of *Iran's Reconstruction Jihad: Rural Development and Regime Consolidation after 1979* (Cambridge University Press, 2020). His articles have appeared in *The International Journal of Middle East Studies, Iranian Studies, Middle East Critique, The Middle East Journal, The Muslim World, Third World Quarterly*, and others.

Mahmood Monshipouri is a professor of international relations at San Francisco State University and a lecturer at the fall program for freshmen at the University of California, Berkeley. Monshipouri is the author of *In the Shadow of Mistrust: The Geopolitics and Diplomacy of US-Iran Relations* (Oxford University Press, 2022). He is the editor of *Why Human Rights Still Matter in Contemporary Global Affairs* (Routledge, 2020), and the author of *Middle East Politics: Changing Dynamics* (Routledge, 2019). He is currently working on book titled *Climate Change, Environmental Refugees, Forced Migration, and Human Rights in the Middle East* (Rowman & Littlefield, forthcoming).

Deepika Saraswat is an associate fellow at the West Asia Center, Manohar Parrikar Institute for Defence Studies and Analyses, New Delhi. Saraswat has a PhD in political geography from the School of International Studies, Jawaharlal Nehru University, New Delhi. Previously, she was a research fellow at the Indian Council of World Affairs (ICWA). Her research focuses on Iran's foreign policy and geopolitical developments in West Asia and Eurasia, and Indian foreign policy. She has the author of *Between Survival and Status: The Counter-Hegemonic Geopolitics of Iran* (ICWA & Macmillan: 2022).

Degang Sun is a professor of political science at the Institute of International Studies, director of Center for Middle Eastern Studies, Fudan University, Shanghai, China. He is the vice president of Chinese Association of Middle East Studies. He was a visiting scholar at the Center for Middle Eastern Studies, Harvard University (2018–19), senior associate member at St. Antony's College, Oxford University, and an academic visitor to the Oxford Centre for Islamic Studies (2012–13), Denver University (2007–8) and the University of Hong Kong (2004–5). His research interests are Middle Eastern politics and international relations; great powers' strategies in the Middle East; and China's Middle East diplomacy.

Index

Abraham Accords, 169, 174, 179; and perceptions of Iranian loss, 186
Afghanistan, 41, 79–84, 101, 103, 104, 105, 139, 170, 211, 221, 250, 255, 256; civil war in, 77, 150; politics in, 9, 16, 77, 80, 83, 84, 140, 258, 259; trade with Iran, 102, 245; US invasion of, 21, 232; US withdrawal from, 138, 144
Africa, 15, 102, 183, 314, 316; and BRI, 134; Iran's relations with, 1, 7, 10, 213, 270, 281
Ahmadinejad, President Mahmoud, 15, 73, 100, 248, 276, 280, 282, 292; on Israel, 284; nuclear issue and, 1; presidency of, 2, 13, 15, 16, 20, 22, 115, 116, 141, 176, 275, 284, 294, 314
Amini, Mahsa, 127, 159, 168, 179, 181, 270
Amir-Abdollahian, Hossein, 25, 75, 124; death of, 4; on relations with Armenia, 213; on relations with India, 105
Argentina, 158
Armenia, 8, 17, 211, 222, 225, 227, 228, 228, 236, 237, 239, 241; conflict with Azerbaijan, 9, 84, 85, 104, 212, 216, 219, 220–221, 225, 227, 231–234, 235, 240; Iran and, 85, 97, 212–214, 217, 218, 230; Israel and, 217; occupation of Nagorno-Karabakh, 219; Turkey and, 218
ASEAN, 16, 278, 281–282, 298, 299; formation of, 281
Ashgabat, 247, 249, 251, 253, 255, 256, 258, 259
Asian Infrastructure Investment Bank (AIIB), 16, 99, 134
automobiles, 55, 59
Australia, 21, 100, 104, 291, 298
Azerbaijan Republic, 8, 96, 104, 211, 219, 222, 225, 226, 229, 230, 236, 251, 252; conflict with Armenia, 9, 84, 85, 104, 212, 213, 216, 219, 220–221, 225, 227, 231–234, 235, 240; relations with Iran, 26, 97, 214–215, 220, 230–235, 237, 238–239; relations with Israel, 213, 216–217, 237; relations with Turkey, 213, 217–219

Badawi, Prime Minister Abdullah, 278, 297
Bahrain, 127, 180, 276

Belorussia, 17
Belt and Road Initiative (BRI), 75, 80, 81, 99, 101, 102, 104, 134, 153, 258, 298; and Iran, 24, 72, 79, 90. *See also* One Belt-One Road
Biden, President Joseph, 4, 8, 82, 132, 139, 151; Biden administration, 4, 21, 107, 112, 133, 142, 157, 171, 217
Biden Doctrine, 4
Brazil, 25, 103, 158, 312
BRICS, 5, 26, 104, 122, 132, 134, 283, 285, 309, 319; Iran's membership in, 19, 103, 104, 116, 158, 318
Britain, 133, 171, 277, 312
Bush, President George W., 94

Cambodia, 298, 299; Iranian gas deal with, 282
Canada, 139; Iranian exports to, 52,
Carter, President Jimmy, 272, 273
Caspian Sea, 9, 25, 79, 80, 91, 96, 201, 215, 222, 249, 252, 255; Caspian Sea Cooperation Organization, 76; Caspian Summit, 259; energy resources in, 214; legal status of, 138, 201, 249, 251; littoral states, 237; transit routes, 101, 236
Central Asia, 10, 18, 37, 75, 76, 78, 79, 80, 83, 100, 101, 102, 105, 140, 143, 144, 149, 213, 235, 236, 258, 294, 301; China and, 153, 157; India and, 82, 104; Iran and, 84, 103, 246–247, 253, 257, 258, 259; Israel and, 216, 230, 256; Turkmenistan as gateway, 9, 249, 252; United States and, 18
Chabahar, 59–60, 80, 82–83, 85, 103, 105, 294; competition with Gwadar, 81, 102; as transit hub, 83, 86, 104, 301
China, 4, 5, 7–10, 13, 17–18, 21, 23–24, 25, 26, 41, 64, 66, 73, 74, 75, 77, 78, 80, 82–84, 86, 90, 91, 95, 99, 100, 102, 104–107, 124, 127–128, 140, 141–142, 143, 149, 151, 186, 195, 212, 213, 235, 237, 253, 257, 258, 269, 270, 277, 291, 300, 315, 318, 319, 320; Ahmadinejad presidency and, 15, 276; culture and civilization of, 5, 22, 77, 274; imports from, 6, 14, 60, 148; Iranian oil and, 16, 98, 135–136, 184; and JCPOA, 121, 148, 155, 156, 225;

333

China (*continued*)
  and new world order, 309, 310, 312;
  Pezeshkian administration and, 4, 94;
  Raisi administration and, 19, 115–116,
    118, 122–123, 126, 159; Rouhani
    administration and, 4, 70, 72, 116, 171;
    and Russia, 93, 314, 315, 317; and Saudi
    Arabia, 122, 123, 125, 132–133, 160, 161,
    179, 181; trade with, 33, 34, 35, 43, 51, 53,
    54, 97, 98, 101, 138, 153, 154, 236, 277;
    UAE and, 172; United States and, 137–138,
    139, 144, 257
China Pakistan Economic Corridor (CPEC),
  81, 102, 104
Cold War, 75
Collective Security Treaty Organization
  (CSTO), 213, 229
COVID-19, 40, 43, 57, 132, 157, 217, 233; and
  Raisi administration, 3; and sanctions, 92;
  and trade, 34, 35, 38, 39, 43, 44, 136
Crimea, 173
Cuba, 16, 25, 120, 237; Raisi administration
  and, 17

dams, 250; Friendship Dam, 248, 250, 257
Danieli, 2
dollar, US, 2, 133, 176; alternative to, 104, 122,
  135, 318, 319; and sanctions, 20, 139
drones, 170, 174, 182–183, 216, 231; Chinese
  sales, 127; sales to Russia, 96, 171–173, 233
Dushanbe, 70, 78, 81

East-West Corridor, 102, 237
Economic Cooperation Organization, 247
Egypt, 38, 135, 143, 144, 148; and BRICS, 158;
  and Turkey, 219
employment, 55–56, 64, 101; informal, 58; self-
  employment, 57
Erdoğan, President Recep Tayyip, 218, 219
Ethiopia, 172, 270, 281; in BRICS, 158; drone
  sales to, 170, 183
Eurasian Economic Union (EAEU), 81, 258;
  Iran and, 16, 75, 93, 222, 235
Euro, 2, 20
European Union, 1, 2, 5, 8, 9, 10, 53, 65, 103,
  134, 137, 139, 212, 221, 311, 318; and Gaza
  war, 320; Rouhani administration and, 16;
  Russia and, 17; and sanctions, 21, 25, 80,
  96, 159
exports, 54, 57, 136, 139, 175, 176, 183, 194,
  214, 219, 252, 318; Chinese, 195; drone,
  170, 205; Indian, 34; Indonesian, 294, 296;
  Iranian, 52, 35, 36, 52–53, 219, 237, 292,

294; oil and gas, 22, 64, 92, 98, 107, 143,
184, 211, 213, 215, 248

Financial Action Task Force (FATF), 24
France, 53, 171, 221, 225, 312; Ay. Khomeini in,
  273; trade with, 54

Gaza, 216; war in, 270, 284, 320
Georgia, 84, 184, 211, 213, 214, 222, 225, 252;
  Iranian exports to, 219; trade with, 222
Germany, 51, 53, 133, 134, 156, 171, 225;
  Iranian trade with, 97; in Northern
  Corridor, 80
Global East, 10, 133, 141, 144
gross domestic product (GDP), 43, 45, 175;
  Asia's, 43; China's, 133; Iran's, 3, 36, 39, 43,
  52, 55, 56, 92, 175; of the United States,
  133
Gülen movement, 172
Gulf Cooperation Council (GCC), 123, 127,
  216; China and, 24, 100, 102, 107, 128
Gulf of Oman, 17, 103
Gwadar, 82, 100, 105; competition with
  Chabahar, 81, 101–102

Hong Kong, 132
Hormuz Peace Endeavor (HOPE), 4
Huawei, 101, 133, 144

India, 4, 5, 6, 13, 14, 16, 22, 23, 25, 41, 60, 64,
  66, 70, 82–86, 102, 103–106, 149, 184,
  212, 213, 236, 269, 276, 291, 298, 300, 301,
  312, 314, 315; and BRICS, 158; Chabahar
  Port and, 80, 81, 102; China and, 143;
  culture and civilization of, 77; exports,
  34; INSTC and, 222, 235; Iranian trade
  with, 33, 34, 43, 51, 53, 79, 80, 95, 97; and
  Salma Dam, 250; and SCO, 318; State
  Bank of India, 2; US-India-Israel-UAE
  Quad, 133
Indian Ocean, 81, 82, 103, 106, 134, 142, 291;
  China in, 143
Indonesia, 9, 10, 16, 41, 135, 277, 280, 283, 290,
  301, 315; and ASEAN, 281; and BRICS,
  283; and GCC states, 295–298; Iranian
  trade with, 33, 43, 274, 291–294; in NAM,
  299–300
Indo-Pacific Quad, 133
International North-South Transport Corridor
  (INSTC), 103, 222, 258
internet, 55
Iran, banking in, 55, 56, 64, 101, 141, 294, 318,
  319; cultural ties, 18, 74, 76, 77, 93, 116,

119, 120, 199, 212, 238, 255, 259, 271, 274, 316; inflation in, 2, 3, 34, 38, 55, 57, 58, 64, 92, 93, 175, 176, 179, 270; ideology in, 4, 10, 14, 15, 19, 20, 23, 25, 73, 74, 94, 99, 106, 199, 212, 227, 238, 239, 273, 275, 276, 279; and JCPOA (nuclear deal), 1, 36, 53, 70, 90, 94, 96, 99, 100, 105, 107, 122, 140, 141, 174, 175, 176, 177, 178, 181, 183, 185, 186, 201, 217, 225, 235; military-industrial complex in, 8, 191; nuclear program, 5, 16, 20, 24, 98, 99, 102, 106, 123, 124, 155, 159, 195, 197, 212, 216, 234, 293; poverty in, 2, 3, 55, 58; protests in, 8, 127, 159, 168, 169, 173, 174, 178–182, 183, 184, 185, 186, 238, 269, 273; sanctions and, 2; security policy, 118, 245; and Syrian civil war, 17, 19, 79, 80, 124, 159, 182, 184, 192, 202, 211, 216, 218, 239; and Ukraine war, 8, 18, 24, 91, 94, 96, 98, 101, 125, 167, 169, 170–174, 182, 185, 186, 192, 196, 198, 200, 202–205, 227–230, 233–234, 235, 236, 239, 318, 319

Iran-Iraq War, 14, 18, 20, 25, 36, 55, 56, 170, 192, 192, 211, 232, 269, 271, 274, 280, 283, 291

Iraq, 14, 20, 25, 75, 80, 107, 134, 144, 171, 192, 211, 235, 237, 238, 239, 273; and China, 143; Ay. Khomeini in, 273; mediation by, 160, 181; Raisi administration and, 17; US invasion of, 21, 150, 194, 221

Islamic Revolutionary Guards Corps (IRGC). *See* Revolutionary Guards

Israel, 8, 103, 126, 185, 200, 202, 212, 226, 230, 231, 237, 247, 270, 278, 284; and China, 143; and India, 106, 133, 301; and Saudi Arabia, 124–125, 128; and threat perceptions, 8, 20, 23, 85, 119, 142, 169, 179–180, 182, 184, 213, 215, 216–217, 219, 222, 229, 232–233, 234, 235, 253, 255, 256, 320

Italy, 53, 54, 134

Japan, 14, 16, 41, 43, 104, 133, 139, 151, 184, 212, 227, 291, 298, 301, 312; Iranian trade with, 33, 34–35, 52, 53, 59, 66, 100

Jebel Ali Port, 105

Kazakhstan, 17, 80, 96, 98, 100, 135, 218, 222, 237, 251, 252, 253, 257; and Caspian Sea, 215; and CSTO, 213, 229; and Northern Corridor, 80; and SCO, 318

Khamenei, Ayatollah Ali, 13, 25, 73, 74, 121, 141, 183, 213, 248, 257; and the East, 15, 72, 309, 315; and the nuclear deal, 2; on Ukraine, 94

Kharazi, Kamal, 137, 257

Khatami, President Mohammad, 13, 16, 94, 248, 280

Khorasan, 247, 255

Kosovo, 221

Kuwait, 35, 97, 127, 184

Kyrgyzstan, 98, 218; and CSTO, 213, 229; and Eurasian Economic Union, 222; and SCO, 318

Latin America, 1, 120, 121, 213, 316; China and, 7, 10; as part of the East, 15; trade with, 237

Lebanon, 144, 185, 211, 237; Iranian proxies in, 216; Israeli invasion of, 270, 320

Libya, 17, 172, 182, 192

Macron, President Emmanuel, 72

Mahathir Mohamad, 269, 274, 277, 278, 282, 285; and Look East policy, 270, 280; and Palestine, 284

Malaysia, 9, 16, 25, 33, 41, 269–272, 293, 315; and ASEAN, 281; and BRICS, 283; neutrality of, 277–278, 282; and OIC, 279; and Saudi Arabia, 296; as Sunni-majority country, 275, 284–285; trade with, 43, 282

"maximum pressure campaign" (MPC), 1, 8, 21, 91, 92, 167–169, 174–175, 177–178, 181, 185, 186, 314

Medvedev, President Dmitry, 201

Mexico, 139

middle class, 92, 93

missiles, 107, 171, 173, 182, 193, 196–197, 200, 202, 203, 231, 233; Chinese, 127; and Israel, 270; SAM-300, 25, 174; Saudi Arabia and, 123; SCUD, 192; UN Resolution 2231, 96

multilateralism, 157, 310; Asian, 6, 70–71, 78, 86; in Eurasia, 75; Iran and, 72; JCPOA, 155, 156; regional, 83

Nagorno-Karabakh, 9, 84, 85, 172, 182, 219, 212, 226, 227, 230–231, 234, 235; and Lachin Corridor, 233; Russia and, 229

National Iranian Oil Company, 248

NATO, 78, 134, 167, 173, 183, 202, 248, 316, 318, "anti-NATO"; 77; and Azerbaijan, 228, 229, 232; and Iran, 167; and Turkey, 172, 218; US allies in, 133; and Ukraine, 200, 202, 228, 229

Nicaragua, 16, 17, 25, 120, 237

Non-Aligned Movement (NAM), 278, 291
North Africa, 38, 91, 175; as East, 15
North Korea, 14, 16, 18, 139, 192, 281

Obama, President Barack, 177; Obama administration, 55, 92, 183, 185
oil, 33, 35–36, 52, 73, 91, 98, 100, 102, 106, 136, 141, 171, 183, 184, 215, 221, 248, 252, 259, 272, 282; and Caspian Sea, 251, 252; China and, 16, 98, 134, 135, 140, 143, 144, 155; deposits, 138; exports, 2, 22, 53, 64, 92, 175, 176, 211, 213, 237; India and, 301; Indonesia and, 291, 292, 294; Israel and, 216; Malaysia and, 282, 285; markets, 201; prices, 34; revenues, 55; Russian, 107, 215, 221, 247; Saudi, 122, 182
Oman, 17, 127, 253, 276; mediation by, 65, 128, 160, 181, 237; trade with, 97
One Belt-One Road, 81. *See also* Belt and Road Initiative
Organization for Economic Cooperation and Development (OECD), 134
Organization of Islamic Cooperation (OIC), 279

Pahlavi, Reza Shah, 217
Pahlavi, Shah Muhammad Reza, 218, 269, 277; Pahlavi dynasty, 216; Pahlavi era, 271, 272, 274, 275, 284–285
Pakistan, 16, 41, 81, 82, 83–84, 85, 103, 104, 105, 142, 143, 211, 232, 233, 235, 237, 269, 270, 298, 301, 318; China and, 24, 81, 82; gas pipeline, 100; trade with, 33, 43, 97
Palestine, 125, 126, 133, 285; China and, 143; Malaysia and, 270, 278, 284
pandemic. *See* COVID-19
Parliamentary Research Center, 92
Persian Gulf, 7, 20, 76, 79, 80, 102, 103, 126, 181, 184, 200, 201, 211, 216, 252, 253, 276, 279; China and, 133, 143, 168, 170, 174, 175; gas fields in, 2; islands in, 23, 73, 102, 124, 136; security of, 106, 144; Soviet Union and, 270; transit through, 80, 85, 258; US and, 177, 179, 186, 202
Pezeshkian, President Masoud, 4, 15, 22, 23, 94; election of, 270
Poland, 80, 173
private sector, 56, 60, 107

Qatar, 17, 127, 143, 276; mediation by, 65

Rafsanjani, President Akbar Hashemi, 13, 14, 22, 195, 247, 274; and Indonesia, 291, 292; and Malaysia, 271, 280; and the Soviet Union, 193; and the West, 94
railways, 19, 80, 105, 134, 252, 253
Raisi, President Ebrahim, 3, 13, 23, 25, 70, 74, 78, 80, 81, 82, 121, 122, 212, 269, 270, 271, 316, 317; administration of, 4, 7, 93, 101, 102–103, 115, 117, 126, 127, 213, 309; on Central Asia, 257, 259; and China, 134, 171; good neighbor policy, 15, 17; and Indonesia, 290; and Saudi Arabia, 125, 128
regionalism, 75, 77, 78; Asian, 6, 70; Iran and, 18, 19, 75–76
Revolutionary Guards, 21, 139, 170, 171, 180, 234; Gen. Qasem Soleimani, 170; Quds Force, 202, 239; and Russia, 191, 193, 194, 198, 199, 203
Rouhani, President Hassan, 13, 116, 122, 156, 171, 179, 180, 231, 246, 276; and Malaysia, 280; Rouhani administration, 3, 7, 16, 20, 70, 71, 72, 73, 74, 93, 100, 248, 255
Russia, 8, 14, 17, 18, 23, 26, 53, 75–77, 80, 90, 91, 93, 94, 95, 100, 106, 107, 121, 133, 134, 151, 186, 191, 192, 204, 205, 212, 213, 215, 219, 220, 221, 226, 227, 229, 230, 232, 234, 236, 251, 253, 259, 309, 310, 312, 314, 315, 317, 318–320; Ahmadinejad administration and, 15; and Azerbaijan, 233; and BRICS, 158; China and, 143, 153, 157, 253; as Global East, 111; and JCPOA, 223; military doctrine and, 198–200; military relations with, 8, 17, 18, 25, 79, 84, 90, 142, 167, 168–174, 182–183, 185, 192–194, 220; military strategy and, 200–202; Minsk Group, 231; Pezeshkian administration and, 4; Rafsanjani administration and, 13; Rouhani administration and, 3, 16, 70; sanctions against, 125; and SCO, 78; skepticism toward Iran, 24–25, 96, 202–204; and Syria, 19; and technology transfer, 195–198; trade with, 53, 66, 98, 101–102, 104, 218, 222, 235; and Ukraine war, 80, 83, 221, 233

sanctions, 2, 6, 19–20, 35, 38, 39, 43–45, 51, 52, 56–57, 62–65, 67, 79, 80, 92, 95, 96, 101, 105, 107, 136, 138, 141, 144, 159, 167, 173, 184, 186, 212, 215, 235, 270, 292, 293, 314, 316; China and, 97, 98, 140, 155–156; evasion of, 5, 90, 98, 120, 237, 253; "extreme"; 149, 154; hard currency and, 55; Malaysia and, 282, 285; and Russia, 125, 318, 319; secondary, 1, 4, 22, 51; and

technology transfer, 59–60; Turkey and, 218; Ukraine and, 236; United Nations, 100; as war, 120
Saudi Arabia, 10, 59, 91, 119, 122–124, 126, 136, 143, 144, 148, 160–161, 184, 226, 270, 297; and BRICS, 158; China and, 7, 24, 119, 127, 140; Houthis and, 168, 174; Indonesia, 294, 295, 296; Iran and, 17, 20, 26, 100, 125, 132, 151, 182, 186, 211; Israel and, 125, 128, 169, 179–180, 181; trade with, 38; Turkey and, 219
Shanghai Cooperation Organization (SCO), 26, 75, 77, 78, 79, 95, 99, 132, 133, 138, 144, 309, 318, 319; Iran in, 5, 16, 19, 70, 74, 75, 81, 82, 83, 86, 93, 100, 103, 104, 106, 121, 132, 156, 158, 235, 258; Saudi Arabia and, 123, 132
Siemens, 2
Silk Road, 33, 134, 136, 144, 255, 257; Maritime, 136, 144; New Silk Road, 100; restoration of, 80
Singapore, 33, 41, 43, 272, 277, 281, 282, 296
South Africa, 25; in BRICS, 103, 158
South Asia, 15, 76, 157, 258; China and, 101
South Caucasus, 6, 8, 9, 10, 91, 212, 213, 220, 221, 222, 225–230, 232, 234–235, 237, 240; and 3 + 3 Model, 84; China and, 101; INSTC and, 104; Israel and, 216–217, 229; Qajar dynasty and, 211; Turkey and, 217–219, 239
South Korea, 14, 21, 100, 151, 184; assets held by, 107; trade with, 33, 41, 43, 53, 55, 139
South Pars, 2
Soviet Union, 77, 133, 139, 150, 193, 215, 247, 250, 255, 273, 314; collapse of, 19, 75, 76, 201, 211, 251, 312, 314, 316; Iran-Iraq War and, 192
strategic ambiguity, 100
Sudan, 16, 17, 180
Supreme National Security Council, 73, 74
Syria, 98, 133, 134, 142, 144, 192, 201, 202, 211, 216, 218; civil war in, 19, 79, 143, 159, 170, 172, 182, 184, 200, 204, 239; extremists in, 124; Iran in, 17, 19, 79, 80; Russia in, 23, 79
SWIFT, 293
Switzerland, 53, 54; sanctions by, 96

Taiwan, 14, 41, 132, 139
Tajikistan, 74, 84, 249, 257; civil war in, 77; in CSTO, 213, 229; in SCO, 318; trade with, 17
Taliban, 16, 79, 80, 83, 84, 104, 259; Iran and, 105, 258

taxi, 55
terrorism, 17, 79, 84, 156, 159, 175, 254; "economic terrorism," 79; SCO and, 78; Terrorism Index, 174; war on, 221, 279
Thailand, 33, 31, 43, 277, 280, 281, 283, 291, 293, 298
Tigray War, 170, 182, 183
Total, 2
Treaty of Amity and Cooperation, 16, 282
Trump, President Donald, 1, 2, 177, 180; election of, 82, 150–151; and the maximum pressure campaign, 8, 167, 176, 314; Trump administration, 18, 72, 84, 90, 91, 92, 140, 142, 149, 154, 171, 225
Turkey, 8, 55, 60, 84, 85, 104, 134, 135, 144, 172, 173, 211, 212, 213, 219, 222, 226, 230, 233, 236, 237, 247, 270; Azerbaijan and, 216, 229, 231, 232; Israel and, 219; as middle power, 182; and the South Caucasus, 217–219; trade with, 51, 53, 80, 97, 101, 253
Turkmenistan, 9, 17, 80, 83, 98, 100, 211, 215, 218, 219, 222, 237, 245–259

Ukraine, 17, 18, 172, 228, 229, 230, 233, 236, 237, 239, 240; war with Russia, 19, 24, 80, 83, 85, 91, 94, 96, 98, 101, 104, 107, 125, 151, 167, 171, 173, 174, 182, 185, 186, 192, 196, 198, 200, 201, 203, 204, 215, 219, 220, 225, 226, 227, 259, 309, 312, 316, 317, 318, 320
United Arab Emirates (UAE), 10, 91, 103, 105, 123, 126, 143, 144, 148, 158, 168, 219, 291; China and, 127; and Persian Gulf islands, 23, 102; and trade, 35, 51, 53, 97, 98, 101, 140
United Nations, 17, 18, 83, 231, 284, 292; UN Resolutions, 18
United States, 1, 2, 3, 5, 7, 9, 10, 15, 17, 21, 22, 24, 64, 65, 71, 74, 76, 78, 85, 91, 100, 103, 106, 115, 119, 121, 137, 139–140, 150–151, 158, 159, 167, 176, 181, 183, 185, 186, 194, 200, 221, 230, 232, 247, 252, 272–273, 275, 281, 291, 293, 298, 311, 312, 314, 316, 320; China and, 132–133, 138, 141, 143, 157, 258; dual containment and, 75; hegemony, 94, 144; Indonesia and, 300, 301; and Iran's nuclear program, 16, 21, 172, 178; sanctions by, 25, 53, 58, 59, 96, 107, 153–154, 169; threat perceptions of, 14, 20, 171–172, 212, 257; trade with, 51, 52, 62, 72, 97
Uzbekistan, 83, 84, 98, 100, 104, 235, 253, 318; and INSTC, 81, 82

Venezuela, 25, 103, 120, 125, 170, 237; Ahmadinejad and, 16; Raisi and, 17
Vietnam, 41, 293, 298; and BRICS, 283; trade with, 33, 43, 282
Vietnam War, 139, 277

Washington Consensus, 25, 99
Women, Life, Freedom. *See* Iran protests
World Health Organization (WHO), 3
World Trade Network (WTN), 35

Xi Jinping, 16, 99, 121, 134, 152

Yemen, 124, 144, 159; Houthis in, 168, 174
Yuan, 122, 133, 135

Zambia, 16
Zanganeh, Bijan, 72
Zangezur, 85
Zangezur Corridor, 84, 85, 104, 222, 229, 232, 236; Azerbaijan and, 219, 221; Iran and, 220
Zarif, Mohammad Javad Zarif, 71, 72, 73, 135, 294; and JCPOA, 177

www.ingramcontent.com/pod-product-compliance
Lightning Source LLC
Chambersburg PA
CBHW030324020526
44117CB00030B/1016